Sean O'Connor is a writer, director and producer in theatre, radio, television and film. He produced the feature film version of Terence Rattigan's *The Deep Blue Sea*, directed by Terence Davies and starring Rachel Weisz and Tom Hiddleston. He edited the BBC's long-running radio drama *The Archers* and also worked as executive producer of the BBC's *EastEnders*. His Shakespeare adaptation *Juliet and Her Romeo* played to great acclaim at the Bristol Old Vic, directed by Tom Morris. His adaptation of John Osborne's *The Entertainer* toured the UK in 2019. In 2013, he published *Handsome Brute* (Simon & Schuster), a study of the 1940s murderer Neville Heath.

'A case study in human frailty, jealousy and desire … fascinating.'
The Times, Best Books of 2019

'One of the most infamous and intriguing cases of the twentieth century is brought to vivid life in this immaculately researched and totally gripping account. Sean O'Connor unfolds the tangled events at the Villa Madeira with a craftsman's skill, laying bare its hothouse atmosphere of regret, passion and suburban despair.'
Mark Gatiss

'Meticulously researched … superbly evocative and gripping … a narrative that builds with the intensity of an approaching thunderstorm.' *The Spectator*

'Sean O'Connor can't resist striking a theatrical note in this "biography of murder".' *Sunday Times*

THE
FATAL
PASSION
OF ALMA
RATTENBURY

SEAN O'CONNOR

**SIMON &
SCHUSTER**

London · New York · Sydney · Toronto · New Delhi

A CBS COMPANY

First published in Great Britain by Simon & Schuster UK Ltd, 2019
This edition published in Great Britain by Simon & Schuster UK Ltd, 2020
A CBS COMPANY

1 3 5 7 9 10 8 6 4 2

Simon & Schuster UK Ltd
1st Floor
222 Gray's Inn Road
London WC1X 8HB

www.simonandschuster.co.uk
www.simonandschuster.com.au
www.simonandschuster.co.in

Simon & Schuster Australia, Sydney
Simon & Schuster India, New Delhi

Interior images ©: pp. 12, 156, 190, 202, 260, 382, National Archives; pp. 44,
138, 370, John Rattenbury Collection, courtesy of the Frank Lloyd Wright
·Foundation; pp. 71, 342, Popperfoto/Getty Images; p. 84, Bettmann/Getty
Images; pp. 96, 114, City of Victoria Archives; pp. 124, 302, 328, Hulton
Archive/Getty Images; pp. 174, 369, courtesy of Yvonne Stoner; p. 258, New
York Daily News/Getty Images; p. 381, courtesy of Alwyn Laddell

A CIP catalogue record for this book
is available from the British Library

Paperback ISBN: 978-1-4711-3272-8
eBook ISBN: 978-1-4711-3273-5

Typeset in Sabon by M Rules
Printed in the UK by CPI Group (UK) Ltd, Croydon, CRO 4YY

For my father, A. J. O'Connor,
who tells a good story.

And I will judge thee, as women that break wedlock and shed blood are judged; and I will give thee blood in fury and jealousy.

– Ezekiel 16:38

Contents

CAST OF CHARACTERS

Bournemouth

Villa Madeira:

Alma Victoria Rattenbury	Musician/composer
Francis Mawson Rattenbury	Architect
Christopher Rattenbury	Alma's son by Compton Pakenham
John Rattenbury	Alma's son by Rattenbury
Irene Riggs	Companion/help
George Percy Stoner	Chauffeur/handyman
Dr William O'Donnell	General practitioner
Alfred Basil Rooke	Surgeon
D. A. Wood	Surveyor
Shirley Hatton Jenks	Barrister, squire of Pilsdon Manor
Frank Hobbs	Chef
Louise Price	Owner of Villa Madeira
Antonia Landstein	Later owner of Villa Madeira

104 Redhill Drive:

George Reuben Russell Stoner	Stoner's father
Olive Matilda Stoner	Stoner's mother
Samuel Richard Stevens	Stoner's grandfather
Elizabeth Augusta Stevens	Stoner's grandmother
Richard Edward Stevens	Stoner's uncle
Christine Stoner	Stoner's wife
Yvonne Stoner	Stoner's daughter

Bournemouth Police:

William Goldsworthy Carter	Detective inspector
William James Mills	Detective inspector
George Henry Gates	Detective constable
Arthur Ernest Bagwell	Police constable
Sydney George Bright	Police constable

Leeds

Mary Anne Mawson	Rattenbury's mother
John Rattenbury	Rattenbury's father
Jack Rattenbury	Rattenbury's brother
Kate Miller Jones	Rattenbury's sister

London

Caledon Robert John Radclyffe Dolling	Royal Welch Fusiliers
Frank Dolling	His brother
Margaret Solly	His aunt
Thomas Compton Pakenham	Machine Gun Corps/journalist
Phyllis Mona Pakenham	His wife
Simona Pakenham	His daughter
Dorothy (Pinkie) Kingham	His sister
Frank Titterton	Singer and broadcaster
Beatrice Esmond	His accompanist
Simon Van Lier	Keith Prowse Music
Yvette Darnac	His mistress, singer with the BBC
Keith Miller Jones	Rattenbury's nephew, a solicitor
Katherine Miller Jones	His sister
Dr L. W. Bathurst	Harley Street specialist
Maude McClellan	Matron, Nursing Home

The Old Bailey:

Richard Somers Travers Humphreys	Judge
Reginald Croom-Johnson, KC	Counsel for the crown
Terence James O'Connor, KC	Counsel for the defence
The Hon. Ewen Montgu	His assisting counsel
Joshua David Casswell	Counsel for the defence
Robert Lewis Manning	Solicitor
E. W. Marshall Harvey	Solicitor
John Bickford	His clerk
Dr Hugh Arrowsmith Grierson	Expert witness
Dr Robert Dick Gillespie	Expert witness
Dr Lionel Alexander Weatherly	Expert witness
Dr John Hall Morton	Governor, Holloway Prison
Reginald Moliere Tabuteau	Governor, Pentonville Prison

British Columbia

Victoria:

Walter William Clarke	Alma's father
Frances Clarke	Alma's mother
Ernest Wolff	Alma's grandfather
Elizabeth Wolff	Alma's grandmother
Florence	Alma's aunt
Matilda	Alma's aunt
Mina	Alma's aunt
Ernest	Alma's uncle
Lionel	Alma's uncle
Emma	Alma's aunt
Marie	Alma's aunt
Amy	Alma's aunt
Dora	Alma's aunt
Ophelia	Alma's aunt
Clement Rowlands	Her husband

Iechinihl:

Florence (Florrie) Rattenbury	Rattenbury's first wife
Francis Burgoyne (Frank) Rattenbury	Rattenbury's son
Mary Rattenbury	Rattenbury's daughter
Eleanor Howard	Florrie's adoptive mother
Foy	Gardener
Sam Maclure	Architect
Margaret Maclure	His wife

FOREWORD

It is Sunday afternoon, preferably before the war. The wife
is already asleep in the armchair, and the children have been
sent out for a nice long walk. You put your feet up on the sofa,
settle your spectacles on your nose, and open the *News of the
World* . . . In these blissful circumstances, what is it that you
want to read about? Naturally, about a murder.

– George Orwell, *Decline of the English Murder*[1]

Now at the very edge of memory and every passing year slipping
further into history, the Rattenbury case of 1935 was one of the
defining British murder trials of the interwar period and was
regarded as 'one of the most dramatic criminal trials of recent history'.[2] The title popularly conferred upon the case, the 'Murder at
the Villa Madeira', immediately conjures up a lost world of steam
trains and railway bookstalls, Wolseley saloons and Craven 'A'
cigarette cards, Helen Wills Moody at Wimbledon and Donald
Bradman at the Oval. It was a time when the rigid calendar of
national life was followed with tribal loyalty; the Derby, the Cup
Final, Christmas, Easter, Whit. The scope of individual lives was
as sharply regimented; men and women, children and grown-ups,
master, mistress and servant – the chasm between them inviolable
in a culture regulated by caste. But holding a startling mirror up
to this apparently ordered and deferential world, the Rattenbury
trial proceeded to expose a salacious and lurid story of adultery,

alcoholism, drugs and murder. It was a 'terrible exposure of the sort of thing that can go on in a quiet, domestic house in England'.[3]

Writing in 1946, in the aftermath of the horrors of the Second World War, George Orwell set out his criteria for crimes he believed made up the canon of classic English murders, 'our Elizabethan period, as it were'.[4] Orwell was acutely aware of the cultural resonances of these cases, what they revealed about Britain and what they revealed about the British public who consumed these stories in daily and particularly Sunday newspapers. For readers with an appetite for blood and lust after Sunday lunch, the Rattenbury trial conformed to the classic 'woman in the dock' cases of the Victorian and Edwardian period: Madeleine Smith, Constance Kent, Florence Maybrick and Adelaide Bartlett. Each of these trials was focused on a female protagonist accused of murder. By reporting the intimate details of these women's lives, the press was able to expose hidden and unsettling truths about the sexuality and behaviour of middle-class women in a period of apparent conformity. But after the Great War, the trope of the woman in the dock had been rebooted for the jazz age on both sides of the Atlantic with the trial of Edith Thompson in Britain in 1922 and Ruth Snyder in the United States in 1927. This latter trial, the inspiration for *Double Indemnity* and *The Postman Always Rings Twice*, mirrored the British case in many aspects and the American press delighted in heightening the similarities between Snyder and Thompson, with both women cast variously as the infamous villainesses Messalina, Clytemnestra or Delilah; bad women who did bad things.

Alma Rattenbury's story was played out on the most public stage in the country; Court Number One at the Old Bailey, long established as an arena for exposing the foibles, fantasies and fibs of middle-class Britain. Every aspect of her life was minutely observed and exhaustively reported to readers throughout the country sitting on chintz or cretonne-covered sofas in the new crescents, vales, drives and avenues that were being erected in the building boom that was sweeping Britain in the 1930s. Newspaper readers had extraordinary access to the most trivial and intimate details of the Rattenbury household; how much housekeeping money Mrs Rattenbury was given by her husband to spend; on what, on whom and when. For as much as the trial exposed the sexual mores of suburban Britain, it also laid bare a new consumer society with headlines about the case jostling for attention with the new full front-page advertisements for houses, cars, vacuum cleaners, clothes, make-up and the new convenient tinned foods. Though the story of the Rattenburys is famously a story about sex, it is as much about money and the invisible, subtle but enduring class divisions that continued after the First World War and were only really to be shaken by the Second.

The jury at the trial were asked to separate the 'natural revulsion'[5] they might feel for Alma's character from the crime of which she was accused. She was, even her own counsel admitted, a 'selfish, designing woman'.[6] But was she a murderess? Even one of her early supporters, the novelist and criminologist F. Tennyson Jesse, dismissed her – 'the cheap strain in her came out in the words of her lyrics'[7] – failing to note that although she composed music, the lyrics of her songs were written by other people.[8] But what sort of behaviour could one *really* expect from a woman – and a colonial to boot – who purchased ready-made cocktails from the off-licence? Francis Iles, the author of the classic tale of middle-class murder and marital malignity, *Malice Aforethought*, enjoyed sneering as much at the Rattenburys' taste (or lack of it) as he did at their morals.

It is depressing, but at the same time illuminating, to learn that the cocktails at the Villa Madeira were bought ready-made. Anyone who has sampled the usual ready-made cocktail, consisting of almost undiluted Italian vermouth, will understand why this information is depressing ... We have no information about the wine that was drunk at the Villa Madeira, and possibly we are spared some rather hideous knowledge.[9]

Like Ruth Snyder and Edith Thompson before her, the media focused obsessively and relentlessly on what Alma looked like, what she wore, how she behaved. Her clothing, even her gestures and sighs were scrutinised as indications either of her guilt or at least of her moral degeneracy. The press colluded in promoting her story to the front pages, somewhere between the launch of the *Queen Mary* and the royal wedding of Princess Marina of Greece and Denmark and the Duke of Kent. She could not have been more perfect fodder for the tabloid newspapers that had been ushered in by Lord Northcliffe following the First World War. He had deliberately targeted the emerging lower-middle class – clerks, shopkeepers and, increasingly, women – by taking the newspaper industry downmarket. He emphasised small features, sport, human interest stories, readers' letters and crime. Crime stories were so popular that Northcliffe became infamous for the motto, 'Get Me a Murder a Day'.[10] By the 1930s, as Orwell observed, crime had become both a popular entertainment as well as a boost to newspaper circulation to such an extent that senior crime correspondents had vast budgets to entertain chief constables, the *Daily Express* even renting a flat in Mayfair for this specific purpose.[11] When Harry Guy Bartholomew took over as editorial director of the *Daily Mirror* in 1934, he had copied the strategy of American newspapers such as the *Daily News*, which focused on human interest stories and murder cases like that of Snyder and Gray. In doing so, he had completely transformed the *Mirror* from a genteel Tory paper to a mass-market tabloid.[12] Like Ruth Snyder, glamorous, depraved and deadly, Alma Rattenbury was perfect casting for this voracious new tabloid audience. Her story dominated the front pages for months, a real-life soap opera with all the elements to keep readers titillated and addicted to the latest twist; sex, drugs, violence and a real-life siren pleading for her life at the heart of the plot. And even in the midst of it unfolding 'live' at the Old Bailey, the *Daily Express* sent not a crime reporter, but the prolific theatre critic, James Agate, to 'review' the drama. As far as the press was concerned, the Rattenbury trial had everything.

In the vast majority of murder cases, the courtroom is the climax – where lies are exposed, truth will out, the innocent vindicated, the villain punished; order is restored. But in the Rattenbury case, the trial wasn't the conclusion of the story at all, only the beginning of an unexpected, darker phase, culminating in a denouement that even the most creative of newspaper editors cannot have anticipated. So sensational was the trial and its aftermath that it very soon inspired writers as well as journalists to wrestle with the questions it raised about modern life in suburban Britain. The version of events described at the time by Tennyson Jesse was to have a defining and enduring influence on the popular representation of the story. The year before the trial, she had published her celebrated *roman-à-clef*, *A Pin to See the Peepshow*, inspired by the life of Edith Thompson. She followed it up by working on an introduction to the Rattenbury case for the distinguished *Notable British Trials* series.[13] Published by William Hodge, these covered historical murder trials such as those of Madeleine Smith and Florence Maybrick, but also contemporary cases like that of Crippen. Each edition – which included a transcription of the trial purporting to be complete – was introduced by a renowned criminologist or legal expert. These editions were widely regarded as the definitive popular text on each case, eschewing the lurid sensationalism of the tabloids. Tennyson Jesse's perceptive introduction to the Rattenbury trial is one of the masterpieces of crime writing and the transcript of the trial has been the basis for all the books, articles, plays and films inspired by the case ever since. But few have looked beyond Tennyson Jesse's introductory essay for further evidence or deeper insight into the murder itself. Consequently, much of the popular perception of the story, including the most celebrated version of it, Terence Rattigan's play *Cause Célèbre*, has been defined by what was available to Tennyson Jesse in the summer of 1935 and little else.

This book explores archive material that wasn't publicly available in the mid-1930s, as well as statements that weren't referred to at the trial and have only been recently opened for study at the

National Archives in Kew. If anything, this new evidence confuses rather than clarifies a case that has already polarised opinion. In 1980, the former attorney general Sir Michael Havers collaborated on a book with Peter Shankland and Anthony Barrett that was the first major examination of the case since the trial, *Tragedy in Three Voices*. The authors had access to several of the most important witnesses and family members who were still alive at the time. Then, in 1988, the flamboyant solicitor Sir David Napley, who had successfully represented Jeremy Thorpe when he was accused of conspiracy to murder in 1979, published *Murder at the Villa Madeira*. These two studies, both written by celebrated legal minds, reached contradictory conclusions as to the identity of the killer at the heart of the Rattenbury case.

In the various British versions of the story, it's Alma Rattenbury who has been the focus, with her husband a supporting player, dispatched somewhat to the footnotes and famed, effectively, as a murder victim. But in North America, Francis Rattenbury's legacy is very different. He is remembered there as one of British Columbia's most important architects, having effectively defined the cityscape of Victoria, the Dominion's capital. Several Canadian studies, including Terry Reksten's *Rattenbury* and Anthony Barrett and Rhodri Windsor-Liscombe's *Francis Rattenbury and British Columbia*, explore his life and work in great detail. Many of the public buildings and domestic houses he created in Victoria remain today, a testament to his creativity and ambition. In British Columbia his fame continues to eclipse Alma's, the end of his life a sad appendix to an extraordinary and glittering career. This book attempts to elevate Rattenbury's story beyond the footnotes and to investigate his background and personality as a crucial part of the story. How is it that the most celebrated architect in British Columbia retired to obscurity in suburban Bournemouth? Having made such a success of his life in an outpost of the empire, where did it all go wrong? And why?

Remembering his parents, the Rattenburys' son John felt that, far from being the lurid tale of sex and violence the press promoted at the time, the story of the murder at the Villa Madeira was 'a trag-edy for all concerned'.[14] For at its heart is a mystery more complex and elusive than the Cluedo-style whodunnit it appears to be on the surface. Was Alma Rattenbury the crass, drunken nymphomaniac depicted by the tabloids? Or was she a passionate, creative woman, trapped between the freedoms initiated by two world wars, and submerged in the uncomfortable conformity of peacetime?

Front door, Villa Madeira

PROLOGUE

BOURNEMOUTH, 24 MARCH 1935

Spring or Summer?

Spring has made her official entry this week, we have felt for
a moment her warm breath on our cheeks, we have smelt
some of her early characteristic scents, we have overheard this
person and that having seen a bee or a butterfly. We have felt
invigorated and tired by turns. Here in the south we receive
spring's caresses the earliest. Last summer it was hereabouts
that the sun made his record of hours. Yes, we are lucky to live
in the south.

– *Bournemouth Echo*, 23 March 1935[1]

Spring arrived punctually in Bournemouth on Sunday 24 March
1935, the weather 'almost summerlike'.[2] The sun was hot, the sea
was calm and the promenading crowd on the seafront was abnor-
mally large for the time of year. On one of the beaches, four men
wearing 'slight bathing costumes and stripped to the waist'[3] lay out
in the sunshine. Deckchairs along the cloistered shelter near the
pier were full of 'lightly-clad people, some knitting, others reading,
while others dozed'.[4] There was only the slightest trace of rain. It
looked like the good weather had arrived and was here to stay.

Late that evening, William O'Donnell, a 66-year-old general
practitioner, received a telephone call at his home-surgery in
Richmond Chambers, just off Bournemouth's central square. He

was needed urgently at 5 Manor Road. Could he please come at once? Dr O'Donnell checked the time on his wristwatch – 11.30 p.m. – and immediately telephoned for a taxi.[5] Shortly afterwards, O'Donnell was picked up by a cab driver, Thomas Plumer, and driven the short distance to the house.[6]

Remarkably little has changed in Manor Road since the mid-1930s. Despite urban planning and a world war, it remains a quiet, broad avenue of private homes, hotels and apartments, slightly down at heel now, but still genteel. The gently winding avenue is lined with the mature pine trees common throughout Bournemouth – of which there were 3 million in 1935.[7] These pines offer a cool, dark shade from the summer heat and protection from coastal showers.[8] They 'throw off a resinous perfume and a balmy, incense-like odour [which] pervades the air'.[9] Only two or three brisk minutes' walk to the south is the East Cliff, which stands 100ft above the sandy Bournemouth beaches and Boscombe Pier, looking out across Poole Bay, with ancient Hengistbury Head to the east and Studland Bay to the west.

Dr O'Donnell had been attending the lady of the house, Mrs Rattenbury, and her children for about four and a half years.[10] She and her husband had settled in Bournemouth, having re-located from British Columbia on the Pacific coast of Canada. He was sixty-seven years old, and a retired architect of some note. His wife was much younger, an attractive woman who was a musician and com-poser of popular songs. They lived with their six-year-old son John, who was at school during the week but spent his weekends at home. Mrs Rattenbury's older son from an earlier marriage, Christopher, only came home during the holidays. The Rattenburys kept two servants: a companion-help, Irene Riggs, and a chauffeur-handyman called Stoner, both of whom lived in.

Known as 'Villa Madeira', number five was on the south side of Manor Road, situated shortly after St Swithun's Church,[11] squeezed in the gap between a modern block of private flats and the Hinton Firs Hotel. The house, also little changed since the time of the crime, was small, white and pebble-dashed, built in 1902 and originally named 'Kelton'. In 1935, it sat among seaside villas, holiday homes and boarding houses typical of the period: Coolhurst, Seabank, Coastleigh, Toft Cottage, Dunholme Manor. It may well have been christened the more exotic-sounding 'Villa Madeira' to appeal to prospective tenants during the summer season. And 'Madeira' had a local topicality, Madeira Road being some five minutes by car and home to Bournemouth Police Station.

The squat two-storey house stood beneath a half-hip slate roof, an entrance door with a stained-glass panel to the left of the ground-floor windows, a drive and garage to the right. The low wooden gates to the driveway were embellished with the art deco rising-sun motifs that were fashionable at the time. A quaint lychgate led into the small front garden and up to the porch. The windows of the house were leaded, typical of the time it was built, giving it an English country cottage look rather than the Mediterranean villa its named implied. But the appearance of the Villa Madeira was as deceptive as its name. Built on a long and narrow plot, the body of the house was not apparent from the road. Contemporary reports described the house in fairy-tale terms, 'small as the witch's cottage in *Hansel and Gretel*'[12] – implying an inherently sinister nature to the building as if suited to the violent events that took place there.

By the time Plumer's taxi drew up outside the house it was about 11.45 p.m. He asked Dr O'Donnell if he should wait for him. O'Donnell said he'd let the driver know, and hurried under the lychgate and up to the front door, which had been left open for him, leading to a square lobby area.[13] The hallway was long, dark and poorly lit. Glazed art nouveau panels with a stylised floral design had been integrated into the top panel of each of the ground-floor doors to allow in daylight. To the left of the passage was the staircase giving access to the first floor. Underneath the stairs, there was a downstairs bathroom and separate lavatory. The staircase to the first floor had unusual glazed doors and glass panels between the banister and the upper floor. There was also an external French window that gave access directly onto the stairs from the side of the house. All the internal glazing was decorated with the same art nouveau motif as the ground floor doors. For such a small house it was an unusual arrangement. Though the glass let in light, the ground floor could effectively be separated from the floor above, almost like two separate dwellings.

There was no central heating and the house smelt a little of damp and a little of dog as Mrs Rattenbury's terrier had the free run of the property. O'Donnell swiftly went past the rooms to the right – the dining room, the kitchen and finally the drawing room, which overlooked the rear garden. At the end of the long hallway, and adjacent to the drawing room, the doctor hurried to what he knew to be Mr Rattenbury's bedroom. Not only did the Rattenburys have separate beds in separate rooms, they also slept on different floors.

As Irene had telephoned the doctor, she and Mrs Rattenbury were expecting him. Stoner, the chauffeur, had been sent in the car to hurry him, not knowing that he had already called for a taxi. When O'Donnell saw Rattenbury, he was lying on the bed partially dressed. Though he had his vest and coat on, his trousers had been removed and he was wearing pants. He had some bedclothes wrapped around him, perhaps to preserve his modesty or perhaps to keep him warm. He was lying on his side and facing the wall, a towel wrapped around his head, wet with clotted blood. The pillow beneath his head was also saturated with blood. His left eye was contused, purple and so swollen that O'Donnell was unable to open it. Rattenbury was unconscious, his breathing rapid and laboured. The doctor tried to assess his condition and asked Rattenbury's wife what had happened. But she was drunk, talking incoherently in a 'wildly excited condition', running about the room barefoot in her pyjamas, a whisky and soda in her hand. 'Look at him!' she said. 'Look at the blood! Someone has finished him!'[14]

O'Donnell presumed that Rattenbury must have fallen and hit his head on the piano in the drawing room. He could see that the injuries were very serious, so decided that they needed to get him to a nursing home immediately. There was a telephone in the bedroom, so he called a local surgeon, Alfred Rooke, and told him to come at once. As they waited for Rooke, O'Donnell was keen to remove the rest of Rattenbury's clothes, but thinking him too heavy, he asked the wife to get the taxi driver to help him. Mrs Rattenbury rushed out of the house, in a very agitated state, still in her pyjamas, and headed for Plumer, who had been waiting outside in his cab.

'Oh, you are not our man, are you? You are the taxi man.'

'Yes.'

'Come quick!'[15]

She was clearly confused, mistaking him for the surgeon that O'Donnell had only just telephoned. Plumer followed her into the house and to the bedroom at the rear. He began to help her and the doctor take off the rest of Rattenbury's clothes.[16] Suddenly Mrs Rattenbury called out in panic, 'Oh my God, his hand is going cold!'[17]

After they had removed the old man's coat and vest, O'Donnell told Plumer to go and fetch Mr Rooke from his home in Wharn-cliffe Road, a short drive away. When O'Donnell entered the adjacent drawing room, Mrs Rattenbury was telling the maid to clear up a pool of blood that had stained the carpet to the side of one of the armchairs. She insisted that she did not want her little boy to get a fright at the sight of blood the next morning. He was sleeping upstairs as usual in her bedroom, which was directly above the drawing room. The maid started mopping up the blood as best she could. She then removed the bloodstained loose cover from the armchair and tried to wash the bloodstains from the back and the arm of the chair.[18]

The drawing room was typical of suburban middle-class homes of the period, a riot of flowers and chintz, reflecting the taste of the lady of the house rather than her husband, for Mrs Rattenbury was 'fond of flowers'.[19] The room was 19ft 7 long by 12ft 3 wide, and contained a sofa and three armchairs. Dominating the room was a grand piano. On the closed piano lid were some candlesticks, some rolled-up architectural plans and a couple of wooden ani-mals. Leaded French windows looked over the south-facing garden. Busy floral wallpaper made the room seem dingy and there was a light fitted carpet, also decorated with a floral pattern. Garden

flowers – chrysanthemums and carnations – were casually arranged
in vases around the room. Some Victorian prints adorned the walls
and above these ran a picture rail shelf displaying a prized china
dinner service. There was a modern fireplace with a tiled surround
and hearth with a wire fireguard. On the mantelpiece were some
china ornaments and on the chimney breast was a contemporary
photographic portrait of a distinguished-looking gentleman with a
moustache, as well as two crossed swords and a pistol with a heavy
butt.[20] A polished radio-gramophone cabinet stood in the alcove to
the right of the fireplace. The sofa under the window and one of the
chairs had loose covers in a modern art deco-style cretonne fabric.
The armchair that Mr Rattenbury usually occupied was placed side
on to the fireplace with its back to the French windows. This was
fitted with an Edwardian damask design, the cretonne cover having
just been removed by the maid and then left in the corner by the
French windows. The blood on the patterned carpet was to the left
side of the chair.[21]

Mrs Rattenbury seemed to be in a state of panic. She told
O'Donnell that she had gone to bed early and was awakened by a
noise from downstairs. She ran down to see what it was and found
'Ratz' – the affectionate name she used for her husband – lying in
the chair with his head leaning over to his left and a large pool of
blood on the carpet. As she rushed into the drawing room in her
bare feet, she had trodden on something sharp on the floor; his false
teeth, lying in a pool of blood.[22]

She then told O'Donnell that she and her husband had spent a
happy evening together and were looking forward to making a trip
the next day to visit friends in Bridport. Mrs Rattenbury then picked
up a library book from the piano and insisted that O'Donnell look at
it. Ratz, she said, had given her a passage in the book to read allud-
ing to suicide. O'Donnell said that he hadn't the time to bother about
the book at that moment. She flicked through it to draw O'Donnell's
attention to the extract, but he insisted that he really didn't wish to
see it. She placed the book face upwards on a small table by the fireplace.[23] At some point Stoner, the chauffeur, had returned from the

doctor's surgery, having realised that O'Donnell had made his own way to Manor Road.

A few minutes after midnight, Alfred Rooke, the surgeon, arrived to find the Villa Madeira in a state of confusion.[24] Rattenbury was restless, with an irregular pulse, but remained unconscious. Rooke noted the considerable amount of blood on the bedding but couldn't establish how severe the injuries were because of the mass of blood and hair around them. At the same time, Rattenbury's wife continued to get in the way, trying to remove her husband's shirt and calling for scissors to cut it off. Rooke thought she was 'in a very abnormal state' and warned her to calm down: 'If you want to kill him, you are going the right way to do it! Do let me get near him and attend to him.'[25] With no sign that she would take his advice, Rooke felt that in the chaotic circumstances the only thing he could do was to get the patient away from his hysterical wife and into the nearest nursing home. Dr O'Donnell called ahead to 'Strathallen', which was half a mile away in Owls Road. He then gave the chauffeur a pound note to pay the taxi driver who had driven Rooke to the house. While O'Donnell waited for the St John's ambulance to arrive, Rooke went ahead to collect his instruments from his house, which was just across the road from the nursing home.

When Henry Hoare, the ambulance driver, arrived at the Villa Madeira, O'Donnell advised him to be careful with the patient as he had a suspected fracture of the skull. Accompanied by O'Donnell in the ambulance, Rattenbury arrived at the nursing home at 12.45 a.m. and was taken directly into the operating theatre. Meanwhile, Mrs Rattenbury told Stoner to follow the ambulance to the nursing home and to drive the doctor back when he had finished there.[26]

In the operating theatre, Rooke cleaned Rattenbury's head of clotted blood and shaved his scalp. The patient was sufficiently unconscious for the whole procedure to be carried out without any anaesthetic, although he was restless enough to need several nurses to control his head, arms and legs. Rooke discovered three wounds to the back of Rattenbury's head. The largest was about

3.5 inches long – above the ear on the left-hand side and with irregular, jagged edges. The bone was exposed in the deep parts of the wound and there was an obvious depressed fracture of the skull. Rooke was able to feel where the bone had been driven into the brain. The next wound was in the middle of the back of the head, a laceration that reached right down to the bone. The third wound was similar to the second, a little further to the right. It was now clear that Rattenbury hadn't accidentally fallen and banged his head on the piano at all; this was a deliberate act of violence. The three wounds were made with great force from a heavy blunt instrument, almost certainly delivered from behind.[27] This was a matter for the police.

Rooke told Dr O'Donnell to telephone the police station in Madeira Road so they could send an officer to inspect the injuries before he carried out any surgery. He continued cleaning the wounds until 46-year-old PC Arthur Bagwell arrived at the nursing home at about 1.30 a.m. Bagwell saw Rattenbury on the operating table and was satisfied that the injuries were no accident. When Bagwell left Strathallen for Manor Road, Rooke continued to investigate the wounds in detail. He turned down a flap of scalp to expose the underlying bone, part of which had penetrated Rattenbury's brain. Rooke freed this and then cut away part of the damaged edges of the skull. He was unable to remove as much bone as he would have liked, owing to the grave condition the patient was in. He then went about sewing up the injuries. At that moment, he had no idea if Rattenbury would survive the attack.

Meanwhile, PC Bagwell had cycled to the Villa Madeira, arriving at about 2 a.m.[28] He knocked on the door, which was opened by Mrs Rattenbury and the maid. Mrs Rattenbury was now wearing a kimono over her pyjamas and led Bagwell into the drawing room at the back of the house. She seemed to him to be very frightened and very drunk. Bagwell informed her that he had just come from the nursing home to see her husband's injuries and wondered how he might have come by them. Mrs Rattenbury told him that earlier that evening, at about nine o'clock, they had been playing cards before retiring to bed. At 10.30 she had heard a yell, so she ran downstairs and found her husband slumped in the chair. She had then sent for Dr O'Donnell.[29] Just as she was making this statement, William Mills, a 29-year-old inspector with Bournemouth Police, arrived on the scene. He could see that Mrs Rattenbury was drunk, but wondered if she could explain what had happened. She said, 'I was in bed when I heard someone groaning. I came downstairs and found my husband in the easy-chair. He was unconscious and blood was flowing from his head.'[30]

Mills noticed that the left-hand door of the French windows was open. 'Was this window open when you came down?' he asked. 'No,' she said, 'it was shut and locked.'[31] Already, it seemed to Mills that whoever had attacked Mr Rattenbury lived in the house. And present that night were only the little boy, the servants and Mrs Rattenbury. The case against her seemed to be writing itself.

Mills and Bagwell searched the house. As well as the blood-stains on the drawing-room carpet, they noted the stains that had been washed from the armchair. The seat of the chair was wet and smelled of urine. In the corner of the room was the loose cover that had been removed from it, saturated with blood. In the downstairs bathroom were a coat and waistcoat that had also been thoroughly washed. A bloodstained collar was found in a dustbin outside the house by the kitchen door. In his examination of the property, Mills also found the library book face upwards on a small side table.[32] It was *Stay of Execution* by Eliot Crawshay-Williams, open at page 296. Mills turned down the corner of the page and took possession of it with the other evidence he had collected. He then left the house and made his way to the nursing home to interview the doctors, leaving PC Bagwell behind with Mrs Rattenbury and her maid.

Now alone in the drawing room with Bagwell, like a character in a play or a novel, Mrs Rattenbury suddenly told him, 'I know who done it.'[33] He cautioned her, but then she said, 'I did it with a mallet.' Bagwell must have asked after the whereabouts of this mallet as she replied, 'It is hidden. Ratz has lived too long.' Then she seemed to change her mind: 'No, my lover did it. It is urine on the chair.' Next she tried to bribe him: 'I will give you £10.' But then as quickly changed her mind again: 'No! I won't bribe you.'[34] Her behaviour became even more erratic. She put a gramophone record on the radiogram, a tenor singing a melancholic love song, 'Dark-Haired Marie'.

Still in her pyjamas and very much the worse for drink, Mrs Rattenbury then began pestering Bagwell and tried to kiss him. Clearly uncomfortable, he wanted to get away from her. At the same time he wanted to relieve himself, but, worrying that she'd follow him into the downstairs lavatory, he decided to go outside, where he might also be able to call a policeman on the beat who would be able to assist him in this awkward situation. Bagwell told her that he was going to find another officer.

Meanwhile, Inspector Mills had arrived at Strathallen and, on the way in, noted the Rattenburys' chauffeur asleep in the front seat of their car. He entered the nursing home and consulted with O'Donnell and Rooke in the anteroom to the operating theatre. They confirmed how serious Rattenbury's wounds were and that he was in a critical condition. Mills said that he had been to Manor Road and that 'that woman' – Mrs Rattenbury – 'was drunk'.[35] Satisfied, Mills decided to return to the Villa Madeira.

Just before 3.30 a.m., Dr O'Donnell got back to the Rattenburys' car. The chauffeur was now awake and courteously opened the passenger door before driving him back to Manor Road. He complained to O'Donnell that the second gear wasn't working.[36]

Mills had been driven ahead of O'Donnell in a police car to find a very agitated Mrs Rattenbury in the hallway.[37] In his absence she had continued drinking and the radio-gramophone was still playing. Mills explained her husband's condition to her. Immediately she asked, 'Will this be against me?' Mills cautioned her. Then, out of the blue, she confessed again.

'I did it. He gave me the book. He has lived too long. He said, "Dear, dear." I will tell you in the morning where the mallet is.'

Nobody thus far had mentioned a mallet apart from Mrs

Rattenbury herself. She continued to make unguarded comments, running around the hallway, staggering about from one policeman to another, making confused and confusing statements.

'Have you told the coroner yet? I shall make a better job of it next time. Irene does not know. I made a proper muddle of it. I thought I was strong enough.'[38]

At this point, the front door opened and O'Donnell arrived, accompanied by the chauffeur. Hearing the doctor's voice, Mrs Rattenbury rushed towards him. O'Donnell tried to explain the seriousness of her husband's condition to her, but she couldn't take it in. He felt that the only way to stop her making an exhibition of herself was to give her a sedative and send her to bed. He took her up to her room, where her little boy John was still trying to sleep in spite of the disturbances that night and with the lights on throughout the house. O'Donnell injected her with half a grain of morphia (30 mg), the usual dose being half that.[39] After treating her, O'Donnell came down the stairs and told the police that he had given her morphia and that she was now quiet. But a few minutes later she rushed down the stairs again and back into the drawing room. Mills asked her, 'Do you suspect anyone?'

'Yes.'

'Whom do you suspect?'

'I think his son did it.'

Knowing that there was a six-year-old boy asleep upstairs, this must have seemed an extraordinary claim to Mills, so he pursued the issue: 'What age is his son?'

'Thirty-six.'

'Where is his son?'

'I don't know.'[40]

At this point, the solicitous doctor intervened again and asked Mills if he had cautioned her. When Mills said not, O'Donnell warned that she wasn't in a fit state to be questioned: 'She is full of whisky and I have given her a large dose of morphia. She is not fit to make a statement to you or to anybody else!'[41] They then tried to get her back up to her bedroom with some difficulty, as she was nearly asleep. Stoner took her in his arms and carried her up the stairs to her bedroom. Once she was safely in bed, Mills asked the chauffeur if he had seen a mallet about the place? But Stoner said no, he'd never seen one.[42]

At 4.30 a.m., 44-year-old Detective Inspector William Carter, a plain-clothes officer, arrived to find the Villa Madeira overrun.[43] The lights were on in every room and the small house was packed with Stoner, Riggs, Dr O'Donnell and Mrs Rattenbury, as well as the police officers searching the premises for the mallet that she had mentioned. These were Mills, Bagwell and PC Canfield, an officer whom Bagwell had alerted on the beat. They were soon joined by PC Bright, who had come to assist Carter. There were ten people in the house in all, as well as Mrs Rattenbury's dog.

In a desk in the drawing room, the police found some architectural plans that confirmed Mr Rattenbury's full name. The maid and chauffeur wandered from room to room on the ground floor and occasionally answered questions from the various police officers. Had they heard a quarrel? Had they ever seen a mallet in the house? Having spoken to the other officers, Carter had made up his mind to arrest Mrs Rattenbury, but wanted to do so when she was fully aware of what was happening. Carter watched silently as she slept, oblivious to the activity around her and unaware of the drama to come.

When she woke at 6 a.m., Carter said nothing for about ten minutes and neither did she.[44] Soon afterwards, she wanted to vomit, so he sent for a bowl. Then he called the maid and asked her to make some coffee. Mrs Rattenbury asked if she could dress and have a bath. Knowing that he would have to leave the room if she were to do so and that, while alone, she might compromise evidence or even harm herself, Carter sent for a police matron. While they were waiting for her arrival, PC Bagwell, who was continuing to search the premises, came into the bedroom and checked under the bed. Finding nothing, he carried on searching the grounds and the downstairs rooms. Just as the sun rose at 6.15 a.m., he was searching in the narrow gap to the left of the front door between the wall of the house and the property next door, where there was a decorative trellis. Bending down under an overhanging tree, hidden behind some boxes, he found a wooden mallet.[45] On it was some hair and a piece of bloody flesh.

When the police matron arrived at around 7 a.m., Bagwell and Mills left. Mrs Rattenbury went to the downstairs bathroom with the matron to bathe, then returned to her bedroom to dress. By 8.15 she had changed into a sober brown dress with a lace collar. At the same time, the maid had been looking after the little boy, John, getting him washed and ready for school, trying to shield him from the very adult events that surrounded him. In the presence of PC Bright, Carter cautioned Mrs Rattenbury and charged her with the attempted murder of her husband. She made a statement as Carter wrote it down. He then read it to her. She asked him if she could read it herself. Calmly, she read it aloud: 'I was playing cards with my husband, when he dared me to kill him as he wanted to die. I picked up the mallet. He then said, "You have not the guts to do it." I then hit him with the mallet. I hid the mallet outside the house. I would have shot him if I had a gun.'[46]

Sitting on the bed, she signed the statement. Bright then arranged transport to Bournemouth Police Station. As Mills had already taken the police car, it was arranged for Mrs Rattenbury's chauffeur to drive her there in their Fiat. She chose a brown hat and a fur coat to complete her outfit. Thinking ahead about the welfare of her children, she made sure to take her cheque book from a drawer in the bedroom and put it in her handbag. She left her room and met the maid and chauffeur at the bottom of the stairs by the glazed doors. The police then overheard a cryptic exchange between Mrs Rattenbury and the servants. 'Do not make fools of yourselves,' she warned. The chauffeur replied, 'You have got yourself into this mess by talking too much.'[47] But as the police had their suspect under arrest, it seemed irrelevant. The chauffeur drove Carter and Mrs Rattenbury the five-minute journey to the police station. On the way there, whatever she might have been thinking, she said nothing. On arrival at Madeira Road, a forbidding Victorian building,

Carter formally charged her with attempted murder. 'Yes, that's right,' she replied in a clear, unemotional voice, 'I did it deliberately and would do it again.'[48] Three days later, Inspector Carter visited her in the infirmary at Holloway Prison where she was being held.[49] He had to inform her that her husband had died from his injuries at 8.15 that morning.[50] Alma Rattenbury was now facing a charge of murder.

ACT ONE

CHAPTER ONE

FROM LONDON TO VICTORIA

For a city, which is in some respects the greatest capital of the world, the approaches to London are of singular and painful unsightliness. The streets are dreary, although so peopled; the sellers of fruit or flowers sit huddled in melancholy over their baskets, the costermonger bawls, the newsboy shrieks, the organ-grinders gloomily exhibit a sad-faced monkey or a still sadder little dog; a laugh is rarely heard, the crossing-sweeper at the roadside smells of whisky; a mangy cat steals timidly through the railings of those area-barriers that give to almost every London house the aspect of a menagerie combined with a madhouse. To drive through London anywhere is to feel one's eyes literally ache with the cruel ugliness and dullness of all things around.[1]

The story of Alma Rattenbury, which culminates in a violent act in a small house in an English seaside resort in the mid-1930s, actually begins deep in the previous century at the heart of a city in a period of extraordinary and unprecedented change. Even in the context of rapid urban growth throughout much of Europe, the expansion of London in the age of Victoria was spectacular. At the beginning of the 1800s the population of the city was under a million; by the end of the century it had risen to 6,586,000.[2] Much of this was due to immigration: by the mid-nineteenth century, over a third of the population of London had been born abroad.

Alma Rattenbury's maternal grandfather, Ernest Wolff, had emigrated to England from Burgdorf, 14 miles northeast of

Hanover in Lower Saxony. In the 1840s, many German states were disenchanted with their monarchies. The liberal middle classes demanded a constitution and the enhancement of civil rights, as well as advocating republicanism and the unification of Germany. This zeal for reform sparked the 1848 revolutions. But the revolutions in the German states only resulted in the re-establishment of the status quo, leaving many Germans disaffected. Added to this, there had been a series of poor harvests across Germany throughout the 1840s and '50s, as well as a population explosion. With a failing economy and chances of work remote, many Germans resolved to emigrate.[3] By 1891, Germans formed the largest immigrant community within England and Wales after the Irish. A wave of Irish immigrants as well as Jewish refugees from pogroms in tsarist Russia also meant that work in London was plentiful but cheap. Most German immigrants made a living as bakers, commercial clerks, seamen or, like Ernest Wolff, tailors.[4] Much of this trade was farmed out by middlemen, known as 'sweaters', to individual tailors or to small groups working in sweatshops – squalid, cramped and ill-ventilated rooms – which remained outside the scope of factory legislation. Tailors would work for twelve to fifteen hours a day for very low wages as they were paid per garment rather than by the hour – 3d, for instance, for a pair of trousers.[5] Most male tailors producing cheap, ready-made clothes – known as 'slopwork'[6] – earned just 13s a week.[7] And though a German branch of the Amalgamated Society of Tailors was formed in London in 1875, there were only sixty-eight members. This is despite the fact that there were about 2,000 German tailors working in London by 1891.[8]

Germans were the most assimilated of all minorities in London in the nineteenth century and, as with the queen and prince consort, there was a long tradition of intermarriage between German men and English women. In 1862, while living just outside London in Hayes, Ernest Wolff had met and married Elizabeth Grace, the daughter of a local blacksmith. Two years later, she gave birth to a daughter, Frances, who would in turn become Alma Rattenbury's mother. The Wolffs relocated several times around London before settling in Reading, 40 miles west of the city. In 1881, they were living at 17 Mason Street, and on his meagre and precarious tailor's income Ernest was supporting his wife and eleven children; Frances, Florence, Matilda, Ophelia, Mina, Ernest, Lionel, Emma, Marie, Amy and Dora. Though by then identifying himself as a British subject, Ernest Wolff continued to have a strong German identity. All his children would speak German at home and whenever the family visited their Continental relatives, the children would officially identify themselves as German, whether they had been born in Germany or not.

Though thoroughly integrated into British life, Germans in London like the Wolffs upheld their national traditions with clubs or societies for everything from amateur theatricals to typography, from cycling to chess.[9] Many of the meetings of these *Vereine* would end with dancing, drinking and singing, the latter being to expatriate Germans an important expression of their native culture.[10] 'No description of German life, be it *Verein* life or home life, can be complete without reference to the *Lied*. Every *Verein* – the Gymnasium included – has its *Lieder-Tafel*, its social gathering for song.'[11]

Membership of these clubs was not exclusively German and some included English members.[12] All the Wolff children played musical instruments or sang and it may have been at one of these musical gatherings that Frances Wolff was introduced to her future husband, Walter Clarke, a printer, who was the son of a local musician.

By 1886, the Wolffs had moved nearer to central London, accompanied by Frances's fiancé. They took a modern, three-storey property in Charles Street, Walworth, south of the Thames. Though the street was described by the social reformer Charles Booth as 'fairly comfortable', the neigbourhood was surrounded on three sides by much poorer districts, the local population crushed by ever-increasing overcrowding and ever-rising rents. The people seemed to be 'quite happy in poverty, hunger and dirt, enlivened with drink.'[13] Booth estimated that Southwark, of which Walworth is a part, was

London's poorest borough, with 68 per cent poverty.[14] The Wolffs' house was a short walk away from what Dickens called 'that ganglion of roads from Kent and Surrey and of streets from the bridges of London ... the far-famed Elephant'.[15]

Dirty and chaotic, Elephant and Castle was a vibrant commercial and transport hub renowned as the 'Piccadilly Circus of south London',[16] with pubs, restaurants and shops lining every approach road to the junction. Though the London, Chatham and Dover Railway had connected Elephant and Castle in 1862, it would not join the Tube network until 1890. Horses were still the common mode of travel and until the twentieth century Elephant and Castle was the centre of London's horse trade. In all, 50,000 horses were required every year to keep London moving, many of them – 300 a week – bought and sold through the Horse Repository at the Elephant.[17]

The Wolffs may have been drawn to southeast London because by the 1880s it was also the heart of the London music hall scene. Frances and her sisters Matilda (or Tilly), Ophelia and Mina all sang professionally and were 'well known in south London for their wonderful musical ability'.[18] The family were billed as 'German melodists, violinists and instrumentalists', an 'unrivalled attraction'.[19] Their brother Ernest Jr was also performing regularly as well as teaching the piano and the violin. Later in their careers, he and his sisters would claim to have graduated from the London College of Music, though there is no trace of their attendance there, or indeed at any of the major music schools in London. It's most likely that the siblings tutored each other.[20]

In 1884, the *South London Press* reported that the twenty-year-old Frances Wolff, now performing as the more exotic 'Franceska', had secured a 'prominent place' in the D'Oyly Carte Opera Company.[21] The comic operas of W. S. Gilbert and Arthur Sullivan had grown in ambition and popularity since their first success, *Trial by Jury*, in 1875. With the impresario Richard D'Oyly Carte they commissioned their own state-of-the-art theatre in which to produce their work. The Savoy had opened in 1881 and was the first building in the world to be lit entirely by electricity. Gilbert and Sullivan were a global phenomenon and between 1880 and 1890 produced a new 'Savoy' opera almost every year that would play in repertoire with revivals of earlier works as well as tours and productions in America. Frances appeared as Lady Ella in *Patience* in D'Oyly Carte's repertory company from August to September 1884, as well as playing Kate, a supporting mezzo-soprano role in *The Pirates of Penzance*. She didn't appear in premieres of the operas and was never to perform leading roles with the company.[22] She was a supporting player, not a star. But the family continued to have an association with the D'Oyly Carte. In 1890, Tilly Wolff toured in *The Gondoliers*,[23] which had been a great success when it had premiered at the Savoy the previous December.[24] Tilly was an understudy to the contralto Alice Gresham and never appeared with the company again; as with Frances, stardom would elude her. But though it didn't advance her career, her involvement in the production was to have a lasting effect on her family. During her engagement with *The Gondoliers*, Tilly had met a young Welsh singer in the male chorus, Clement Rowlands, whom she introduced to her sister, Ophelia.[25] Rowlands and Ophelia Wolff then started courting.

A living could certainly be made by the 2,000 professional musicians working in 1880s London,[26] but the work was irregular, as theatres would often close for up to four months a year. Most of the opportunities for musicians were provided by music halls, which played all year round. The challenge for novice professionals like the Wolffs was finding regular work. This was primarily done through trade publications like *The Era*, which carried advertisements for actors, musicians and music hall artistes. Performers looking for engagements would also rendezvous on Monday mornings at the corner of York Road and Waterloo Road, where managers of clubs and music halls would look to fill up their programmes for the coming week. A short walk from Charles Street, this was wryly known among the profession as 'Poverty Junction'.[27]

Charles Street was also within walking distance of the most important music halls,[28] including the South London Music Hall on New Kent Road, and the first purpose-built music hall, the Canterbury, on what is now Westminster Bridge Road. Music halls had evolved from taverns and singing saloons, and alcohol remained key to their popularity and profitability,[29] but by the 1880s they had established a distinct and hugely popular form of entertainment. A series of acts or turns played every performance, comprising a variety of acrobats, ventriloquists and illusionists, but the defining acts of music hall were the singers and the comics:

> [Music hall] gave the people exactly what they wanted. It did not concern itself with uplift or education, but with warmth, friendliness, and understanding, singing to them about problems ... It took as its subject the neighbours, the landlord, the dire necessity and difficulty of paying the rent; it discoursed of mothers-in-law, husbands and wives, the joys or sorrows of married life, the lodger and that staple article of diet, the humble but tasty kipper.[30]

At the peak of their popularity in the 1880s, music halls across London played to 45,000 people a day. The halls would present up to four programmes daily with many acts dashing between various venues to perform two or three times. As the century came to a close, they grew in size and grandeur, reaching their most extravagant in the Empire, Leicester Square and the vast Coliseum in St Martin's Lane, both still standing today as a cinema and an opera house. They were sumptuous and gilded palaces of variety, in marked contrast to the living conditions of the majority of the audience.

The Wolffs' home was next-door-but-one to the local church, St John the Evangelist, known locally as the 'Costermongers' Church' because the majority of worshippers worked on nearby East Street market. The church, which had been built in 1860, had originally attracted a broad range of worshippers: law stationers, music teachers and skilled tradesmen such as cabinet makers and wheelwrights. But by the time the Wolff family were living there in the 1880s, the core of the congregation was in decline, with more and more working-class families moving into the area. This local church reflected the swiftly declining fortunes of the Wolffs' local neighbourhood: 'The parish had been greatly neglected and the congregation was growing smaller by degrees. The church was dilapidated, and the schools about to be given up, the Mission Room was overrun with rats, and there was little or no parish organisation.' The area was infected by physical and spiritual poverty.[31]

Alma's parents, Frances Wolff and Walter Clarke, were finally married at St John's on Christmas Day 1886.[32] Many working couples married at Christmas, Easter, Whitsun or on the August Bank Holiday, as these were their only days off.[33] After the wedding, Frances and Walter rented rooms at 28 Hercules Buildings on Hercules Road, between the present Imperial War Museum and Lambeth Palace. The Clarkes' neighbours worked in the service industries and provided consumer goods – coffee-house proprietors, French polishers, waiters, dressmakers, musicians, collar makers and perfumiers – for this was a district with aspirations. The street was 'well-to-do middle class', though the households were not sufficiently wealthy to keep servants.[34] Shortly after they were married, Frances found she was pregnant and a daughter was born on 23 September 1887. Eight weeks later the Clarkes rushed to have her baptised at Holy Trinity, the church nearest to their home. She was named Amy Elizabeth, after Frances's sister and mother. Later that day, the child died of malnutrition. Though the overall death rate was declining in the late Victorian period, infant mortality was as high as it had been fifty years before, and a quarter of all funerals in London were those of babies. This was a combination of overcrowding, neglect and lack of hygiene. In London's poorest boroughs, babies stood a 20 per cent chance of dying before they reached their first birthday. But as there is no indication that the Clarkes lived in abject poverty, the child's death may have been due to what is now known as intrauterine growth retardation. The

baby may have been born small and weak due to poor nourish-
ment from the placenta during pregnancy. A common cause of
this is high blood pressure, or pre-eclampsia, which is common in
a first pregnancy. Improvements in modern antenatal care mean
that today IUGR is picked up early and can be successfully treated.
Despite her own mother's continuous fertility, it would be five years
before Frances would carry a child to term again – a much-wanted
daughter, Alma.

* * *

In the last years of the nineteenth century there was a widespread
fear that Britain and the empire were in apocalyptic decline.
Britain's economic position was no longer pre-eminent and high
immigration from Europe and Russia led to mass unemployment
in British cities. By the 1880s, life for London's poor was becoming
increasingly desperate. The city was riven by angry demonstra-
tions, strikes and riots by working people. In 1882, the *Oxford
English Dictionary* first listed the word 'unemployed'. In 1888, it
then listed the word 'unemployment'; the new nouns were here to
stay.[35] Unemployment was high throughout the winter of 1885/86
and several marches and public meetings took place across the
city, drawing attention to the developing crisis. On 10 February
1886, a crowd of rioters was expected at Elephant and Castle from
Greenwich, Deptford and New Cross, and the area's shops were
all quickly closed. The *South London Press* reported of 'terrorised
south London':

> From London Bridge to Greenwich, a distance of 7 miles, nearly
> every shop was either closed or barricaded. Messrs Tarn whose
> great warehouse is by the Elephant and Castle were among
> the first to set the example. Then from Elephant and Castle to
> Clapham on the one road, and to New Cross on the other, a
> similar state of affairs prevailed until at the smallest computation,
> there could not have been less than 30 miles of shops which had
> been closed against possible riot and pillage.[36]

A large body of police, including mounted officers, later broke up the crowd that had gathered at Elephant and Castle junction, minutes away from the Wolffs' house.

After a moment of celebration for the queen's Golden Jubilee in the summer, the winter of 1887 was the coldest for thirty years and newspapers began to report on the large number of homeless people living rough in public places like St James's Park. After continued unrest, public meetings in Trafalgar Square were banned. In response, an affronted left-wing press announced a rally on Sunday 13 November and 10,000 protestors (though contemporary newspapers claimed over 100,000) with various grievances assembled around Nelson's Column. Opposing them were 2,000 police and 400 soldiers equipped with bayonets and rifles. In the riot that followed, the campaigner Annie Besant was appalled that 'peaceable law-abiding workmen, who had never dreamed of rioting, were left with broken legs, arms, and wounds of every description'.[37] Three hundred rioters were arrested and there were two fatalities. 'Bloody Sunday', as it became known, was a symbol of the increasingly polarised communities in 1880s London, now a vastly overpopulated, vexed and anxious stew.

The most chilling and potent symbol of the schism at the heart of late Victorian London was an extraordinary *fin de siècle* demon who went on to define his historical moment and continues to shape the iconography of the East End today: Jack the Ripper. Was he, like Stevenson's recently minted Dr Jekyll, a West End toff preying on vulnerable and needy working-class women? Or was he one of the army of immigrants who had come to the overpopulated East End to bleed it dry? The Wolffs' local newspaper deplored the horror that had taken place in Whitechapel as well as the social conditions that had nurtured the Ripper's autumn spree of terror: 'If it be possible that these atrocities have been perpetrated by a sane person, London contains, if it did not produce, a more inhuman monster in human shape than has hitherto been known among men, savage or civilised.'[38]

Riots, strikes, unemployment, poverty, unsolved murders – the

tapestry of life for a working-class family like the Wolffs as London
approached the end of the century seemed increasingly grim. Even
the collaboration between Gilbert and Sullivan had lost its magic
touch. The duo ended their relationship with Richard D'Oyly Carte,
and with no new opera since *The Gondoliers* – now an unexpected
flop on Broadway (christened 'The Gone-Dollars') – it felt like the
end of an era. Then, in September, Frances's mother found that
she was pregnant again – another mouth to feed, another child to
provide for in an already cramped house. Perhaps Elizabeth's late
pregnancy and the death of Frances's own baby brought the family's worries about their finances and their future to a head. With a
large family of young women with uncertain careers in music and
their father's poorly paid tailoring to support them, what were their
prospects in the next century? With all their practical and musical talents, might they not have more success where competition
was less keen, and where there would be new opportunities for all
of them? Should they return to Germany where they had family
and history?

* * *

In the 1890s, Canada was a colony of the British Empire, the greatest and oldest of the self-governing overseas territories. Despite
being larger than the whole of Europe, it possessed no sovereignty
of its own. Its laws, signed in the name of Queen Victoria, could
theoretically be overridden by the imperial parliament 3,000 miles
away in London. Tradition held that the queen herself had chosen
the site of the Dominion capital Ottawa by closing her eyes and
stabbing a map with a hatpin.[39]

An ocean and a world away from Charles Street, the Canadian
Pacific Railway had been planning to connect the thriving cities of
eastern Canada with the sparsely populated west. But the company's
ambition was not simply to build a railway, but to create transport
links that would span the world. They would join the Atlantic and
Pacific Oceans with Canada acting as a land bridge between Asia
and England. The railway had been built as a consequence of the

declining days of the gold rush in British Columbia on the west coast. By 1864, gold-rush fever had dwindled and the construction of the Cariboo Road, which was built to provide access to the gold fields, had left British Columbia in huge debt. The cost of living had risen, revenues declined, road building was suspended and schools were closed. The boomtown days were over and the fortunes of the capital, Victoria, had rapidly declined as the gold prospectors deserted her. The general feeling among British Columbians was that the only way to secure the Dominion's economic future was annexation by the United States. But in March 1867, the British government had finalised the British North America Act, which gathered the colonies of Ontario, Quebec, New Brunswick and Nova Scotia into the new federal union of Canada. In return for joining the confederation, Canada promised to absorb all of British Columbia's debts and to build a railway from Montreal in the east to the Pacific coast within ten years. Queen Victoria gave assent to the Union and British Columbia was admitted to Canada on 20 July 1871.

Even as it was being built, all along the route, from the Rocky Mountains to Vancouver Island, the railway brought prosperity, with new towns sprouting up and formerly inaccessible lands being opened up for cultivation. As well as anticipation, though, there had been disappointment. The railway was originally planned to follow a northerly route, across the island bridges to Nanaimo and down to Victoria as the western terminus. But in 1880 it had been announced that the terminus was to be situated in a place on the mainland with the unpromising name of Gastown. To the chagrin of many British Columbians, this was rebranded as the City of Vancouver. The Canadian Pacific Railway's William Van Horne was determined that this new city would be 'the metropolis of the west, the London of the Pacific'.[40] Soon Vancouver established itself as the centre of commerce in British Columbia, deposing Victoria as the province's largest city. The railway had opened five years ahead of schedule in 1887, making the Pacific accessible for the first time. The journey from Liverpool to the western coast of Canada would now take a miraculous ten days. Many forms of temptation were used to lure potential immigrants; brochures, posters and newspaper advertisements portrayed Canada as an already populated and prosperous nation. British Columbia was promoted as a raw country, full of possibility. Throughout the 1880s, regular articles and letters appeared in British newspapers from settlers who had already emigrated and made a successful life for themselves.

The Dominion was 'a land of the second chance – a country most suitable for those who had the courage to begin again in toilsome struggle toward material success.'[41]

For the Wolffs of Walworth, they'd share their language and culture with British Columbia, which needed workers with practical skills – printers like Walter and tailors like Ernest. There was gold in the Yukon and the Cariboo, there was land to farm – and a developing population who would need entertainment and tuition, which the rest of the family could provide. It seemed a land of milk and honey, in stark contrast to dark, dirty and dangerous London. In a handbook aimed at settlers, the travel writer Frances McNab enthused about the promise of life on the Pacific coast:

> The condition of British Columbia is one of gradual unfolding. There is no other word which will describe the process taking place in that country ... This generation may not gather the fruit or harvest the seed, but at least it will see a wholly new and distinct branch of life produced with all its hopefulness and promise.[42]

Plans were made for the family to emigrate. Frances and her husband would travel out to acquaint themselves with the country first and make sure it had all the advantages that the promotions promised. They would be joined on the trip by Frances's father and her sister, Florrie. When they arrived in Victoria, if they were satisfied, the rest of the family would follow.

Frances, Walter, Ernest and Florrie made the trip to Liverpool and then across the Atlantic to Quebec. After arriving in Victoria, the family shared rooms in a lodging house in Johnson Street. Staying there at the time was a fellow immigrant, a young widower called John Harbottle, whose wife had only recently died. Single-handedly, he was struggling to look for work while taking care of his five children, the youngest being just six months old. While the Wolffs waited for the rest of their family to arrive, they struck up a warm friendship with Harbottle, Florrie and Frances helping with the motherless children.

Meanwhile, back in London, on 1 May 1891, Elizabeth gave birth to her twelfth child, May. Frances's sister Ophelia and her fiancé Clement Rowlands, who planned to emigrate with the family, were married at St John the Evangelist on 26 May. In the absence of her father, Ophelia's brother Ernest and her sister Mina were witnesses. At the ceremony, Elizabeth was still nursing baby May, who was not yet a month old. After a honeymoon, the new Mr and Mrs Rowlands would follow the rest of the family to Victoria a little later in June. With extraordinary determination, two days after the wedding, the remaining Wolff family packed their belongings – including their babe in arms – and made the trip to Liverpool, the first stage of their journey to a new country and a new life.

The Wolffs had passages for 28 May 1891 on the SS *Mongolian*, a new ship that had only been launched earlier that year. Allan Line Steamers, the 'old pioneer line to the loyal Dominion of Canada',[43] left Liverpool twice a week, promising a journey of no more than six days from coast to coast. The *Mongolian* carried 100 first-class passengers, eighty second-class and 1,000 steerage. First- and second-class passages cost from 12 to 21 guineas, intermediate steerage cost £8 and steerage was £4. Steerage passengers were commonly divided, with the front compartment reserved for single men, the middle for married couples and families, while single women were accommodated at the rear of the vessel, as far from the single men as possible.[44]

The majority of passengers on the *Mongolian* were migrants fleeing poverty in Ireland, Scotland, Poland, Russia, Finland, Norway and Sweden. All were seeking a better life abroad. Despite the close

confines of the ship, each nationality kept to itself. The Russians
in steerage brought their own bread from home to last the whole
voyage, while in first class the ladies brought their own tea and a
supply of cream that was kept for them in cold storage. Intermediate
passengers were provided with two meals a day and supper. Though
there were no luxuries, intermediate passengers were at least provided with beds, bedding and 'all necessary utensils, wash basins
etc.'. Steerage passengers weren't provided with any utensils or bedding at all for the six-day voyage.[45] But Frances McNab noted that
the conditions of the Allan Line for intermediate and steerage passengers compared favourably with other lines and that the experience
was made comfortable by 'the extraordinary civility and readiness
to oblige of the whole ship's company'.[46] There was a Church of
England clergyman on board who held a service on Sunday in the
saloon and took care of the emigrants during the voyage, deliver-
ing them to the chaplain at the Emigration Bureau on arrival in
Quebec.[47] On the journey across the Atlantic there were 'the usual
icebergs, fogs and whales'.[48] On 6 June 1891, the prospect that
greeted Elizabeth Wolff and her children when they arrived on the
east coast of Canada was extraordinary:

> It is scarcely possible to convey any idea of the magnificent effect
> of the St Lawrence [River]. Other rivers may be larger, but few
> possess such a stirring history; moreover, it is in future the direct
> highway over British territory to the ancient splendour of the
> Orient. Of Canada it may be said that the Canadians themselves
> appear unaware of the riches and grandeur of their own country.
> The beauty and magnificence of the scenery is certainly more
> appreciated by the emigrant than the native.[49]

They then made the four-day train journey from the east to the
west coast, where the family were reunited at last. Victoria must
have seemed a far cry from Elephant and Castle, the sky was clear
and the weather temperate; 'the people look quiet and respectable
and everything is intensely English'.[50] Rudyard Kipling visited the

city at around this time and was wildly enthusiastic about it, as it reminded him of refined British seaside resorts such as the Isle of Wight, Torquay and Bournemouth:[51] 'Real estate agents recommend it as a little piece of England – the island on which it stands is about the size of Great Britain – but no England is set in any such seas or so fully charged with the mystery of the larger ocean beyond.'[52]

Despite missing out as the terminus of the Canadian Pacific Railway, during the 1880s Victoria had flourished. The old wooden gold-rush structures had been replaced with permanent buildings of brick and stone. A postal service was initiated and a sewage system was finally constructed. Telephones had been introduced in 1878 ('People standing 15 miles apart can hear each other speak!'[53]) and in 1883 it had become the first town in British Columbia to light its streets with electricity. This period saw the emergence of a new middle class of merchants and, with no income tax, the city had quickly developed into a paradise for the rich, who showed off their wealth and status in magnificent, architect-designed homes. The city was enticingly beautiful, populated by a charmed society that, like many colonial communities, became 'more English than the English'.[54] A *New York Sun* reporter wrote that Victoria was the 'quaintest English town in North America with no more hustle than a summer resort', the residents being 'more idle than the visitors'.[55] There were dances, tennis parties, picnics and boating regattas. But an assistant district commissioner to the British Columbian governor-general thought Victorians 'lethargic and impolite',[56] overly concerned with class distinctions and the importance of precedence. 'It was an insult to seat a "lady" next to a small tradesman's wife, and names of guests invited to a social function were eagerly scanned for any who might have been left off.'[57] The isolation of the community from Britain led to clannishness, reinforced by intermarriages between middle-class families.[58] This resulted in a rigid social code that fiercely monitored its mores and behaviour, particularly those of women. It would punish any infraction of established convention with a relentless and unforgiving severity.

Alma Belle Clarke

CHAPTER TWO

MISS CLARKE

9 June 1892–23 July 1913

Do you know what Alma means in Latin? It means life-giving, bountiful. In olden times they used it about goddesses, like Venus. Well, I'm not Venus, God knows, but apparently it also means kind and comforting, and that I am.

– Terence Rattigan, *Cause Célèbre*[1]

My name is Alma and Alma is Spanish for soul.

– Tennessee Williams, *Summer and Smoke*[2]

Even before the arrival of the rest of the family, Alma's parents had started to prosper in Victoria. Immediately, they had found that life in the city was much cheaper than in London: 'On 1,000 a year a man would be a millionaire in these parts, and for 400 he could live well.'[3] Walter had secured a job as a printer for the Victoria *Daily Times*, British Columbia's first liberal newspaper. At the same time, Frances had thrown herself into the local music scene, and by February 1891 she was producing a charity concert in aid of a recent local disaster. She performed as an elocutionist, while her sister Florrie sang.

Elocutionists in the late nineteenth century had little to do with phonetics and *My Fair Lady*. Coming to prominence in 1850s

North America, they recited dramatic monologues – poetry, plays, famous speeches – often accompanied by music to create a new performance art form. Speech was a regular feature of what we would now call concerts and these accompanied recitations were something between a musical composition and performed literature. The genre was hugely popular in North America until the advent of radio and cinema in the early twentieth century. Public recitation was deemed to be more respectable than acting and elocutionists were not suspected of dubious morality as actresses routinely were. Consequently, this new profession was particularly attractive to women. Female elocutionists dominated the art form to such an extent that by the end of the century it was thought too effete for men, *Werner's Magazine* complaining of male elocutionists 'curling their hair' and 'truckling to women' at 'pink teas'.[4] As the art form developed, practitioners began to include gesture and posture as ways of enhancing their performance. They became famous for particular texts in the same way that musicians and singers would become associated with a signature piece or song. As 'Miss Franceska Wolff', Alma's mother was renowned for reciting 'The Maniac', a piece of lurid gothic by Ella Wheeler Wilcox ('Laugh and the World Laughs With You, Weep and You Weep Alone'), which she had performed 'so successfully in London'.[5]

> *A strange noise sounded in my brain;*
> *I was a guest unbidden.*
> *I stole away, but came again*
> *With two knives snugly hidden,*
> *I stood behind them. Close they kissed,*
> *While eye to eye was speaking:*
> *I aimed my steels, and neither missed*
> *The heart I sent it seeking.*[6]

Reunited, the Wolffs quickly became the focus of Victoria's music scene, with concerts and recitals of the 'celebrated Wolff family'[7] held all over the city, gaining the sort of celebrity, success and prominence that they could only have dreamed of in the over-crowded music scene in London. Florrie, Mina, Tilly and Ophelia would sing while Ophelia's husband Clement ('from the D'Oyly Carte Opera Company') directed. Their brother Ernest would accompany on the piano and play the violin; Frances and Mina would recite. The family claimed to have performed 'in all the principal halls in London, England and had the honour of appearing before HRH the Prince of Wales and the Lord Mayor of London'.[8] There's no evidence of the family performing for royalty, but thousands of miles away, who could confirm or deny their achievements? Who in Victoria would know? Soon, the Wolffs were headlining the concerts at which they appeared, the Von Trapps of Victoria.[9]

Once established in the city, Frances, Ernest Jr and Clement Rowlands founded their own music school, the Victoria School of Music, at 115 View Street. It was very much a family affair, with Rowlands teaching singing, Ernest teaching piano, organ, violin and music theory and Frances teaching elocution and deportment.[10] As well as advancing professionally, the family began to prosper personally, too. In the autumn of 1891, Frances found that she was pregnant. In December that year, Tilly married Hudson Charles Aldin and moved to Yale in the Cariboo. In May 1892 Florrie married John Harbottle, the widower she had met in the boarding house they shared when they first arrived in the city. She would be stepmother to his five young children. Alma's father was now working for the government printing office in Victoria; at last the family was settled, secure and solvent. Finally, on 2 June 1892, Frances gave birth to a daughter. She would be named for the Latin meaning 'nourishing, cherishing' or the Spanish for 'soul'. She was christened Alma Belle – a beautiful soul.

Alma's date of birth caused great confusion at the time of her arrest. Even in her earliest statements to the Bournemouth Police, she variously gave her age as thirty-eight or thirty-one. Both British and Canadian newspapers stated her age was thirty-one, thirty-three or forty-three. This confusion stems from the late registration of her birth, which only took place in 1897, but also to a touching vanity on Alma's part, who shaved four years off her age in her 1929 passport.[11] Alma was forty-two at the time of her trial, much older than the press generally assumed. She had been registered at birth as Alma Belle Clarke, but within a few years her middle name had changed to Victoria. This may possibly have been in honour of the British queen, who celebrated her Diamond Jubilee in 1897, as well as a nod to the city of Alma's birth.

By 1897, the family had fully integrated into life in Victoria. Frances's younger brother Lionel had followed his siblings onto the stage, though not as a musician, but as a mind reader and hypnotist ('fun, laughter and science combined').[12] In August of that year, Amy Wolff married a professional lacrosse player, George Snider. Theirs was a society wedding, in some contrast to Frances and Walter's ceremony in the backstreets of Walworth. The 'two popular Victorians' were married 'under a fragrant bell of white roses and maidenhair fern at the home of the bride's parents on Quadra Street', before starting their married life in Seattle.[13]

After six years running the Victoria School of Music, and having gained a certain local celebrity as teachers and performers, Frances and her brother Ernest, together with her husband and daughter, decided to leave behind the sophistication of Victoria for Kamloops, a former fur-trading post at the confluence of the two branches of the Thompson River.[14] Again, this move seems to have been inspired by the arrival of the Canadian Pacific Railway to what had formerly been a place in the wilderness. Kamloops had originally been settled by the First Nations Shuswap (Secwepemc) tribe. Fur traders had arrived in the area in 1811 but a trading post was not built – by the Hudson's Bay Company – until 1843. This was a fort surrounded by a 15ft-high palisade, an indication of the fraught relations with the Shuswap. Though there had been a flurry of gold-rush activity in the 1850s, by 1874 Kamloops could only boast a population of 200, with just seventy-four adult males. But with the coming of the railway, the town had been transformed. By 1889, the population had risen to 368. Hotels, schools, churches, a hospital, fire department, telephone lines, water and electricity soon followed. By 1893, the population had risen to over 500 and the town was incorporated as a city. With the population growing rapidly, there was an increasing demand for culture. Alma's father and uncle saw this as an opportunity. Walter became co-owner of the *Kamloops Standard*, a conservative weekly newspaper that he would administer, edit and print single-handedly. Frances, Walter and Alma settled in a house on Victoria Street overlooking the river. Just as Walter pursued his new venture, so too did his wife and her brother. They set up another music college, the Kamloops School of Music at Ravens Hall, along the same lines as the school they had successfully run in Victoria. In the context of a developing city like Kamloops, a celebrated musical family such as the Wolffs was welcomed as 'an acquisition to musical circles'.[15]

It is most likely that Alma began to learn the piano and the violin under her uncle Ernst, but she also received tuition at school. Zetland House was a private girls' school run by Lily Beattie and her five sisters, who had emigrated from Ireland to Kamloops in 1893. Subjects were taught to a high standard and included English, mathematics, French, Latin, drawing and painting. They also offered preparation for examinations for the Royal Academy of Music and the Royal College of Music in England. It may have been this expertise in music that persuaded Frances to send her daughter there, and thus began Alma's formal musical education. On 14 April 1898, Alma's mother and uncle organised a gypsy-themed concert at the Kamloops Musical and Athletic Association Hall. Though she appeared on stage with several other children, this event may have been Alma's first public performance. According to the *Kamloops Standard*, 'The children were all dressed in pretty red skirts, black stockings and white blouses with small velvet jackets, trimmed with coins and charms. They all carried tambourines and sang and danced with great effect.'[16]

In 1900, Ernest Wolff left Kamloops to work at the Grand Opera House in Seattle, leaving Frances and the Beattie sisters to tutor Alma. By now Frances had grown eccentric and taken to dying her hair red and filling the house with stuffed animals.[17] A family anecdote claims that Frances would beat Alma if she didn't practise her music for the requisite number of hours a day.[18] One of many talented sisters, Frances had never established herself as a leading performer and had channelled her creative energy into teaching. Now her ambition was focused on her adored only child. An early photograph shows Alma poised with a violin, the image of a child prodigy. At a Burns Night concert in 1900, Alma played 'Robin Adair' on the violin, perhaps her first public solo performance. It must have been her own father who reported so proudly of his daughter's achievement and talent in that week's *Standard*: 'So many children, when they play, play mechanically, but not so this little girl. It was evident from the moment she drew her bow across the strings that her soul was in it and the performance was that of a musician.'[19] At her debut, Alma was eight years old.

* * *

As well as performing, Alma soon began to compose her own music, 'suddenly thinking of an air and jotting it down on anything handy'.[20] She was an imaginative, precocious only child – a bit of a tomboy used to running wild.[21] She was loved and perhaps indulged by proud parents, with whom she had a warm relationship; her mother was always 'chum' and her father, 'my only dad'. Alma recalled her Kamloops childhood some years later in an interview with Mary Lomas in *Westward Ho!* magazine:

> What an odd little girl I must have been in those days … I remember I was always imagining I could see little people in the woods: they really appeared to be there, but I couldn't make anyone understand. I used to put a portrait of Beethoven on the music stand and say to him, 'Now just you hear what I'm going to [com]'pose. Then I'd go out on to the verandah with my violin – I always liked playing out-of-doors best – and would try to play all sorts of little airs out of my head. We lived on the bend of the river, and away through the trees I really thought I could see tiny little figures like fairies dancing about. There were the good

ones on the left hand side – they were white and pretty – and the black, ugly ones on the right. If I played wrong notes, I was sure the bad fairies were doing it to tease me, so I would turn my back on them and try to forget them while I played to the good ones. I expect the sunlight filtering though the leaves took shape and, in my imagination appeared like tiny figures.[22]

One of the formative influences on Alma's early life was a concert tour in June 1901 to Kamloops of the celebrated violinist Camilla Urso.[23] Urso, herself a former child prodigy, had been the first female violinist to play in concert in America and throughout her career had argued the case for women musicians to have the same professional status as their male counterparts. Urso's visit to Kamloops was a great event for the burgeoning city. Alma was asked by her mother if she'd like to hear the concert that evening. Alma worried that she wouldn't be able to see the great virtuoso, a woman who had made her passion her career, and was now, Alma believed, 'the greatest player in the world': 'I don't believe I can wait till tonight to hear her play. 'Sides there'll be such a crowd there, and I'm so little perhaps I won't see her well.'[24]

Determined to meet Urso, Alma, without telling her mother, made her way to the local hotel where the violinist was staying. She located Urso's room and when the forthright young Alma knocked on the door, it was opened by Urso's manager.

'Please, does the greatest player in the world live here?'

'Yes. Madame Urso lives here. What is you name, little one?'

'Alma Victoria Clarke, and I've come to ask her to play to me.'[25]

Alma was told that Madame Urso couldn't be disturbed, but she was given 'the best seat in the house' for the performance that evening at the Victoria Theatre. She left the hotel 'the happiest little girl in Kamloops'[26] and that night watched as Urso played Mendelssohn's Violin Concerto, a female virtuoso centre stage, the very image of Alma's own ambitions.[27]

The Clarkes' fortunes were to turn again. In early September 1899, Alma's father had received a telegram announcing that he had been left a fortune of over £10,000.[28] He had travelled to England to collect his inheritance and, with this financial security, he gave up Kamloops and *The Standard* to become a travelling journalist. For the next twelve years the family would move frequently, Clarke gaining himself a nickname, 'The Rambler'.[29] Frances now had the time and Walter the money to focus on Alma's musical career. They were able to send her to the very best schools and in 1902, while living in Toronto, Alma was enrolled at Havergal College, the most exclusive girls' school in Canada. The school had been opened in 1894 by Ellen Mary Knox, an Oxford graduate and former teacher at Cheltenham Ladies' College who was a 'startling replica of Queen Victoria'.[30] A feminist, Knox ran the school with determination and vision and often posed the question to her female students, how could women get the most out of their lives? What could they offer the world? What did they want to do? In her book advocating the various options open to young women, Knox articulated the value of music as a profession, a sentiment that was absorbed by the young Alma Clarke: 'If you love music, you will instinctively be drawn to her, and agree with Adam Bede that your muscles never move better than when you are making music; that is to say, your life work and ambition, will never move better then when you, too, are making music.'[31]

For Alma, it was clear what she wanted to do. Her passion and her vocation was music and she was determined to make it her career. She had the talent and ambition to follow her mother's side of the family as a professional musician and her father's inheritance would enable them to support her in realising her dreams. And perhaps Alma might have more than mere talent. Her mother and aunts had always been supporting players, never leading artistes. Perhaps Alma might have the ability to become a star of the concert stage? Again, Miss Knox encouraged her girls to adopt a defiant self-belief: 'If you are a genius, your lot is already cast. You will burn until you can reveal your inspiration to the whole world.'[32]

By 1902, Alma's musical education was dictating where the family would live. They had returned to Victoria where Alma attended St Ann's Academy, a Catholic convent school that had been set up by the sisters of St Ann with the intention of providing education for girls in rural Canada. Alma's teacher at the school thought her 'brilliantly clever ... a vivid little thing full of happiness and music, with a special attraction of her own'.[33] At the same time, Alma was sent to a professional music teacher, Miss F. M. Smith, who taught at a studio in Dallas Road. Miss Smith had already successfully tutored pupils who had entered the Toronto College of Music, which bore 'favourable comparison with the great music schools of Europe and America'. At the time, Alma was 'a tiny little thing whose feet could barely reach the pedals',[34] but what she lacked in stature, she made up for in ability and ambition.

After studying with Miss Smith, the fourteen-year-old Alma was to be examined by the director of the Toronto College of Music, Frederick Torrington. Torrington was British, from Dudley near Birmingham. He had emigrated to Canada, originally settling in Montreal where he had taught music privately, while frequently performing as a concert soloist. Moving to Toronto, he had quickly established himself as a prominent figure in the musical life of the city. He was ultimately appointed as conductor of the Toronto Philharmonic Society and had founded the College of Music in 1888. By the time he met Alma, Torrington was widely regarded as the 'father of good music in Toronto' and his fame was known all over Canada.[35] Alma was aware that her performance before Torrington on 9 July 1906 was to be life changing. She played Gounod's *Serenade*, Wagner's *Spinning Wheel* and Beethoven's Nocturne No. 5, executing the pieces brilliantly.[36] After the performance she was awarded the Torrington Medal and offered a scholarship to attend the Toronto College of Music. Torrington advocated that pianists should study professionally at an early age and it was suggested that Alma begin her studies in piano and music theory at the beginning of the fall term in September 1906, while she was still only fourteen. She was to study for three years under Torrington and he was to have a formative influence on her musical education and the first steps in her career.

Chaperoned by her mother, Alma moved to Toronto to take up her studies.[37] The college was situated in a commanding building on Pembroke Street, 'one of the most attractive residential streets in Toronto; quiet, beautifully shaded, and leading directly to the Allan Gardens'.[38] However, during the spring term of 1907, Alma started to have stomach cramps, pain in the abdomen, vomiting and nausea. Her health continued to decline and her mother called Walter to their daughter's bedside. She was taken into hospital and there were 'grave fears for her life'.[39] She was diagnosed with appendicitis. The concerns about Alma, who was now something of a local celebrity, even made the press in her hometown of Victoria.

W. W. Clark [sic], a prominent newspaperman of British Columbia, more familiarly known as 'The Rambler' and formerly of Victoria has left for Toronto, where he was called on account of the serious illness of his daughter, Miss Alma Clark. Miss Clark is well known amongst musical circles in the east, having some time ago won the Dr Torrington musical scholarship, of which master she was formerly a pupil. Recently she underwent an operation for appendicitis and as a result of this her life is now despaired of.[40]

Appendicitis had only been first diagnosed in 1880 and could still be fatal. As recently as 1902 the coronation of Edward VII had been postponed due to the king needing an emergency appendectomy, his surgeon firmly warning him that if the operation didn't go ahead the only event taking place in Westminster Abbey would be a royal funeral.

Alma was taken to hospital and an emergency operation was performed, but at the beginning of May the press was reporting that the procedure had not gone well. The appendicitis – or the complications following the surgery to correct it – lasted throughout the summer months, with Alma's life held in the balance. At the beginning of August she was finally discharged from hospital and began her convalescence. But she was determined not to let the illness interrupt her studies. She resumed the course, applying herself assiduously to her work as well as attending concerts by the many musicians who visited Toronto's famous Massey Hall. She was 'constantly hearing good music'.[41]

Despite her illness, she won the Mason and Risch scholarship in 1908 and was awarded the Torrington Gold Medal in 1908–09. She gave many recitals in the college hall on Saturday afternoons as well as public recitals with a full orchestra in Massey Hall – a 3,500-seat venue – which she remembered with pride: 'I gave several recitals in Toronto, and received splendid support. The people were lovely to me, and the Press gave me such good notices, I am very proud of them. At one concert I played Mendelssohn's Concerto with the Toronto Symphony Orchestra and I think that was the most difficult thing I have done yet. It carried me away playing with the orchestra. I loved it.'[42]

She was a born performer with an instinct for music: 'Strike a chord on the piano and she could identify every note in it.'[43] Despite her youth, she was technically very accomplished and without any debilitating nerves. She played the European classical repertoire and all from memory, throwing herself into the pieces she played, giving herself up to the emotion in the music. 'I don't always feel in the right mood, and when I am not I am disappointed in myself, because I know I should have played better. That is just the beginning of a concert, for I usually lose myself and forget everything.'[44]

She later recalled that one of the highlights of her professional career was, at the age of seventeen, playing both a violin concerto and a piano concerto in the same concert. Finally, in 1909 she graduated with her diploma and became an Associate of the Toronto College of Music. Torrington proudly boasted to the press that 'this young western girl is a musical wonder'.[45]

* * *

By 1910, Alma and her parents had settled in a spacious modern house in Pendrell Street, Vancouver, where her father had taken a job with the local newspaper *The Sun*, while at the same time dealing in property. He presented Alma with a special reward for

her success: a brand new grand piano. At eighteen years old Alma
had matured into a 'tall finely built' girl with 'questioning eyes that
displayed a frank, open nature'.[46] Mary Lomas, a journalist for
Westward Ho! magazine, wrote a feature about 'Canada's Musical
Prodigy'[47] in February that year. Alma was the 'embodiment of
youth at the threshold of life, eagerly awaiting for Time to reveal to
her the great human secret in the music of the masters'. But by now
she had given up the violin in order to concentrate fully on studying
the piano. Lomas was completely charmed by Alma, who played
passages from Beethoven, Chopin and Liszt for her: 'Her style of
playing is as unaffected as she is herself; she executes the difficult
passages with an ease and artistic skill that are the result of splendid training: her touch is delicate and clear; her manner at attack
displays a force and intensity of feeling that is unexpected in one so
young. It is the sudden revelation of this power, combined with a
sympathetic tenderness in the softer movements, that betrays a temperament without which it is impossible to become a great artist.'[48]

Lomas was convinced that Alma had an extraordinary future
ahead of her as a concert pianist, well equipped as she clearly was
with the essentials to overcome the difficulties on the road to success and fame: 'health and a deep love of nature: a great capacity for
hard work; and ambition with the aid of temperament, to achieve
great things'.[49]

Finally, on Friday 28 April 1911, Alma made her formal professional debut in Victoria as a concert pianist. She was no longer a
prodigy, but hailed as a genius – an exceptional home-grown talent
with worldwide fame and fortune in her grasp: 'There are many
pianists but there are not many of the calibre of Alma Victoria
Clarke.'[50]

But despite the reputation of teachers like Torrington and schools
like the Toronto College of Music, North America suffered from a
deep-rooted inferiority complex regarding its native music culture.
Audiences wanted to hear the best of European music played by the
most celebrated European players and by the end of the nineteenth
century, importing musicians and opera companies from Europe

had become a thriving industry. The latest sensations in European music would tour Canada and America, preceded by intensive publicity campaigns. The American concert pianist and near contemporary of Alma, Olga Samaroff (née Lucy Hickenlooper), realised that she would need some sort of European pedigree if she wanted to sustain a successful concert career in America.[51] Samaroff spent five years in Europe before she could return to America as a commercially viable performer. With such prodigious talent, and with Walter's inheritance to support her, Alma's parents now planned to send her abroad to complete her studies in Germany, the home of her grandfather.[52] For the still very much German-defined Wolff family, this would have seemed like an inevitable next step and the closing of a circle. Alma would become that rarest of things, a home-grown concert player with an international reputation; the youthful, accomplished embodiment of the young nation she came from.

* * *

The flamboyantly named Caledon Robert John Radclyffe Dolling was born on 10 August 1886, the eldest son of Caledon Josia Dolling and his wife Harriet. The Dollings were an ancient French Huguenot family who had settled in Maralin in County Down. Caledon's mother Harriet Crace was part of a celebrated family of interior designers who had worked for every British monarch from George III to Queen Victoria. Their work included the decoration of Buckingham Palace, Windsor Castle and the Royal Pavilion in Brighton. Caledon and his younger brother Harry attended Tonbridge School as day boys. He left school in 1904 to train as an officer in the Indian Army. Although he passed the entrance examination for Sandhurst, he was rejected because of his poor eyesight. Two years later, like the Wolff family, he was lured to British Columbia by the Canadian Pacific Railway's breathless accounts of the province's booming economy and unparalleled opportunities. Like many young men at the time, he tried his hand at farming in Saskatchewan. His attempts proved a failure, however, so in 1910 he

moved to Vancouver, in a year that saw the city's population growing at a rate of 1,000 per month. He opened a real-estate agency in
partnership with a fellow immigrant from England, Robert Stark,
and by 1911 they were advertising themselves as property specialists. Though the occasion that Alma met Dolling is not recorded,
with her father now dealing in property too it may well have been
her father who introduced Alma to her future husband: a tall,
bespectacled Irishman with a sandy-coloured moustache and a
unique accent, 'a native of Ireland who [had] knocked about in
Canada, his speech savour[ed] of both countries'.[53] Alma charmed
him with her warmth, vivacity and depth: 'At one moment she
would be wildly gay, and would fling her arms in the air to empha-
size her voluble flow of words. The next moment she would be silent
and subdued. Her eyes – so grey and magnetic – compelled attention to everything she said. [One] noticed particularly ... the very
intense way in which she looks into one's face and how her eyes
become large with emotion or excitement.'[54]

Dolling's patrician background must have appealed to Alma – and
particularly to Alma's mother, for whom the squalor of Walworth
was sharp in her memory. Alma's relationship with Dolling further
justified the Clarkes' decision to leave England for Canada all those
years ago. Here was the granddaughter of an immigrant tailor being
courted by an aristocrat. It was a textbook example of the upward
social mobility that British Columbia had afforded them. Alma later
claimed that the couple's youthful romance had culminated in elope-
ment, though their marriage licence records that Dolling's friend and
colleague Robert Stark was a witness at the wedding, as was Alma's
mother, who also gave her daughter away.[55]

The couple were married at five o'clock on 23 July 1913 at St
Mark's Church in Seattle, then home to Alma's Aunt Mina. Dolling
was twenty-seven and Alma twenty-two. She wore a travelling suit
and hat and carried a bouquet of lilies of the valley.[56] They toured
British Columbia for their honeymoon. Dolling's younger brother
Harry, who arrived too late to attend the service, remembered
seeing the couple from Dolling's office in Grenville Street as they

returned from the honeymoon. 'I saw Alma first. She was dressed in a white suit and she looked absolutely radiant – a sight I have never forgotten. She looked superb.'[57]

For Alma, the future looked extraordinarily bright. She was on the cusp of a lucrative and fulfilling concert career and was married to a man she loved.

On the day the Dollings celebrated their wedding, the *Colonist* headline also celebrated a new innovation in communication as the newspaper was able to contact a ship '1,000 miles distant' by wireless telegraph.[58] They were on the verge of the modern world of mass communication; the youthful twentieth century looked full of possibility and hope. Still on the front page, but fighting for space, there was minor news thousands of miles away in Europe. Prospects for peace were brighter in the troubled Balkan states, with First Lord of the Admiralty Winston Churchill stating that 'spring and summer were marked in Europe by an exceptional tranquillity'.[59]

CHAPTER THREE

MRS DOLLING

4 August 1914–21 August 1916

> Mankind ... has got into his hands for the first time the tools
> by which it can unfailingly accomplish its own extermination.
> Death stands at attention, obedient, expectant, ready to serve,
> ready to sheer away the people en masse; ready to be called
> upon to pulverize, without hope of repair, what is left of
> civilisation.
>
> – Winston Churchill, *The World Crisis: The Aftermath*[1]

In 1914, Canada was a self-governing dominion of the British Empire, but did not control its own foreign affairs. As during the Boer War, the Canadian government could decide the nature and extent of Canada's war effort but, fundamentally, it would immediately be drawn into any war should Britain declare one. In 1910, the Canadian prime minister, Wilfred Laurier, had stated that 'when Britain is at war, Canada is at war. There is no distinction.'[2]

Germany had long recognised the strategic importance of Vancouver and its adjacent coalfields. And Canada's meagre defences were a militia of only 3,110 men backed by 74,606 'citizen soldiers', all mounted in the nineteenth-century manner. When the German light cruiser *Leipzig* was spotted ominously patrolling the Pacific coast, the *Vancouver Province* asked, 'If Great Britain and Germany are drawn into a European War, what is going to happen to British Columbia? How will this defenceless province protect herself from raids by hostile cruisers?'[3] In July 1914, a Seattle shipyard had completed two submarines for the Chilean Navy, but Chile had been hesitating to pay the bill until all its specifications had been met. On 3 August, when Germany declared war on France and invaded neutral Belgium, the shipyard offered both the submarines to British Columbia for just over $1 million. The prime minister of British Columbia, Richard McBride, accepted with alacrity. Britain, which had long pledged to defend Belgium's sovereignty, issued an ultimatum to Germany on 4 August demanding the withdrawal of German troops. When this ultimatum expired at midnight, Britain and Germany were at war. Consequently, so too was the British Empire. The next day, above a front-page photograph of George V alongside an image of the battleship HMS *Iron Duke*, the *British Colonist* announced, 'British Empire Declared War on Germany'.[4] The message was loud and clear; the empire was all in it together.

Most Canadians greeted the outbreak of war with enthusiasm. When word reached Victoria the crowds outside the *Colonist*'s office burst into cheers, followed by heartfelt renditions of 'God Save the King' and 'Rule Britannia'. In Ottawa, thousands stood in the streets and sang the national anthem, 'The Maple Leaf Forever', and 'O Canada'. In Toronto, the official declaration came with a shock: 'Immense crowds gathered at the newspaper offices waiting for definite news. When the bulletins were finally posted placing the matter beyond doubt and the intelligence was disseminated, it was at first received in silence. Then all possible consequences were forgotten in an outburst of patriotism and the streets resounded with cheers for the empire.'[5]

Eighty per cent of Vancouver's population had British origins and an angry mob attacked the German consulate there, tearing down the double-headed eagle from above the door and burning an effigy of the Kaiser.[6] Ironically, the second largest ethnic group in British Columbia were, like Alma's family, German. Suspicion about German spies among the German immigrant population became common. On 10 August, the German assistant manager of the famous Château Frontenac was arrested as a German reservist and three Germans suspected of spying were arrested in Nova Scotia.[7] For Alma's German-speaking family, who had always been proud of their background and heritage, the war with Germany must have made life deeply uncomfortable.

British Columbians were ready for the fight, 'not just for the lust of conquest but because we one and all think that there is grave danger to our Empire, and to the motherland whence the majority of us came'.[8] Throughout the province, British Army reservists scrambled to book passages to England to re-join their regiments and recruitment offices were swamped. In all, 619,636 Canadians would enlist to fight on behalf of the empire. On 19 August, Canada formally declared war and three days later passed the War Measures Act, providing the government with new and expanded powers. Alma's husband applied for service and was given a commission in the 11th Royal Irish Fusiliers of Canada. Dolling was disappointed not to be offered a role in combat because of the poor eyesight[9] that had already thwarted his military career and was sent instead to the port of Prince Rupert, where he was appointed second in command in a training division. Though a strict disciplinarian, he was much admired by his men, and never asked them to do more than he would do himself. Many of the recruits he trained subsequently won commissions and promotions. Alma accompanied her husband to Prince Rupert and was remembered for devoting all her spare time to organising singing, boxing, athletic and football competitions for the men. But Dolling was dissatisfied with training and after a year in Prince Rupert he was still keen to see action on the front line. Having re-applied to the War Office, he finally secured a role in combat. On 27 August 1915, Dolling and Alma set sail from New York for England on a wave of imperial fervour.

On 8 September, Dolling was offered a temporary commission with a reserve battalion – the 2nd – of the Royal Welch Fusiliers.[10] The Royal Welch was one of the oldest British infantry regiments, with a rich tradition going back to the seventeenth century. The history of the Fusiliers in the Great War is well documented and both

Siegfried Sassoon and Robert Graves served with them. The experiences of the 2nd Battalion are described in Sassoon's *Memoirs of a Foxhunting Man* and *Memoirs of an Infantry Officer*, as well as in Graves's autobiographical *Goodbye to All That*. They were also recorded by Frank Richards in his memoir *Old Soldiers Never Die* and by J. C. Dunn in *The War the Infantry Knew*. Shortly before war was declared, the Fusiliers' regimental mascot, a white goat, unexpectedly died. Dunn wryly observed that 'he must have known something'.[11]

By the time Dolling arrived in northern France on 8 October 1915, the new fighting system of what became known as trench warfare was already a year old.

> Much labour was needed to repair and remake trenches that collapsed with time and weather as well as from damage by shell-fire ... Hundreds of miles of duckboard were laid to mitigate the mud and the consequent wastage by trench-foot ... To live in trenches in the winter months some stoicism, a little experience, and a good deal of individual resource are needed ... The life is sociable, and there's always occupation, there are some visitors, there's shop and gossip, and rumour unending; but it's a succession of interruptions, and too communal not to be irksome. There's interest at first for the intelligently interested, but interest flags in that atmosphere; the deprivation of individual preoccupations is the worst of it, and so life becomes monotonous to the active-minded ... the rats and the lice are always with us.[12]

The Royal Welch Fusiliers had engaged in a number of major battles from the outset of the war and by 1915 they were involved in all the major engagements in the British section of the Western Front. Dolling's battalion was part of the 19th Infantry Brigade, which in turn was part of the 33rd Division that took over the line at Cuinchy and Cambrin in late 1915. Robert Graves recalled, 'Cuinchy bred rats. They came up from the canal, fed on the plentiful corpses, and multiplied exceedingly ...'[13] Graves also wrote of the brick-stacks that dominated the flat landscape – thirty or so brick structures that had been built by a local brick factory just prior to the outbreak of war. Each was about 16ft high, a formidable obstacle in an attack and equally as useful as shelter in defence. The majority of the brick-stacks were within German territory, though some lay behind British lines. The six brick-stacks in Dolling's unit's sector became a byword for a deathtrap as they were heavily targeted by the Germans day and night by *Minenwerfer* bombs, mortars and 'flying pigs'.

Early in 1916, the 2nd Battalion experimented with a new form of engagement: the raid. These had to be organised with extreme precision by officers like Dolling: issuing maps, siting machine guns and mortars correctly, digging mine galleries, cutting wire, carefully placing barrages, setting up bombs and assessing aerial intelligence from the General Staff.

At the end of January, the Germans had blown and occupied the third of three overlapping craters in the neighbourhood of Givenchy, just north of La Bassée Canal. Givenchy had a reputation among the men as a sort of living hell: 'The fire of bitter antagonism never died down to ashes in such places ... the wind of every passing shell would fan the embers into a blaze of fury.'[14] The topography was exposed, dangerous and – some men felt – cursed. From the middle of these craters, the Germans continued to dominate part of the British line. In the early hours of 6 February,[15] an engineering platoon led a raid to bomb the Germans out. At the same time, Dolling and his men went into No Man's Land to protect the flanks, facing artillery and machine-gun fire, bombs, rifle-grenades and trench-mortars. By dawn, Dolling's company had turned the Germans out of the crater, inflicting heavy losses on the enemy and driving them completely out of position; the raid was a success. On inspecting the crater, the British realised that the Germans had only been thirty-five yards away from their own lines. They christened it the 'RWF crater'. Dolling had been badly wounded but forty other men had died taking it.[16]

Meanwhile, Alma was working in the War Office in Whitehall,

while commuting to Chislehurst on the outskirts of London
where she was living at 'Sunnyways', the house of Dolling's aunt,
Margaret Solly. On 9 February, she received a telegram about
Dolling's health following the raid: 'wounded on 5th Feb but
remains at duty'.[17] Telegrams cost 6d for every nine words, and
a penny for each extra word after that, so unimportant words
were left out and messages were very short. Alma's letters to her
husband – and his to her – do not survive, but even officers like
Dolling were not permitted to describe the events they were living
through. Alma would have had little idea of what he was enduring
and no idea at all where he was.

On 13 February, Alma received another telegram indicating that
her husband had been admitted to Meerut British General Hospital
in Rouen,[18] but he was discharged two weeks later. For his bravery,
Dolling was awarded the Military Cross, which was announced in
The Gazette, the official public record, on 13 March:

> Military Cross awarded to Temp. 2nd Lieut. C R J R Dolling,
> Royal Welch Fusiliers, for conspicuously gallant leading during
> a night attack. It was mainly due to his promptness and coolness
> in handling his men that the assaulting party took the posi-
> tion aimed at. He was wounded in three places, but kept up the
> morale of his men. On a previous occasion he led a successful
> bombing raid against an enemy working party and accounted for
> several of them.[19]

Vera Brittain observed in *Testament of Youth* that, in 1916, the
MC 'meant a good deal; it was still a comparatively rare decoration, awarded only for acts of really conspicuous courage'.[20] Alma,
despite anxiously waiting in London, at least could take some comfort from the fact that her husband had been hailed as a hero.

Two days after Easter on 25 April, Dolling was involved in
another raid on the German trenches at Cuinchy. This time he was
injured with multiple wounds and admitted to the Lahore General
Hospital in Calais. Again, a telegram to Alma on 28 April offered

scant information: 'Condition satisfactory. Will send any further news.'[21] He was hailed as 'the leading light of the show' and his company commander commended him warmly: 'I cannot say enough of his conduct and the good work he has done since he has been with us.' On Saturday 29 May, Dolling attended an investiture at Buckingham Palace where he received the Military Cross from the king.[22] Though a proud Alma accompanied her husband to the palace, she was not permitted to attend the ceremony and was obliged to wait outside.

* * *

Dolling returned to the front early in July. Three years into the war, he was now a veteran, and for him, as for so many men in his battalion, the fighting was taking its toll. He had been re-posted to the 9th Battalion, but his commanding officer wanted him as company commander in the 2nd Battalion. At last he received the promotion for which he had several times been recommended, being promoted acting captain in command of B Company on 3 August.[23] He joined them at a new location, alongside the River Somme. The Somme offensive had begun on 1 July when the British Army suffered nearly 60,000 casualties in a single day, including 20,000 dead, equivalent to the total British losses during the Boer War. One hundred and forty-one bloody days of attack and counter-attack followed over the slopes of an insignificant range of hills in Picardy.[24]

On 25 August, a telegram was sent to Alma in London, but as she wasn't there it was redirected to Dolling's aunt's house at Chislehurst: 'Deeply regret to inform you that CRJR Dolling 2nd Welsh Fusiliers was killed in action August 21st. The army Council offers their sympathy.'[25]

On the night of 20 August, Dolling had been killed instantaneously by a shell during a raid on High Wood, between the villages of Bazentin-le-Grand and Bazentin-le-Petit.[26]

Grieving Alma received many letters from Dolling's brother officers and men showing how great a blow his death was to them. They told of his great kindness, the value of his friendship, the encouragement of his example. 'The Regiment', wrote one, 'has lost a splendid soldier. I have not known a man possessed with a higher sense of duty.'[27] His commanding officer wrote directly to Alma. 'You have the whole Regiment's sympathy. They were all fond of him and relied on him and trusted his leadership ... He was such a man and had no fear and loved his work ... I have lost a brilliant Company Commander and a friend.'[28] On 7 August, writing on simple black-bordered notepaper, Alma instructed the army to send her late husband's kit to her 'as soon as possible please'.[29] Widowed at twenty-four and her heart broken, for Alma, and for hundreds of thousands of women like her, what was there to live for? Vera Brittain shared her sense of loss and despair: 'I wondered how I was ever going to get through the weary remainder of life. I was only at the beginning of my twenties; I might have another forty, perhaps even fifty, years to live. The prospect seemed appalling.'[30]

To make matters worse, as Dolling was registered as a temporary second lieutenant on his death certificate, Alma was only offered the corresponding widow's pension. She challenged this, stating that Dolling had been a captain, commanding B Company for two months before his death, and was therefore entitled to a captain's pension.[31] Alma's case was passed to the War Office, but the process was painful and protracted. On 21 October, they wrote to Alma's solicitor advising that a declaration in support of her plea would be needed, together with proof that she had actually been married to Dolling: 'Should Mrs Dolling be unable to obtain the signature of an officer not below the rank of Lt Colonel, that of Major, a Captain of some years' service, a Justice of the Peace, a Minister of Religion or a medical practitioner will be accepted.'[32]

Exasperated, but not defeated, Alma wrote to the former Canadian prime minister himself, Sir Richard McBride, who had resigned his post in 1915 and had since worked as agent general of British Columbia in London. McBride, aware of Alma's fame as a concert pianist in Canada before the war, was only too happy to support her plea and vouch for her. He wrote her a personal, handwritten letter: 'As to your bona fides and good standing I shall be only too pleased to be of assistance to you. You may say to the authorities that my name can be had as a reference with regard to your case.'[33] On 6 November, Alma's solicitor wrote to the War Office that Alma was 'rather at a loss as to who can sign the form as she is a stranger over here'.[34] However, they offered McBride's assurance and, perhaps disingenuously, wrote that they trusted 'that in the circumstances this will be sufficient for your purposes'.[35]

Alma was staying at Sunnyways in Chislehurst when Dolling's brother Harry visited her there. He had been invalided out of the army with dysentery since 1915. One day a parcel arrived addressed to Alma from the War Office. In it were Dolling's few remaining possessions, 'small articles of specially sentimental or intrinsic value',[36] which had been carefully sent back from France, wrapped in his sleeping bag. Harry helped unroll it. The first item Alma came across were Dolling's glasses, broken in pieces; 'that was a terrible sight to her'.[37] It would be all she had left of her husband and her marriage. She had no funeral arrangements with which to distract herself. In contrast to the bodies of American soldiers who were all shipped home for private burial, Alma would not be permitted to bring her husband's body home. There was a strong sentiment in all ranks that the dead rest with the main body of their comrades. The result was what we have today – a vast number of cemeteries, strung like beads on a rosary the length of the British part of the Western Front.[38] On 23 November, Alma finally received a letter informing her that Dolling had been buried at Flatiron Copse British Cemetery near Bazentin: 'The Military Secretary ventures to send this information now, in case Mrs Dolling has not previously received it.'[39] Alma had not been informed of her husband's final resting place for three months. Now that she knew where he was, the only thing that seemed to matter to her was to visit his grave, to pay her respects. To say goodbye.

Finally, on 18 December, the matter of the pension was settled and Alma was granted a £250 gratuity and £100 a year.[40] The pension was more than a disagreement about a war widow's rights. Crucially, it was to give her the financial independence to fund her next move. Rather than retreat into despair or spiritualism – the number of registered spiritualism societies doubled between 1914 and 1919 – Alma was determined to visit Dolling's grave. With her income secured and no responsibilities, she would not remain alone in London or in Chislehurst with Dolling's aunt. She would seek out her husband's grave by volunteering to help men just like him. And in order to do so, she would travel into the horror of the world itself – the Western Front.

Orderly Dolling

CHAPTER FOUR

FRANCE

5 January 1917–6 January 1918

Perhaps you need the close proximity of death to experience
that intoxicating sensation of being alive, and of performing
every hour of the day some vitally necessary task in the
service of life.

– Elsie Butler, Scottish Women's Hospitals[1]

In August 1914, millions of able-bodied men at home in Britain and
across the empire had rushed to join the services to fight for king
and country. At the same time, millions of women set about raising
funds, establishing medical units or organising help for refugees.
In Edinburgh, at a meeting of the Scottish Federation of Women's
Suffrage Societies, Dr Elsie Inglis had suggested that the Federation
might offer their support to the Red Cross. Such a venture could
promote the cause of women's suffrage while the suffragettes'
more militant action was suspended for the duration of the war.
Writing to the suffragist campaigner Millicent Fawcett, Dr Inglis
explained that by volunteering to support the war effort, she felt the
Federation might help to secure votes for women when the war was
over: 'I cannot think of anything more calculated to bring home to
men the fact that women can help intelligently in any kind of work.
So much of our work is done where they cannot see it. They'll see
every bit of this.'[2]

Initially it was mooted that an Edinburgh school could be turned into a hospital for the war wounded, staffed entirely by women. When the school building was found to be unavailable, Dr Inglis offered the proposed 100-bed unit to the Red Cross and the War Office. Both offers were swiftly turned down. There was no interest in a hospital staffed by women. Dr Inglis was told to 'go home and sit still'.[3]

Undaunted, Inglis wrote to the French ambassador in London offering hospital units to the *Croix-Rouge Française* 'officered by women doctors and staffed by fully-trained nurses and qualified dressers'. She made a similar offer to the Serbian authorities. Recognising that their own medical services were inadequate, both France and Serbia accepted Dr Inglis's offer. In Edinburgh, she convened a Scottish Women's Hospitals Committee to raise funds and recruit volunteers. By the end of August, they had raised over £5,000 – an incredible sum – which would fund three units at a cost of £1,000 per hundred-bed unit.[4] By 27 November, Madame de la Panouse, the president of the *Croix-Rouge,* was able to offer the women an ancient and empty abbey, situated on the edge of the forest of Chantilly, 30 miles north of Paris and just behind the front line.[5]

Founded in 1229 by Louis IX, Royaumont Abbey was a picturesque Cistercian building, with a cloistered garden and a fountain in the middle. It was situated on an undulating plain, surrounded by woods with a river that ran through the grounds and into a lake. It had been evacuated in 1905 by the Sisters of the Holy Family when a law was passed against religious orders and had remained empty until the owner had offered it to the *Croix-Rouge* at the outbreak of war. In September 1914, the seemingly unstoppable German forces were only a few days' march from Paris and had just reached the abbey, when they were swept back by the Allies, leaving Paris safe and Royaumont unscathed. This, the Germans' first major defeat, would turn the war of movement into a state of bloody paralysis. When the Germans retreated, they began to dig the trenches that were to define a new and horrifying style of warfare. By the time

Alma arrived at the abbey, long lines of trenches ran from Verdun in the east, westwards through Reims, Soissons and Noyon, then turned northwards to Albert, Vimy Ridge, Loos, Neuve-Chapelle, Armentières and Ypres, all the way to the coast south of Ostend.[6]

The first selection of women volunteers had arrived at the abbey in the middle of November 1914:[7] seven doctors, ten nurses, seven orderlies, two cooks, a clerk, an administrator, two maids and four chauffeurs.[8] They were faced with an extraordinarily impressive but hugely impractical building in appalling condition. The vast rooms were filthy with dirt and cluttered with heavy masonry, straw and rubbish. Broken windows needed mending, drains needed fixing and the rudimentary electricity needed repairing, too. The water supply was practically cut off, so buckets of water had to be carried up and down the seventy-one stairs to the second floor. A local bylaw prevented sewage from being discharged into the river, so arrangements were made to open up the ancient cesspits underneath the abbey.[9] Sourcing fresh water and fuel continued to be major issues throughout the women's stay at the abbey. They received their first patients in January 1915 when Royaumont was officially recognised as a military hospital: Hôpital Auxiliaire d'Armée 301.[10] The first ward to open was named 'Blanche de Castille', after the mother of the founder of the abbey,[11] and this was followed by wards named after Millicent Fawcett, Joan of Arc and Mary Queen of Scots. Finally, the abbey was 'a little corner of Britain; and without leaving their own country, the French [soldiers] would be breathing the free restorative air of England'.[12]

Soon after the outbreak of hostilities, British GHQ had issued a circular alerting the medical services to the particular challenges they would be facing in northern France, many of them conditions never experienced before in previous conflicts. Most of the casualties came directly from the trenches, the wounds having been received six to twenty-four hours earlier. Wounds from high-explosive shells and multiple injuries from machine-gun fire resulted in soil and clothing as well as metallic fragments being driven deep into the tissue where they formed the focus of infection. This

new type of wound, together with the agricultural land prevalent
in northern France, was a lethal combination. The well-manured
and heavily contaminated soil of the area – all too often a sea of
mud – harboured bacteria that allowed life-threatening conditions
to thrive, such as tetanus, streptococcal infection and gas gangrene.
The latter spread very quickly after injury and symptoms included
cracking or popping sounds in the tissues indicating gas formation,
discolouration of the muscles, bronzing of the skin, swelling and the
weeping of a foul-smelling liquid. Gangrene – death of the tissues –
would follow.[13] The patient would experience often-severe vomiting,
then collapse, followed by death. In an era before antibiotics, the
women at Royaumont were fighting these aggressive infections with
the most rudimentary of medicines – morphia and aspirin.

On 6 January 1917, with neither training nor medical experience, Alma Dolling arrived at the railway station at Creil to start
work as an orderly at Royaumont. On landing in wartime France
for the first time, like Evelyn Proctor who also arrived that winter,
Alma must have felt 'alone and homesick, far from England and
home and safety. [But she] was on a great adventure – the greatest
of [her] life.'[14]

> At every station that we went along in the slow train by which we
> journeyed from Boulogne to Creil, the platforms were crowded
> with bayoneted solders, fresh from the trenches with the soil still
> fresh upon them, others going back clean and spruce, accoutre-
> ments shining, their fond women giving a last adieu. They were
> so honest, so staunch-looking a set of men, that one felt it was
> good to have them for Allies. On arriving at Creil in the dark we
> found the station thickly thronged with its blue uniformed men,
> all the paraphernalia of war on them, waiting for the train to take
> them back to the firing line.[15]

Alma was typical of many of the orderlies who found their way to
the abbey. They came from a variety of backgrounds but each had
to be of sufficiently independent means as their services would be

voluntary. Only their uniforms, travel costs, board and lodging were provided.[16] Some women already had professions and a few, like Alma, were war widows. Many of them, empowered by the war as well as the pre-war activities of the suffragettes, yearned for independence and a taste of adventure. For Elsie Butler, volunteering to work for the Scottish Women's Hospitals was an antidote to staying at home in England, raising funds or knitting socks:

> To begin with there was the release from the fearful strain of living under the cloud of war as a useless civilian. However terrible the sights, however fearful the situations, however intolerable the pity wringing one's heart, that cloud at least had lifted. Then too being in a strange land among strange people gave a sense of remoteness from reality; yet everything one did was vital, urgent and exacting.[17]

Whatever their language abilities, all the women were expected to speak French, as the majority of the men they would be treating would be French soldiers.[18] Some of these were colonial forces from Senegal, Morocco and other French African colonies, and for most of the women this was their first engagement with non-white men. The orderlies were the 'lowest rank in the hospital hierarchy'[19] but were recruited 'for the most part from a privileged stratum of society'.[20] The orderlies were enthusiastic, undaunted, but untrained 'raw material', remembered one senior member of the staff, 'most of them lacking even the personal discipline that comes from going down into the world's arena and competing there for a living':[21] 'They were dreadfully reckless in their conversation and even in their behaviour. No doubt about it, they would have been called fast at home; for they swore, they smoked, they drank … they even flirted with men.'[22]

Alma's job as an orderly was physically and emotionally gruelling. In their blue-grey uniforms and mob caps, the young orderlies worked the wards, stores, kitchens and laundry. There were long hours, heavy lifting and stomach-churning tasks day after day:

dragging bags of dirty, blood-soaked linen along corridors, washing down the floors and operating tables.[23] Apart from their specific
tasks as hall porters, drivers, pharmacists, X-ray and theatre assis-
tants, all orderlies had to help to carry stretchers upstairs on the
arrival of the casualties, and subsequently from the different wards
to the X-ray room and operating theatre; this could entail mounting
six or seven flights of stairs.[24] But despite the often-horrific conditions, these young women, far from home and the comforts of their
ordinary lives, soon got used to them. On 24 July, Alma wrote
home about her workload and her life at Royaumont:

> We chop and change from post to post, but are never kept 'up'
> for more than three weeks at a time, the strain's too great ... I
> do all kinds of work ... We never know one day from another
> except by Mass every Monday morning then yesterday must
> have been Sunday. There is a fearful French push on at the
> moment and one can hardly think straight for noise. Every
> other night am 'Night orderly' – hours running something like
> this – Woke up at 4 a.m. on duty by 4.15, off duty at 4 p.m. in
> afternoon, Sleep till 8.45, on duty 9 p.m. till 8 a.m. next morn-
> ing. Sleep??? Till 12.45, duty at 1 o'clock, off at 6.30 when I
> have a night's rest till 4 next morning. It's a limit of a time and
> dreadful hours; I hardy know what I'm doing, for naturally one
> does not sleep *solidly* those few hours off. Am supposed to be
> asleep now ... but the noise is dreadful ... there's a bally fight
> going on over head – they quite intend finishing us this time –
> but they've tried before – and outside a few casualties and a bit
> o' damage – we still remain.[25]

Cicely Hamilton remembered the intense activity of the workload,
with 'rushes when the ambulances went again and again to the station ... where the trains from the front discharged their wounded,
when every ward was full, and the doctors and nurses were never
out of the operating-theatre, and you wondered how they kept
going'. And there would be other times – long stretches – when

beds were vacant and operations few, and the staff in general had 'plenty of leisure to remark on each other's shortcomings'.[26]

Being so close to the front line, the women were always aware of the danger they were in. The front was often a fluid place to be and the hospital could at any point slip into enemy hands, potentially resulting in the women being taken as prisoners of war.[27] But a feature of the Scottish Women's Hospitals was their unbreakable spirit. When the soldiers poured in through the doors, all the staff worked as one. António de Navarro noted in 1916 that 'perhaps the most admirable characteristic of this body of young women is an invariable light-heartedness which has survived their many months of grinding work'.[28] The orderlies were as keen as the doctors to prove what women could do on their own with no men to fall back on to do the unpleasant tasks. The orderlies also knew that those in charge were observing their work and determining where their particular talents lay. It was possible for an orderly to train as a radiographer or a laboratory technician or to take charge of a department – such as the pharmacy, the stores or housekeeping. Those who proved themselves particularly proficient in the wards would be upgraded to the rank of auxiliary nurse. Alma certainly assisted at emergency operations. She later told her sons that she frequently had to hold down men as they had their limbs amputated with a saw. The first time she had to hold a leg on her shoulders as it was sawn off, the smell of blood and anaesthetic sickened her to the point that she thought she would faint. On one occasion, she performed a mastoid operation herself on Tranche, the camp cat. This was strictly forbidden and the operation had to be performed in secret, after dark. Tranche's miraculous recovery was noticed immediately and Alma suspected of being responsible. The cat gave the game away by following her around like a grateful dog.[29]

As the war continued, the women at Royaumont explored ways of reaching casualties earlier so that they could reduce the delays that so greatly increased death rates from gas gangrene. What they needed was a hospital nearer the front line. In the summer of 1917, they came across a deserted evacuation centre, two rows of wooden huts right next to the railway station at a village called Villers-Cotterêts, near the town of Soissons, 5 miles away. Villers-Cotterêts had been battered in the preceding months and the surrounding countryside was a wasteland, stripped of trees and with trenches lining the roads. Shell holes some 30ft deep splattered the fields and the surrounding local villages had been reduced to piles of stone. Refugees tramped the roadside, begging for help as German prisoners of war attempted to mend the roads. Soissons was still under fire and, alarmed at the women's plans, the French considered that Villers-Cotterêts was a dangerous site for a hospital and 'very far for women to go'.[30]

Alma was one of the first women to travel to Villers-Cotterêts to establish the new field hospital. The 'dirty barracks' was an 'awful mess', but the women 'worked like the dickens with never a moment off to get the place repaired'. The wooden huts that were to become wards and accommodation for the hospital were basic: corrugated iron roofs, oil-papered windows and duckboards for paths laid across ever-present mud. But the wards were soon clean with whitewashed walls, 211 beds with red blankets and a staff of thirty-three. The wards in the front row of huts were named after the Allies: Serbia, Belgium, Italy, Portugal, Romania and Britain. A covered walkway linked the wards to the railway station so that the wounded could be lifted directly into the hospital without exposure to the elements. In the second row of huts were three more wards – Russia, France and America – as well as an operating theatre, X-ray installations, offices and accommodation for the staff, which was also very basic.

We slept on the floor as far as I can remember – I suppose we had a palliasse or something – something that raised us a bit from the rats. The things I remember about the huts were the rats. At night time bombs used to drop – I didn't wake – awful noises they used to make – some not very far away – but if a rat came – just a scratch – I jumped up and threw my shoes all over the place trying to get these rats – I was much more afraid of the rats than the Germans.[31]

By early August, the hastily adapted huts were functioning as a frontline hospital.

Each ward has one sister and one orderly and one 'infirmiere' [a lightly wounded soldier capable of some work]. Really we are nurses and not orderlys [sic] and they call us nurse up here – So you see I am really doing the [same] work as people who have been here for months as the other two orderlies on the ward are old hands – But I don't know how we are going to exist in winter as we have to go out for everything as the huts do not communicate. I must have some warm clothes sent. I am hoping they will interchange us with people at Royaumont as camp life is much harder in lots of ways.[32]

Though the staff were fewer and the work harder at Villers-Cotterêts, the hospital was more informal, with nursing sisters not strict about uniforms and doctors and orderlies living harmoniously together, with a greater fluidity in their roles and responsibilities: 'One realises these women – extraordinarily brilliant women – are just the same as ourselves and are so simple and nice and kind – we call each other by our surnames – but we are otherwise entirely feminine! Which might astonish some people who might imagine the Scottish women to be suffragettes of the most rabid type!'[33]

* * *

In December 1917, despite the continuing horror and exhaustion, another Christmas approached on the front line. As she had done at Prince Rupert, Alma would have been heavily involved in the events to celebrate the festive season, a moment of warmth and normality among the dark days of the winter, approaching the fifth year of a war that was supposed to have been over years before.

While we were having tea some beautiful carols were sung by 6 of the staff … the lights were turned out suddenly and out of the darkness from the double doors that led from the refectory to the carpenters' shops lanterns came held by the carolers who were dressed in long military French blue waterproof capes with the hoods over their heads round which was put white cotton wool pieces so that it looked like snow and the storm lanterns were trimmed with holly and mistletoe of which there is an abundance here – they came singing and sang three carols then walked out singing as they went through the hut with the snow and continued in each ward in turn. The men (Canadians) seemed quite touched. We forget they are so far from home and things like that must bring it very near to them.[34]

Alma left the hospital at Villers-Cotterêts in October and returned to Royaumont for a short time before returning to England. She served with the Scottish Women's Hospitals from 5 January 1917 until 6 January 1918.

Today, a worn and inconspicuous plaque on the walls of Royaumont commemorates the work that Alma and hundreds of other brave and determined women did there: '10,861 wounded French soldiers received from an exclusively feminine staff, the benefits of a devotion without limits.'[35]

Alma's children remembered that she talked about being awarded the *Croix de Guerre* for her war work. Though there's no record of the award, on 14 December 1921 the *Vancouver Colonist* reported that Alma 'was wounded during one of the raids and was awarded a special medal from the French government'. The *Vancouver Daily World* also reported on 19 December 1921 that Alma had 'abandoned her musical career during the late war and volunteered as a field orderly with the Scottish Women's Hospital at the Abbaye de Royaumont, France, and later drove an ambulance. She was wounded during one of the raids, and was awarded a special medal.'[36]

A year later, the same newspaper added further detail to the circumstances under which Alma received the *Croix de Guerre*, reporting that as well as saving lives, Alma had risked her own life, resulting in being injured herself: '[She had] served voluntarily throughout the entire war, first, at the war office in London, and later with the *Croix-Rouge Française* as a field orderly and ambulance driver, and was decorated by Marshall Joffre after doing heroic work at Soissons, where she was wounded whilst dressing the wound of an Arab, who was killed by the same shell.'[37]

If Caledon Dolling had died a hero, his widow had matched his courage, committing herself to tending the wounded and saving lives on the front line. At one point when Royaumont was being bombarded by the Germans, Alma wished she could retaliate – to be a man and fight like one. But then she remembered the obligation towards the red cross on her arm, 'precious little protection, I'm sorry to say, but *c'est la guerre*'.[38]

There is no record that Alma achieved her wish to visit her husband's grave, but she was a determined young woman and not averse to using either her charm or her connections to get her own way. Organised tours for war widows to visit their husbands' graves were not coordinated until 1919, when the St Barnabas Society was set up, subsidising the pilgrimages of women who would not otherwise have been able to afford it. If she managed to visit the grave independently before she left France, she would have found Flatiron Copse Cemetery a little to the east of Mametz Wood where Dolling had died. As in Kipling's story of a bereaved woman tracing the grave of her lost loved one, in 1918, the cemetery would not have been completed and the plot Alma was searching for difficult to find: 'All she saw was a merciless sea of black crosses, bearing little strips of stamped metal at all angles across their faces. She could distinguish no order or arrangement in their mass; nothing but a waist-high wilderness of weeds, stricken dead, rushing at her. She went forward, moved to the left and the right hopelessly, wondering by what guidance she would ever come to her own [grave].'[39]

When she located it, Alma would have seen that Dolling lay among the regimented democracy of 1,572 other husbands, fathers and sons who had died in the bloody summer of 1916.[40]

Alma Pakenham

CHAPTER FIVE

MRS PAKENHAM

26 January 1918–29 December 1923

> Why couldn't I have died in the war with the others? Why
> couldn't a torpedo have finished me, or an aerial bomb, or
> one of those annoying illnesses? I'm nothing but a piece of
> wartime wreckage, living on ingloriously in a world that
> doesn't want me.
>
> – Vera Brittain, *Testament of Youth*[1]

The loss of her first husband was the defining crisis of Alma
Dolling's young life. Her heart broken, she became 'a cynical
woman of the world, taking her pleasures where she could find
them'.[2] On her return to England from France in January 1918,
within a matter of days she found herself in a relationship with
another man. Like Dolling, he had served with some bravery in the
war. He was also married.

Known as 'Compy' to family and friends, Thomas Compton
Pakenham had an exotic and patrician background, related as
he was to the Earl of Longford. Born in Japan in 1893 to the
British naval attaché there, Pakenham spoke Japanese before he
learned English. He had a brother, Hercules Ivo, and three sisters,
Hermione, Cynthia and Daphne, known as 'Pinkie'. He attended the
China Inland Mission School in Chefoo in northern China, which
had been established in 1881 as a boarding school for the children

of missionaries. A quarter of the pupils were, like Pakenham, the children of British government officials. Frank McCarthy, himself the son of a missionary, joined the school as headmaster in 1895 and his ethos was spartan, puritan and evangelical, offering a 'useful rather than ornamental education preparing boys for business rather than for professional life'.[3] Games were taught and taken with 'English seriousness'. In his thirty-five years as head, McCarthy steered the school through some anxious times, including the Boxer Uprising of 1900, when Pakenham would have been a pupil at Chefoo. Encouraged by the Empress Dowager Cixi, the Boxers, a cult-like force, rebelled against the encroaching western colonisation of China and attacked foreigners, Christians and missionaries, so Chefoo School, with 250 foreign men, women and children, was a potential target. Throughout the crisis, the children kept a pillowcase with a complete change of clothes next to their beds in case they needed to abandon the school in a hurry during the night. During the rebellion, Chefoo had been threatened for a week and the parents of nine of Pakenham's fellow students had been killed.

Raised in the height of the colonial period, Pakenham developed a fascination with the structures and culture of the British Empire and in 1929 he would write *Dreamers of Empire*, a study of some of the pivotal characters who had defined the period of imperial expansion, such as Charles George Gordon, Richard Burton and Cecil Rhodes. But only a year later, Pakenham published an autobiographical novel, *Rearguard*, in which he depicted the Langdale family, a 'mutinous rearguard to a famous line' in pre-war Shanghai.[4] Though full of clichés in its depiction of the British behaving badly abroad, a world of tiffin, 'chop chop' and days at the club, *Rearguard* is a cynical depiction of the expatriate class who administered the British Empire. Relations between men and women are faithless and guided only by self-interest; attitudes to the locals and servants are superior and racist. Pakenham was clear that the whole Langdale dynasty – the very aristocracy he himself came from – was feckless and corrupt, their values selfish and empty.

Despite his later claims that he went to Oxford, Pakenham did not go to university at all and, intent on working in the law, he attended the Inns of Court, where he joined the Officers Training Corps as a private. When war broke out, he had joined the 5th Coldstream Guards, who were typically recruited from the upper classes. But this was only a reserve battalion that conducted guard duties in and around London and never saw active service. Shortly after his commission in 1915, Pakenham had married Phyllis Price,[5] in one of the many thousands of hasty wartime weddings that both parties would live to repent at leisure. Phyllis's mother had seen in this handsome Guards officer 'the kind of son in law she was looking for and firmly pushed him, with [Phyllis], towards the altar. As firmly, at a later date, she pushed him out of the house again, threatening him with a poker, because he had taken no time at all to reveal himself as a most unsatisfactory choice.'[6]

A daughter, Simona, was born on 25 September 1916, but she was destined never to actually meet her father. In her memoir *Pigtails and Pernod*, she recalled that he 'disappeared out of my life before I had time to notice him. Nobody told me anything about [him] beyond the fact that he was a Bad Man who had married Five Wives'. Years later, when Simona asked her mother what she ought to tell her friends at school about her father, she was advised to tell them, 'in a voice shaking with drama, "that he was a very brave solder and was recommended for the VC"'.[7]

Like Caledon Dolling, Pakenham was eager to take an active part in the war. By the time he joined the 142nd Machine Gun Company in October 1916, they had already been involved in the German attack on Vimy Ridge in May 1916 and in the Battle of Flers–Courcelette, capturing High Wood at the Somme. Once he joined them, Pakenham was engaged in the Battle of Transloy Ridges, in which they captured Eaucourt l'Abbaye. He then took part in the attacks on the Butte de Warlencourt, then the Battle of Messines, the Third Battle of Ypres and the Cambrai Operations, where his company captured Bourlon Wood.[8] In the *London*

Gazette on 17 September 1917, it was announced that Pakenham was to be awarded the Military Cross for his bravery:

> For conspicuous gallantry and devotion to duty when in command of a raid. Having been informed that it was important to obtain a prisoner, he remained with his party for three-quarters of an hour in the enemy's lines, until he discovered an occupied post, which he attacked, killing six of the enemy and taking one prisoner. His coolness and determination were remarkable.[9]

Pakenham was on leave from 12 to 26 January 1918 and it is during this time that he met Alma, who had only left Royaumont days before. With the looser conventions of wartime, the relationship became intimate quickly and by the summer the couple were living in a hotel in Grantham near Pakenham's base at Harrowby Barracks. Alma must have known that Pakenham was married and that he had a family, but this didn't stop her from pursuing a relationship with him. Aware that her husband was not on active service, Phyllis tracked him down and reminded him of his obligations to her and their young daughter.

24th September

Dear Compy,

I have not seen you since January last, and my letters to you are left unanswered. I have had no money since June last year, and had it not been for my people, both I and our baby might have starved. This state of things cannot go on and I must beg you to come back to me as my husband and live with me and maintain a home.

I will do my best to make things go happily.

Yours

Phil

PS I shall expect your answer within a week from now.[10]

Pakenham's reply was short and uncompromising. Already in a relationship with Alma, he made it clear that his marriage to Phyllis was over:

1st October 1918

> *Dear Phil*
> *I have read your letter asking me to go back to you, but really cannot see how, in any way, it is possible. I am sorry, I can't say anymore, but the idea would be too absurd a mockery, and I can only hope you can see it in this way.*
> *Yours,*
> *Compy*[11]

The breakdown of the Pakenhams' marriage was typical of many failed marriages at the end of the war. After rising slowly between 1858 and 1913, the divorce rate per thousand married couples jumped sixfold between 1913 and the post-war peak in 1921. There was a sharp but short-lived change in the sex ratio of divorce petitioners from about 55 per cent husbands before the war to about 75 per cent immediately after it, reflecting the fact that many men returned from the war to find that their wives had committed adultery in their absence. In an attempt to facilitate divorces for this unprecedented number of broken marriages, Lord Buckmaster introduced a private bill into the House of Lords adding desertion to adultery as a valid reason for divorce. In 1918, couples were not allowed to part simply because the relationship had broken down. Since 1857, men had been able to divorce their wives because of adultery, but women had had to prove adultery as well as another fault, which included cruelty, rape and incest. The bishop of Durham agreed that the laws relating to marriage would need to change under the influence of 'modern conditions, social and intellectual': 'We live in a time of revolutionary change, nowhere more far-reaching than in the region of sexual morality.'[12] Phyllis instigated divorce proceedings as Pakenham and Alma continued their affair.

* * *

On Monday morning, 11 November, the war was over. London went wild with delight when the news came through: 'Flags fluttered out from windows and balconies and roofs, and from the waving hands of the teeming multitude that swarmed the streets in an outburst of delirious, irrepressible joy.'[13]

In Downing Street, at exactly eleven o'clock, the prime minister, Lloyd George, appeared from No. 10, his face 'wreathed with smiles', a cue for a 'huge howl from the waiting crowd': 'I am glad to be able to tell you that the war will be over at eleven o'clock today. The British Empire has done a great share towards the winning of the war and we are now entitled to shout.'[14]

On the stroke of eleven, the crowd thrilled to the long-absent sound of Big Ben tolling the hour for the first time since 1914. But, like Alma and many other women whose men had been killed during the war, Vera Brittain was subdued on Armistice Day, the celebrations surrounding her at odds with the deep sense of alienation and loss she felt.

> I walked slowly up Whitehall, with my heart sinking in a sudden cold dismay. Already this was a different world from the one I had known during four life-long years ... And in that brightly lit, alien world, I should have no part. All those who I had really been intimate with were gone; not one remained to share with me the heights and depths of my memories ... The war was over; a new age was beginning; but the dead were dead and would never return.[15]

Though British forces had officially suffered around 750,000 deaths during the war, a further 1,663,000 men had been wounded and many of these subsequently died from their injuries on demobilisation. For years after the armistice the ghost of the war would haunt daily life on British streets, with amputee or blind ex-servicemen selling matches and bootlaces, or simply begging; a generation of men crucified with shell shock. Thirty per cent of all men between twenty and twenty-four had been killed. Consequently, as soon as the war ended, newspaper headlines speculated about 'Our Surplus Girls',[16] the *Manchester Evening News* reporting about 'Husband Hunting'. When the National Census was published in 1921, the statistics were devastating; in England there were 19,803,022 females and only 18,082,220 males, a difference of 1,750,000 and almost twice the number of women that had been anticipated.[17] In the tabloids, the word 'surplus' soon mutated into 'superfluous'; 'Britain's problem of 2 million superfluous women'.[18] For months the census story was never out of the press, with the *Daily Mail* asserting that 'the superfluous women are a disaster to the human race'.[19] Many of these women would also now lose their livelihoods as men returning from the war reclaimed the jobs they had given up in order to fight. Having made their contribution to the war effort, women had to patiently step aside. For a young war widow like Alma, even a reliably unreliable man like Compton Pakenham must have seemed better than no man at all.

On 23 January 1919, a notice was served on Pakenham at the officers' mess at Harrowby Barracks that he was guilty of deserting his wife, naming Alma as his mistress.[20] At the time he gave his address as Mrs Solly's home in Chislehurst. The decree nisi was issued on 17 June 1919. Pakenham was then issued with a bill of £44 10s 3d from Phyllis's lawyers – their costs for the divorce.[21] This would be followed by another bill of £9 19s 5d in October; divorce was an exacting and expensive business.

Alma and Pakenham were determined to leave England, to go away from Europe with its memories of destruction and death. On 12 September, they sailed on the *Caronia*, arriving in New York twelve days later. On their arrival at Ellis Island, the information that Pakenham and Alma gave the immigration authorities declared they were both Irish, the Pakenhams being Irish peers. Pakenham stated that his father was Sir William Compton Pakenham, a senior naval commander in the British fleet. Sir William was actually Pakenham's uncle, who was unmarried and had no children. These half-truths, embellishments and lies may well have been agreed by the couple in order to disguise the fact that they weren't married, as Pakenham's divorce had not yet been finalised. The decree absolute completing Pakenham and Phyllis's divorce was issued in January 1920, leaving Pakenham free to marry Alma, which he did in Brooklyn that July. They rented an apartment on 11th Avenue and Pakenham worked as a writer for magazines. Moving to Long Island, he made a living as a travelling lecturer, giving talks on economic conditions in Japan as 'Dr Pakenham', a title for which he wasn't qualified. Alma started to give piano lessons, a far cry from her career before the war as a concert soloist. A son, Christopher, or 'Toffy', was born on 8 July 1921. But the Pakenhams' financial problems were acute and Alma was no better at holding down a relationship with Compy than Phyllis had been. Sadder and wiser, she wrote to her mother, who, in March 1922, duly came to collect Alma and Christopher and took them back to her home in Vine Street, Vancouver. Now nearly thirty, Alma resolved to focus on teaching music and raising her son.

By 5 December 1923, Alma was performing as 'Mrs Compton Pakenham' at the Arion Club at the Empress, the pre-eminent hotel in Victoria that overlooked James Bay, and was very much the centre of the local social scene. This recital may have been her re-launch as a concert player. She had only taken to performing recently; despite her former fame as a soloist before the war, few in the audience that night remembered her. 'Mrs Pakenham was a stranger to the majority of the audience when she first came on the platform, but after listening for a few minutes, no one had the slightest doubt about her assured place as a pianist of the first rank.'[22]

The concert was a great success and enthusiastically reviewed by the *Colonist* the next day. Once again, Alma was hailed as 'brilliant', with a 'big concert style and polished technique combined with much individuality'.[23] With a renewed confidence, perhaps a return to the concert career that she had always dreamed of was a possibility?

Later that month, on the evening of 29 December, Alma was

chatting with a friend in the lounge of the Empress, having given another concert in Victoria. There were celebratory noises coming from the nearby banqueting hall, 'the sounds of revelry and men singing. Whoever they were, they were putting some real enthusiasm into the song':[24]

For he's a jolly good fellow, for he's a jolly good fellow
For he's a jolly good fellow, which nobody can deny![25]

But the song, Alma noted, wasn't the usual raucous din. She felt that 'every word was meant'. Alma's friend suggested that they should look into the banqueting hall and see who all the fuss was about, so they did. The friend was surprised to see that she knew the guest of honour who had inspired the outburst of singing: it was Francis Rattenbury, the famous architect.

Soon afterwards, the offstage party having finished, some of the men strolled into the lounge to finish their cigars and pipes. Alma's friend took the opportunity to introduce her to Mr Rattenbury. He was tall, vigorous and still handsome despite his fifty-five years, with thinning red hair touched with grey. He had designed the hotel they were standing in and from almost any of the windows she looked from, Alma could see the magical form of the parliament buildings he had designed, its outline lit with fairy lights as it had been since Queen Victoria's Diamond Jubilee. Rattenbury explained to her that they were celebrating as he had been given the go-ahead to build a new amusement centre behind the hotel. There'd been much discussion about it in the local newspapers, so Alma would have been aware of it. As they were talking, it became apparent that Rattenbury and Alma had mutual acquaintances. He was a great friend of her Aunt Emma, who had been widowed in 1909. Indeed, he had been a witness at her marriage to Percy Criddle in 1919, when Alma had still been in Europe. Victoria certainly was a small world.

And so it was that Alma first met Francis Rattenbury, the man she was destined to marry. The circumstances of this first meeting took on a romantic, even fated quality for Alma: 'The memory of that singing had gone to my head, and though I had resolved never to marry again, but to devote myself to my music, that song seemed to make all the difference.'[26]

Alone together for a moment, and heady on the festive atmosphere, with the lights twinkling across the bay, Alma was emboldened to compliment Rattenbury: 'Do you know that you have a lovely face?' Rattenbury was 'knocked out' by her words. 'Great Scott. Have I? I am going right home to have a look at it. I've never thought it worth looking at yet.'[27]

But Alma wasn't making small talk or flirting; she was sincere: 'I'm not joking. You have the kindest face I ever saw.' After the heartache and disappointment she'd had – the war, the death of her husband, the ill-advised marriage to Pakenham – Alma needed a little kindness. She was quite taken with him; 1924 was going to be a very happy New Year. Shortly after meeting Rattenbury, Alma admitted, 'If I don't love him, I simply don't know what love is.'[28]

Francis Mawson Rattenbury

CHAPTER SIX

Mr Rattenbury

11 October 1867–29 December 1923

> The greatest game in life is to set out to do something, strive against all difficulties, and win.
>
> – Francis Rattenbury[1]

Like Alma, Francis Rattenbury had both German and English ancestry. He could trace the history of his family in England as far back as the fifteenth century, when Johannes Von Ratenburg had escorted a bride from Bavaria to be married in the Devon town of Okehampton. Rather than return home, Von Ratenburg settled in England and anglicized his surname. The Rattenburys subsequently 'played a great part in the days of Henry VIII and Charles I' and, with the drive of an immigrant family, by the mid-seventeenth century a John Rattenbury had reached the esteemed office of mayor of Okehampton.[2]

Francis Mawson Rattenbury was born in Leeds to a family of Methodists on 11 October 1867. His life was dominated by his relationship with his mother, Mary Ann Mawson, the daughter of a successful Bradford printer who promoted merchandise produced by the local woollen mills.[3] She was a 'wonderful mother'[4] with a lively sense of humour and a strong will that her son would inherit. As an adult, Rattenbury wrote to her about the powerful influence she'd had on the development of his personality and ambition: 'Day by day I learned my lessons from you and hope and know I shall be a better man from what I learned. As I listened to you on every topic that came up I instinctively endeavored to gather from you a truer view of life.'[5]

He had little regard or warmth, however, for his father John, a professional artist who copied famous paintings of the day for the middle-class market. He had an older brother and sister, John – known as Jack – and Kate. The family had moved to a more modest house in Headingly when their father had given up a secure but dull job with the General Assurance Company in order to pursue a mediocre career as a painter. So Rattenbury was educated at Leeds Grammar School, which provided a free classical education for local boys whose parents couldn't afford to send them elsewhere.

On leaving school, Rattenbury was enrolled into the Yorkshire College with a view to joining his mother's family business, but he had little enthusiasm for the textile industry and left without graduating. However, in December 1884, Mary Ann noticed her son drawing a number of Christmas cards; he certainly had creative talent. She brought the cards to the attention of her brothers, William and Richard, who were partners in one of the leading architectural practices in Yorkshire, Lockwood and Mawson. Many years later, Rattenbury remarked that, for him, the Christmas cards had been 'a lucky thing'.[6] His mother's intuition was to change and define the course of his life.

The reputation of Lockwood and Mawson had been built on the commission to design a model manufacturing community for the progressive industrialist Titus Salt. As well as a factory, Salt had envisioned building an entire town on the banks of the River Aire, with schools, churches, a hospital and a library as well as neat dwellings for his workers. Lockwood and Mawson started working on Saltaire in 1851 and it kept them busy for the next twenty years. At the same time, they designed important civic buildings in Harrogate, Keighley, Boston, Wakefield and particularly Bradford, where they were responsible for St George's Hall, the Exchange and, the pinnacle of Lockwood and Mawson's partnership, Bradford Town Hall.

But by the time Rattenbury joined his uncles' practice in 1885, Henry Lockwood, the key creative figure in the partnership, had died some years previously. Without his creativity and ambition, Rattenbury realised that the firm's most successful years were behind them and that there was little more he could learn from his surviving uncle. At the time, there was much in the press about the huge building boom in Vancouver on the western coast of Canada. With demand for a new infrastructure and few designers and architects resident in the province, the ambitious young Rattenbury emigrated to British Columbia.

On 5 July 1892, an article appeared in the *Vancouver Daily World* announcing Rattenbury's arrival there: 'Attention is directed to the advertisement of Mr F. M. Rattenbury, architect, who has opened an office in the New Holland Block, Cordova St. He has been for ten years erecting all classes of buildings in connection with the well-known firm of Lockwood and Mawson, Bradford Town.'[7]

In this self-promotion, Rattenbury claimed to have trained under Henry Lockwood, the most talented architect at Lockwood and Mawson. In reality, he had only been eleven years old when Lockwood died. On the same page was a notice for a competition to design new parliament buildings for Victoria. The prime minster was allocating $600,000 for a new, aspirational symbol of British Columbia.[8] Freshly arrived from England, with extraordinary self-belief, Rattenbury entered the competition.

Rattenbury's design for the parliament buildings was more than a plan for a civic utility; it was a statement, defining British Columbia as an important outpost of the British Empire but also as a governing territory in its own right. A blending of the Romanesque, classical and Gothic in design, it was confident, commanding and refreshingly distinct from the neoclassical designs favoured by the state capitals in America. On 15 March 1893, Rattenbury received a telegram from the deputy chief commissioner of Lands and Works: 'Accept Congratulations. Come to Victoria by tomorrow's boat if possible.'[9]

At the age of twenty-five Rattenbury had won the most prestigious building commission in the history of British Columbia.

Within a month, Rattenbury had completed working drawings and a local builder, Fredrick Adams, was appointed as contractor. He predicted that Rattenbury's design would cost $61,000 over budget, but Rattenbury blithely promised that the building could be completed for less – $555,000.[10] The relations between Rattenbury and Adams were to be fraught with disagreement, difficulty and drama from the start. Rattenbury continued to clash with the city bureaucrats who vexed him throughout the life of the project. Finally, the parliament buildings were opened on 10 February 1898 to great acclaim. For Rattenbury it was a triumphant justification of his vision and his uncompromising tenacity as the public and the press applauded his work: 'The beauty of the structure calls forth the admiration of everyone who has seen it, while the perfection of the work and the thoroughness in which the details have been carried out is a surprise to visitors. In general design and in the choice of the stone for the buildings the good taste and judgment displayed has been decidedly happy, the result being a harmonious picture delightful to the eye.'[11]

Once the celebrations had died down, certain flaws in Rattenbury's design became apparent. Though the grand hall of the Legislative Assembly was indisputably imposing, it was very difficult for members to hear each other as the acoustics were so poor. At the same time, the lieutenant governor's suite of entertaining rooms, though offering a fine view of the harbour, were not functional either, as was noted by the caretaker: 'I would respectfully draw your attention to the entire absence of anything in the shape of Lavatory accommodation for either Ladies or Gentlemen, it has been found very akward [sic] at times when Entertainments were in progress we are compelled to furnish the crudest kind of accommodation, for the Ladies and Gentlemen have a long way to travel before reaching a Lavatory, which on such occasions are always crowded.'[12]

Such teething issues aside, just as Rattenbury had intended, the 'marble palace'[13] had elevated him from unknown immigrant to the most celebrated architect in the province, leading to many more domestic and commercial commissions, helping him amass a large personal fortune. But though an extraordinarily impressive achievement, the parliament buildings were delivered to the British Columbian government vastly over budget – just as Frederick Adams had forecast – at a cost of over $1 million.[14] The first great challenge of Rattenbury's career revealed him as an uncompromising and charismatic visionary with an ability to articulate the complex relationship between crown and colony in monumental architecture. But it had also exposed him as an arrogant self-publicist, intransigent when challenged, vituperative when wronged, sly and disloyal under pressure.

* * *

The construction of the parliament buildings had a seismic effect on Rattenbury's career, but it was also to mark a pivotal change in his personal life. During the first stages of construction, Rattenbury was a frequent visitor at the lodgings of Forbes G. Vernon, who was chief commissioner of Land and Works when the building was commissioned and had sat on the board that had selected Rattenbury's winning design. Vernon lodged in a boarding house for bachelors in Rae Street, run by a Nellie Howard and her adopted daughter, Florrie.

Florrie was the daughter of Captain George Herman Nunn, who had served with the British Army in India for several years and had married Florrie's mother, Helen Alpin, in Bombay in 1853. Nine years later, news of the Fraser River gold rush lured Nunn to British Columbia. He had arrived in Victoria with his family (and a parrot) to find that while the gold-rush excitement had ended, the free port of Victoria was thriving. He signed on as an officer on a ship sailing between Victoria and San Francisco, but later abandoned his whole family in Victoria. Florrie's mother decided to live with one of her older daughters in Oregon, leaving Florrie and her brother to an uncertain future in Victoria. Florrie went to live with the 'widowed' Nellie Howard. Mrs Howard treated Florrie like her own daughter, effectively adopting her.[15]

Florrie was a far from natural match for the outgoing and ambitious Rattenbury. While he was tall, dashing and handsome, she was quiet, short and plain, with a prominent nose, square jaw and large, frog-like eyes. She brought to her relationship with him neither extreme beauty, wealth nor status. Shy and retiring, she was known to many as a sweet and kind young woman but, judged by the standards of the day, as a spinster at twenty-six her options were limited. But marriage to the most successful architect in the province would secure Florrie a comfortable future. However, neither she, a single woman with no fortune, nor he, a celebrated architect with a prosperous future ahead of him, could risk the disapproval of the strict Victorian society. So when Florrie announced that she was pregnant, Rattenbury was obliged to marry her. Whether Florrie entrapped Rattenbury is unclear, but their relationship seems to have been characterised by a lack of romantic feeling, even from the earliest days of their married life.

A quiet evening wedding took place at Christ Church Cathedral on 18 June 1898. Florrie wore a 'very becoming travelling dress of green cloth with a white velvet picture hat' as well as a crescent of diamonds, a gift from Rattenbury. She carried a bouquet of white roses and stephanotis, a gift from Rattenbury's older brother Jack, who attended the ceremony.[16] Perhaps an indication of Rattenbury's attitude to the marriage, the morning after the wedding there was no romantic pause. Accompanied by Rattenbury's brother and some friends, the couple sailed to Vancouver by steamer en route to Dawson City via Lake Bennett. 'Every arrangement has been made in advance to secure comfort on the trip and make it as interesting as it is un-common.' Newly married and two months pregnant, Florrie was to accompany her husband on an arduous journey to the 'new El Dorado', the gold fields of the Klondike. Whatever Florrie had expected, she was soon to learn that this wasn't a honeymoon; it was a business trip.

Armed with the fortune he had earned from the parliament buildings and other commissions, Rattenbury realised that there were great financial returns to be made in providing transportation to the gold fields. Rather than prospectors carrying supplies, Rattenbury had the idea of drafting a fleet of shallow riverboats to transport cattle and supplies there. With financial backing from London he set up the Bennett Lake and Klondike Navigation Company and had three steamers made in Victoria. *Flora*, *Nora* and *Ora* were named after Florrie, her forenames being Florence Eleanor. *Flora* had been launched before the Rattenburys arrived in the area, but on their working honeymoon, Florrie was on hand to christen the *Nora* on 27 June. But by 1899 the Klondike gold rush was over, almost as soon as it had started. Prospectors abandoned the area and instead travelled to Alaska in search of gold. Rattenbury's boats were sailing half empty. He decided to cut his losses and sever his connection with the Bennett Lake and Klondike Navigation Company. His venture in the north had been a disaster.[17]

Returning to Victoria, the Rattenburys rented *Hochelaga*, an elegant home in the fashionable Rockland Avenue,[18] and, perhaps bruised by his failure in the Klondike, Rattenbury cultivated his domestic and social life, writing to his sister Kate about the house or visits to the Union Club, where he was a regular and enthusiastic member; 'We really have one of the most sociable clubs here possible, a lot of good chaps. It adds a great deal to the attractions of the town as a place to live in.'[19] The Union was the first gentleman's club founded west of Winnipeg. It had been founded in 1879 and was notoriously rowdy, known for the heavy drinking that accompanied the many political, business and social contacts made there.[20] Anecdotes of afternoons at the club or days in the garden now filled Rattenbury's letters home, rather than the architectural plans that had formerly filled his correspondence.

Somehow the mornings creep on, dodging around the garden, in the woods, and along the beach, sometimes potting away at the ducks, so that before one can tear oneself away it is about 10 p.m.; and then I get away down town after a little tiffin. Is not that a shocking way to go to 'biz'?[21]

But Florrie was not comfortable living among the wealthy matrons of Rockland Avenue. Despite their wealth and her husband's status, she was still the adopted daughter of a woman who ran a boarding house with a brother who earned his living as a waiter. So Rattenbury preoccupied himself with designing and building a house for her in the more relaxed district of Oak Bay on a plot overlooking the sea. There were few permanent residents at the time and many of the houses in the neighbourhood were summer holiday homes. Rattenbury built the relatively modest house on Beach Drive, with two storeys and gables in the Arts and Crafts style, with fashionable Tudor references such as half timbering and wooden verandahs.[22] In the main hall there was an ornate Tudor-style fireplace with an inscription, 'East, West, Hame's Best'.[23] He had the house decorated with Turkish carpets, tapestries, oak tables and chairs, and glass and silverware imported from England. In the garden Rattenbury planted trees and bulbs, broom, jasmine, honeysuckle and a dense mass of climbing roses around the house. It was an idyllic English country cottage by the sea. When it was finished the Rattenburys finally decided on a name for it, 'Iechinihl', 'pronounced softly', Rattenbury clarified, 'Eye-a-chineel'.

> It is an Indian name, and has a story connected with it. In one part of our garden I have often noticed there was a good many clam shells and there is also a spring of fresh water. Mentioning this to an old timer, he told me that for centuries our particular garden has been an Indian camping ground and that they had a legend that formerly all men were dumb and looked at each other like owls. But one day on this very spot a good spirit conferred on them the gift of speech. The name means 'the place where a good thing happened'.[24]

On 14 January 1899, Florrie gave birth to a son, Francis Burgoyne Rattenbury. 'Snookie' was born with equinus, or 'horse feet', which affects the upward movement of the ankles. An anxious

Rattenbury and Florrie consulted various doctors and tried several treatments in order to correct them: '[His] boots have at last arrived from England (eight months getting them – Good Old England – but better late than never), and I hope they will put him alright.'[25] But the boots didn't solve the problem. In letters to his mother and sister Kate in England, Rattenbury worried that his son's disability might be permanent and that he may never be able to walk properly. His letters from this period also express a frustrated restlessness. Despite having only recently settled at Iechinihl, he frequently contemplated travelling or even moving abroad: 'I do not think I should care to anticipate always living here [in Victoria]; I have notions of trying Rome or some continental city for a time, so as to have a complete change of life, surroundings and interests.' But in the end, he resolved that he had 'always found so far that when away from Victoria one wants to get back very badly'.

When the Canadian Pacific had terminated the railway line at Vancouver, the population and economy of Victoria, despite being the capital of the province, had dwindled in comparison with their arch-rival across the strait. What Victoria needed was a specific identity to attract business and tourists. The Chamber of Commerce agreed that with all its natural advantages, its temperate climate and coastal position, the city should become the 'leading health and pleasure resort in the northwest'. But before Victoria could appeal to well-heeled travellers, it would need to clean up the James Bay mudflats, a stinking tidal rubbish dump that sat on the city's very doorstep adjacent to Rattenbury's parliament buildings. In 1900, a group of local businessmen agreed with the Tourist Association to reclaim the 9-acre site and develop it as a civic asset. At the same time, Sir Alfred Shaughnessy, the president of the Canadian Pacific Railway, was keen to advance the company's interests in the area. Eager to secure a deal with the CPR, the city offered Shaughnessy half of the 9-acre site for development. At considerable expense, they agreed to fill in the mudflats and to maintain the streets and pavements around the hotel site. They would also prevent the building of any unsuitable buildings on the remainder of the former mudflats. Fresh water would be supplied to the hotel free of charge for fifteen years and the CPR would be exempt from taxes for the same period. A delighted Shaughnessy promised that he would turn the eyesore of the mudflats into the 'beauty spot of Canada'.

As the most celebrated architect in the province, Rattenbury was asked to draw up plans. Having designed the parliament buildings that also overlooked James Bay, he now planned a hotel to complement his most celebrated work, a seven-storey building with 350 bedrooms. He skilfully adapted the CPR's signature Franco-Scottish style, adding Elizabethan, Jacobean and Gothic features, so that Victoria could boast another uniquely iconic building. On 19 September 1905, Shaughnessy declared that the hotel would be called the Empress, identifying it with the late Queen Victoria as well as the CPR's own Empress line that sailed between the west coast and the Orient. When it finally opened on 2 January 1908, late and vastly over budget, the hotel was a class by itself – no dark Victorian fussiness within, but lots of light, extensive grounds and an extraordinary open view of the harbour and Rattenbury's majestic parliament buildings. The CPR press office lauded their new destination hotel as a great advance for their business. 'The CPR will take you and care for you from the far east to the far west. You can go under the CPR flag from Liverpool to Hong Kong, half the circuit of the world.'

Once again, Rattenbury's vision successfully defined the tenor of the imperial age.

* * *

Meanwhile, the Rattenburys continued to investigate treatments for their son's condition, which meant many extended trips for Florrie and Snookie to San Francisco to consult specialists there. Despite exhaustive treatments, Snookie was to wear special shoes for the rest of his life. Rattenbury began to notice that when they'd first been away from home, Florrie had written to him once a day.[26] Latterly, she was writing once a week at most. In his letters to his mother and sister, Rattenbury revealed a deepening sense of dissatisfaction, 'all enthusiasm had vanished and could not be reawakened'.[27]

But in 1903, Florrie announced that she was pregnant again; for the moment, all seemed happy at Iechinihl: 'We jog along in the same way, quiet and jolly: the garden in the morning, business, the Club, where there are some ripping good fellows and where I have some friends I think a great deal about, and usually a quiet evening in with Snookie.'[28]

Rattenbury was delighted to report to his mother that, on 11 May 1904, Florrie had given her another grandchild.

Well, you have another granddaughter, with huge blue eyes and a big crop of curly black hair – we were hoping for red! It also has a powerful pair of lungs and knows how to use them and this makes Snookie quite jealous. Snookie was very amusing when he first saw the new arrival. His eyes opened wider and wider then he quietly walked up to it and gave it a kiss.[29]

Though Florrie had favoured the name Stephanie, their daughter was named Mary after Rattenbury's adored mother. Though it had never been a love match, it seems that after the birth of Mary a deepening rift began to develop between Rattenbury and his wife. He had built Florrie a beautiful home, surrounded with expensive furniture, paintings and objets d'art. They employed a large staff including several Chinese servants – the cooks Wee, Sing and Chew and Foy the gardener.[30] There were also maids, a nurse for the children and a uniformed chauffeur called Hall. Rattenbury even bought himself a dog and named it Moses. But though he was at home among the middle-class merchants and their wives who commissioned homes from him in Oak Bay and Rockland Avenue, Florrie was not. She had always lacked the confidence, elegance and charm that would have enabled her to join the elite society in

Victoria and, as she grew older, despite her own humble history, she became prim and judgemental. When she heard that her neighbour Mrs Bowker Senior[31] might be of mixed race, she avoided her and, when a friend of Snookie used the word 'bloody' in front of her, he was banished from the house.[32] More and more the differences in the character and background of Florrie and Rattenbury began to grow into antipathy.

In 1902, Charles Melville Hays, the visionary president of the Grand Trunk Pacific Railroad and rival to the Canadian Pacific, had announced that they were planning a transcontinental line with a terminus on the north Pacific coast. Rattenbury was asked by Hays to design a chain of hotels along the GTR route as well as in the terminal cities of Prince Rupert and Victoria. The project promised to be the most creative and lucrative of Rattenbury's career, his lasting legacy in British Columbia to stand alongside the parliament buildings and the Empress Hotel. At the same time as reinvigorating his career and professional standing, he also saw the GTR as an opportunity to get rich and fund his retirement. He quietly began to buy up land along the likely route of the railroad. By 1907, he had purchased over 40,000 acres of crown-granted land all along the possible GTR route, costing $150,000, committing the bulk of his earnings from the parliament buildings and the Empress Hotel commissions. Rattenbury was a classic opportunist who had expertly negotiated the possibilities and pitfalls of the empire, but in this case, he had gambled his entire fortune on one single investment.

On 30 September 1911, Rattenbury's mother died. He had known that she had been ill for some months, but her death brought an end to a long and intimate correspondence between mother and son. He had thought her a 'wonderful mother' and even though he admitted to her that he was 'not of a demonstrative nature', having 'seen life' he felt he had begun to appreciate her better and once wrote to her to try to express his feelings, despite his instinctive nature of self-repression.

It is rather hard to write down, in plain words, one's thoughts and when you do, it seems theatrical. I have sometimes thought that the gift of being entertaining and having tact was a great source of being believed, but I know now that whilst these go a long way, still, that back of these there must be a great heart and a true ring. The gifts you have, we can't all have, but the loving nature I suppose we can get. I only hope that my youngsters will, in some small degree, have the same feeling for me that I have for my charming mother.[33]

The loss of Rattenbury's mother was shortly after followed by the death of his brother, Jack. Now his only trusted confidante was his sister Kate, thousands of miles away in Yorkshire, with whom he shared his growing sense of isolation: 'I don't get much pleasure out of the family and don't see much of them – but I have got used to that long ago.'[34]

With the Grand Trunk railway commissions, Rattenbury's career promised to be entering a golden period. But at Iechinihl he and Florrie had stopped speaking to each other and now only communicated by sending notes via their daughter. Mary had attended St Margaret's School where she had shown some creative flair and even won prizes for drawing, but had dropped out because of her nerves. She was subsequently tutored privately at home, Rattenbury insisting that the tutor focus on teaching his daughter history and geography so that she would appreciate the many countries he planned to visit with her. But Mary had become a highly strung child who had developed a speech impediment as she sensed the tensions and hostility that were growing between her parents.[35]

In 1912, now that Nellie Howard was retiring, by giving up the Rae Street boarding house she was losing both her home and her income. So Florrie insisted on moving her into Iechinihl, where she was much loved by Florrie's children and regarded by them, if not by Rattenbury, as part of the family, known as 'Grannie' Howard. Rattenbury did his best to avoid them both and started taking his meals in his room, as the rest of the family ate in the dining room. He found Nellie's devotion to Florrie suffocating, and her ever-clacking knitting needles torturous. Soon he began spending evenings at the Union Club or drinking whisky in his room night after night, alone.[36]

In July 1914, he had bought tickets for himself and Mary for a European tour where he hoped she would be rewarded by the education he had given her. They would first travel to England where they would catch up with Snookie, now known as Frank, who was by then attending Wylie's School in Hampstead, which offered 'special tuition for boys to whom Preparatory or Public Schools may not be suitable'.[37] He hoped to train for the diplomatic service. But Rattenbury was disappointed when Mary suddenly changed her mind. She felt that going off to Europe with her father was a 'treacherous disloyalty'[38] to her mother and Grannie Howard and she would remain at home. Sensing Florrie's malign influence in his daughter's decision, an irate Rattenbury went to Europe alone. He arrived in London in August and was dining with Frank in a hotel when the orchestra leader interrupted dinner to announce that war had been declared. The band then played 'God Save the King'.[39] Rattenbury rushed home to Victoria to enlist, but was told that, at forty-six, he was too old.

As soon as the war in Europe started, life in Victoria changed drastically. Huge numbers of men left the city – builders, designers, contractors. The flow of tourists dried up, major building programmes were suspended and businesses folded. Prospects for architects were particularly bleak. Even Rattenbury's friend Sam Maclure, one of the most sought-after architects of the day, closed his office and worked from his home. Work on the Grand Trunk railway's hotels all along the new rail route stopped. In Prince Rupert, only the foundations of Rattenbury's hotel were built; overnight it became an almost forgotten town at the end of the line. The Grand Trunk Pacific was bankrupt. Any hope of young men emigrating from Britain to settle on the lands along the GTR route were quashed, as they were all joining recruiting offices and headed for the front. The land Rattenbury had carefully acquired at great expense was suddenly worthless. His professional ambitions, his reputation, his future security – and his marriage – were all in free fall.

* * *

In 1918, Florrie's sister Mary Brenner had contacted her to say that their mother was destitute and would she help? Still resentful about being abandoned by her to Nellie Howard's care, Florrie refused to intervene. Her hand forced, Mary brought legal proceedings against her sister in the Oregon courts, but Florrie steadfastly refused to be compelled to help and wrote back to Mary saying that she did not believe in charity. Florrie's mother died in poverty in 1919. Rattenbury now lived in completely separate quarters in the place where, once upon a time, a good thing had happened. Past fifty and beyond his prime as an architect, his huge statement buildings were out of fashion in the more anxious and uncertain world of the 1920s. Still raw from the death of his mother, Rattenbury was stuck in a joyless marriage and even his investments were under threat. As the war had drawn to a close, the British Columbian government had determined to provide opportunities for returning soldiers to buy their own land. Having identified various areas of undeveloped land, the government set up a Land Settlement Board. One of the areas of future development was where Rattenbury had bought land along the GTR route. In June 1921, the board informed him that they were buying up his lands by compulsory purchase. A stunned Rattenbury claimed that he would be facing a staggering loss of $520,000, almost his entire fortune.

But there was the possibility of better times ahead. The Chamber of Commerce was trying to find ways of attracting tourists to Victoria in winter and had been contemplating the development of an entertainment complex behind the Empress Hotel. Local voters had already rejected the plan, but city councillors hoped to revive enthusiasm for the scheme by canvassing the support of the now-veteran Rattenbury, the seductive showman who had been so pivotal in transforming the waterfront of the city and putting Victoria on the map. Inspired by Sir Joseph Paxton's famous Crystal

Palace, he mooted a huge amusement centre for sport and leisure, all accessible under one large glazed roof. A huge press campaign encouraged local taxpayers to vote in a second ballot in favour of the project, insisting that 'by voting for the amusement centre, we can start the road to Victoria's prosperity'.[40] Another vote was taken on 29 December 1923. This time the scheme was passed by a majority of 2,909 votes to 352. Rattenbury's Crystal Garden would go ahead. That evening a banquet was held at the Empress Hotel in his honour. He was once again the man of the hour and there was much to celebrate. 'For he's a jolly good fellow, that nobody can deny!'

Writing to his sister some days later, and clearly energised by that night, Rattenbury mused on his relationship with women, before going on to tell her about the 'young married woman' he had met, 'about twenty-six, the belle of the ball and a marvellous musician'.[41]

> The funny thing is that whilst I have had very little to do with women in my lifetime, the whole blessed lot, married and single, from twenty-five years old up, made a chum of me, and it is jolly nice whenever I go out to have them all making themselves as agreeable and pleasant and even affectionate as they possibly can, paying *me* compliments.[42]

Rattenbury rapturously confided to Kate the extraordinary impact Alma had had on him as soon as they met. For a few hours that evening she had made him forget that he felt old and tired and disappointed. 'I danced every dance until two in the morning and enjoyed every minute.'[43]

At fifty-five, and perhaps for the first time in his life, Francis Rattenbury had fallen in love.

Iechinihl

CHAPTER SEVEN

THE SECOND MRS RATTENBURY

29 December 1923–18 December 1929

> Mitch: You need somebody. And I need somebody, too. Could
> it be – you and me, Blanche?
>
> Blanche: Sometimes – there's God – so quickly!
>
> – Tennessee Williams, *A Streetcar Named Desire*[1]

Alma had written that it was love at first sight when she first met
Rattenbury, but though he seemed genuinely smitten, there's a suggestion from her later writings that the motivation for her relationship
with him was more mercenary than romantic. She was a widow with
a young child and only her piano lessons to support them, and it was
well known in Victoria society that Rattenbury's marriage had broken
down as long ago as the war. Much older than Alma – he was fifty-
five, she was thirty – Rattenbury was a pillar of society in the city, and
he seemed, at least, to be rich. For a single woman with an uncertain
future in a world devastated by war, he could offer her security and
status. So, early in 1924, Alma moved from her mother's house in
Vancouver to live with her Aunt Emma Criddle – and Rattenbury's
friend – in Victoria at 514 Dallas Road.[2] Shortly afterwards she
moved into a house on Niagara Street in Beacon Hill Park.[3] She had a

pressing need for wanting a place of her own; she required privacy to carry on the clandestine affair she was having with Rattenbury, whom she had taken to calling affectionately, but perhaps with not much love, 'Ratz', a chummy, schoolyard name.

The contrast between the two women now in Rattenbury's life couldn't have been sharper. Though 'a woman of breeding and education',[4] Florrie had conventional tastes and values, whereas Alma was very much a modern woman. She was vivacious and outgoing, smoked, drank and bobbed her hair, wearing fashionable clothes that the stern Florrie wouldn't countenance. When he met Alma, Rattenbury felt that he had 'struck oil' and he quickly became infatuated with her. She looked like 'a fragile Madonna, rather sad', yet was 'really full of fun, ready for any prank' and 'intensely in earnest'. He was hugely impressed by her past achievements and the way she had met the challenges in her life. She told him that she had been a music prodigy at the age of five,[5] 'practised under the best masters "de Packmann etc" some ten hours a day for nearly fifteen years, won every diploma and prize. Gave a piano recital, one after the other, with Samaroff at 25. Musicians say she is a divine player, that there is none can surpass her.'[6]

Unaware that she was using the house in Niagara Street for assignations with a married man, Victoria society at first welcomed Alma, the widow of a brave soldier lost in the European war, and she was taken under the wing of architect Sam Maclure's wife, Margaret, a leader of the city's artistic and musical community. Though known to be a strict disciplinarian, Mrs Maclure was indulgent towards Alma when they first met and on one occasion watched tight-lipped as Alma's son Christopher caused chaos in her parlour, throwing the sofa cushions in a heap on the floor, 'Mummy doesn't want you to do that, Toffy,' Alma protested weakly, but without chastising her son. When he started reaching for the pictures on the wall, Margaret could hold her tongue no longer and pleaded, 'Don't let him get at the pictures!'[7]

But Rattenbury's frequent visits to Alma's house had not gone unnoticed by the conservative matrons of Victoria. One day, on hearing that she had been unwell, Margaret Maclure took soup and a hamper to Niagara Street. An acquaintance who lived across the road then reported back to her that she had seen Alma leaving the house with Rattenbury and that they had enjoyed her hamper together in Beacon Hill Park. Mrs Maclure telephoned Alma and confronted her: 'People have been saying things about you. And now I can see that they were right.' Alma was dismissive.[8] The same people who were censuring her would soon be begging to be guests at her home one day; it was clear that she meant to be Rattenbury's next wife. Now that his relationship with Alma was public knowledge, Rattenbury acquired a box at the opera and started to take her with him. Sam Maclure, who had known Rattenbury for nearly thirty years, was stunned by the audacity of their behaviour. Rattenbury, he felt, was 'bewitched'.[9] His relationship with Alma now fuelling gossip in the salons of Oak Bay, Rattenbury requested a divorce from Florrie, but she adamantly refused.

Rattenbury moved out of Iechinihl and set about harassing Florrie. Known for his intransigent nature, fuelled by his desire for Alma, he became uncharacteristically cruel. He sent vans to remove the better furniture, but as quickly as his possessions were removed, Florrie and one of the servants secured them in the maid's room, the only room to which Florrie had a key. Between them they managed to keep the most valuable pieces of furniture as well as Rattenbury's stock of imported champagne. He retaliated by laying siege to the house, ordering the lights and heating to be turned off. Margaret Maclure provided food hampers for Florrie as she and Mary remained in the house. Florrie filed an injunction against her husband that ruled in her favour on 28 July 1924, securing her right to stay. But Rattenbury would not be defeated by mere legal directives. He now began inviting Alma into the drawing room at Iechinihl, thus forcing Florrie to retreat to her room upstairs. One night, Alma was playing the piano and Mary Rattenbury came downstairs and asked her to stop because Florrie was upset and unable to sleep. According to Mary, Alma responded by playing the funeral march as loud as she could.[10] Exhausted by this battle with Rattenbury and Alma, Florrie could fight no more and agreed to a divorce on 28 January 1925, with Rattenbury required to pay her $225 a month and to provide her with a home of her choice. But rather than move as far away from them as possible, Florrie dug her heels in. With the estate agent Charles Pemberton, she selected a $1,200 plot at the top of Prospect Place just off Oak Bay Avenue where Sam Maclure would build her a new house. Pemberton remembered that she was 'very definite' where she wanted it built – in full sight of Iechinihl.[11] Alma may have won Rattenbury's heart, but Florrie would not step quietly into the background; she would haunt them as long as she remained alive.

Alma and Rattenbury married in Bellingham, Washington on 8 April 1925. The discreet service was arranged away from Victoria in an attempt not to provoke the wrath of Florrie and the likes of Margaret Maclure. Alma and Christopher moved into Iechinihl, together with Alma's piano. She was now the lady of the house with money, servants and a secure future. She might have hoped that over time Victorian society would begin to forget the machinations of her journey to becoming the second Mrs Rattenbury.

Two months after the wedding, Rattenbury wrote enthusiastically to his sister: 'I've hesitated writing until I saw how it was going to work out, altho' I have known her over two years. She is the niece of a great friend of mine.' Alma was 'full of sympathy and keen to see the nice side of everyone and flares up with rage over any meanness. Talented in literature and poetry and gets a world of amusement out of any living thing, from bugs upwards; butterflies eat out of her hands.'[12] With the difference in their ages, he could not tell why she had married him:

> [A]t her age it seems unreasonable, for she had the world at her feet. Perhaps the restful life appealed. And she seems to find all kinds of qualities in me that she likes that I never knew of. It looks like some years of happiness and interest instead of the loneliness that I see so much around. I look years younger.[13]

But Rattenbury's love-struck appreciation of his new wife's character was not shared by his family. As soon as she entered their father's life, Frank and Mary saw only 'disaster ahead'.[14] Though they appreciated that she was certainly talented as a musician and had 'physical attractiveness',[15] they worried that Alma had developed 'an extraordinary influence' over their father. He was now becoming an elderly man and 'strange in his manner like some geniuses'. But though they believed she had 'acquired a little surface culture'[16] from her marriages to Dolling and Pakenham, Alma had only a 'shallow sort of refinement'.[17] In contrast to the reserved and respectable Florrie, Alma was 'vulgar'.[18] As far as Rattenbury's children were concerned, their father's marriage culminated in nothing but him yielding complete control to Alma; she seduced money from him and 'drank continually' but managed to keep their father's favour by 'flattering him'.[19] By 16 October 1925, relations between Rattenbury and his daughter had completely broken down.

> After a good many years of vulgarity you began and for five years have not tried to be pleasant and the last two years you have done every blessed thing that you could think of to be unpleasant and vindictive as you know how ... I am glad to inform you that I have a delightful home full of kindness, merriment, music and everything that is delightful in life. There is no happier home in the universe – I don't want even to be reminded of the rotten past life.[20]

But in contrast to the fractured relations with his children, Rattenbury was blissfully happy with his new wife, a sentiment he shared with his sister Kate:

> We are very happy, Alma is a brick and a wonderfully bright and loveable companion. I can't imagine life without her and fortunately she seems as contented with me. With the disparity in years, it seems astonishing to me. We seem to enter everything together, as if we were the same age. I don't know when we will

come to England – it is an expensive trip and I think it will have
to wait until I can get some compensation from the govt. which I
hope I do before long – They certainly robbed me in good style. In
the meantime we have already renovated the house – and added
on a music room – which acoustically is marvellous – I built the
walls and ceiling on the principle of a drum – and a huge concert
grand piano – sounds almost like an organ – This really is a wonderfully happy home – Alma has the knack of eliciting love – and
the servants are devoted to her – and the place is full of animals
and birds – all of them – next door to human ... I hate to think
what my life would have been like – had she not come along – it
was pretty hateful & of course – have got much worse .[21]

But though the marriage with Alma seemed idyllic to Ratz, just
as his relationship with his children had become toxic, the social
ostracism that he and Alma were enduring began to affect his business relationships and professional standing. He had collaborated
on the design of the Crystal Garden with a junior architect, Percy
James. In May 1925, James wrote to him demanding a greater
share of the commission for the work that he had done. Rattenbury
dismissed James's appeal in typically high-handed manner: 'You
were not only satisfied with the terms – but very pleased to get the
job.'[22] Peeved with Rattenbury's attitude, the ambitious James now
wanted not just his fair share of the commission, but his fair share
of the credit, too. Canvassing support, he found many people who
were prepared to say that he had designed the bulk of the work, but
that Rattenbury had taken the credit. The intemperate Rattenbury
took his grievances to the press, insisting that he was the sole
architect of the Crystal Garden. He then called Basil Gardom, the
Canadian Pacific Railway's superintendent of construction who
had hired Rattenbury in the first place. But Gardom had already
promised to support James. As well as the argument about the
Crystal Garden, Rattenbury must have felt snubbed and bruised
when the CPR, looking to redesign the Chateau Lake Louise, the
Banff Springs and the Calgary Station Hotels, did not even consult

him. In 1927, he brought a legal case against the government about the compulsory purchase of his land along the GTR route, suing them for $500,000. But though it reached the Supreme Court, the case was dismissed.

With Rattenbury's professional status compromised and his and Alma's social standing ruined, in the spring of 1927, Alma attempted to build bridges and negotiate her readmission to Victoria society. As Margaret Maclure had been supportive when she returned to Victoria after the war, Alma telephoned her, introducing herself as 'Mrs Rattenbury'. If she could charm Mrs Maclure, there was a chance that she could salvage some sort of standing in the community. But Margaret played faux confusion and asked, '*Which* Mrs Rattenbury?' When Alma attempted to clarify, Margaret insisted that she knew of only one Mrs Rattenbury, Florence Rattenbury of Prospect Place.[23] If Alma had assumed that marrying Rattenbury would elevate her status in the community and secure her future, she was hugely misguided. She had failed to account for the uncompromising severity of the social mores in Victoria. Having betrayed them, she and Rattenbury were now social pariahs. Arguments continued between Rattenbury and his children, with Frank Rattenbury later commenting that there were terrible scenes: 'If I were to tell you, you couldn't print it. It was that bad.'[24] Their tongues firmly in their cheeks, some Oak Bay locals began to refer to Iechinihl as 'Bluebeard's Mansion'.[25] Then Alma's health declined.

> [She had] had an abscess on the brain and at least a pint of evil smelling clotted blood and mucus passed out of her nose and ears – lost 12lbs in weight – but today has just gone out motoring feeling as happy and light-headed as a sand boy. It is unbelievable, and how she kept going is beyond me.[26]

After months of ill health and bad news, in May 1928 there was something joyful for Rattenbury to report to his sister – Alma was pregnant.

Just as she had beautifully recovered she slipped and has badly sprained her ankle; kept her a month in bed and it will bother her for months but she does not seem to mind it a bit, getting rid of her nightmare has been a wonderful thing. And now all the poison is out of her system, lo and behold, her great wish of years is coming true and she is going to be a mother. She is delighted beyond measure and the child will certainly get lots of love *showering* – he ought to be some child ... I've had a wonderful five years.[27]

A son was born on 27 December 1928. He was named John after Rattenbury's father and brother Jack, but Rattenbury may well have been thinking further back in history to when the status of the family had been assured in Okehampton in the seventeenth century; his ancestor John Rattenbury had served as mayor of Okehampton four times, and in 1644 had even welcomed Charles I as a guest to his own home.[28]

On 13 October 1929, at the age of fifty-nine, Florrie Rattenbury died of a brain haemorrhage. Alma naively assumed that her rival's death removed the impediment to her being readmitted to polite society in Victoria. After her telephone exchange with Margaret Maclure she must have realised that she and her sons would never be accepted into society unless she made some significant gesture. If Mary Rattenbury is to be believed, the day after her mother's death, she received a visit from Alma, who, with what seems extraordinarily insensitive timing, attempted to offer her condolences. But Alma had failed to account for the bitter resentment that Mary had nursed for her. Even fifty years after the event, when interviewed about the incident in 1974, Mary's revulsion for Alma had fermented into a deep and abiding hatred. She claimed that Alma had been 'high on drugs' at the time of the visit and recalled that when referring to Rattenbury, Alma had said, 'I simply loathe him – I hate him.'[29] Mary dismissed Alma from the house, marking the end of Rattenbury's fraught relationship with his two older children. The confrontation with Mary also brought an end to Ratz and Alma's lives in British Columbia. Cold-shouldered by his former friends and business associates at the Union Club, he was 'unable to stand the animus of the Victoria people'[30] any longer, so decided on a fresh start in England.[31] Though they must have discussed the option of living in London, they settled on Okehampton, a small town on the northern edge of Dartmoor in Devon, which was the ancient home of the Rattenburys. As well as the refreshing winds to stabilise Alma's health, the area was full of legend and romance. Okehampton Castle, standing on the summit of a bank of rock near the Launceston Road, was now a romantic ancient ruin. It even had its own ghost, a certain Lady Howard who had murdered at least two of her husbands and was said to have been condemned to take the form of a hound that raced nightly between Okehampton and Tavistock as punishment for her crimes.[32] In Okehampton the Rattenburys would have history and, perhaps most importantly for this later branch of the family, respectability. Baptising John in the Rattenburys' ancestral church would help to wash away the recent tawdry past and mark a new start for them and their sons.

On 18 December 1929, Rattenbury changed his will, completely disinheriting Frank and Mary. His assets in British Columbia would be administered through a trust on his behalf by his colleague F. E. Winslow. His entire estate – approximately $40,000 – he left to Alma's children. If she were ever widowed again, Alma would be secure for the rest of her life with an income of $4,200 a year and the right to resort to Ratz's capital.[33] At the same time he arranged for Foy, who was both a loyal family friend as well as the gardener at Iechinihl, to receive an allowance for the rest of his life, which must have added even more salt to Mary and Frank's wounds.

When he went to see off his father and new step-family at the docks, Frank Rattenbury later recalled that 'Alma was in a stupor, booze, I suppose, or something else', echoing his sister's suspicions that Alma might have been taking drugs. According to Frank, his father looked 'pretty blue', realising 'what a frightful mistake' he had made.[34] Christopher, by then nine years old, remembered the family being waved off by Foy who was 'crying when we departed'.[35] There was no sense of celebration when the Rattenburys left British Columbia for England. This was not the start of a joyous adventure. It was exile.

Edith Thompson

Holloway, 9 January 1923

Mrs Thompson

> When a married woman who has a lover kills her husband, she
> does not really wish to kill the husband; she wishes to kill the
> situation.
>
> – Thomas Hardy[1]

A 5.15 a.m. on 9 January 1923, a 29-year-old woman waited in her cell at Holloway Prison; she had less than four hours to live.[2] She knew that she would be dead shortly after nine o'clock. But there was no way for her to check the passage of her last moments as she was not permitted her wristwatch and the prison clocks had been disabled that morning. She had been transferred to the condemned cell the night before when it was clear that there would be no last-minute reprieve from the home secretary. After she had heard the news, she had painted her nails.[3] In the corner of the cell was a vase with three arum lilies she had requested. These would be placed on her body in the coffin that she would occupy before lunchtime that day.

Shortly after 5.15 a.m., she was given a cup of tea, which, despite the circumstances, she enjoyed. She then smoked a cigarette. At 6 a.m. crowds began to gather outside the prison, undeterred by the drizzle that continued from the previous evening. Some of the

4,000 people who would be gathered by 9 a.m. were protesting about the execution and against capital punishment generally. Many more would come because they were curious to be there at the precise moment when the most notorious woman in Britain would be hanged. Such was her infamy that, three days earlier, the eminent novelist Thomas Hardy had composed a poem, 'On the Portrait of a Woman About to be Hanged', knowingly conjuring images of his infamous rural murderess, Tess:

> Could subtlest breast
> Ever have guessed
> What was behind that innocent face[4]

The *Daily Express* observed that 'no trial in the records of the Central Criminal Court [had] gripped the public mind and imagination in such a manner',[5] while *The Times* sneered at the 'artificial and unhealthy excitement which had surrounded the trial and the announcement of the verdict'.[6]

At 6.30 a.m. the wardresses thought the prisoner was cheerful. One of them helped her into her silk slip and underclothes. Over them she wore the mourning dress her mother had loaned her for the trial. She was offered a piece of toast and an apple, but had no appetite. By the time the governor called in at 8.15 a.m., it was clear to him that she had been crying. Dr John Morton,[7] also the chief medical officer at Holloway, gave her a stimulant, 1/32 grain of strychnine, and offered her a large measure of brandy. He was only away for fifteen minutes when the wardresses asked him to return as the prisoner's condition had declined. Morton then gave her a strong sedative, scopolamine and morphine. This was thought to be enough to send a normal person to sleep. But this was no ordinary woman: 'She [was] one of those amazing personalities only met with once in a generation.'[8] Shortly after the medication she became dazed and was barely conscious.[9]

At 8.58 a.m. she seemed to have fallen asleep. Sixty seconds later, the executioner and his assistant entered the cell at speed, followed by the chaplain, to find her 'in a sort of stupor'. The woman moaned as if realising, after weeks of agonising waiting, that her time had finally come. She collapsed. The executioner's assistant lifted her up, gently encouraging her, 'Come on mate – it'll soon be over.'[10] Her hands were swiftly pinioned behind her back and strapped together by the executioner while his assistant tied her skirt and her ankles. The chaplain was appalled at what they were about to do: 'My God, the impulse to rush in and save her by force was almost too strong for me.'[11] But he did nothing and continued to intone from the burial service; cold comfort for the young woman whose life was about to end in a matter of seconds.

She was carried out of the cell, with the two prison officers making a seat with their arms under her. They carried her briefly through the open air, January drizzle touching her face one last time, and into the execution shed where the scaffold awaited. The execution room 'smelt strongly of a hospital'.[12] The executioner and his assistant 'did the necessary', putting the white cap over her head and then the noose around her neck. 'She looked as if she was already dead ... it was agonizing just to see her being held up by the four men, her bound feet on the trap doors'. She tried to say something to her executioner, but 'couldn't get it out'. He kicked the lever, the trap opened and she fell almost 7ft into the void below. Nine men and one woman witnessed her neck breaking instantaneously.[13]

As the law dictated, the woman was left hanging from the noose for an hour, a practice going back to the times when the bodies of criminals were publicly exposed on the gibbet; a warning to other potential miscreants. Her body was stripped and washed in readiness for the post-mortem. Her slip and underwear were sent to be cleaned, but her dress was heavily stained so would be burnt. She was laid in the prison's standard elm coffin in the hastily cleaned underwear ready for her parents and sister to visit her. As well as the lilies, there was a bright cross of seasonal holly laid at her feet.[14]

Her family visited the body to say their last goodbyes and asked permission to kiss her. They were allowed this final kiss, but 'only on the forehead'.[15] After the devastated family left, she was covered with lime to hasten the process of decomposition and buried in the prison grounds in an unmarked grave.

Margery Fry, Holloway's education adviser, noted the strain that the execution had taken on Dr Morton: 'I have never seen a person so changed in appearance by mental suffering as the governor appeared to be.'[16] Later, John Ellis the executioner claimed that 'everybody present was upset to vomiting point'. He remarked to his assistant, 'I hope I never have to hang another woman.' A year after this execution, Ellis attempted suicide by shooting himself with a revolver. He survived. He was then arrested, tried and warned not to do it again. On 20 September 1931, 'in a frenzy of madness', he cut his own throat with a razor. His son claimed that his father's death had been inevitable because he had been 'haunted'; though he had executed 200 men, it was 'the recollection of the hanging of two women that drove him to suicide'.[17]

* * *

Edith Thompson had been a vivacious, romantically inclined professional woman from Ilford, a suburb of east London. She was the manageress of a hat shop in Holborn and had lived an unhappy, dissatisfied life with her husband Percy until she embarked on an intense relationship with their lodger, twenty-year-old Frederick Bywaters, a virile and handsome merchant seaman. They conducted a clandestine affair over fourteen months, though for much of that time, Bywaters was away at sea. A voracious reader of popular romantic novels, Edith had indulged in a parallel fantasy world as a way of sidestepping the banality of her life with her husband as well as a means of cementing her relationship with Bywaters; when he was away, in their letters the lovers discussed the books they were reading in detail.

Around midnight on Tuesday 3 October 1922, the Thompsons had been walking home from Ilford railway station after a night at the theatre. Bywaters, who had been lying in wait for the couple, rushed past them from out of the dark and stabbed Thompson.

Edith called out, 'Oh, don't! Don't!' Bywaters ran away from the scene into the night, leaving Edith hysterical and desperately calling for help as her husband slumped on the pavement. In the few minutes it took to rouse a local doctor, Percy Thompson was dead. Edith and Bywaters were arrested and tried together for murder at the Old Bailey in what the press proclaimed 'the most compelling crime story of the century'.[18] And though Bywaters wielded the knife, it was Edith who was the focus of media attention, the *Daily Express* observing that 'the woman in the dock was without question the personality of the court'.[19]

The prosecution had claimed that the sixty-seven letters from Edith to Bywaters – she had destroyed his – indicated that the lovers had been complicit in a plot to murder her husband. There was a suggestion in her letters that she had ground a light bulb and laced Thompson's food with arsenic, but the post-mortem on his body revealed no traces of glass or poison. It was the nature of Edith's relationship with Bywaters that was at the heart of the trial and dominated national debate throughout the winter of 1922. Was she, in fact, being tried for murder? Or was she being judged for immorality, daring to challenge the values of post-war suburbia? When quoting one of the letters in his summing up, the judge, Sir Montague Shearman, sneered at it: '"He has the right by law to all that you have to by nature and by love." Gentlemen, if that nonsense means anything it means that the love of a husband for a wife is something improper because marriage is acknowledged by law, and that the love of a woman for her lover, illicit and clandestine, is something great and noble. I am certain that you, like any other right-minded persons, will be filled with disgust at such a notion.'[20]

Given the generation of men who had been physically scarred or psychologically damaged during the war, the tabloids tended to fetishise vigorous youths like Bywaters; he was a 'handsome youth, with a clear skin, a keen, finely carved profile, a trenchant high forehead, brilliant eyes ... virile and vigorous in gait'.[21] He 'stood like a soldier on parade, head up, eyes steady, and never flinched'.[22] In contrast, the press articulated their disapproval of a particular type of post-war woman whom Edith Thompson seemed to personify – the 'flapper'.[23] These young women were regularly attacked in the popular press such as the *Mail* and the *Express* for prioritising leisure and pleasure over the responsibilities of marriage. 'The supreme obsession of the modern young woman is to have a topping time ... it is not long before her strongly-developed craving for thrills, variety and excitement drives her into immorality, alcohol, drugs and nightclubs.'[24]

The elegant and fashionable Edith had her hair cut in a bob, drank cocktails, smoked cigarettes and continued to use her maiden name after marriage. All these freedoms had been opened to her – and women like her – in the wake of the First World War. The war had been crucial in empowering women economically due to the expansion of jobs available to them that hitherto had been the preserve of men. Between 1914 and 1918, the number of women workers in Britain increased from 3,277,00 to 4,936,000.[25] During the war women had worked on the railways, trams and buses, on the land, in munitions factories, offices and banks. But on demobilisation the female workforce found themselves at the heart of an ideological battle, with conservatives arguing that women's first duty was to returning soldiers who had done their bit for the past four years and now expected to resume their pre-war occupations.[26] A year after the armistice, some 775,000 women had left their posts, largely due to the Restoration of Pre-War Practices Act of 1918, which had put an end to munitions factories and restored jobs to men. By 1921, the female workforce in Britain had dwindled to 2 per cent – smaller than it had been in 1911.[27]

This recalibration of the position of women in the labour market after the war came – ironically – at the same time that women were empowered politically. In 1918, after nearly a decade of organised protests up to the outbreak of war, the suffragettes finally succeeded in their campaign to secure votes for women. But this was a partial victory, enfranchising only women over thirty. Women aged between twenty-one and twenty-nine – effectively the very flappers and munitions workers who had fuelled the war effort – remained disenfranchised. Despite owning her own home on equal terms with her husband, Edith Thompson was never able to vote in her lifetime.

At the same time, following the First World War traditional ideas of motherhood and domesticity were promoted in the new women's magazines that prospered in the 1920s. This ideology was encouraged by various scientific experts, with even the progressive Havelock Ellis stating that unless she became a mother, no woman could have a 'complete human life'. Since the 1870s there had been concerns about the steady decline in the birth rate in Britain from thirty-five per thousand to twenty-four per thousand by 1914.[28] For a great industrial nation at the centre of a world empire, this seemed to prophesy an apocalyptic decline. Edith Thompson was fertile (we know she had an abortion) but remained childless, *Reynolds News* reporting that she had 'stead-fastedly refused to have any children'.[29] She was the embodiment of the emancipated, modern young women who were putting the future of the empire in jeopardy. And for that, she must pay.

The jury comprised eleven men and one woman, the first to sit on a murder trial in British legal history. Before they retired to consider their verdict, Shearman had to remind them that, despite the press furore about the case encouraged by the tabloids, the trial was not an entertainment: 'You should not forget that you are in a Court of Justice trying a vulgar and common crime. You are not listening to a play from the stalls of a theatre.' Despite the large number of letters and the testimonies of thirty witnesses to consider, the jury took just two hours and ten minutes to reach a verdict of 'guilty'.[30] Thompson and Bywaters were both condemned to death. Subsequently there was 'not a home in Britain where [Edith's] name was not familiar and where people not only spoke of her but of the larger question – should women hang at all?'[31] Though the defence admitted that he had wielded the weapon that killed Percy Thompson, 832,000 people petitioned the home secretary to spare Bywaters,[32] the public feeling that he was a misguided youth, 'an immature Samson seduced by a modern Delilah'. There was no such campaign to save Edith's life. Public opprobrium was focused on her, as much for her failure as a wife as for inciting Bywaters. Francis Iles observed that it was 'the women of England' in particular who were determined to see Edith ritually punished: '"Away with this vamp!" they are reputed to have said in their hearts. "Away with this wrecker of the sacred Home, which is our chief means of livelihood! Away with this blot on our profession of wife! We will teach all such that they had better be content with their allowance of one man apiece, or it will be the worse for them."'[33]

Appeals by both Edith and Bywaters were dismissed by the recently appointed Lord Chief Justice Hewart, who felt the case 'squalid and rather indecent'.[34] Their executions would go ahead in the New Year of 1923.

Christmas Day of 1922 was Edith's last birthday. She was twenty-nine. After a desultory lunch, she became hysterical and had to be sedated. She appealed to the wardresses – 'Why did he do it? Why?' – but they were silent. On Boxing Day she was calmer and wrote to a close friend:

> Yesterday I was thinking about everything that has ever happened – it seems to help in all sorts of ways when I do this. I realise what a mysterious thing life is. We all imagine we can mould our own lives – we seldom can, they are moulded for us – just by the laws and rules and conventions of this world, and if we break any of these, we only have to look forward to a formidable and unattractive wilderness.[35]

* * *

Some hours after Edith's body was unceremoniously buried in the precincts of Holloway Prison, in that night's *Evening Standard* there began the first indication of a controversy regarding the execution: 'Mrs Thompson showed the deepest distress as the hour of her execution approached and restorative had to be administered by the doctor and warders.'[36] This was picked up by the following morning's *Daily Mirror*, which claimed, 'At five o'clock she was unconscious and when the hour for the execution arrived she was in a dazed state and hardly able to walk, so that she had to be practically carried to the scaffold.'[37] The headline of the *Daily Herald* on 10 January announced:

SCENE OF HORROR AND SHAME
WOMAN CARRIED TO SCAFFOLD
PITEOUS CONDITION OF MRS THOMPSON
REPORT OF SCREAMS[38]

'Such was Mrs Thompson's condition,' the *Herald* claimed, 'that certain of the officials refused to take their part in the proceedings.' The next day, the *Herald* published a report entitled, 'Abolish the Scaffold', as it claimed that the public had been 'revolted by [the] horror of Tuesday's hangings'.[39] That weekend, the *News of the World* further reported the 'distressing condition of Mrs Thompson'.[40] Rumours continued that Edith had 'disintegrated as a human creature' and that she 'fought, kicked and screamed and protested her innocence to the last, and that it required about five men to hold her down while she was being carried to the gallows and having the noose put over her'. Most shocking of all was a rumour that her 'insides fell out'. This was understood to mean that she had had a prolapse or miscarriage at the moment of execution. Unusually for a condemned prisoner, she had put on weight in the weeks following the trial, which only added to the speculation. Later, Violet Van der Elst, the eccentric millionaire and anti-capital punishment campaigner, claimed that 'the end [of Edith Thompson] was terrible ... In the last few days of her life, her hair was going grey, and her sufferings had been so great, that she had a complete collapse. They carried her to the scaffold and had to hold her up while they fixed the cap round her head; she was moaning all the time. They hanged a practically unconscious woman.'[41]

The controversy about the execution of a modern woman who had apparently met her end in the most traumatic, medieval way increased in the years that followed, with the press and public

engaged in intense debate about Edith's death and a growing lobby
in favour of the abolition of capital punishment altogether.[42]

Edith Thompson had been the first woman to be hanged in
Britain since 1907. Between 1900 and 1949, 130 women were sentenced to death for murder in England and Wales. Only twelve of
these women were eventually executed; 91 per cent of them had
their sentence commuted, compared to 39 per cent of male murderers. But these figures hide a more complex truth. The vast majority
of these female murderers, 102 in all, had killed their own children,
a crime peculiar to women. The second largest group of female
killers in this period were women who had killed their lovers or
husbands; the majority of these *were* executed. Despite the popular
belief that female murderers were less likely to be executed than
their male counterparts, if the women who killed their children are
removed from these statistics, women like Edith Thompson found
guilty of killing their spouses had less chance of a reprieve than
male murderers. This discrepancy between how male and female
murderers of their partners were treated in the twentieth century
stemmed right back to the Middle Ages in the arcane statutes of
British Law. From 1321, women who killed their husbands were not
actually tried for murder at all, but for *petit treason* (petty treason),
a crime considered worse than ordinary murder as it involved the
betrayal of a superior by a subordinate; effectively it was a crime
against the state. Women tried and found guilty of *petit treason*
were punished, not as murderers, but as traitors. The penalty for
petit treason was to be hanged, drawn and quartered, but because
the 'natural modesty of [women's] sex' forbade 'the exposing and
public mangling of their bodies'[43] they were offered a less indelicate
fate; to be burned alive at the stake. In practice, convicted women
would usually be strangled before the flames were lit. It was only in
1828 that women won the right to be tried for murder like men and
the right to be hanged if they were found guilty.

Throughout history, both in the reporting of real murder cases
and in their dramatisation in novels and plays, from *Agamemnon*
to *The Arden of Faversham*, it is suggested that the murder of a

husband by his wife at home, where both the wife and home represent all that is safe and comforting, is particularly deviant and abhorrent and deserving of a correspondingly severe punishment. In her study of criminal women and British justice, Helena Kennedy observes, 'Sympathy is not a commodity often granted to women who break the rules. Bad wives are also women who break the rules. They do so by being dissolute or unfaithful or by not fulfilling the wifely functions. Wives who betray their husbands offend against the notion of women as keepers of the hearth.'[44]

As Ann Jones points out in her pioneering study of the subject in 1980, 'the story of women who kill is the story of women'.[45]

By 1935, of the twenty-two women who had been condemned to death in Britain since the execution of Edith Thompson, only two had actually been hanged. In the intervening years, her death had accumulated power as a dark warning to British courts and British juries. But with Alma Rattenbury's arrest in March that year, the controversy was resurrected and 'the memory of the earlier trial haunted the court-room like a ghost'.[46] A dozen years on, were British juries better able to distinguish between immorality and criminality? Had the British press replaced an Old Testament lust for vengeance with a New Testament clemency? Or would they be sending yet another woman to swing at the end of a rope?

ACT TWO

Alma, John and Christopher Rattenbury

CHAPTER EIGHT

A THIRD ENGLAND

England is the most class-ridden country under the sun. It is a land of snobbery and privilege, ruled largely by the old and silly.

– George Orwell, *The Lion and the Unicorn*[1]

The Rattenburys did not take the most direct route from Victoria to England. Their itinerary, it seems, evolved as they went. Accompanied by a nursemaid, they sailed through the Panama Canal to Havana. On the voyage from Havana to New York, Christopher Pakenham recalled that Ratz became involved in a card game with some professional gamblers. By the time they reached their destination, he owed a large sum of money. Unable to pay his debts, he roused the whole family in the middle of the night and made a run for it. They left New York travelling by train to Montreal from where they sailed to Europe. Having visited Venice, they settled for a while in northern France long enough for Christopher to go to school there.[2] It was here that Ratz bought a right-hand drive Fiat saloon that they would take with them to England, sailing from St Malo on 28 June 1930. The journey from Victoria had taken six months.

In *English Journey*, J. B. Priestley identified a new, post-war England emerging in the 1930s, distinct from the quaint highways and byways of medieval Old England and Queen Victoria's industrial nation of coal, steel, textiles and railways. Socially and economically, it was a country in the midst of transformation: 'a third England of arterial and by-pass roads, of filling stations and factories that look like exhibition buildings, of giant cinemas and dance-halls and cafes, bungalows with tiny garages, cocktail bars, Woolworths, motor-coaches, wireless, hiking, factory girls looking like actresses, grey-hound racing and dirt tracks, swimming pools and everything given away for cigarette coupons.'[3]

In many ways, the England that greeted the Rattenburys was recognisably the country we have inherited today. But it was more diverse and complex than the dark corridor to war that has often been depicted, though the pressure of international events – first in America and then in Europe – was keenly felt throughout what seems a short but full decade. W. H. Auden famously dubbed the 1930s a 'low, dishonest decade',[4] Ronald Blythe labelling it 'the Age of Illusion'[5] and William McElwee the 'Locust Years'.[6] For despite the post-war promise to returning soldiers to create a Jerusalem 'built for heroes to live in', the period was characterised by deep divisions across classes and regions. A shocking symbol of the times took place in Oxford in 1934, where private and council housing estates were being developed side by side. The private homeowners complained that the council estate would adversely affect the quality of their lives and the value of their properties, so as the schemes reached completion, two brick walls were erected, topped with revolving spikes.[7] At the same time, the two roads connecting the estates were blocked off, effectively segregating the two communities. One local councillor protested that council tenants were being 'herded behind walls and barbed wire like Germans in a concentration camp'.[8] These walls, and many of the attitudes that built them, were to remain in place – both literally and figuratively – until long after the Second World War.

On 31 August 1930, the Rattenburys finally visited Okehampton in order for John to be baptised, an event that, given the family's ancient relationship with the town, made the local newspaper.[9] Rattenbury's nephew, Keith Miller Jones, the son of his sister Kate, was thirty-one years old, 6ft 4 and working as a solicitor in London. He attended the service and was to be John's godfather.[10] But despite the welcome that the family were afforded, Rattenbury was bitterly disappointed. The guidebook vision of Okehampton was fiction, and he dismissed the town as 'ugly, dirty and stupid'.[11] They would not settle here. It may have been concerns about Alma's continuing ill health that first suggested the benefits of living in Bournemouth.

Situated in the extreme southwest corner of Hampshire, and just over 100 miles from London, Bournemouth stands about 100ft above sea level on a high plateau that extends to the edge of the cliffs and down along the several sheltered and wooded valleys or 'chines', which here and there break the cliffs and run down towards the sea. Set between two double-tidal estuaries, the town is swept by year-round breezes, which moderate the summer heat and the winter cold, allowing it to boast in one 1930s guidebook 'the most equable climate of any seaside resort in the kingdom'.[12] Bournemouth had only come into being at the beginning of the nineteenth century, not in response to the needs of commerce and industry, but solely to meet the demands of those in search of health, leisure, or somewhere pleasant to live. 'In its very newness and cleanness, and in its elegant detached houses, its sheltered gardens luxuriant with flowers and shrubs and foliage, and its many broad tree-lined avenues, the town has great attraction and charm.'[13]

So beneficial was the town's climate thought to be that in 1855 the Brompton Hospital had established the Royal National Sanatorium for Consumption and Diseases of the Chest there.[14] Soon afterwards the town became a centre for convalescent homes, particularly for cases of tuberculosis, which led to its reputation – which still lingers today – as an 'invalid's paradise'. By the 1930s, Bournemouth was a 'true garden city by the sea' of some 117,000 inhabitants. But since the First World War, it had also developed as a tourist and holiday destination, gaining a reputation for relaxation and amusement, with sports like tennis, bowls, golf, cricket and croquet as well as water-based pursuits such as fishing, boating and bathing. And there was culture, too. The town had been the first in England to establish a permanent orchestra. Since 1929 it had been based at the new Bournemouth Pavilion and led by Sir Dan Godfrey. The Pavilion was a modern entertainment complex at the heart of the town providing concerts and theatre performances as well as dining and dancing. There were also two piers, at Boscombe and Bournemouth, the latter hosting performances by the municipal band seven days a week and open-air dancing every evening.[15] But as well as a holiday and convalescent destination, Bournemouth was also an attractive and popular place for the middle classes to retire.

For the Rattenburys, if not a home from home, Bournemouth was as near as England could offer. They decided to stay in the town for a while before selecting a more permanent residence. Christopher was sent to board at Cliff House School in Southbourne, where he'd be known as Christopher Rattenbury, though Alma and Ratz didn't change his name officially. Cliff House was a large, red-brick mansion built in the 1880s, a couple of minutes from the sea. Under the headmaster Captain F. Gidney, the school took boys from the ages of seven to thirteen to prepare for the major public schools and the Royal Naval College. It offered a classic middle-class education, with rugby, cricket and rowing considered as important as the academic subjects, though innovations such as basket-weaving and wireless classes indicated that the curriculum was also up to the minute.[16] Ratz would drive Christopher to Southbourne on Monday mornings and pick him up on Saturday to spend the weekend in Bournemouth. John would stay at home with his parents and the nurse until he was old enough to join his brother at school.

Through Hankinson's, a Bournemouth estate agency,[17] the Rattenburys found the Villa Madeira, a small house on a quiet road on the East Cliff, very much secluded from the holiday crowds. The landlords, Louise and Alfred Price, ran a local tobacconist's in Old Christchurch Road and had owned the Villa Madeira for some seven years, latterly living in it themselves and only vacating it in order to accommodate the Rattenburys. They agreed to take it fully furnished for £6 6s od a week.[18] The global economic crisis may have persuaded Rattenbury to rent such a modest property that was just big enough for their needs. Alma had a 'horror of white', so decorated the house in the busy, feminine floral designs of the period. 'It is so chilly,' she said. 'I will not have anything white in the house.'[19] She took the back bedroom, which she would share with John; it had a cottage-style sloping ceiling and a balcony with a leaded French window overlooking the garden. Christopher would take the room next door when he was home from school. Ratz took a bedroom on the ground floor next to the drawing room, where they had a telephone installed. The Rattenbury household would be one of over a million telephone subscribers in Britain at the time – though private telephone use, as much else in the 1930s, was an indicator of status. In middle-class Epsom, one in 3.5 households had a telephone, while in Merthyr Tydfil, the ratio was just one in every forty-seven.[20] With such rapid technological advances, Leon Simon, the director of telegraphs and telephones, prophesised that 'almost anything' could be achieved in the near future. 'The day is coming when you will be able to call up anybody on an aircraft in flight' and 'through the application of television to the telephone service, caller and called will be able to see one another while speaking over any distance'.[21]

With Ratz settled with all his conveniences on the ground floor, there was an unspoken agreement that any sexual relationship between him and Alma was now over. Symbolically, the master bedroom at the front of the house would remain empty and was only used by guests. Finally, Alma decided to get a little dog, naming her Dinah, perhaps after Alice's kitten in *Alice in Wonderland*, though Bing Crosby had recently had a popular hit with the song, 'Dinah (Is There Anyone Finer?)'. But in contrast to the big, airy rooms, handmade exotic furnishings, expansive grounds, large domestic staff and sea views at Iechinihl, the Villa Madeira was squat, dark and suburban; quite a come-down for the formerly celebrated architect and his once-famed wife.

The Rattenburys had chosen a particularly turbulent time to

start a new life in a country that was in the midst of financial crisis as well as great technological change. The resulting political instability prompted a rise in the popularity of fascism across Europe and within Britain itself. After the stock market crash on Wall Street on 29 October 1929, many countries across the globe had tried to protect their domestic markets by taxing foreign imports. Consequently, the value of British exports halved, which drastically affected traditional British industries like textiles, shipbuilding and coal. This disproportionately affected industrial areas like south Wales and northern Britain, which would experience enormous hardship during the 1930s. By the end of 1930, unemployment had more than doubled, from 1 million to 2.5 million – 20 per cent of the British workforce. By the autumn of 1931, anxious middle-class families like the Rattenburys expected that the pound would go the way of the mark and the rouble, that their savings would be lost and their investments worthless.

In 1931, Britain came off the gold standard and the pound was devalued to 25 per cent against the US dollar, helping exporters by making their goods cheaper abroad. Though prices rose, interest rates, which had risen to 6 per cent in the 1920s, were kept low and building societies eased their terms, offering for the first time 25-year mortgages with 5 per cent deposits rather than the fifteen-year terms with 25 per cent deposits they had offered the decade before. With mortgages more accessible, the building industry boomed. Four million houses were built during the 1930s, largely in the private sector.[22] There was huge competition between building firms to attract buyers, so house prices dropped, making a regular salary of about £200 a year enough to secure a mortgage on a house worth £500.[23] The growth in house building also kick-started a boom in consumer goods and, by 1935, the British middle-class home emerged as a national symbol: 'The home is by far the most important institution in the lives of the British people. It is a centre of interest, not only in the immediate family life, but equally in the wider hustling world of trade and commerce, for its influence is far-reaching and all-embracing. For the average British man and woman, each day begins and ends in the family centre. The influence of a happy, harmonious home is therefore a national asset.'[24]

The housing boom stimulated growth in all sorts of sectors: roads, cars, shops, schools, civic buildings and cinemas. Living standards rose, encouraging growth in domestic appliances such as cookers, vacuum cleaners, heaters and, the most popular domestic electrical appliance of all, radios (the second most popular was the humble iron). The rise of hire-purchase also contributed to this, increasing twentyfold between 1918 and 1938, though married women were still not legally permitted to make hire-purchase agreements without their husbands' consent.[25]

This desire for new consumer goods was also encouraged by the growth of electricity, which had first been generated for sale in Britain in 1881 but had not managed to challenge the domination of gas in domestic homes. By 1920, only 6 per cent of houses had been wired for electricity, but, by the end of the 1930s, electricity was used in 66 per cent of British homes. Consequently, the desire for new electrical appliances mushroomed throughout the decade.[26] By the end of the 1920s, there had been 30,000 vacuum cleaners in Britain; by 1935, there were 400,000; by 1939, there would be nearly a million. In 1922, when the BBC was first formed, there had been only 36,000 radio licences issued; by 1931, there were 4.3 million. By 1939, there would be 8.8 million as the radio industry expanded.[27]

Though radio was extremely popular, some listeners were disturbed by the sounds and voices brought directly into their homes. One of the first successful radio dramas, Richard Hughes's *Danger*, convinced some listeners that, like the characters in the play, they were trapped in an underground mine.[28] By the 1930s even the poorest families could afford a radio set. At first, customers' interest was in the technical properties of 'wireless' sets – the valves, diodes and resistors – so radios were crude in terms of design. But as the technological advances slowed down and one manufacturer was essentially offering the same apparatus as another, radios began to be housed in cabinets or pieces of furniture that harmonised with everyday life. One radio manufacturer even produced a wireless set that was housed in an easy chair. The domestication of this alien art form went some way to calm the fears of listeners who were genuinely confused by it. Radio became, quite literally, part of the furniture, with E. M. Delafield declaring, 'If I were to name a symbol of modern homelife I should chose the wireless.'[29]

John Reith, the first director general of the BBC, believed that radio was 'potentially as important as the printing press'[30] and was determined that the corporation offer its listeners 'all that is best in every department of human knowledge, endeavour and achievement, and to avoid things which are, or may be, hurtful. It is occasionally indicated to us that we are apparently setting out to give the public what we think they need – and not what they want, but few know what they want, and very few what they need'.[31]

Before it secured its place in the hearts of the nation during the Second World War, throughout the 1930s the BBC – and Reith personally – was the focus of intense debate, with his agenda dismissed as too elitist. Reith responded to adverse criticism by introducing more populist programmes, such as dance music in the evenings and soon the Savoy Orpheans, Paul Whiteman, Jack Hylton, Jack Howard, Jack Payne and Henry Hall broadcast every night for an hour before midnight, except, the Calvinist Reith insisted, on the Sabbath.[32]

When the conception of the BBC was first mooted, there had been considerable pressure from the newspaper industry to prevent the corporation from broadcasting news. The potential power of the infant BBC was quickly identified by Henry Hamilton Fyfe, the editor of the *Daily Herald*, who was concerned that radio would bring an end to newspapers altogether: 'We shall all carry earphones about with us and be able to pick up messages. Those who regard newspapers merely as a help to passing the time would find wireless news enough for them.'[33] Consequently, the Newspaper Proprietors Association had joined forces with the news agencies to lobby against the BBC developing its own news service. As a result, when it was launched, the BBC was not allowed to broad-cast any news bulletins at all before 7 p.m. so as not to damage the market for newspapers.[34] Such were the restrictions on what news could be broadcast that, famously, on Good Friday 1930, the BBC news announcer reported that 'there is no news tonight'. To Reith's chagrin, the BBC remained an ineffective news service for much of the 1930s and only developed its first, very inhibited, news programme in 1934. This continued right up to the Munich Crisis in 1938, when the BBC argued that the provision of regular news bulletins during the darkening crisis in Europe was of national importance.[35]

The wireless had a particular impact on women like Alma. Women made up only 16 per cent of the British workforce so were by default the largest radio audience. This generation of women was exposed to many subjects that would have been outside the experience of most of their mothers and grandmothers, such as English literature, history and science. A 1939 survey of women's listening habits reported that 'the housewife learns [from radio] what she had no time to get from books'. As a result, in the 1930s housewives across the social spectrum were generally much better informed than their husbands.

As well as listening to the wireless, the cultural lives of middle-class women were also enhanced by 'serious reading'.[36] During the 1920s and '30s, a generation of British novelists such as Elizabeth Bowen, Winifred Holtby, Rose Macaulay, Rosamond Lehmann, Virginia Woolf, Storm Jameson and Rebecca West wrote about the lives of women like themselves, elevating the concerns of the home and domestic life as a suitable subject for fiction. Many of these books, the 'feminine middlebrow', explored the pressures and frustrations of ordinary women's lives: 'Every morning you awake to the kind of list which begins; Sink-plug. Ruffle-tape. X-hooks. Glue. And ends; Ring plumber, Get Sweep. Curse laundry. Your horizon contracts, your mind's eye is focused upon a small circle of exasperating detail. Sterility sets in; the hatches of your mind are battened down.'[37]

In an age before the introduction of the paperback, most middle-class families borrowed rather than bought books. But public lending libraries were considered to be dubious institutions with 'an unpleasant whiff of charity about them'[38] and not suitable for middle-class ladies. Public library books were thought to be dirty and carry disease, so until the Second World War, many women were members of private lending libraries such as W. H. Smith or Boots. By the mid-1930s, Boots was the largest circulating library in Britain with over 400 branches and 500,000 subscribers.[39] By 1939, 35 million books would be issued by branches of Boots, who catered for 'suburban shoppers as much as fashionable ladies'.[40] In 1933, Boots library in Poole, just next to Bournemouth, with a population of 43,000, issued 6,000 books every week.[41] Women made up 75 per cent of Boots' members and membership was structured, effectively, by social class. 'Class A' subscribers could take out books 'on demand' for 17s 6d a year and choose from all the books in circulation, regardless of popularity or date of publication. 'Class B' subscribers paid 10s 6d for the 'ordinary service', which restricted them to choosing from books that were more than a year old.[42] All Boots library books had a distinctive green shield embossed on the cover and there were eyelet holes at the top of the spine into which a tag was inserted when the book was borrowed – a green tag for first-class and a red tag for second-class subscribers.[43]

With such a voracious female readership, there were 200 new fiction titles published in Britain every week during the 1930s.[44] The vast majority of books that Boots issued were mysteries (45 per cent) and romance (30 per cent), in contrast to the more downmarket W. H. Smith libraries, which issued 50 per cent romance and 25 per cent crime.[45] The publisher Michael Joseph astutely identified the crucial role that books and particularly fiction played in the lives of millions of middle-class women: 'Women seek in the various realms of fiction the wider range of human experiences which a complex and narrowed life denies them. Having neither the time nor the opportunity in this crowded, hustled existence to taste the joys and sorrows, the vicissitudes and triumphs of a more elemental experience, they turn to fiction to satisfy their natural craving ... for emotional satisfaction.'[46]

As well as borrowing books from Boots, women would also consume 'light fiction' as short stories and serials in magazines. Sixty new women's magazines were launched between 1920 and 1945 and most of them were aimed at housewives, such as *My Little Home, Home Chat, Mother, Woman and Home* and *Good Housekeeping*.[47] They played a major role in reinforcing the domestic role of women, with household tips on how to get stains out of shoes, how to make potted meat and how to make lampshades;[48] marriage was 'the best job of all'.[49] As well as flattering the reader by describing domestic work as a profession, these magazines also accessed a receptive market for consumer goods. In February 1919 an advertisement for face cream had promoted the slogan, 'Back to Home and Duty', advising readers that 'Now the war is won, many women and girls are leaving work, their war job finished. They are naturally desirous of regaining their good complexions and soft white hands freely sacrificed to the national need. Oatine is invaluable for this purpose.'[50]

The message had been clear and uncompromising; after the war women should step back into the kitchen and the nursery; domesticity, not work, was the primary destiny for them. Added to this, during the period of mass unemployment in the 1930s, it was felt that women shouldn't occupy jobs that could be taken by men. In teaching and in many clerical organisations, marriage bars meant that women were compulsorily dismissed when they got married. In 1930, Winifred Holtby was horrified that the majority of female employees in the civil service had actually voted to maintain the marriage bar: 'Who are the girls who have voted for the marriage bar? Nine out of ten swing daily to their offices in suburban trains, trams and buses, carrying in their suitcases a powder puff and a love-story or *Home Chat* ... they think on foggy mornings when the alarm goes, that they loathe above everything the scramble to the office. They think if only they could marry and have a little home of their own all will be well.'[51]

In 1932, the BBC, which had hitherto been a fairly progressive institution, also introduced a marriage bar.

As well as dictating what women should do (or more often not do), women's magazines also established what women should look like and how they ought to behave. In October 1932, *Woman* clarified that wives were subject to their husband's approval: 'No matter what your circumstances might be, you cannot afford to neglect your appearance, nor must you ever forget that to look your best at all times is your duty – towards yourself and towards the man you married.'

The masculine fashions of the 1920s – bobbed hair, the Eton crop and short skirts with their memories of war work and independence – gave way to a more feminine look, encouraged by the example of the Duchess of York.[52] Hems were lowered, there were more bows, frills, ruffles and chiffon, 'rounded slenderness and lissomness [were] the chief characteristics of the 1934–5 silhouette'.[53] The development of rayon and artificial silk initiated a strong ready-to-wear fashion trade that meant that ordinary women could dress like film stars or titled ladies.[54] Women's clothes were indices of class and status and the prevailing social codes extended to the appropriate dress for particular functions or for certain times of day. Women regarded the clothes they wore in the morning as 'work' clothes and advertisements in magazines for domestic machinery no longer featured maids, but the housewife herself ironing or vacuuming. Though they might wear aprons, these would be decorated with flowers or coloured trim to distinguish them from the plain white aprons of domestic staff.[55] Many women would take off their aprons as soon as they heard the doorbell ring as it was considered 'the height of bad manners and bad taste' to answer the door wearing one.[56] They would generally change at least once during the day – certainly for their husband's return for dinner in the evening.

Alma often wore pyjamas and kimonos around the house during the day, an unusual bohemian flourish in the conventional suburbs of Bournemouth at odds with the usual middle-class uniform that had evolved for middle-class matrons like her – tweeds and tartan in the country and cocktail dresses in town. Coats were frequently fur and hats were de rigueur for all daytime occasions.[57] These ranged from the toque popularised by Queen Mary to turbans, berets and snoods. Women were not permitted, however, to wear hats for dinner in restaurants or at nightclubs, where evening dress was obligatory and hair was expected to be 'as polished and shiny as brushing and brilliantine could make them'.[58]

The pressure on Alma and women like her, with limited budgets but appearances to be kept up for their peers as well as their husbands, resulted in a market among middle-class women for good-quality second-hand clothes. They would never buy these from a market stall due to anxieties about cleanliness and the social embarrassment if they were observed. Many women would buy and sell their clothes anonymously through classified advertisements in magazines such as *The Lady*.[59] One correspondent explained that 'having expensive taste, but greatly reduced income', she would be grateful if another would sell her 'exclusive wardrobe regularly and cheaply; only really good things; privately'.[60] Another woman, a young widow 'income reduced' was 'accustomed to buy from the best houses, would take entire wardrobe, day and evening, undies, from lady same age ... must be moderate price'.[61]

Throughout the 1930s, there was great ambivalence about the use of make-up, and much of this was about how it reflected on men. Many advertisements for cosmetics aimed at married women acknowledged that some men didn't approve of them: 'There's one thing a loving husband won't forgive ... a cheap painted look!'[62] *Good Housekeeping* ran a piece in 1931 entitled, 'Do Women Dress to Please Men?' castigating the habits of the 'modern woman, her paints, and powder, her reddened nails ... and plucked eyebrows ... [Do] many women realise how men are revolted by some of their habits?'[63]

The vicar of Belper in Derbyshire caused controversy in May 1935 when he threatened to withhold the chalice from women wearing lipstick who presented themselves for communion, provoking a debate in the press about 'the Ethics of lipstick'.[64] And yet in *Miss Modern* in 1932, Godfrey Winn was outraged when the Bank of England banned make-up altogether: 'The majority of business men, from chief down to office boy, delight in pretty, varied clothes and the lovely (though artificial) complexions of the women members of staff ... they introduce glamour and romance into our humdrum routine.'[65]

In a *Good Housekeeping* survey, only 20 per cent of correspondents admitted to using lipstick, 7 per cent rouge, and 7.5 per cent claimed to use no make-up at all.[66] But with the glamorous images from Hollywood in cinemas across the country, there was a huge surge in demand for cosmetics.[67]

Marie Stopes had forecast as early as 1918 that 'the greatest social influence since the discovery of printing is the cinema'.[68] Glamorous films from Hollywood warned female audiences that they must 'keep young and beautiful if [they wanted] to be loved'. Music hall was dying fast and variety theatres were being turned into cinemas across the country. Sound had eclipsed the silent film and the fleapit was being replaced with great speed by purpose-built super-cinemas. These were luxurious palaces with marble staircases, cut-glass chandeliers, velvet curtains, Wurlizter organs and uniformed staff. The number of picture houses grew from 3,000 in 1926 to 5,000 in 1939. By 1937, 20 million people went to the cinema every week, the majority of them women. Going to the pictures soon became 'as standardized as a church service or a daily newspaper', and women would walk into a cinema 'as easily as into [their] own kitchen'.[69]

There was a mutual interchange between films and fiction in the interwar period, with many features aimed at the female market – musicals, romances and tear-jerkers. And though the cinema was a place of escapism and fantasy for women, it was also able to explore their domestic preoccupations – family, money, duty, love, fidelity – even if these issues were dramatised in the many popular historical films of the period.

As well as exerting a great influence on British women in terms of fashion and beauty, cinema also promoted smoking. By the mid-1930s, 41 per cent of women and 80 per cent of men smoked.[70] Alma was a chain-smoker and would even smoke during meals,[71] often with a cigarette holder, while Ratz smoked a pipe. Uniquely, smoking crossed all social and gender barriers, so cigarette manufacturers were soon investing in huge advertising campaigns, with many of the advertisements declaring the health-giving properties of smoking. Craven 'A' were 'made specially to prevent sore throats' and Kensitas claimed that they helped with weight loss: 'When tempted to overindulge ... say, "No thanks, I'll have a Kensitas instead."'[72]

By the 1930s, shopping habits in British high streets had changed enormously since the time before the First World War and offered women like Alma extraordinary choice. Chain stores had grown up all over the country, many of which are still familiar to us today, such as Boots and Marks & Spencer. There were also Sainsbury's the grocer, Burton's the tailor, Dorothy Perkins and Dewhurst the butcher as well as a roster of half-forgotten high street names such as Home & Colonial, C&A, Lilley & Skinner, Freeman, Hardy & Willis, Timothy Whites and MacFisheries.[73] Woolworths, the once-great bastion of the great British high street, had first opened in 1909 and by 1937 had 711 shops, selling 'nothing over sixpence'.[74] Goods were now all displayed in open-plan departments for customers to touch, no longer secured in drawers or on shelves and policed by floorwalkers. Department stores were designated along class lines, with Debenhams grading their stores A – 'high class', B – 'popular to medium class' and C – 'just popular', the classes being reflected in the standard of the merchandise sold.[75]

Small local shopkeepers like the newsagent Mrs Price resented the expansion of the chain stores, but independent shops still dominated the sale of fruit, fish, vegetables and bread. But in the same way that housewives had to adjust to a new way of shopping, shopkeepers had to accept a new way of working, selling branded goods with prices set by the wholesalers and manufacturers, offering prepackaged foodstuffs rather than blending their own tea, or weighing sugar, butter or flour as they used to. The dominance of the big food companies had led to the growth of pre-packaged, branded and processed foods. These were backed by ubiquitous advertising campaigns promoting tinned products by Heinz and Crosse & Blackwell such as peas, beans, ham, pilchards, peaches, pears and pineapples, as well as many familiar brands such as Bird's custard powder, Rowntree's and Chivers jellies, Marmite, Bovril, Horlicks, Ovaltine and Nestlé's instant coffee.[76]

By the time the Rattenburys were settled at the Villa Madeira in September 1931, Alma's ambitions had dwindled and her horizons narrowed. The new labour-saving devices and convenience foods allowed her the leisure to enrich her inner life with the books she borrowed from Boots, the films she watched at the picture house and the wide variety of programmes she listened to on the wireless. But these distractions did little to disguise the fact that the ambitious young woman once hailed as a genius of the concert stage in British Columbia was now defined entirely by her relationship with her husband and children. She had become a frustrated, middle-aged, provincial housewife.

Drawing room, Villa Madeira

CHAPTER NINE

VILLA MADEIRA

29 June 1930–26 September 1934

> Ours is essentially a tragic age, so we refuse to take it
> tragically. The cataclysm has happened, we are among the
> ruins, we start to build up new little habitats, to have new little
> hopes. It is rather hard work: there is now no smooth road into
> the future: but we go round, or scramble over the obstacles.
> We've got to live, no matter how many skies have fallen. This
> was more or less Constance Chatterley's position. The war had
> brought the roof down over her head. And she had realised that
> one must live and learn.
>
> – D. H. Lawrence, *Lady Chatterley's Lover*[1]

Six years old at the time of the murder, John Rattenbury retained
fond, 'keen but disconnected memories'[2] of life at the Villa Madeira
when they first arrived there. He had a 'great sense of love'[3] for his
mother, who would wake him and his brother at dawn and take
them swimming in the sea as the sun rose, with him riding on
his mother's back. She'd call him her 'Chipmonk' and his brother
'Toffy'. There would be picnics in the New Forest, where Alma
would play the violin as the boys swam in the river.[4] On very hot
days they would play in the garden and Alma would ask for the
canvas sun shelter that they stored in the garage to be put up so
that John could sleep outside.[5] Alma taught John how to read, how

to dance for his father and how to help her in the garden, growing the pink flowers she loved. Much of the time, it was an idyllic childhood – mornings on the beach and afternoons in the garden. In the evenings they would play card games, listen to the wireless or read library books, *Peter Pan*, *The Midnight Folk* or *Winnie-the-Pooh*. One of his strongest memories was, as a four-year-old, hearing his mother playing the grand piano in the drawing room: 'I came in from the garden where I had been industriously digging up her flowers. Near the piano was an easel, low to the ground, with a drawing of a building that Father had designed: clean, straight lines drawn on crisp white paper. An entrance door and steps. Trees on either side. Some hand lettering.'[6] He felt 'some awe'[7] for his father, who even gave John a model house to play with made of wood.

Housekeeping was the main focus of Alma's life at the Villa Madeira. Though she had an account at Harrods in London,[8] much of her shopping was in local stores in Bournemouth and Boscombe. Ratz gave her a cheque for £50 a month from his account at the Bank of Montreal to pay the household bills, including doctor's fees, the laundry, the children's clothes, their own clothes and to maintain the car, but Alma felt it was 'never enough'. Her attitude to household accounts was chaotic and vague, and she 'had difficulty counting to ten because she would run out of fingers'.[9] Consequently, she was always finding herself in debt or overdrawn, even though her mother would send her money every now and again, perhaps £25 for her birthday or at Christmas. Ratz guaranteed her overdraft up to £100. Every six months or so, Alma would ask him for extra money to pay off her debts.[10] Ratz, though, was becoming increasingly concerned about the economic climate, and had become tighter with the purse strings, so Alma would have to prime him to get the money when she needed it, choosing the right moment. She also had to pay the servants' wages from her household budget. The Rattenburys kept a small staff – a chef called Davis to do the cooking[11] and a nanny for John.[12] The staff were engaged through advertisements that Alma placed in the local newspaper, the *Bournemouth Echo*.

After the First World War, middle-class families had found it increasingly difficult to secure and keep domestic staff, and in 1919 even the British government had investigated what became known as 'the servant problem'. There was a strong feeling among the middle classes that it was the government's responsibility to restore supplies of servants to private households and that as long as there were vacancies in domestic service, women should not be allowed to receive unemployment benefit. Throughout the 1920s practical books had started to appear such as *Life Without Servants* and *The Servantless House*. But as the depression took hold, many women reluctantly returned to domestic service. By 1931, there were as many servants working in Britain as there had been in 1890. Twenty per cent of British households had at least one servant living in and a daily maid was well within the means of a grammar-school teacher who had paid off their mortgage. But domestic workers in the 1930s were much less reliable than they had been before the war. They were more prone to quit and resentful of poor working conditions. This was particularly the case with women who had enjoyed the freedoms and good wages of factory work during the war. Margaret Powell, who went into service in 1924, articulated the new attitude of servants to domestic service after the war, which was no longer gratefully deferential: 'The very name "service" meant that you'd said goodbye to all personal freedom – the same as it did for men in the Army.'[13]

By 1931, Davis the chef had left the Villa Madeira and was not immediately replaced. Alma took an advertisement out in the *Echo* for a companion-help. This was answered by Irene Riggs, a 22-year-old Bournemouth girl who was an experienced domestic servant who had worked since leaving school at fourteen, serving in one household for five years, then another for three.[14] She would be paid £1 5s a week and would live in, taking the middle bedroom on the first floor above the kitchen.[15] Sunday and Wednesday afternoons she would have off. Irene had never met a woman quite like Alma before – relaxed, flamboyant and unpredictable. But she soon got used to Alma's eccentric behaviour – wearing pyjamas around the house in the day, playing the gramophone or the piano late at night, chain-smoking and lying in bed until midday. Alma would have sudden mood swings, becoming 'very excited and used to run about a good deal', then she would get drowsy and go to sleep, 'just as if she had taken something'.[16] Despite Alma's unusual disposition, Irene found her a warm-hearted and kind woman and, for her, the relationship was much closer than that of employer and employee. Alma was 'the most kind-hearted woman in the world' and equally as generous, often giving Irene clothes and money.[17] She would frequently ask Irene to accompany her on trips away, to restaurants and to the theatre. They were 'two great friends rather than ... mistress and maid'.[18] Irene called her 'darling', rather than 'Mrs Rattenbury', thus muddying the distinction between the family and the staff at the Villa Madeira.[19] Perhaps because of her colonial upbringing or the social mobility her family had enjoyed in their move from southeast London to the centre of society in Victoria, Alma didn't feel beholden to the class divisions that tightly bound middle-class behaviour in Britain in the 1930s.

Though Alma had found a friend and confidante in Bournemouth in Irene, Ratz had not. In contrast to his former rich and rowdy social life at the Union Club in Victoria, he had few local friends. On the rare occasions that the Rattenburys left the town together, they'd visited Shirley Hatton Jenks, a wealthy barrister and the squire of Pilsdon Manor in Bridport. D. A. Wood, who lived on Poole Hill, was a surveyor and had been employed by Ratz professionally.[20] He visited the Villa Madeira almost daily and was 'practically his only local intimate'.[21] Other than their landlady Mrs Price, the Rattenburys' only other regular visitor was Dr O'Donnell, who first started attending Alma and the children in 1932. William O'Donnell had qualified as a doctor at Trinity College Dublin in 1893 and was a Licentiate of the Royal College of Physicians of Ireland and a member of the Royal College of Surgeons. He had married his wife Alice in 1878 and they had two sons and a daughter. He had practised in Dublin, Malvern and Fishguard before setting up his home and practice at Richmond

Chambers in central Bournemouth in 1924. Alma had continued to have health problems since arriving in Bournemouth, despite the sea air, so O'Donnell decided to send her away for two weeks of tests and X-rays in order to assess her condition. Finally, Alma was diagnosed with tuberculosis. She was in frequent need of medical attention as she was particularly troubled by suppurating glands. Lymph nodes would swell in her neck and have to be drained, a painful, unpleasant process. Between 1932 and 1935, she would be operated on under anaesthetic four times by Alfred Rooke, a local surgeon.[22] O'Donnell made over 100 other visits to the Villa Madeira over a period of two years,[23] during which there evolved a much closer relationship between him and Alma than might have been expected between general practitioner and patient. He became a family friend. Again, Alma confused the boundaries between her personal and professional relationships.

In the 1930s, keeping middle-class patients happy was crucial to operating a successful general practice. Affluent private patients like the Rattenburys provided most general practitioners with the bulk of their income. Visiting the surgery, poor patients would enter through the side door and sit in the waiting room, whereas private patients would use the front door and wait in the dining room 'amongst the polished silver and mahogany'.[24] They would have their prescription bottle sealed with wax, wrapped in white paper and delivered to their home by an errand boy after evening surgery. Hypochondriac and neurotic patients, a category in which Alma might have been included, tended to be indulged rather than dismissed as timewasters, and one doctor who practised at the time stated that his business depended on neurotic patients as they required regular visits and regular medicine and would pay willingly and dearly for them. He estimated that, though they made up less than 10 per cent of his total patients, the well-off supplied half his income and would subsidise the poorer patients on his list.[25] The successful GP was one who cultivated a good bedside manner and helped ease pain, rather than cure conditions, so there was a growth in the use of sedatives and painkillers such as

morphia, heroin, barbitone and phenobarbitone.[26] Cocaine could
be taken hypodermically, by the mouth or as snuff, sometimes
mixed with boric and lactose. The medicine cupboard in Alma's
bedroom contained prescription drugs as well as over-the-counter
remedies, including the hypnotic drug Soneryl and Stannoxyl, a
treatment for the bone condition osteomyelitis, which may have
been a side effect of Alma's tuberculosis. The cupboard also contained Chlorodyne, one of the best-known patent medicines made
up of laudanum, cannabis and chloroform, as well as the sedative
potassium bromide.[27]

Several prominent British drug scandals in the 1930s involved
middle-class women. In 1933, Chelsea divorcée Diana Dorothy
Willis was jailed for eight months for stealing fur coats from shops
in order to fuel her drug habit.[28] Many female addicts had served
as nurses during the war or ran nursing homes. In October 1934
sisters Mary and Edith Hiscock – both nurses – were convicted
in Cheltenham for procuring heroin to feed their own addiction[29]
and in the same year well-connected society nursing-home matron
Veronica Heywood, who had become a heroin addict following
surgery, had charges against her dropped, though her GP, Dr
Valentine Hirsch, was fined £15 for supplying her.[30] In 1937, Ellen
Ruddle died of morphine poisoning and before her suicide she
was 'found wandering without proper clothing' and had become
'entirely uncontrollable',[31] just as Irene observed Alma 'run about
a good deal' in the garden, dressed only in her pyjamas. Alma
may have used cocaine or morphia to combat the symptoms of
her tuberculosis, to heighten her mood or to help her sleep. And
GPs like Dr O'Donnell found it hard to refuse patients what they
wanted when it was they who paid their bills and subsidised their
livelihood.

* * *

2 June 1932 was Alma's fortieth birthday and her son Christopher
remembered her being very distressed at the prospect.[32] The hopes
she had once nursed of a concert career had been dashed. Gone

were the days when she was the toast of Victoria society, with her name regularly appearing in the newspapers. She was middle-aged, putting on weight[33] and living in a modest house with an ageing husband who worried about money and was becoming increasingly tight-fisted. Perhaps sensitive to the mid-life ennui she was feeling, Ratz had Alma's piano shipped over from Victoria. It was placed in the drawing room, completely dominating it. Alma had no ambition to pursue a career as a classical pianist, but after buying several records by contemporary singers and playing them on the radiogram, just as she had done in her childhood, Alma started to write her own tunes again. Perhaps this revived memories of Miss Knox from deep in Alma's past when she had first imagined that music might be her vocation: 'If you love music … your muscles never move better than when you are making music; that is to say, your life work and ambition, will never move better then when you, too, are making music.'[34]

Ratz thought Alma's tunes might make very good popular songs and encouraged her to have them published. He spent several months trying to find a publisher who might be interested. He travelled up to London to discuss Alma's work with the newly formed music publisher Boosey and Hawkes in their Regent Street office, but he was told that there was no use trying to sell Alma's music at the moment. Times were hard and music was a luxury; they weren't publishing anything. They didn't even want to look at the pieces she'd written. This sent Alma into despair. It was 'like hitting a stone wall'.[35]

Meanwhile, Alma was concerned about her son Christopher. He had an issue with his legs that needed treatment. She consulted a Dr Basker in Southbourne, who prescribed a series of injections that Alma would give Christopher at school with a hypodermic syringe she kept in the medical cupboard in her bedroom. She had also noticed that the boy, by then eleven years old, had started drawing disturbing images and leaving them all over the house. One of the sketches was of a boy sitting up in bed holding a sixpence with a man leaning over and threatening him with a stick, as if the man

had put a long hypodermic needle right through the boy's arm.[36]
So, in September 1932, Alma decided to consult a phrenologist.
Phrenology was a pseudo-science that involved the observation of
the skull to assess an individual's personality or temperament. Alma
located a practitioner in nearby Boscombe called W. G. Clarke. She
was impressed with Clarke's reading of Christopher's personality,
sending him an extra £5 as an appreciation of how accurate she
thought it was. She was so pleased, in fact, that she asked Clarke to
give her an assessment too.[37] Clarke's reading of Alma's character
was only given after the trial and was surely influenced by contemporary attitudes towards creative people, particularly women, as
well as what he had read about her in the press:

> She was one of those people who, when they come under the
> influence, give way to temptation easily. I told her that she had
> not much fight in her, and warned her that she must guard against
> emotional excitement. She agreed with me and told me her emo-
> tional condition was due to being overworked when she was
> young. At that point Mr Rattenbury intervened and said that he
> agreed with his wife. He said that she had appeared before large
> audiences in Canada when she was only eight years of age, and
> the strain and excitement was too much for a child of that age.[38]

* * *

Though the Rattenburys had been used to a large staff at Iechinihl,
for such a small household at the Villa Madeira it seems somewhat luxurious to have employed a chef, particularly given Ratz's
frequent concerns about the housekeeping budget. But shortly
after the Rattenburys' visit to the phrenologist, in October 1932,
34-year-old Frank Hobbs saw one of Alma's advertisements in the
Bournemouth Echo for a chef. According to a statement he gave to
police but never used as evidence at the trial, Hobbs telephoned for
an appointment and later arrived at the house to meet Alma. The
next day, he received a letter offering him the job of Alma's cook

general.[39] The following day he started work at the Villa Madeira and was given the spare room next to Alma's. 'Practically from the first day' he entered service at the house, Alma would spend a great deal of her time talking to Hobbs in the kitchen and taking him into her confidence. She wrote songs and then asked him for his opinion about the lyrics. She confided in him that she had been married before and that her mother had arranged the marriage between her and her husband.

After two or three weeks, Hobbs went out for his half-day off one Wednesday afternoon. On his return he found Alma in the kitchen where she was clearly anxious to see him. She said, 'I have been waiting for you to come in.' Thinking that she had some orders for him, he said, 'Yes, madam.' But Alma replied, 'Don't call me madam, you are the same equal as myself. Don't you realise that you were one of the many applicants for the situation? The other applicants' references were far superior to yours but I chose you because you have sex appeal.' Hobbs maintained that Alma was not herself and didn't know what she was saying. But she was insistent: 'I know what I am saying quite well. I want you and I mean to have you.'[40]

Hobbs asked her if she was aware that her husband and children were in the house? He insisted that he wasn't that sort of man and wouldn't even think of sleeping with her. He left the kitchen and went up to his bedroom. Only a couple of minutes later, Alma came into his room. He tactfully pushed her out and locked the door. Throughout the night she continued to tap on his bedroom door, but eventually she gave up and went to bed.

The next morning, Hobbs carried on with his work as if nothing had happened. Alma never got up before noon, but after this incident she stayed in bed for three or four days. When she finally appeared, she came to Hobbs in the dining room where he was preparing breakfast and apologised. She had lost control of herself. He was a 'perfect brick' for not doing what she'd wanted him to do. Hobbs assured her that the matter was closed as far as he was concerned and carried on with his work.

Around this time Mrs Price, the Rattenburys' landlady and frequent visitor to the house, had been invited to lunch and tea. Before she left after tea, Alma asked her if she wanted to come to dine that evening as well, as Dr O'Donnell was coming for dinner. Once Mrs Price had left, Alma had become very excited and started running about the house. She had then become drowsy and gone to bed. Later, when Mrs Price arrived for dinner, Irene told her that Alma was not at all well and could not see her. With the mistress of the house upstairs in bed, O'Donnell and Irene dined alone, both concerned about Alma.[41] Alma's retreat to her room after her sexual overtures to Hobbs may simply have been due to the embarrassment of his awkward rejection, but her boldness and erratic behaviour might also be an indication that she had taken some sort of drug that had heightened her mood, which was then followed by a reclusive come-down.

Two weeks after the awkward incident with Alma, Hobbs was approached by Ratz, who said that, owing to the economic depression, they could not afford to keep him. Alma would do the cooking and she would get a woman in to do the housework. He then gave Hobbs two weeks' wages in lieu of notice. The Rattenburys clearly wanted to get rid of him as soon as possible. Hobbs was convinced that Ratz knew nothing of the incident that had occurred between him and Alma. Ratz had always been pleased with Hobbs's work, so there was no reason to dispense with his services. Hobbs was convinced that Alma, hurt or embarrassed at being rebuffed, must have persuaded her husband to dismiss him. That afternoon, Hobbs packed his things and left, saying nothing about the incident to Alma or Irene.[42]

Ratz could see that Alma was still hurt and disappointed that her songs had been rejected by Boosey and Hawkes, but, never a man to be defeated, he had an inspired idea. He asked a friend to introduce them to Sir Dan Godfrey, who led the Bournemouth Symphony Orchestra. In turn, Godfrey advised him to exploit his contacts to get an introduction to the music publisher Keith Prowse, whom Godfrey felt were the right people for Alma's music. So Ratz contacted the agent general of British Columbia in London, Frederick Parker Burden, and asked if he could arrange a meeting for them. Alma and Ratz duly travelled to New Bond Street in London on 8 December 1933 to meet the general manager of the publishing division of Keith Prowse, 53-year-old Dutchman Simon Van Lier.[43]

After waiting in an outer office full of busy clerks, they were ushered into Van Lier's inner sanctum.[44] He chatted to them and asked if Alma would play one of her songs, the one she thought the best. After two minutes of her playing it, Rattenbury felt Alma had enthralled the music publisher. After ten minutes, Ratz wondered what he thought. Van Lier said he was 'greatly impressed' and would publish one of the songs, have it orchestrated and broadcast. Rattenbury was so delighted that he clasped Alma's hand and 'almost danced with joy'.[45] Van Lier said that he would also have another two of Alma's numbers published as sheet music for the piano. She would need a music arranger and Van Lier would introduce her to a lyric writer, but he thought she had enormous potential. He then invited the Rattenburys to dine with him at the weekend.

That Saturday, Van Lier hosted dinner with the Rattenburys at the ultra-modern and fashionable Mayfair Hotel ('the most beautiful and fashionable hotel in London'), together with his 'fiancée' (Van Lier was married at the time), the BBC singer Yvette Darnac. Van Lier told them all about the challenges of the music industry that Alma was so keen to join. He confided that his office was always full of anxious composers waiting to get a break and that he had 200 compositions sent to him every week. But Alma, he told Ratz, was a genius: 'She is marvellous! I have travelled all over the world and into all kinds of places for tunes, there are few of them. It is one of the greatest gifts of humanity – and here is your wife – her mind teeming with exquisite tunes.'[46]

The dance floor at the Mayfair Hotel that night was 'brilliant with the gorgeous costumes of the dancers' dancing to Bert Ambrose and his orchestra, one of the stars of the dance band era.

Ambrose's orchestra was 'the best that London had to offer' and broadcast on the BBC in the prestigious Saturday-night slot from the Mayfair with vocalists Sam Browne and Elsie Carlisle.

That evening, Van Lier had evidently sent word that 'a great new composer was present',[47] so soon Ambrose himself came over to Van Lier's table and was introduced to the astonished Alma and Ratz. He was charmed to meet them and promised to broadcast some of Alma's music on the radio. Yvette Darnac said to Alma, 'Do you realise in future – that when you enter this room – the band will break off and play your music to you?' Alma was thrilled by the experience and by the prospects that were being outlined to her. This was her dream come true. After the evening with Van Lier, Ratz wrote excitedly to his sister from their hotel: 'The Greatest Publisher in London is absolutely at Alma's feet – acclaiming her as a genius – on the centre of London life – said they would spend thousands of pounds putting out her work – and anxious beyond words that we won't trot away.'[48]

Van Lier promised to mentor Alma, giving her an hour of his time every day, 'putting her wise to all the tricks of the trade'. There was talk of radio broadcasts, music for theatre and film. It seemed inevitable that they would have to move to London; the possibilities for Alma were endless. Alma herself was 'dizzy with it all'.[49]

Van Lier put the Rattenburys in touch with a musical arranger and introduced Alma to the lyricist Edward Lockton,[50] who had been writing popular parlour songs since 1900, such as 'Where My Caravan Has Rested' and 'Stars That Light My Garden'. He had had a particularly big hit with 'Because', which had been recorded by Caruso. A music industry hack, Lockton quickly added lyrics to several of Alma's melodies, many of the same longing, sentimental quality.

Alma decided to publish her work under a pseudonym and chose the exotic-sounding 'Lozanne'. She had bought more new records, including some by the tenor Frank Titterton. As soon as she heard his voice she declared, 'That is the voice for my songs!'[51] Titterton was 'one of the best equipped and most popular tenors of the day' and had an expansive singing career from Gilbert and Sullivan to the concert stage. He had been conducted by Sir Edward Elgar in the *Dream of Gerontius* in 1928 and had a busy recording and broadcasting career as well as appearing in films such as *Song at Eventide* with Fay Compton and *Waltz Time* with the West End star Evelyn Laye. He 'brought to the music something of the Caruso touch in his voice and in his management of it'. Alma asked Ratz to write to Titterton and arrange a meeting to discuss her songs.

The Rattenburys met Titterton for lunch at a London hotel where he was accompanied by his secretary and accompanist, Beatrice Esmond: 'We found Mr and Mrs Rattenbury to be a striking-looking couple. Mrs Rattenbury was very smartly dressed, and her conversation was that of a well-travelled cultured woman with keen powers of observation. Her intense emotionalism, which since has impressed itself on [us] over and over again, was apparent at that first meeting.'[52]

Titterton agreed to record some of Alma's songs and between 1932 and 1935 they would make twelve records together, on two of which she accompanied him herself at the piano.[53] The relationship between him and the Rattenburys was very warm. He was 'a man of the most genial personality' and told 'a good story as well as he [sang] a romantic ballad'. He and Beatrice would meet Alma and Ratz for lunch in town or dinner at Titterton's home, Shelmerdene in Surrey. They would arrange 'little gala evenings for dancing and the theatre' and over the four years he got to know her, Alma told Titterton about her past life. He observed that, though she was fond of a party, in his company she didn't drink anything stronger than orange juice, except on one occasion when she had some champagne to celebrate the success of one of her songs. In September of 1933, Alma earned £47 9s 2d from her songwriting. At last she was earning a living from something she loved doing. She was creatively fulfilled and was paid for it, too.[54]

As Alma's star was clearly rising, and perhaps to find an interest that they could share, Ratz suggested that *he* should write some lyrics for her songs. Alma wasn't keen, perhaps not only because of the quality of Ratz's writing, but because she wanted to hold onto this unexpected success for herself. Undaunted, and an indication that Ratz was still as stubborn as he ever was, at a party given by Titterton, Ratz proceeded to recite one of the lyrics he had written, 'with great feeling'. The result wasn't what he had anticipated: 'There was a moment's awkward silence, then everyone burst into laughter. They could not control themselves – it was such sheer doggerel.'[55]

But Ratz took it very well and joined in the laughter himself, saying, 'Well, perhaps I had better stick to architecture and not become a poet.'[56] Titterton gave the Rattenburys a signed, framed photograph of himself. Alma was so pleased with this gift from her celebrated friend that she had the photograph hung in pride of place on the chimney breast above the fireplace in their drawing room. Now he would watch over her whenever she played the piano.

But the glorious career, fame and fortune that Simon Van Lier had promised for Alma never materialised. In the fast-moving world of popular songs, Alma's yearning, romantic ballads, very much pre-war in sentiment, were out of step with the fast rhythms of the jazz-influenced music that was dominating the dance halls and wireless programmes of the day. Her music seemed old fashioned, the laments of another era. Her royalty payments began to dry up and in September 1934 she earned only £1 7s 11d from her songwriting.[57] At the same time, Ratz was becoming an old man. He had had all his teeth out and had started wearing dentures. As a companion, he was 'stolid, unintellectual ... and for an architect ... had surprisingly little imagination or sense of beauty'.[58] The difference in age and temperament between Alma and Ratz seemed more and more acute. John Rattenbury remembered that, by now, the Villa Madeira was 'not a happy house': 'My father was reclusive and wasn't a happy man ... the age gap between my parents was a problem. He was fast becoming an old man; she was a vibrant, beautiful woman and wasn't only getting into drink, I think she might have been getting into drugs too. And by the time of his death I think my father was probably impotent.'[59]

Despite Dr O'Donnell's warning that with her TB she shouldn't drink, a disappointed and bored Alma started drinking more: 'My life ... was so what we call monotonous that at times I used to take too many cocktails to liven up one's spirits – take them to excess, say, or wine.'[60]

Ratz, too, was depressed and was drinking alone at night, as he had done when he had become estranged from Florrie at Iechinihl. As the difference in their ages began to feel like a growing chasm between him and Alma, Ratz suggested that perhaps she should start 'living her own life' and seek out a lover.[61] But even if Alma had wanted to do so, Bournemouth was a conventional place and the memory of being publicly reviled in Victoria was too strong. Then the morbid Ratz began to talk of suicide.

After threatening to kill himself several times, things came to a head on 9 July 1934. Ratz declared that he was going to put his head in the gas oven. Exasperated, Alma had had enough. She told him to go ahead – why didn't he just kill himself? An astonished Ratz hit her in the face, but she retaliated. She grabbed him by the arm and bit it. Ratz stormed out of the house and a concerned Alma phoned Dr O'Donnell.[62] When the doctor arrived at the Villa Madeira, he found her very distressed. She had a black eye and a cut above her eyebrow. She told him that she and Ratz had had a quarrel, he had lost his temper and hit her. O'Donnell dressed her eye and sent her to bed, having given her a quarter of a grain of morphia. Then he and Irene went out looking for Ratz, concerned about the threats of suicide he had made and worried that he might jump from the East Cliff. Failing to find him, they called the police. Ratz was eventually found safe.

Alma was exasperated and frustrated by Ratz's behaviour, but she was aware that there were few options open to her. Having experienced divorce already, she knew it was expensive and difficult. In 1934, adultery was still the only grounds on which a marriage could be dissolved. Couples whose marriages had broken down couldn't release each other even if they wanted to.[63] The 6 January 1934 edition of *Woman's Own* suggested that women should put up with any of the difficulties of married life because 'a bad husband is better than no husband'. Unhappy wives like Alma should accept their lot. There were also the children to think about. John would be going to pre-prep school at Cliff House in September and Christopher would be moving up to Canford School. John would board during the week and return home at weekends.[64] While this needed a considerable outlay, it would also mean that they would no longer need Mrs Almond, the nurse. However, equally, with both sons away at school, Alma would be left at home, living a much emptier life, with now only Ratz and Irene for company. For Alma, the prospect of autumn at the Villa Madeira that year must have seemed bleak.

The international situation was no more cheering either. At the stadium in Nuremberg, 60,000 girls and boys, some younger than Christopher, had assembled to be reviewed by Hitler.[65] On 5 September, the front page of the *Bournemouth Echo* reported on the seventh congress of the Nazi Party, pointing out that it was no mere party congress – it was a 'gigantic demonstration to celebrate the Leader's triumph in last month's plebiscite, and to honour him as the First Citizen of the Reich'. Hitler had declared that the Nazis were now the 'complete master' of the German people.[66] The former prime minister Lloyd George warned darkly, 'The world of today ... is a jungle, and the nations are prowling though it, baring their teeth at each other. Any moment, a mistaken gesture or a misunderstood arrangement may make them spring at each other's throats.'[67] Could the unthinkable be true? Might there be another war?

As a way of combatting his depression, Ratz decided to return to what he knew best. There was a building boom in Britain. Why didn't he come out of retirement and start working as an architect again? His original plan was to build a new type of residence combining four houses. He showed this to a big building firm but they stole his idea and advertised it in the *Daily Express*. He then designed a new type of apartment block and had even secured a £350,000 order for them, but the scheme was abandoned after an issue with the planning application.[68] He wrote to F. E. Winslow, who administered his affairs in British Columbia, that he had had 'rotten luck' but felt he was on to a good thing. He developed a strategy of locating exceptional sites to build on and borrowing the money himself to finance the build. 'It has taken a lot of working out for financing was a "terra incognita" to me, but wish me luck I want to leave the wife and kids something outside of dead assets.'[69]

He was hoping to secure the money for his scheme after Christmas 1934. Assuming that the Union Club 'must be almost played out' and seeing no possibility of his ever returning to British Columbia again, he enclosed a letter resigning his membership. 'Life', Ratz wrote sadly, 'is strange.'[70]

Now that they were losing Mrs Almond, Alma worried about taking John to and from his new school as it was too far by tram. Ratz agreed for Alma to hire a driver who could also help around the house. Recalling the awkward experience with Hobbs, Irene subtly suggested that perhaps they should advertise for a youngster? As usual, Alma placed an advertisement in the *Bournemouth Echo*, which appeared on Wednesday 26 September.

The headline that day celebrated the new Cunard Liner No. 534, 'the most-talked-of vessel in the English-speaking world', which had been named the *Queen Mary* by the queen at a ceremony witnessed by 200,000 people in the pouring rain in the 'drab, drear little Scottish township' of Clydebank.[71] 'Britain's wonder' was, at 1,018ft long and 73,000 tonnes, the largest and fastest liner ever built in a British shipyard. It was already a national symbol, a 'ship of hope', a challenge to the world for supremacy of the Atlantic and a seductive image of all that seemed most exciting about Britain in the modern age – travel, glamour and speed. Tucked away on the bottom of page two in the classified section was the advertisement that Alma had placed:

Daily willing lad, 14–18, for housework.
Scout-trained preferred.[72]

George Percy Stoner

CHAPTER TEN

STONER

26 September–31 December 1934

There are few human relationships more complicated than a
love-affair between a young man and an older woman, and
there are few more summarily dismissed by the world at large.

– Francis Iles, *As for the Woman*[1]

George Percy Stoner was 5ft 6, with well-brushed blonde hair,
blue eyes, long fair eyelashes, a frank, open face, clean-cut features
and pale, clear skin.[2] He was fit from working as a labourer for
his grandfather's building firm and from the work he'd done as a
mechanic for a local garage. As soon as she saw him, Alma was
smitten: 'We loved each other from the moment we met, we just
came together because it was fate.'[3]

In late September of 1934, when Alma interviewed him for the
situation at the Villa Madeira, Stoner told her that he was twenty-
two.[4] She took the interview in her pyjamas, her frequent daytime
attire, though she wore underwear beneath. Her manner as ever was
theatrical, warm and generous, offering him a cigarette as was her
wont. A local boy, Stoner had probably never met such a glamorous and sophisticated woman as Alma before, a famous songwriter
with an exotic Canadian background and accent. She told him that
what they needed was a chauffer-handyman. John's school was

some distance away and took too long to reach by public transport. A chauffeur would relieve Ratz of the responsibility of driving the boy to and from school every week. Stoner would be required to arrive for his duties every morning at 7.45 a.m. On Mondays he would take John to school in Southbourne. During the week there'd be errands to run – driving Alma to the shops, household jobs to attend to as well as some work in the garden. Then on Saturday mornings he'd bring John back to Bournemouth for the weekend. Every Monday he'd be paid £1. With no bills to pay, Stoner would have considered this a fortune, the average British salary being £150 a year. He could also count himself incredibly lucky considering the number of unemployed young men at the time.

The position at the Rattenburys would be Stoner's first job and was a symptom of the rapidly escalating motor industry. In 1914, motoring had been a very exclusive occupation in Britain and there had been only 132,000 private cars on the road. By 1935, this had exploded to 1,477,000. Cars had become much more affordable, the average factory price having dropped from £308 in 1912 to £130 by 1935. By the mid-1930s, 10 million people would rely on the motor business as mechanics, salesmen and, like Stoner, chauffeurs; in less than twenty years, the motor trade had become the second largest employer in the country. But up to 1934, motoring remained unregulated, there was still no driving test and, in 1930, the speed limit of 20 miles an hour had been scrapped. At the same time, the small number of roads had been built for horse-drawn traffic so were dangerous, uneven and unsuitable for motor traffic. The total British road network had only increased by 4 per cent between 1899 and 1936.[5] Consequently, there were huge numbers of traffic accidents, reaching a record number of casualties in 1934 with 7,343 deaths and 231,603 injuries; four people a day were being killed on London's roads alone. When Leslie Hore-Belisha was appointed as Minister of Transport in June 1934, he had condemned these traffic casualties as 'mass murder on the roads'[6] and was determined to revolutionise road awareness in Britain. Against tough opposition from the AA and the RAC, he introduced a driving test and a

30mph speed limit in built-up areas. But he is best remembered for the introduction of the road crossings identified by orange flashing lights known as Belisha Beacons. These were soon to become familiar items in the urban landscape across Britain, but in the first four months of their appearance, 3,000 of the 150,000 beacons in London had been vandalised. By the end of 1935, they were so popular that they even inspired a board game.

Though Stoner was older than she'd stipulated in her advertisement, Alma waived the issue. He told her that he was an only child and Alma told him that so was she; they had something in common already. Showing him around the house, it would have been clear to him that Mr and Mrs Rattenbury not only had separate beds or even separate bedrooms, they had rooms on different floors. With bathrooms on both floors and the unusual glass partition that encased the stairs, they could lead separate lives. At the front of the house, Alma showed him the master bedroom that overlooked Manor Road; it was empty.

* * *

Stoner lived a couple of miles away in Ensbury Park with his grandparents. His father, George Reuben Russell Stoner, had been born in Brighton on 21 February 1882, the son of a bricklayer. The family had moved around the country in search of work, so Stoner's father was baptised in Stoke Newington on the same day as his older brother Percy, who died from a bout of measles a few years later, aged six. When George senior grew up, he followed his father into the bricklaying trade and would also travel long distances for work. By the time he was twenty-five, he had fathered a child with Mabel Steer, a farmer's daughter from Steyning in Sussex. They married shortly afterwards in Chipping Norton and by 1911 the couple had three more children. When war broke out, Stoner's father had joined the Machine Gun Corps and then the Tank Regiment.[7] But though married with young children, by the spring of 1916, he had started a relationship with 23-year-old Olive Stevens, the daughter of a carpenter from Bournemouth. By the summer it was clear that she was pregnant, and she gave birth to one of the many thousands of illegitimate war babies on 19 November. During the war, in the context of the deaths of thousands of young men, attitudes to unmarried mothers were changing from the generation before. 'Patriotism covered a multitude of sins'[8] and it became excusable for a woman to 'give all' to a soldier before he went back to the front.[9] The National Council for the Unmarried Mother and Her Child was set up by the Child Welfare Council in 1918 with the intention of reforming the ancient laws that discriminated against illegitimate children, as well as seeking to provide accommodation for mothers and their children, which had hitherto been the workhouse.[10] Olive's child was born on 19 November and was named after his father and his father's dead brother, George Percival Stoner.

After the war was over, George married Olive, though without divorcing his wife first. Mabel Stoner also married again at Chipping Norton in 1920, claiming that she was a widow. These second marriages were both bigamous. Following the increase in martial breakdowns in wartime and the high cost and complexity of divorce, the incidence of bigamy was increasingly common in the years after the war and by 1920, there were 500 per cent more prosecutions for bigamy than there had been prior to 1914.[11] Returning to civilian life, George drank and suffered from occasional 'brainstorms', perhaps the result of shell shock. Unlike his fruitful relationship with Mabel, he and his second wife would have no more children. Their son had a solitary childhood and seemed to his parents to be 'very, very backward'.[12] He didn't learn to walk until he was three and was regarded as 'a sort of weak boy'.[13] The education he received was limited as his parents travelled around the country in search of work, his father designing and erecting buildings as well as working as a surveyor. 'In my business', Stoner's father claimed, 'we have to go from one part of the country to the other, and, of course, he was with us, and it interrupted his schooling.'[14] Because of his father's erratic occupation, from the age of three Stoner went to live with his mother's parents, Samuel and Elizabeth Stevens, at 109 Pine Vale Crescent in Ensbury Park, a suburb of Bournemouth, ultimately calling them 'Mother' and 'Dad', rather than his real parents. Eventually, the extended Stoner family were all settled in the neighbourhood and maintained close relationships with each other as well as working for the family business. Stoner's parents lived at 'Johoba', a three-bedroomed bungalow at 104 Redhill Drive, which they had built themselves. Their rear garden backed onto Pine Vale Crescent, so the families were able to access each other's houses within seconds. Stoner's Uncle Richard, a carpenter by trade, lived next-door-but-one at 108 Redhill Drive, known as 'Bridgemore'. At the rear of Stoner's grandparents' house were some sheds and a workshop that housed the family's collection of tools, planes, chisels and mallets.[15]

Stoner had only received a few years' schooling, though two teachers who had taught him between the ages of ten and twelve felt that, though he was not above average intelligence, he was not 'very backward'. When he did go to school, he attended Winton and Moordown Council School,[16] three-quarters of a mile from Redhill Drive. With class sizes of fifty or more, as was the norm, there was little time for the needs of a child who might benefit from more attention. He grew up a loner and would rather stay at home and repair his bicycle or conduct mechanical experiments than play out in the road with the other local children. A member of the family later blamed his mother for his reticence: 'He wasn't allowed to play with anybody because his mother felt that they were different to other people. As a boy, he had to go straight home from school. He was never allowed to go to parties. It's not natural for a child to be kept away from other children.'[17] But his father felt that the boy was just shy by temperament: 'He was rather keen on staying in – rather reserved – if he had friends he would have them younger than himself.'[18]

Stoner left school at the age of fourteen and started working with the family building firm. He was prone to fainting fits, which he seemed to have inherited from his father, and on one occasion in 1933 he hurt himself when he collapsed while on the scaffolding of a house he was helping his uncle to build next door to 104

Redhill Drive.[19] He learned to drive when he was fifteen while he was working for his father,[20] but he still didn't mix with the local boys, nor did he drink or court girls. Mollycoddled by his mother, by his late teens he was slightly prudish and, in all probability, a virgin.

Stoner started working at the Villa Madeira at the end of September 1934. When not engaged in his work, he'd sit in the front dining room with Irene, leaving the drawing room for the use of the Rattenburys, and then returning home to Ensbury Park every night. It seemed that it was not only Mrs Rattenbury who was impressed by him, but Ratz as well. Stoner's family were involved in the business of designing and building houses, so Ratz shared common ground with his new employee. Ratz's friend Mr Wood, a frequent visitor to the Villa Madeira, felt that he was 'kindly disposed' towards Stoner, regarding him 'more as an object of sympathetic charity than as a servant. Stoner was not of bright intellect and he had difficulty in obtaining employment. Mr Rattenbury was asked to do something for him, and therefore took him into his house and treated him in the most considerate way.'[21]

* * *

Monday 19 November marked the beginning of the Christmas period for the big department stores in Bournemouth, such as Allen's, Bobby's, Bright's and Beale's. Each would try to outdo the other with enticements over the holiday season. Schools closed early so children like John Rattenbury could be at Bournemouth railway station for 3.30 p.m. when Father Christmas arrived by train to an expectant and exultant crowd. Twenty riders accompanied Father Christmas's state coach from the station to Beale's, with cheering crowds lining the route. The Boscombe Silver Prize Band of thirty instrumentalists marched ahead of the procession. As well as Father Christmas, Beale's offered a variety of seasonal showpieces to entertain the children. Entrance to 'Christmas in Many Lands', showing how the season was celebrated in other countries, was 'both entertaining and educational'. 'From the deep winter of Labrador you travel by stages to the summer in Australia and back via Japan and China. You finish up with a glimpse at Europe and a visit to parties and pantomimes.'[22]

19 November was also significant as it was Stoner's birthday. Given her generous nature, Alma would certainly have marked the occasion in some way. But she was shocked when he confessed his real age to her; he was now eighteen, not twenty-two as he had said at the interview. When they first met, he had been seventeen years old; not much older than her son. A couple of days after his birthday, Alma planned a trip to Leeds with Irene. Stoner would drive them there in the Rattenburys' Fiat. This was the first time that she and Alma were joined on one of their excursions by anybody else. Irene immediately felt the difference; three was a crowd.

Though they aimed to drive to Leeds, they only drove as far as Oxford with Stoner complaining that his watch didn't keep the right time. They stayed the night at the Randolph Hotel, Alma taking two communicating rooms for herself and Irene and a third for Stoner.[23] It may have been on this trip to Oxford, away from the Villa Madeira and away from Ratz, that Alma first articulated to Stoner how she felt about him. She later claimed that the attraction was entirely mutual, but it seems most likely, given her very direct overtures to Hobbs ('I want you and I mean to have you'), that it was Alma who initiated relations between them. Stoner was a working-class teenage boy in his first job, which he would be unlikely to jeopardise by flirting with his mistress. On 22 November, days after his eighteenth birthday, they had sex for the first time. For centuries in Britain, the age of consent had been twelve years of age, until it was raised to thirteen in 1875. Ten years later it was raised to sixteen, so in 1934 Stoner could have been legally sexually active. The age of consent for marriage had only recently been raised to sixteen by the Marriages Act of 1929; prior to this, some marriages took place with bridegrooms of fourteen and brides as young as twelve. Stoner was, however, still ineligible to vote for another four years – twenty-one was considered the age of majority for both men and women. But if Stoner's youth might have been a factor in arresting the attraction Alma felt towards him, it was too late. From then on Stoner would stay overnight at the Villa Madeira and shortly afterwards, in order to make their liaison more convenient, he moved in, taking over the master bedroom. Soon Stoner got into the routine of undressing in his bedroom, then crossing the landing – the light upstairs always left on – to spend the night in Alma's bed, keeping the French doors open to let in the night air to help Alma's chest. Just as she had confided to Hobbs, she told Stoner she hadn't wanted to marry Ratz, 'but pressure was put on her by her parents ... she was very uptight about being married' to him.

Very soon Stoner was cashing cheques for Alma, paying bills on her behalf as well as Ratz's; all too quickly he became a trusted member of the family. As his wristwatch did not keep good time, Alma loaned him her father's gold hunter watch to use in the car. It was valuable and of great sentimental importance to her, a keepsake to remind her of her 'only dad'. Keenly watching the accelerating relationship between him and Alma, Irene began to feel sidelined and hurt. It was obvious to her that Alma was Stoner's mistress in both senses of the word. But Ratz seemed oblivious to the adulterous relationship that was taking place right under his roof.

Having not had a sexual relationship with Ratz since the birth of John, Alma was now faced with the sexual appetite of an inexperienced eighteen-year-old. The last thing she could risk in her precarious position was an unwanted pregnancy. Abortion was illegal, and though fairly easy to arrange privately, was expensive, costing as much as £50.[24] After the war, women were hungry for information and guidance about their sex lives. There had been a wave of manuals about sexual fulfilment in marriage and family planning, such as Marie Stopes's bestselling *Married Love* and *Wise Parenthood*.[25] Stopes, who was not a doctor but a fossil plant specialist, had opened the first Mothers' Clinic for Constructive Birth Control in the Holloway Road in 1921 despite great opposition from the establishment. Most doctors at the time were opposed to birth control and the Home Office even considered banning all advertisements for contraceptives and leaflets that promoted family planning. Stopes's clinic was prosecuted for obscenity over a leaflet that had a diagram showing a finger pointing to the womb on the grounds that it might not be the woman's own finger. The bishop of Bradford condemned family planning clinics as 'infinitely worse than the unnatural vices that were practiced in the wicked cities of Sodom and Gomorrah'. Despite the hostility towards them, family planning clinics were popular among ordinary women and gradually spread throughout Britain. In 1930, the Lambeth Conference gave permission for married Anglicans to practice birth control, but Pope Pius XI expressly prohibited Catholics from doing anything that could hinder the 'natural power of creating life', declaring artificial contraception a 'grave sin'. But by 1930, 40 per cent of middle-class couples were estimated to be using some sort of artificial birth control. Marie Stopes recommended a 'racial cap', a small rubber dome that fitted over the cervix and was held in place by suction. Dutch caps were 'thick heavy things made from something like car tyres', until latex came along in the 1920s from America and was then used for diaphragms or condoms, though many men complained that they disliked wearing condoms, comparing the experience to 'washing your feet with your socks on'. The London Rubber Company started to manufacture latex condoms in 1932 and by 1935 were producing 2 million a year. The more expensive latex condoms were disposable, costing 2 or 3 shillings a packet. Re-usable ones cost about a shilling, but they needed to be washed after use, inspected for tears or holes and stored in a box covered in talcum powder. By the 1930s a unisex sheath was available to be used in conjunction with a spermicidal jelly or paste such as Volpar (Voluntary Parenthood paste), which was 'guaranteed to last for years'.[26]

Alma later insisted that Ratz 'must have known' that she was having a sexual relationship with Stoner, and that in order to keep the peace at the Villa Madeira, he had turned a blind eye to the situation. But Ratz's friend Wood, who visited the house frequently, was adamant that he knew nothing at all about his wife's affair with their chauffeur.

Soon the situation at the Villa Madeira developed into a routine. During the day Stoner would frequently drive Alma for trips in the car and on one occasion they drove out to Christchurch and walked along the water meadows there. He pointed out the railway arch at Three Arches Bend and told her that he had once almost jumped out of a train just as the railway line crossed the bend in the river. At night, he would sleep in Alma's bed. He would continue to do so when John was back from school at weekends, the boy being a heavy sleeper and too young to notice anything untoward.

Still a mother's boy, Stoner would call and see his parents almost every day. He would drive over in Ratz's car, always asking permission to do so, and sit with his mother as she did her housework. If his father was away, he would make a point of going to see her at some point during the day and chat to her about life at the Villa Madeira, how he would play patience with Mr Rattenbury and discuss an idea that Ratz had been mulling over to build a block of flats.[27]

In November of 1934 Alma was a little troubled when Stoner mentioned that he had something 'queer about his brain' and had been taking medication two or three times a year for it. He didn't say what the issue was, and insisted that he would outgrow it if he carried on taking 'the medicine'.[28] In all probability this was adolescent attention-seeking fuelled by Alma's own self-dramatising habits. But as time went on, it seems that Stoner began to have a positive effect on her. He didn't drink and didn't like her to do so either, so she stopped drinking alcohol altogether. He may also have persuaded her to stop taking any drugs that had been prescribed by O'Donnell. Alma spoke admiringly of Stoner's strongly held convictions: 'Never have I known any one with so much determination & strength of opinion, & character.'[29] Despite everything that was against them – her marriage, the difference in class and age – Alma and Stoner were happy. A young, inexperienced man, new to sex and adult relationships, he was intense and passionate. And perhaps he reminded Alma of her more hopeful self when she too was on the threshold of life and had not been bruised by war and loss and disappointment. Stoner certainly saw their relationship as a grand passion: 'I feel I have not earned this love, it has dropped into my hands too easily and I must surely have to pay the price for it someday, somehow.'[30]

Whenever he left her, he'd never say 'goodbye'.[31] In a romantic pact, he promised that it was the one word he couldn't say to her. And Alma felt that perhaps their happiness was a reward for the sadness she had experienced. Despite the many differences between them, she and Stoner never argued because they were 'too happy'.[32] Without considering the repercussions of the situation they were in, they would often talk of an imagined future in an idyllic other world where they would be together. As unlikely as it seemed, just like the emotion she intuited in the music she had played since her youth, Alma's passion, infatuation, love – whatever it might be – for an eighteen-year-old boy had finally given her life purpose and the melodies she wrote meaning.

* * *

The headlines in the *Bournemouth Echo* in the weeks leading up to Christmas 1934 focused on a local murder story. Reginald Woolmington was a 21-year-old farm labourer and amateur boxer from Dorset, who had become estranged from his teenage wife Violet shortly after their wedding. He was, according to some, jealous and had a violent temper. For the first six weeks of their marriage they lived in cramped conditions with his parents. They later moved into their own cottage where their son was born. Violet found the responsibilities of her new life extremely demanding. She was alone for most of the day with a new baby who cried too much and she felt that Woolmington was away at work far too long. Violet's mother started to visit her daughter, taking with her the materials for the gloves that she made up, which was a local industry. Mother and daughter would make the gloves while the baby slept. These visits by his mother-in-law began to cause tension between Woolmington and his wife and on 29 November a row took place between the three in which Violet accused Woolmington of ill-treating her, using his fists against her and trying to strangle her. When Violet stated her intention of leaving him and moving back home with her mother, he said, 'You bugger, I'll do you in.' Woolmington told his mother-in-law to stop interfering before he stomped off to work. When he arrived home that night, Violet had gone, leaving a note: 'I've gone home. Don't come up. I've asked my mother to have me, I've made up my mind to go into service.' Woolmington went to some lengths to persuade her to come home, asking his employer to visit her with him, even asking a lay reader at Sherborne Abbey to write to her on his behalf. But Violet was adamant. She would stay with her mother until after Christmas, then go into service.[33]

On the evening of Sunday 9 December, events took a tragic turn. Woolmington met Violet's brother who told him that she had been seen at the cinema the night before with another man. In reality, she hadn't, she had simply been talking to her girlfriend's acquaintance in the queue outside the picture house. But the jealous Woolmington was heard to say, 'I shall do her in.' The next morning, he sawed the barrels off a shotgun, looped some wire over it to make it easier to carry and cycled over to his mother-in-law's house in Milborne Port, where he found Violet in the kitchen doing the washing. Her mother was out and the baby was asleep in a cot by the wall. He pleaded with her to come home, but Violet refused. He brought the gun from under his coat and said, 'Perhaps this will help.' He was heard to say, 'Are you coming home or not?' followed soon afterwards by a gunshot. He raced out of the house and cycled frantically up the road, leaving Violet slumped by the washtub with a gaping shotgun wound in her chest. He did little to cover his actions, telling his employer, 'I shan't be coming to work any more, I've been up and shot my wife.' When he was later arrested, a note was found in the pocket of his overcoat that seemed to imply that he had been intending to kill himself if he could not persuade Violet to return to him:

Goodbye All,
   It is agonies to carry on any longer. I have kept true hoping

she would return. This is the only way out. They ruined me
and I'll have my revenge. May God forgive me for doing
this, but it is the best thing ... Her mother is no good on this
earth but I have no more cartridges, only one for her and
one for me. I am of sound mind now. Forgive me for all the
trouble caused.

   Goodbye all,
   I love Violet with all my heart.
   REG

To the magistrates and the *Bournemouth Echo*, it seemed an undoubtedly tragic, but commonplace story of a man who had murdered his wife and had meant to kill himself, but had lost his nerve at the last minute. Reading about the tragedy in the *Echo*, local readers in Bournemouth like Alma and Irene must have been moved by it. That poor girl and her now-motherless child. But what had provoked an ordinary lad to such violence?

Just before Christmas, Stoner's uncle Richard boxed some wheels in the workshop at the back of his parents' house. He used a wooden mallet with a cylindrical, octagonal head, 6.5 inches long and 4 inches in diameter. The work resulted in some distinctive marks on the head of the mallet.[34] The next time he would see it, in Bournemouth Police Court, it would be labelled Exhibit No. 7 and identified as a murder weapon.

*   *   *

Christopher Rattenbury came home from school for the Christmas holidays and took up his room next to his mother. John also broke up and for the first time since the summer, the Villa Madeira felt full and lively again. With the children, Alma dressed the house with paper chains and decorated the tree in the drawing room. Every edition of the *Bournemouth Echo* throughout December was filled with the anticipation of Christmas, exhorting the public to 'Shop Locally', to 'Buy British' and 'Buy Now';[35] extra staff in the department stores, the mayor suggested, would mean fewer of the 2,000 Bournemouth unemployed:

> The shops are doing their Christmas magic; and they are doing it remarkably well. This promises to be the busiest Christmas since the war ... Let this Christmas be a record for buying presents. During the past dark years which are now passing away it was inevitable that there should be much Christmas economizing. Now things are brighter, so let us be more generous. Let it be a bumper Christmas both in good things and in good will.[36]

The trains were packed, the roads hectic and hotels fully booked as 25,000 people were expected to stay in Bournemouth over the holiday.[37] There was a huge variety of events in place to entertain them in the hotels, shops, cinemas and theatres. There were four local pantomimes to see but Alma had bought tickets back in November to take the boys to *Dick Whittington* at the Little Theatre with W. H. Lester and Neville Kennard, which would open on Boxing Day.[38] In the weeks before Christmas, the local shops stayed open until 7 p.m.[39] and, on 10 December, Alma gave Stoner £10 – a large sum – to buy Christmas presents for the children and told him to use any money left over to buy something for himself. He bought John a child's set of garden tools so that he could help in the garden in the spring. Alma also bought Stoner a cigarette lighter and a cigarette holder from Mrs Price's tobacconist shop as stocking fillers. By Christmas Eve, Alma was £30 19 10d overdrawn again. That day, the weather was mild and 'the casual observer might have thought he was on the French Riviera', as some locals were to be seen in 'abbreviated costumes, sunning themselves in front of their huts'.[40]

On Christmas Day, the BBC broadcast the festive service live from St George's Chapel, Windsor. At 1.30 p.m. the Empire Exchange began, a prologue to the king's broadcast at 3 p.m.[41] He had first addressed the empire on Christmas Day in 1932, when his speech had been written by Rudyard Kipling, though the royal broadcast would not become a regular fixture of the Christmas calendar until the outbreak of war. As well as looking forward to his jubilee in 1935, the king referred to the continuing bleak economic situation and unsettled political times, observing that 'the world is still restless and troubled. The clouds are still lifting, but we still have our own anxieties to meet.'[42]

Over Christmas, Alma informed Ratz that she had taken him at his word and was 'leading her own life', though she made no indication that she was doing so under his roof with a man whose wages he paid.[43] Ratz didn't appear to respond or, it seems, mind. Meanwhile, even though there seemed little hope of publishing them, she carried on writing her songs, which prompted Stoner to ask why she didn't write one for them? She told him that she could never write such a song. How could she write a love song while she was living one?[44]

In Ensbury Park that Christmas, Stoner's grandmother worried to his mother that the boy looked pale.[45] His uncle agreed that he looked 'very, very white'.[46] Perhaps he was driving too much? Or maybe he wasn't working outdoors enough since he had started working for Mr and Mrs Rattenbury? As an only child, the subject of Stoner's appearance and demeanour became a regular topic of discussion among the family over the festive season. Watching him asleep in the chair one day, they observed how drawn he looked, how sunken his eyes were. Something wasn't right.

Francis Rattenbury

CHAPTER ELEVEN

NIGHT BRINGS ME YOU

1 January–22 March 1935

Collyer: But how in the name of reason could you have gone on loving a man ... who can give you nothing in return?

Hester: Oh, but he can give me something in return, and even does, from time to time.

Collyer: What?

Hester: Himself.

– Terence Rattigan, *The Deep Blue Sea*[1]

With a new year ahead, Alma worried about the age difference between herself and Stoner. She wanted to end the relationship, but he wouldn't hear of it and would lose his temper whenever she broached the issue. She admitted to Irene that he was becoming 'absurdly jealous' of Ratz and had even threatened her a couple of times. She was worried when he took to carrying a knife with a 4-inch blade. She became even more concerned when he brought a gun into the house. Was this adolescent bravado, with Stoner copying the Hollywood films he saw? Or something more sinister? But rather than challenge Stoner about why he carried the weapons, Alma seems to have indulged him. She dismissed the issue and, as was her wont, hoped for the best.[2]

At the end of January, Rattenbury was writing again to F. E.

Winslow, the administrator of his business affairs in Victoria. He was pleased to say that after being unable to sell Iechinihl for years as it had been dubbed 'Bluebeard's Mansion' by the locals, his solicitor thought he might be able to sell it and the attached land for $40,000. But as Rattenbury didn't expect to return to Victoria again and wanted to offload his property, he was happy to sell it for $30,000. If he could sell the house, at last he'd be free of his unhappy past with Florrie, Frank and Mary. In a personal letter that he'd attached, Rattenbury updated Winslow on his domestic situation and his professional ambitions, outlining how hard he'd been working to try to get back into architecture, in the context of the building boom in England, 'the greatest ever known'. On 29 January, he had an appointment with a loan company from whom he was trying to borrow £116,000. He had some private backers who had 'verbally agreed' to invest the other 50 per cent of the money he needed to finance the purchase of the land and build some flats. This may well have been arranged by his friend F. S. Long, who was 'wonderfully popular and trusted in London with the biggest people'. He was feeling optimistic about the prospects for 1935:[3]

I have enjoyed life over here and the wife has been a cheery courageous companion making life interesting, she is a truly grand character in spite of the fact that she has had a great deal of severe illness and many operations, cheerfully borne. Her many songs were all composed when ill and she is a devoted mother.[4]

But he was clearly very worried about money, his friend Mr Wood observing, 'During the last few months [Ratz] was considerably worried as to his financial position owing to the drop in the value of his various securities.'[5] So he concentrated on raising the money for his building project, seemingly unaware of the simmering tensions that surrounded him at the Villa Madeira.

One night in February, between 11 p.m. and midnight, Irene was witness to a fight between Alma and Stoner that had started in

Alma's bedroom. Again Alma was insisting that they should end the relationship – he was too young, she was too old – she was married and was the mother of two children. The argument continued as Stoner stormed off to his room in a fury, followed by Alma. As the altercation continued, Irene went into the master bedroom to find Stoner with his hands around Alma's throat. She separated them and sent Alma off to bed, shaken by the incident.[6] Ratz remained downstairs, oblivious.

Stoner had mentioned to Alma in November the issue he had with his brain and the medication he needed for it. Though she had been worried at the time and tried to get him to clarify exactly what he was talking about, the issue had gone away. He now claimed that he was taking illegal drugs. He said he was taking them less frequently than he used to and hoped in a few years he wouldn't have to take them at all. Alma wasn't sure at the time if he was telling the truth.[7] It might all be more adolescent posturing to excuse his violent behaviour and to persuade her to stop threatening to end their relationship. But she was a staunchly protective mother and, though she was doubtful, she was concerned about the impact on her children if what Stoner was saying was true.

On 12 February, Stoner told Alma that he needed to go to London to buy more drugs. Alma begged him not to go, but he insisted, leaving her very distressed. She decided to telephone Dr O'Donnell and explain the whole, messy situation to him. She must have trusted him hugely to admit that she had been sleeping with the chauffeur, who had recently tried to strangle her and was now claiming that he was a drug addict. She wanted O'Donnell to have a word with Stoner and find out what drugs he was taking, if any, and to warn him about the dangers. The next day, O'Donnell met Stoner and said that he believed he was taking drugs. Stoner answered, 'Yes, cocaine.' O'Donnell wondered where he had picked up the habit from and Stoner told him that he had found some cocaine at home. He'd tried it and he'd enjoyed it, so he carried on taking it whenever he could. He told O'Donnell that he had just been up to London to buy some more, but had failed – rather conveniently –

to get any. The doctor asked him where he had tried to buy the drugs, but Stoner refused to say. Though he was no expert, O'Donnell warned him about the dangers of drug addiction and offered help if he wanted to give it up, but Stoner wasn't interested.[8] The conversation ended unresolved, but afterwards Stoner seemed better, things settled down and Alma never brought up the subject again: 'Everything was all right.'[9]

Whatever his motivation for making it, Stoner's claim wasn't true. He may have been inspired by Alma's casual use of opiates given to her by Dr O'Donnell, but he would also have been aware of the sensational coverage of drug trafficking and addiction that had regularly featured in the British press since the death of the actress Billie Carleton in 1918. She had overdosed on cocaine and was found dead in her suite at the Savoy Hotel the morning after the Victory Ball. The subsequent trial of her friend and dealer Reggie de Veulle exposed a hedonistic and destructive drug culture that became fixed in the public imagination throughout the 1920s.[10] Drugs were seen to be part of the 'moral deterioration of post-war upper-class society in its search for mindless escape and forbidden pleasures'.[11] In newspapers, books and films, the public were deluged with a mass of facts and opinions about narcotic drugs, which were no longer confined to grimy opium dens in Limehouse, but had reached London's West End and beyond. Certainly, Tennyson Jesse suspected that Stoner's 'fantastic story' had 'emanated from a cinema-nourished mind'.[12]

The naive and inexperienced Stoner may simply have been trying to promote the image of himself as a glamorous, sexually potent, seductively dangerous lover to his mistress, who was a mature woman with great experience of the world. If he were buying drugs on his trips to London, and there's no evidence that he was, he may simply have been purchasing aphrodisiacs in Soho, which might account for the changed pallor and demeanour his family had noted at Christmas. But it was now not only his family that were noticing a change in Stoner. When he visited Mrs Price's tobacconist's shop, she too thought him very pale, sleepy and peculiar.[13]

Around this time, the family dog Dinah came into season and, always anxious about money, Alma decided to breed her. At least they'd have some return when they sold the pups. But always in her mind she wondered if perhaps she could write more songs she could establish some real financial independence, beholden as she was to Ratz to get her out of debt. Every few months she would have to persuade or cajole him, just to clear her overdraft and pay the bills. She always agreed to everything with a smile: 'All he saw was a smile, all he heard was the "yes darling – no darling" – a mask that agreed with his every mood. And heaven help one if they did otherwise!'[14]

She determined to write some more songs and see if she could get them published herself. So in early March, she telephoned Beatrice Esmond a number of times and told her that she was writing again. She wanted to start afresh as Ratz had taken up a new building scheme and had lost interest in her career. She invited Beatrice to meet her at a London hotel and they discussed two of the new songs she had written.[15] Beatrice was delighted to see that Alma seemed excited and enthusiastic about her music again. Alma hoped that Ratz might regain his former interest in her work. The great promises of Simon Van Lier had come to nothing, so Alma planned to sell the new songs to Peter Maurice, a rival music publishing company to Keith Prowse. She now began to collaborate with another lyricist, Edith Rutter-Leatham, who wrote the words to 'Avelette' and 'By Some Mistake', the lyrics of the latter seeming to articulate Alma's growing concerns about her relationship with Stoner:

> By some mistake you filled my empty days
> But now I wake to face the parting ways
> I see you smile, I hear the words you say
> With no reply I hush your voice away
> By some mistake, by some divine mistake
> I dreamed awhile, but now I wake, I wake.

In Bournemouth, as Dinah was about to give birth, Alma arranged for her to have the pups at the Tree Top Kennels. It was at this time that acquaintances of the Rattenburys were beginning to realise that the living arrangements at the Villa Madeira were quite unusual and to question what was going on, with Ratz's friend Wood very perturbed by what he saw: 'The whole position of Stoner in the house was amazing. Although I visited them regularly, I did not know that Stoner was only a chauffeur. Whenever I called, he was always smartly dressed in a blue suit. He was usually sitting about the house smoking cigars and reading a book. He was more like a guest than a servant.'[16]

Mrs Price, the owner of the Villa Madeira, then made a call to the house and attempted to raise a delicate issue with Alma. She was concerned about Alma's relationship with Stoner. He had come into the tobacconist's in February and she noted that there was 'something peculiar about him'. She felt that this peculiarity was due to his familiarity with Alma: 'Are you not getting too fond of that boy?' Alma did not consider it Mrs Price's business to interfere with her private domestic affairs and politely told her so. Mrs Price later claimed that Alma had said, 'I told you I would make him love me and I have',[17] though Alma absolutely denied this. But there seems no reason for Mrs Price to lie and, whether Alma had set out to entrap Stoner or not, the result was the same; he had fallen in love with her.

Alma was now even more overdrawn – by £67 10s. She still had bills to pay, owing £25 to Tarrant's the dress shop, £9 17s to Plummer's the department store and £10 to Williamson and Treadgold the grocery store. So she lied to Ratz and told him that she needed another operation in London. She would have it done a couple of weeks ahead of Easter before the boys broke up from school. She needed an extra £250. This was a much larger sum than Alma normally asked for on these occasions and she knew Ratz would have to make considerable sacrifices to give it to her, reducing the balance of his current account by half.[18] However, he duly wrote her a cheque for £250, which she paid into her Barclays Bank account in Bournemouth on Monday 18 March. Given their conversation at Christmas that she was now leading her own life, for all he knew she may well have been going to London to meet a lover, though there was no indication that Ratz had any suspicion about who would actually be accompanying her. On the same day, Stoner cashed a cheque of £50 for Alma at Barclays Bank in Bournemouth – a year's salary for Stoner – and was given nine £5 notes and five £1 notes. Alma duly paid off her outstanding debts with the local shops, but in order to add credibility to the story of her operation, she needed to leave Bournemouth for a few days. This afforded her and Stoner the opportunity to spend some time together away from the Villa Madeira and from Ratz, who was depressed that the 50 per cent investment that he needed for his building project had failed to materialise. This time, Irene was not invited on the trip and would stay at home, feeling bruised and sidelined.

On Tuesday 19 March, Alma and Stoner drove as far as Southampton, but the car broke down, so they decided to make the rest of the journey by train.[19] Back at the Villa Madeira, Ratz started to read a new book that Alma had borrowed from Boots library, *Stay of Execution* by Eliot Crawshay-Williams, the parliamentarian-turned-novelist. It was the melodramatic story of Stephen Clarke, a depressed older man who was planning to commit suicide.

> Bitterness crept into [his] soul. He hoped less and trusted less, and desired less, and descended gradually, as most men do under the influence of age and experience, from the lofty levels where his young spirit used to dwell. Where once had been the joyous desire for adventure, came a restless seeking for sensation. His old energy began to weaken; his capacity for steady and good work diminished with his belief in its worth doing. He failed himself, and others failed him. There had been an attempt at marriage, but it had ended in disaster.[20]

The book felt like an uncanny echo of Ratz's own anxieties. Was he too old for Alma? Had he been fair marrying her? Would his building project ever happen? Would he ever work as an architect again? Or is this how the rest of his life would play out? Long, empty evenings alone beckoned. As Alma sped off to London, Ratz settled down for the night with only his library book and one of the servants for company, little suspecting that his wife was being comforted by another.

That night, the London *Evening Standard* reported on the new 30mph speed limit, which had only resulted in most drivers erring on the side of caution and driving at 20mph, leading to dense traffic jams. 'What advocates of the speed limit forget,' bemoaned the *Standard* diarist, 'is that traffic delays inflict a serious burden on trade and therefore the prosperity of the country.'[21] Motorists driving over the new limit were warned by plain-clothes police-women striking gongs. Meanwhile, in Berlin, the first mass air-raid rehearsal took place with worryingly realistic detail – bombers, fire officers and 'casualties'. Images from Berlin triggered an unseasonal chill across Britain, the *Daily Sketch* warning darkly that 'the Germans are nothing if not thorough'.

Arriving in London at Waterloo, Alma and Stoner took a taxi to the fashionable Cumberland Hotel in Marble Arch. Unable to accommodate them, the concierge recommended another hotel in Kensington. Standing at 6 Kensington High Street on the corner of Palace Avenue, the Royal Palace Hotel had been built in 1894 on the 'finest hotel site in London' in the red-brick 'Elizabethan' style by the Arts and Crafts architect M. H. Baillie Scott. An excited Alma and Stoner signed the register as 'Mrs Rattenbury and brother'.[22] They were given rooms 530 and 532 on the fifth floor on the same landing, almost opposite each other. For Stoner, the hotel must have seemed extraordinarily luxurious, a world that people like Alma and Ratz inhabited and he could previously only have dreamed of entering. It had a 'club-like quietude induced by the extraordinary thickness of the Axminster carpeting its grand staircase', with long, wide corridors decorated with marble, French and Japanese murals. On the upper ground floor was a drawing room commanding won-derful views across Kensington Gardens towards Kensington Palace. And there was a lounge 'decorated in an eastern fashion with a lazy luxury quite in keeping with the Occidental portion of the globe'.[23] At any hour of the day or night, there were staff to attend to Stoner's every need. And they addressed him as 'sir'.

Alma then decided that Stoner needed a new suit and took him up the road to Knightsbridge, where she had an account at Harrods. She wore a blueish dress, her fur coat and a hat.[24] While they were there, she bought Stoner two pairs of shoes and two pairs of shoe trees. In the men's clothing department she asked to see some crêpe de Chine pyjamas, and bought three pairs at 60s each. She also bought three shirts, three ties and a dozen linen handkerchiefs. In the men's underwear department she bought three pairs of socks, two pairs of gloves and two suits of underwear. She wrote down her purchases on a shopping card, which was used by 'country customers' who lived beyond the radius of Harrods delivery vans.[25] The items would be dispatched on Saturday and would arrive at the Villa Madeira the following Monday. Alma and Stoner then went to the gentleman's ready-to-wear department, where shop assistant Albert Jarvis asked if he could show Stoner anything. Assuming him at first to be Alma's son, he took Stoner into a fitting room and measured him, to all intents and purposes treating Stoner like the gentleman he appeared to be. They chose a light grey suit with a broad stripe. Alma then picked out a darker blue suit and asked if it was Stoner's size. Jarvis told her that it wasn't but he found her one that was in stock. She said they'd take it. To complete Stoner's new wardrobe, they bought a fawn-coloured mackintosh. He said he'd like to wear one of the suits that evening, so Jarvis arranged for it to be altered and sent directly to the Royal Palace Hotel. Alma gave her room number as 230, but Stoner corrected her; their room numbers were 530 and 532. In all, Alma spent £40 14s 6d on new clothes for Stoner, only buying for herself some belts and one dress for £2 9s 6d from the 'Inexpensive Dresses Department'. She then gave Stoner £20 to spend in five-pound notes. He visited Kirby and Bunn, a jeweller in Old Bond Street, and said he wanted to buy an engagement ring for about £12 or £13. He bought a single stone diamond ring with diamond shoulders costing £15 10s, leaving it to be altered.[26] This was also to be sent that evening to 'Mr G. Rattenbury' at the Royal Palace Hotel. Stoner left one of the hotel's cards with the flourish of a gentleman.

That night Alma wore the ring and Stoner dressed in the new suit she had bought for him. They rehearsed some sort of engagement or commitment ritual. The love between them, Alma later wrote, 'was beautiful'.[27] Now that they had time alone with each other, perhaps they talked about the future and what it would be like if Ratz weren't around. He was an old man, after all. When he died, they could be together properly. Perhaps the naive Stoner, if not Alma, began to believe that one day they could marry, the Happy Ever After to their grand romance. But who knew when that would be?

For the next few days they went out to dine and to the theatre and cinema, like any smart couple enjoying the attractions and excitement of the capital. That week, the Mayfair Hotel offered dinner and dancing with Harry Roy and his band and Kettner's restaurant in Soho offered an alternative – 'perfect food and perfect wines', reassuring potential diners, 'There is no band to disturb you in your social intercourse.' If they couldn't agree on what to go and see at the theatre or the pictures, Stoner would toss a coin – why not leave it to Fate to decide? And there was so much to see. At the Cambridge Theatre, Hermione and Angela Baddeley were appearing in *The Greeks Had a Word for It* decades before it was to find a global audience as *How to Marry a Millionaire*. The pre-*Mousetrap*, 'London's longest run', *The Wind and the Rain*, was now playing its second year at the Queen's Theatre with Celia Johnson and Robert Harris. At the cinema, Ronald Coleman and Loretta Young starred at the Tivoli in *Clive of India*, which John Betjeman reviewing in the *Standard* felt was 'a modern love problem in an historical setting'. The Carlton prompted 'visitors to London' not to miss 'Jubilee year's greatest film', *The Lives of a Bengal Lancer* with Errol Flynn.

Thursday was the first day of spring and in London there was a cloudless sky and the temperature rose rapidly, reaching 19°C in the afternoon.[28] By the evening, the *Standard* editorial reassured readers that 'the European turmoil created by the actions of Germany will subside peacefully'.[29] All the time she was away, Alma kept in touch with Ratz and Irene at the Villa Madeira by telephone and also wrote to the children, sending letters including stories she had written, drawings and fragments of songs. On Friday, she wrote to Christopher at school,

> *If this weather continues, we'll be swimming in the sea soon.*
> *Returning home tonight. God bless you, darling.*
> *Much love,*
> *Mother*[30]

For Alma and Stoner, the trip to London was an idyllic few days of sunshine, shopping, sex and cinema. But by the end of the week it was time to face the realities and responsibilities of life in Bournemouth again. By Friday 22 March, Alma was overdrawn once more. That night, having collected the car at Southampton, Alma and Stoner were back at the Villa Madeira at about 10.30 p.m. When they arrived, Alma saw that Ratz was drinking, as usual. He didn't ask how she was or how her operation had gone. Perhaps he suspected that she had been entertained in London by another man, but if he did, he said nothing. Alma went to bed, kissing Ratz goodnight as usual, leaving him to drink his whisky in the armchair, his dark thoughts preoccupied by the library book he'd been reading: 'Life's a tragedy from its very nature. It couldn't be anything else. We grow old. Get worse. Decay. Go downhill. Isn't that a tragedy? Would *you* invent a process like that? Would *you* see men and women lose health and hope and looks and life and laughter and sink down into rottenness and misery?'[31]

Drawing room, Villa Madeira

CHAPTER TWELVE

THE PLACE WHERE
A BAD THING HAPPENED

24 March 1935

Alice: Fetch water and wash away this blood.

Susan: The blood cleaveth to the ground and will not out.

Alice: But with my nails I'll scrape away the blood; the more I strive, the more the blood appears!

Susan: What's the reason, Mistress, can you tell?

Alice: Because I blush not at my husband's death.

– *Arden of Faversham* (1592)[1]

The national newspapers on Saturday 23 March reported the Conservative MP for Epping's grave warnings about the 'hopelessly inadequate' expansion plans for the RAF in the face of the bullish Hitler, who had that month taken the first salute of the Luftwaffe in Berlin. 'We have', Winston Churchill declared from the obscurity of the back benches, 'entered into a period of great peril. We are faced not only with the prospect of a new war, but with a resumption of the war which ended in November 1918. From becoming the least vulnerable of all nations, we have become the most vulnerable.'[2] Nearer to home, the *Bournemouth Echo* looked forward to the new trolley-bus service that was to start on Monday, displacing the tram-cars that had formerly served the town. Tramlines across Bournemouth had been removed as technology moved on.[3] The headline, though, in the *Echo* that evening and in the *News of the World* the next morning, reported the appeal to the House of Lords against the conviction of Reginald Woolmington, who had killed his wife shortly before Christmas. He insisted that he hadn't deliberately pulled the trigger and that her death was an accident. A trial at Taunton Assizes in January had concluded with the jury unable to reach a verdict. At a second trial in Bristol, on 13 and 14 February, Lord Justice Swift had ruled that it fell to Woolmington's defence, J. D. Casswell, to prove that the shooting was accidental. Consequently, Woolmington was found guilty and sentenced to death, though the jury made a recommendation to mercy on account of his youth.[4] But Casswell insisted that he must be presumed innocent until the prosecution proved otherwise. He wrote to the attorney general asking if he could present the case before the House of Lords, insisting that it posed a legal point of exceptional urgency.[5] Meanwhile, a tense Woolmington awaited the outcome of the appeal from his condemned cell, the date set for his execution only days away on 2 April.

On Saturday morning, Stoner drove Alma to pick John up from school in Southbourne and to watch Christopher play football there. Though the car had recently been fixed in Southampton, Stoner was having problems with the gears. As the weather was unseasonably warm, Stoner was asked to find the canvas sun shelter in the garage and put it up in the garden.[6] In previous years, they'd knocked the four wooden pegs into the lawn with a hammer, though the pegs had a habit of slipping out.[7] Ratz stayed at home. He was still worrying about how to raise the £116,000 to finance the flats. Alma tried to cheer him up, but it seemed impossible to lighten his mood. Ratz's friend Mr Wood visited him that evening:

> [Ratz] spoke in very affectionate terms of his wife and said he did not regret the fairly considerable sums of money he had advanced her in respect of operations she purported to undergo

at some places unknown to him in London. He told me that Mrs Rattenbury said she had benefited greatly by the expensive treatment, in respect of which she had the week before drawn a considerable sum from him before going to London, ostensibly for medical treatment.[8]

Wood was later insistent that on the Saturday night before the murder, Ratz had no idea whatsoever that Alma was having a relationship with Stoner. Once Wood had left, the Rattenburys settled down to play cards as they listened to the wireless. After *In Town Tonight* at 7.30 p.m., there was a music hall programme with Roy Fox and his band from the Café de Paris, comedians Collinson and Dean, 'Fiddle Fanatics' Stanelli & Edgar, as well as Mrs Rodney Hudson's *Eight Step Sisters*. After a concert of the Glasgow Choir, Henry Hall and the BBC Dance Orchestra finished the evening from 10.35, playing until midnight.[9] Ratz fell into a drunken sleep in the armchair in the drawing room and, as usual, Stoner joined his mistress in her bed. After the warm day, Stoner opened the French window onto the balcony to let in the evening air. He and Alma made love for the last time.[10]

* * *

On Sunday, in an effort to raise Ratz's spirits, Alma suggested they drive over to the kennels to see Dinah's puppies and bring her back to the house.[11] The trip to see the litter didn't have the desired effect and Ratz still seemed very depressed. After serving lunch at midday, Irene went off at about 4 p.m. to spend the evening with her parents as usual. Ratz went to sleep in his chair in the drawing room as Alma played with John, dressed as was her habit, in her three-piece pyjama suit, a long sleeveless pyjama top and bottoms beneath an 'Yvonne' three-quarter coat. It was, Alma later remembered, an ordinary Sunday.

At about 5.30, as it was Irene's afternoon off, Stoner brought tea, sandwiches and cake up to Alma's bedroom for her, Ratz and John. They would have a more substantial high tea later on. John was in and out of the room playing and Ratz had brought up with him *Stay of Execution*, which he had nearly finished reading. While they were having tea, he read some of it to Alma, a passage from page 296:

'You don't think marriages between young girls and men a good deal older than themselves are possible?'

'They're possible all right. For some reason, elderly men have a peculiar attraction for young girls. That may be due, nowadays, to the quality of the young men of the day; but I don't think it is. It's always been so. And – the old men like to marry the young girls; and after a bit it's hell for both.'

'Why?'

'Because it's naturally annoying to a young girl to see her husband mouldering, while she still feels frisky. To see the bare patch on the back of his head growing bigger and shinier. To have the shock, one day of coming across most of his teeth grinning at her out of a glass of water. And – there are other things, besides.'

'What things?'

'Well – if you will have me enter into physiological details – a woman, let's put it, always wants more than a man. And when the man is a good deal older, then she wants a good deal more than him. A good deal more than he can give her. It takes all his time for a young man to keep pace with a young girl. And an old man hasn't a chance of doing it. And then – she generally goes somewhere else to make up the deficiency.'[12]

The extract Ratz had chosen to read aloud – down to the detail of the false teeth – was particularly pertinent to their situation. He told Alma that he admired a person who could commit suicide as the character in the book planned to do, but he did not have the guts to do it himself. Concerned that Ratz was so maudlin, now a regular occurrence, Alma tried to cheer him up. What about a trip to London? Ratz wasn't keen. But when she suggested they should go and visit Shirley Hatton Jenks, his wealthy friend in Bridport, Ratz agreed. Perhaps they could discuss the financing for the flats?

Might Jenks match the £116,000 from the loan company? This finally excited Ratz's interest. With the extra expenses he'd had to pay for Alma's operation, it was even more crucial that he secured the money for his building project. What if they went to Bridport tomorrow?[13]

There are discrepancies between the accounts of those involved about what took place in the next crucial half-hour leading to Rattenbury's death. Stoner later claimed that the bedroom door, which was usually left open, had been deliberately closed and that he saw, or claimed he saw, Alma 'living' with Ratz.[14] This was a euphemism for intercourse. Terry Reksten, in her biography of Rattenbury, accepts that Alma and Ratz enjoyed 'some form of marital intimacy'[15] that afternoon in order to help shift Ratz's malaise. But Ratz and Alma had ceased sexual relations years before and she stated at the trial that if Ratz had insisted on his rights as a husband, she would not have granted them. Knowing how jealous Stoner was, nor would Alma deliberately antagonise him by closing the door to initiate marital relations with Ratz in the middle of tea. And what could he see anyway if the door was closed?

According to Alma, at tea, Ratz made her a proposition. He wanted her to seduce Jenks and sleep with him while they were at Pilsdon Manor so that he could secure the £116,000 for the flats he was planning to build. Given that Alma had already told him that she was leading her own life, Ratz clearly had no issue with her sleeping with other men. He may even have suspected, as she and Ratz always had separate rooms when they visited Jenks, that Alma had slept with him on a previous trip. But as fate would have it, Stoner was outside the bedroom door when this exchange took place. Effectively, Ratz was planning to pimp out his wife in order to secure a business deal. And Stoner had heard every word.[16]

After tea, Alma went directly downstairs to Ratz's bedroom to telephone Shirley Jenks. As she was making the arrangements for the trip to Pilsdon Manor, an angry Stoner came into the room armed with a gun: if she insisted on going to Bridport, he would kill her.[17] Given that Ratz was only next door in the drawing room by now, Alma led Stoner to the dining room at the front of the house and told him to put the revolver away and not to make a fool of himself. Stoner insisted that she must never shut the bedroom door like that again. He was furious about the unsavoury proposition Ratz had made to Alma. But he also took issue with the visit to Bridport because, for the first time, Stoner realised he'd be outside the lax conventions of the Villa Madeira, and he would have no choice but to take his meals in the kitchen and sleep in the staff quarters with the other servants. Stoner had only just returned from London where he had been waited on, bought crêpe de Chine pyjamas and been treated as Alma's equal. He had bought her an engagement ring, there had even been talk of marriage; he did not relish this hard reminder that he was a paid houseboy. As Violet Firth, a middle-class woman turned servant, observed in *The Psychology of the Servant Problem*, 'being a servant is very painful to one's self-respect and no amount of money can compensate that injury to anyone who has independence of spirit'.[18] The petulant Stoner was adamant: Alma could go to Bridport if she wanted to, but he wouldn't drive her there.

After their conversation, however, Alma felt that she had reassured Stoner somewhat and that everything would be all right.[19] She doesn't seem to have been much fazed even by being threatened with the gun. These histrionics were typical of Stoner, she felt. She went back to the drawing room where she enthused to Ratz about their trip. She then went into Ratz's bedroom and started putting out some clothes for Stoner to pack. At 7.15 p.m. she bathed John and put him to bed at about 7.45 p.m., ready for school the next day. Later that evening, Ratz seemed in a much happier frame of mind as he and Alma played cards in the drawing room, listening to the wireless. Stoner was nowhere to be seen.

As it was Sunday, the BBC only broadcast devotional programmes, church services and sacred music, so Alma is more likely to have been listening to the independent stations such as Radio Luxembourg and Radio Normandy, which played dance music on

Sunday evenings. Ratz was dozing in his chair, with his back to the French windows, the library book to his side. At 9.30 p.m., as she wanted to get ready for the journey the next day, Alma decided to retire for the night.[20] She let Dinah out of the French windows and closed the door as usual, otherwise the dog would come straight back in without having done her business.[21] Before she left the drawing room, Alma leaned down, saying 'goodnight darling' to Ratz, and kissed him. She went to the upstairs bathroom and by the time she came into her bedroom, Dinah had already been let in and had come upstairs. Alma assumed that Ratz had let her in as usual. She began to pack her suitcase for the trip, getting in and out of bed as she remembered things to take and then leafing through a woman's magazine. But it was not Ratz who had opened the window and let the dog in; it was Stoner.

Directly after the altercation about Bridport in the dining room, Stoner had taken the bus to Ensbury Park, dressed in his new fawn-coloured raincoat and trilby. He had arrived at his grandparents' house at 8.30 p.m. and asked Mrs Stevens, 'Mother, will Dad lend me a mallet?' When she asked what he wanted it for, he told her that he needed to drive in some pegs as he was going to erect a tent in the garden. She went to the workshop and sheds at the back of the house. Groping around the chisels, planes and saws in the dark, she found a wooden mallet with a cylindrical, octagonal head.[22] She asked him, 'Will that do, Percy?' Taking the mallet, Stoner said it would.[23] A few minutes later he had gone.

On returning to the Villa Madeira, still wearing his driving gloves, Stoner took the mallet in his hands. Standing outside in the rear garden, through the French windows he saw Alma kiss Ratz goodnight – an ordinary domestic scene. His resentment and jealousy bubbled over into fury: Ratz was a procurer, treating Alma like a whore and belittling him like a servant. After watching her go off to bed, Stoner entered the drawing room through the French windows, the dog slipping in as he did so. Seeing the back of Ratz's head as he dozed in his chair, Stoner raised his fist as he gripped the mallet and brought it down with great force on the back of Ratz's head, cracking it open and driving the skull into his brain. He then struck again as blood oozed from the wounds. Finally, he hit the old man a third time, with such force that Ratz's false teeth fell out onto the floor. Having attacked him, Stoner dropped the mallet by the sofa, then went up to his own room to change into the crêpe de Chine pyjamas that Alma had bought for him.[24] Downstairs in the drawing room, an elderly man was bleeding to death.

* * *

At 10.15 p.m., Irene returned to the house and let herself in with the key that was secreted outside the front door. The lights were off in the hall, so, presuming that the household had gone to bed, she went straight upstairs to her room.[25] After a few minutes she went across the landing to the lavatory and saw Stoner leaning over the top of the banisters looking downstairs. She asked, 'What's the matter?' and he replied, 'Nothing, I was looking to see if the lights were out.'[26] Irene went back to her room. She then went downstairs to the kitchen and, as she did so, she heard someone breathing, so went to Ratz's bedroom and listened at the door and at the door of the drawing room. Both doors were ajar. She had an unsettling premonition that something was wrong.[27] Not able to work out where the sound was coming from, she switched on Ratz's bedroom light and saw that he wasn't there. Assuming that he'd been drinking and had fallen asleep in the armchair, she didn't go into the drawing room, but went back upstairs to her room. She dressed for bed before going to the bathroom, passing the open door of the bedroom opposite, where Alma was standing, getting her things ready for the next day. Irene said a quick 'hullo' to her before retiring to bed. A few minutes later, Alma came in for a chat as she often did. She told Irene that she had spoken to Jenks and that they were going to Pilsdon Manor the next day. She still wasn't sure if Stoner would be driving them there or not. She then said goodnight and went back to her own room.[28]

If Alma's estimate of her retiring to bed at 9.30 p.m. and Irene's arrival at 10.15 p.m. are to be believed, Stoner must have left Ratz bleeding in the drawing room for an agonising forty-five minutes. Then, like an apologetic child, he went to Alma's bedroom in his pyjamas and got into bed with her. She had not seen him since the argument that afternoon and would have been keen to know whether he would be driving them to Bridport or if they had to make other arrangements. But, knowing his temperament, she didn't push the issue straight away. Then she noticed that he seemed a little strange, rather agitated. She asked him, 'What's the matter, darling?' He said he was in trouble and couldn't tell her what it was. 'Oh, you *must* tell me,' she said and they skirted around the issue for two or three minutes.[29] She assumed that he had had some trivial trouble with his mother. She told him that she was strong enough to bear anything. He then told her that she was not going to Bridport the next day as he had hurt Ratz. Alma said, 'I will go and see him.' But Stoner tried to stop her: 'No, you mustn't. The sight will upset you.' Then he told her that he had hit Ratz over the head with a mallet.[30] At first, a stunned Alma was silent. She didn't quite take in what he was saying. Then she heard a groan from downstairs, the sound of somebody in pain.[31]

Suddenly, she leapt out of bed and raced down the stairs. There in the drawing room she found Ratz, slumped in his chair, covered in blood. Experienced in the treatment of severe wounds during the war, Alma must have gauged the severity of Ratz's injuries; a man of his age would be unlikely to survive them. She rubbed Ratz's hands but they were cold. She tried to take his pulse but felt nothing. She shook him, but he was limp. She tried talking, but he didn't answer.[32] Stepping back, she trod on his false teeth. Suddenly she was hysterical as she tried to force the dentures into Ratz's mouth so that he could speak. Alma raced back up the stairs and told Stoner to go back to his room. He was not to come downstairs until she called him. As soon as she'd seen Ratz, Alma was riven by a sense of responsibility. If the police were to get involved, Stoner would be up on at least an assault charge and the whole situation at the Villa Madeira would be exposed. The only thought in her 'bewildered mind' was, 'God, how can I help this boy?'[31] Alma had to think of a strategy, and fast.

Back in the drawing room, feeling as though she were going to vomit, she poured herself a glass of neat whisky and screamed, 'Irene!'[33]

Irene had not been asleep, so as soon as she heard the cry, she rushed downstairs to find a terrified Alma and Ratz in the chair with a black eye covered in thick and congealed blood. She asked him, 'Whatever is the matter?'[34] Meanwhile Alma was moving around the room, hysterically throwing her arms about and drinking. She shouted at Irene to call Dr O'Donnell. After ringing him from the telephone in Ratz's room, Irene went to the kitchen and the downstairs bathroom to get a bowl of water and a cloth to bathe Ratz's head and try to make him more comfortable. She went into the hall and shouted up to Stoner to come downstairs before returning to the drawing room to bathe Ratz's eye. Stoner came into the room to find Alma crying and screaming, 'Help me get Ratz into bed. He has been hurt.' Seeing the bloody mallet still on the floor, Stoner discreetly kicked it behind the sofa so that Irene wouldn't see it. The three of them lifted Ratz and carried him into his bedroom. Alma then instructed Irene and Stoner to start clearing up the blood from the drawing-room carpet. She didn't want John to see it when he came down in the morning. They removed Ratz's trousers and Alma wrapped a towel around his head, raving all the time, 'Oh, poor Ratz. What has happened? What have they done to you?' She was impatient for the arrival of the doctor and appealed to Irene, 'Can't somebody do something?'[35] She then told Stoner to get the car out of the garage and pick O'Donnell up. Already she was suggesting that she had no idea who was responsible. At the same time, she was removing Stoner from the scene of the crime. With Irene and Alma preoccupied with Ratz, Stoner took the mallet from behind the sofa and hid it outside behind some boxes by the trellis near the front door before going to fetch the doctor.

When he arrived at the Villa Madeira, O'Donnell was shocked at the condition in which he found Ratz. He must also have wondered what might be exposed to the wider world if the police were to become involved. The ramifications would affect him personally; he knew about Alma's affair with her chauffeur and about Stoner's apparent drug addiction. If O'Donnell had also been supplying Alma with any drugs himself, he knew he could be struck off for doing so. At this point, he would have had the opportunity to remove any drugs that Alma might have had in her possession. Rather than call the police straight away, perhaps he felt that they could contain the problem without involving them, so he called Alfred Rooke, the local surgeon. With the help of the taxi driver, he removed Ratz's coat and waistcoat. When he went into the drawing room, Irene was washing up the blood from the chair and the carpet, apparently unaware that she was cleaning up the crime scene. Alma told O'Donnell about the evening she had spent with Ratz and their plans to go to Bridport. She explained that they had spent a pleasant afternoon and that Ratz had been reading a book about suicide. She drew his attention to *Stay of Execution* that was on the piano. By doing so, she seemed to suggest that Ratz might in some way have tried to kill himself, which was clearly unlikely despite his frequent threats to do so, but Alma was clutching at any straws she could to protect Stoner. Rooke arrived at about five minutes past midnight. After he examined Ratz, frustrated by Alma's now hysterical behaviour, he arranged for an ambulance and went ahead to Strathallen Nursing Home. O'Donnell accompanied Ratz in the ambulance, followed by Stoner, who went after him in the Rattenburys' car so that he could bring him back later.[36]

When PC Bagwell arrived at the house from the nursing home to ascertain how Ratz might have come by his injuries, Alma repeated the same story that she'd told O'Donnell. She continued to drink. When Inspector Mills arrived, he too asked her what had happened. When he asked her to clarify if the French windows had been open or not, Alma had the opportunity to suggest the possibility of an unknown assailant. But she wasn't thinking quickly enough and admitted that the doors had been locked shut. Whoever was responsible for the attack must have lived in the house. Alma put one of Frank Titterton's records on the radiogram:[37]

I am far across the waters,
But I hear you call to me,
In my dreams your eyes are shining,
Dark-haired Marie.

I shall come to claim you someday,
In my arms at last you'll be
I shall kiss your lips and love
Dark-haired Marie.

After Mills had searched the premises, Alma told PC Bagwell that she knew who had done it, so she was cautioned. Her mind clearly racing to try to find a way of protecting Stoner, she admitted that *she* had done it and had hidden the mallet. She had, of course, no idea where the mallet was. Remembering sections from the book Ratz had read to her and the conversation they'd had that afternoon, she said that he'd lived too long. Then she said, 'My lover did it,' but without naming Stoner.[38] Her mind oscillating between admission and fear, she tried to kiss Bagwell, then tried to bribe him.[39]

After the police left, Alma tried to escape in pursuit of them, trying all the doors, front and back of the house. Irene quickly locked them and took the keys. She then seated Alma in a chair in the dining room and sat on her so she couldn't move.[40] When Mills returned having assessed Ratz's condition in the nursing home, he told her that her husband was now in a critical condition. The situation seemed to be getting worse and worse. Alma asked, 'Will this be against me?'[41] He cautioned her before she made a hasty confession. 'I did it. He gave me the book. He has lived too long,' which was again an echo of the passage that Ratz had read to her. 'He said, "Dear, dear".' But having confessed, she knew she'd have to tell Mills where the mallet was, so she tried an inept delaying tactic: 'I'll tell you where the mallet is in the morning. Have you told the coroner yet?' In reality, she didn't really know what a coroner was or what they did and may just have been repeating words and phrases she'd read in newspaper crime stories like that of Reginald Woolmington. She wanted to be clear to the police that she had attacked Ratz, that she had done it alone and was determined to do it again. 'I shall make a better job of it next time. Irene doesn't know. I made a proper muddle of it. I thought I was strong enough.'[42]

Meanwhile, upstairs in his mother's bedroom, John was confused and frightened by all the activity in the house. Years into the future he would still be able to recall that night: 'I remember the night my father was murdered because the lights went on in the house – and I woke up. Nobody would tell me what had happened but I had this cold feeling that something terrible had occurred.'[43]

When O'Donnell arrived back at the house with Stoner, he must have thought that it would be best for all of them if Alma would just go to sleep. He gave her half a grain of morphia, a substantial dose, just to make sure. When he had given her a quarter of a grain in the summer, she had slept solidly for eight hours. But almost as soon as she had gone upstairs, she came down again, declaring that Ratz's son was the assailant. O'Donnell was insistent that Alma could not be questioned in her present state as she was drugged and drunk. Stoner carried her up the stairs. He put her to bed and kissed her goodnight. Nothing was said. The kiss was reassurance enough and she would cherish this moment in the long weeks ahead. By this point, Stoner still had no idea that she had confessed to the crime, nor that she had made a statement about it. O'Donnell sat with her until the morphia began to work and she fell asleep. He then left for home.[44]

By the time Inspector Carter from CID arrived it was already 4.30 a.m. He explored the house and grounds as Alma slept, but he checked several times with Irene to see if she had woken. In the drawing room, Carter saw that the French windows were open, that there was a glass of whisky on the mantelpiece and that on the carpet there was a wet stain of 30 square inches. Alma woke at 6 a.m. She was given a cup of coffee but could barely hold the cup. She wanted to have a bath and get dressed but Irene was exasperated by the heavy police presence in her room (perhaps safety in numbers after Alma's forward behaviour with Bagwell earlier): 'The lady can't get up with three men in the room. Give her a chance!'[45] The officers withdrew, but Carter insisted on staying until the police matron arrived. As Alma was lying on the bed, she started talking, but as Carter didn't think she was fully recovered, he didn't caution her: 'I picked up the mallet and he dared me to hit him. He said, "You have not guts enough to do it." I hit him. I hid the mallet. He is not dead, is he? Are you the coroner?'

Again, Alma seemed to be utilising elements of what Ratz had said earlier and altering it for her own purposes. But, heavily sedated or not, she was determined to take the blame. While she was in the downstairs bathroom, supervised by the police matron, Irene was alone in the kitchen with Stoner. He said to her, 'I suppose you know who did it?' Alma had been talking wildly all night, making confessions and accusations, so there'd been no reason for Irene to suspect that Stoner was involved thus far. She said, 'Well?'[46] But there were too many police in the house to have a discussion about it. Irene needed to keep Alma's confidence and even if she didn't like Stoner, Alma did.

As Alma was dressing, Carter questioned Irene and then took a statement from Stoner, who was still in the kitchen. But he had nothing significant to add: he'd seen nothing, he'd heard nothing, he knew nothing.

I retired to my bedroom at 8.50 p.m. ... leaving Mr and Mrs Rattenbury and the boy John in the drawing room. About 10.30 p.m. I was aroused by Mrs Rattenbury shouting to me to come down. I came down into the drawing room and saw Mr Rattenbury sitting in the armchair with blood running from his head. Mrs Rattenbury was crying and screaming and said to me, 'Help me get Ratz into bed, he has been hurt.' I then took the car and went to Dr O'Donnell's house. He had left before I got there. When I returned, I cleaned the blood from the floor on the instructions of Mrs Rattenbury. Mrs Rattenbury was sober and, as far as I know, she had not been drinking. When I went to bed she was in a normal condition. I have never seen a mallet on the premises. Until I was aroused I heard no sounds of a quarrell or noise of any kind. Since September 1934, I have been employed by Mr and Mrs Rattenbury; they have been on the best of terms. I said to her, 'How did this happen?' And she said, 'I don't know.'[47]

At 8.15 a.m., now that Alma was dressed, Carter cautioned her and she made a statement, almost word for word what she'd said at 6.15 a.m. 'I was playing cards with my husband when he dared me to kill him as he wanted to die. I picked up the mallet. He then said, "You have not the guts to do it." I then hit him with the mallet. I hid the mallet outside the house. I would have shot him if I had a gun.'[48]

The statement about the gun was perhaps inspired by the revolver that Stoner had threatened her with the afternoon before. Alma arranged with Irene to take John to school that day as normal. As she was preparing to leave for the police station, concerned that her story should be convincing, Alma needed to establish the whereabouts of the mallet she'd said she'd used. Nobody would be convinced that she was the assailant if she couldn't locate the weapon. She whispered to Irene, 'Tell Stoner he must give me the mallet.'[49] Irene duly relayed the message to Stoner, but he said nothing and Irene didn't pursue the matter; it was pointless anyway as the police had already found it.

Putting on her fur coat as she left the bedroom, Alma met Irene and Stoner at the bottom of the stairs by the glazed doors. She told them, attempting flippancy, but also hinting not to challenge the decision she had made, 'Do not make fools of yourselves.' Stoner replied, 'You have got yourself into this mess by talking too much' – an exchange that was overheard by the police.[50] As she was escorted from the house to the car, Alma caught sight of her young son at the doorway ready to go to school, confused about where his mother was going and when she'd be back. They would never see each other again.

CHAPTER THIRTEEN

CAUSE CÉLÈBRE

25 March–14 April 1935

An East Cliff Sensation
Attempted Murder Charge
Woman in the Dock

– *Bournemouth Echo*, 25 March 1935[1]

Alma had admitted the charge of attempted murder and as far as the Bournemouth Police were concerned it was a straightforward case – a middle-class, middle-aged marriage gone wrong. She now needed legal representation, so Dr O'Donnell consulted the best legal firm in Bournemouth on her behalf; Other, Manning & Tredinnick. Thirty-nine-year-old Robert Lewis Manning was a proud Welshman, Welsh being his first language. His father had died when he was three and when his mother remarried, the family emigrated to run a cattle farm in Southern Rhodesia. On the outbreak of the First World War, he returned to Britain and joined up, despite being underage. He was wounded on the Western Front while serving with the London Scottish Regiment. When he recovered, he was transferred to the newly formed Royal Tank Corps, but was very seriously wounded at Cambrai. On being invalided out of the army, he returned to Southern Rhodesia, but when the family herd was wiped out by tsetse fly, the Mannings moved back to Wales where Lewis Manning decided to become a solicitor. On relocating to Bournemouth, he had bought his practice from a Mr Other at 118 Old Christchurch Road and was soon joined by Mr Boileau-Tredinnick. By 1935, he'd built a solid reputation as one of Bournemouth's leading solicitor advocates. He'd married in 1927 and as a father and husband was ahead of his time, ensuring that his daughter Anne received the same educational opportunities as her brother and helping his wife with household tasks decades before such egalitarian practices became the norm.[2] It may have been this progressive attitude towards women that convinced O'Donnell that Lewis Manning was the right solicitor for Alma.

Later that morning, Alma appeared at the Bournemouth Police Court in Stafford Road represented by Lewis Manning. Inspector Carter stated that she had confessed to attacking her husband and had even clarified, 'I did it deliberately and would do it again.' Alma 'appeared dazed' throughout the three-minute proceedings and was remanded in custody until 2 April. That evening, the story made the front page of the *Bournemouth Echo*, but it was a low-key press story, subsidiary to the headline concerning the conference in Berlin between the British foreign minister, Sir John Simon, and Adolf Hitler, 'a vital day for Europe, and indeed, for the world – the most vital and fateful since the Great War'.[3]

Dr O'Donnell had made a request to see Alma and he visited her at the police station in Madeira Road at 1 p.m. She could barely walk and had to be helped into the interview room by Inspector Carter and the police matron.[4] Clearly still under the influence of the large dose of morphia she had been given early that morning, she couldn't stand up properly. Her pupils were contracted and at one point she tried to vomit. O'Donnell spent about twenty minutes with her during which they discussed what to do with the children. They agreed that both would stay at school for the time being and John would board over the weekends. She wrote two cheques for £5 for O'Donnell to give to Irene and Stoner. She was then transferred to Holloway Prison in London.

When a new prison had been mooted by the City of London

in the 1840s, Holloway was a desirable suburb and local house-holders objected to the idea of a prison being built in their midst until it was suggested that the building would look less like a penitentiary and more like a medieval fortress. Consequently, the central tower was designed as a copy of Warwick Castle. The famous entrance was built of large blocks of grey stone, 'Victorian gothic in its most overpowering form'.[5] The great doorway was surmounted by two enormous dragons, the emblem of the City of London, each holding a key and a pair of manacles. The prison was built in a star shape with seven wings radiating from a central hub. Each wing was four storeys high and contained a different category of prisoner. Holloway was London's largest prison, and could accommodate 975 female prisoners, having been designated for women only since 1902. The prison had a working gallows where Edith Thompson had been executed in 1923. Her body lay in the precincts of the prison in an unmarked grave, a chilling reminder of what might lie in store for Alma.

On arrival at the prison, Alma was taken to a room where an officer took down her age, religion and the details of the charge against her.[6] She was then taken upstairs and locked in a small metal box topped with wire, about 4sqft, and given two slices of bread and margarine and a pint of prison cocoa. She was seen by a nurse who went through her hair with a comb for lice and asked if she had 'had any discharge'. She then joined the queue to see the doctor. She looked at Alma's hands for scabies and used her stethoscope to check Alma's chest. After about an hour and a half, she was taken to a room where an officer took her handbag and made an inventory of the contents while she was told to strip naked. She was asked to sign the inventory of her clothes and possessions. She was given a cloak to put around her and was weighed and measured before being told to have a hot bath. A towel and toothbrush were provided, but no soap. Alma's prison uniform was thrown on top of the door and she was told to put it on. Each prisoner wore a 'Sister Dora' cap and a checked apron with a bib. The dresses worn beneath the aprons indicated which category of prisoner the women were. Those awaiting trial like Alma wore a grey dress with a thin white stripe.[7] She was given black knitted stockings and calico knickers that tied around the waist with a tape. Shoes were made by prisoners and had straps and flat heels.[8] After she was dressed, she was taken to pick up a bundle containing pillow slips, sheets and a thick calico nightdress with long sleeves that was 'very hard to lie on'. She was also given a Bible, a hymn book and the Book of Common Prayer. She was to be held in a ward in the hospital on E Wing for prisoners on remand and awaiting trial, known as 'aliens' by the rest of the prison community.[9]

Prisoners rose at 6.10 a.m., breakfast followed at 7.25 and, like all meals, was consumed by the women locked in their cells. It consisted of two slices of bread and margarine, a pint of tea and some porridge tasting of 'mould and decay'. Chapel was at 8.40 followed by exercise and work. Lunch was served at 12 and might be bacon and haricot beans, fish ('indescribable') or stew followed by pudding ('Constitution unrevealed. Brown in colour, doughy in consistency, rumour has it that jam is in it, occasionally prunes are found.'). More work was followed by tea at 5.50 p.m. This was three slices of bread and margarine and some sugar. On some days there was a baked potato or a small piece of cheese. Tea was accompanied by a pint of cocoa. This consisted of a layer of grease on top and 'a murky and solid bottom'. Many of the women would let the cocoa cool, then skim off the grease with some toilet paper and then use it as a face cream. Lights out was at 9 p.m.[10] Joan Henry wrote about the end of her traumatic first day in Holloway in *Women in Prison*: 'My light went out. I turned over. The iron bars on the high window cast their shadows on the floor. I laid my head on the unyielding pillow ... the walls seemed to be closing in on me; the terror of being locked up.'[11]

Prison was a shock to Alma, a dehumanising process completely beyond her experience. On Tuesday 26 March, she wrote to Stoner in despair:

Oh Darling this is awful.

I must see you I'm so ill. Tell me how Ratz is, also is Dr O'D, Long [Ratz's financial backer in London] or someone arranging bail. Am writing small – cos not too much paper. But Bail must be arranged by April 2nd. I keep thinking this is some ghastly night mare from which I must awake. Oh! Darling I'm going potty. In your foggiest dreams you couldn't imagine life here. All letters are censored. So can't write much even though long to. But Oh! Just to see you darling, why did this awful thing happen. I couldn't keep my handbag or anything, tell Irene. I must see my babies – simply must. My head is going round in circles, if they'd only let me sleep. But you know I'm not strong enough for this rough life and work. I'm so weak. Oh! Darling why why why did this ghastly thing happen. If only I could die. Please let me die. When I go home on Tues can't you arrange to see me. Dr O.D could find out details for you. Perhaps I could see you here. Why did they bring me here? Couldn't I have stayed in Bournemouth? Why bring me here? Do write to me darling. I do love you so. Why why oh! Why did this have to happen. I am in a sick ward here – 10 beds – but not allowed to lie down and I'm so weak I can hardly stand. If only I could have a smoke. If if if. Oh! God why am I here, it all seems some ghastly joke. Find out about my bail. The lawyer Dr O D sent should be able to tell you something. Keep your chin up darling – will meet again. My God its cold, oh for a hot water bottle. Find out how Ratz is – everything (as far as my muddled brain will allow) depends on how Ratz is. Oh make him pull through. Please send me some papers. Tell Irene to write. Tell Dr O.D also. Perhaps he could arrange I could have a smoke. The grey uniform and cape about kill my mind. I want to write so much – but knowing one's letters are read – crabs one's number. I do pray Rz pulls through – all depends on that. I must get out of here – it's all so wrong. My babies – everything. Did you arrange for

[Little John] to stay at school next Saturday. Two things in
this ghastly nightmare stands out. LJ's face at the front door.
And your kiss. Oh God will I never see either again. Will my
brain stand the shock. Tell me everything that has happened.
Send me the papers. Oh! God darling why did this happen,
is it only last Tues. we were going to town laughing, with not
a care in the world? And now I'm a criminal. Awful clothes,
dreadful food – a bath once a week. Not even a watch. No
mirrors – no face powder – nothing allowed – and not seeing
you or hearing your voice – yr dear voice – oh! Why did
this happen. Why can't I even cry. And my children, will I
be out by the 3rd? That bail must be arranged. Oh I wish
to God I were dead. Nothing could be bigger hell for me,
than to not see you or my children. They wouldn't let me see
you before I left. Oh! Darling, darling can't something be
done – Please please help me. I'm so desperate. Perhaps you
could get Dr O. D to find what train that woman policeman
comes to town on, and which she returns to Bournemouth
on with me. Oh! The clang of keys. You might get on the
same carriage, Oh! Darling, I want to see you so. – I don't
think you'd recognize me. I can hardly walk for weakness.
God bless you God Bless you God Bless you – & my babies.
My love is always with you, please write often. I do love you
and want you so, just the comfort of your dear arms for five
minutes. Angel Angel, why am I here – and why did this have
to happen to us? Let me know how Rz is – so much depends
on that. Au revoir – my precious one. Give my love to
Irene – only allowed to write three letters a week. So explain
to Irene – for I must write to you my beloved.
    Yr Lozanne[12]

She signed herself by her professional name, something she'd
never done before with Stoner, Irene or the children, but would do
throughout her time in prison.

The next day she was called in to see the prison governor.

Fifty-two-year-old Dr John Hall Morton was born in Limerick and had studied medicine at Trinity College Dublin. He had joined the prison service in 1909, and was made governor and chief medical officer at Holloway in 1921. He was hugely popular, loyal and unselfish with an untiring energy, a constant devotion to duty and always keenly promoted the welfare of the women in his care. He lived in a Tudor-style lodge at the front gates of the prison with his wife, son and daughter. He had been very shaken by the execution of Edith Thompson, which he had witnessed, and was determined to help Alma avoid a similar fate. Morton found Alma 'very depressed and somewhat confused ... repeating the same sentence over and over again'.[13] He examined her and saw no evidence that she was a drug addict, other than the hypodermic marks from the recent injections O'Donnell had given her. Morton was convinced of her innocence and impressed upon her the necessity of telling the whole truth. Alma told him, 'The truth is, is that it was my fault absolutely.'[14] Having read the desperate letter she intended to send to Stoner, Morton suggested that she rewrite it when she was in a calmer frame of mind, which she did the next day.[15]

> *Darling,*
> *This is torn from part of a letter I wrote to Irene today.*
> *The letter I wrote you yesterday, the gov told me was a little*
> *too morbid! – So as I[rene]'s was of the same tone, it seemed*
> *the only thing to scrap that also. Sorry you couldn't have my*
> *1st letter, though. I was desperately worried about you – but*
> *Irene cheered me up this morning.*
>
> *It was rather unfortunate she came at the same time with*
> *Katherine [Miller Jones, Ratz's niece], it made it more difficult*
> *to talk. But oh! I must see you tomorrow with the lawyer.*
> *I think he could advise Oh! Darling I am so desperately*
> *miserable – Why should this have happened – oh! Why why.*
> *All letters are censored – both coming in and going out. Do*
> *you think the lawyer can arrange bail? Will you be in court on*
> *Tuesday? I must see you even if we can't talk. If you came to*

town with lawyer he might advise you and make it alright for us 3 to talk together. I hope this letter reaches you in time, for as you can see by the enclosed – he is coming tomorrow. Also, it is customary to ask permission of the governor before seeing a prisoner. If you hav'nt already done that, Manning could do it for you darling one. God bless you my sweet one, may God make the time speed away and get us all out of this awful nightmare. Two things stay in my mind – L.Js dear little face, as he was leaving for school, and yr last kiss.

My love be with you always,
Lozanne.[16]

This was sent to Stoner at the Villa Madeira, but, receiving no word from him, she wrote him another at 7.30 a.m. the next day (28 March).

I am trying to have the lawyer's letter I received today sent to you darling, so that you can make arrangements to come up with him, or make arrangements with the governor. But I must see you darling. Please write to me. This is the 3rd letter have written – hope you receive this. I hardly know how to write now. Let me know how Ratz is getting along. No more now. God bless you – my love be with you always.

Lozanne
Have you talked with Dr O'D about how Ratz is? Goodness there is much I want to know. Please ask Irene to give you a few bobby pins for my hair. I think they should be allowed.[17]

* * *

Having charged Alma at the police station on Monday morning, Carter returned to the Villa Madeira and took possession of the armchair, the carpet, the cretonne chair cover, the glass of whisky and a pack of playing cards from the mantelpiece, Ratz's clothes, Alma's pyjamas and kimono, some cloths from the kitchen and two cushions he had found drying on top of the shed in the garden.[18] He also took Alma's bloodstained slippers from her bedroom before securely locking the drawing-room door. Irene had taken John back to school, so when Stoner returned to the Villa Madeira from the police station, they were in the house alone. At 11.45 that morning, the ambulance driver called to collect his fee for transporting Rattenbury to the nursing home. Stoner answered the door and said that he'd pay the bill of £1 1s. He wondered if Hoare could change a fiver?[19] During the day, there was a large delivery for Stoner from Harrods; a suit, pyjamas, underwear and shoes, a reminder of the innocent time, just days ago, before everything changed.

On Tuesday, Stoner drove himself and Irene on a trip to Wimborne. On the way back to Bournemouth, they passed a house in Ensbury Park. Stoner made a point of saying that an ex-policeman lived in the house who had seen him in the area on Sunday night around 9.30 p.m. Shortly afterwards, they passed Stoner's grandparents' house and he mentioned that he had fetched the mallet from his grandfather's workshop. He then showed Irene his parents' house, which was around the corner. While they were driving, Irene asked him if his fingerprints would be on the mallet, but Stoner said no, he had worn gloves.[20] Effectively, by telling her when he'd fetched the mallet, where he'd got it from and how he'd handled it, he'd admitted responsibility for the crime.

On Wednesday, Irene bought a box of flowers for Alma and hoped to get them to her in Holloway the next day. That evening at around 9 p.m. she left the house to go to confession. Irene was an Anglican but specifically went to a Catholic priest because she knew she could share her anxieties without them being repeated to anybody else. She knew that Alma did not attack Ratz and she also knew that Stoner had. But she couldn't share the information with the police without revealing the nature of the relationship between Alma and Stoner. Irene arrived home at about 10.30 p.m. to find Stoner in his bedroom, very drunk. This was completely out of character as he never touched alcohol. He was rambling, saying that Alma was in jail and he was the one who had put her there. He then said, 'Irene, you know I killed Mr Rattenbury, I should never have let her gone. You must get me up early in the morning as I want to go to London to see Mrs Rattenbury and give myself up.'[21]

Irene was so concerned about the state that he was in that at 11.20 she went downstairs and called the police. She wanted someone to come to the Villa Madeira as Stoner was drunk and saying 'mad things'. PC Gates and PC Beale arrived to check on the situation.[22] Irene told them that she did not 'like to stay here alone with' Stoner. When the police talked to him, Stoner was drunk and had clearly been vomiting. He was very talkative and only seemed concerned about Ratz's condition. Neither Stoner nor Irene said anything relating to the events of Sunday night. Irene may have felt it best that Stoner go ahead with his plan to visit Alma the next day, say goodbye, then give himself up. The police noted that as they talked with Stoner, Irene remained at the foot of the stairs eavesdropping, giving them the impression that she was apprehensive about what he might say. When they left, Irene asked Stoner if he could take the flowers and the bobby pins with him that she had bought to give to Alma. That night, unhappy to be left alone with Stoner, Irene asked her brother to stay in the house. About 6.30 a.m. the next morning, Stoner drove Irene's brother to work. He arrived back at the Villa Madeira just after 7 a.m. to collect the box of flowers and the pins before going to catch the 7.25 a.m. train to Waterloo station.[23]

At 8.15 a.m. that morning (Thursday 28 March), Ratz died. Inspector Carter went to view the body, then contacted Lewis Manning and asked to meet him at Holloway Prison later in the day. He also informed Keith and Katharine Miller Jones, Rattenbury's nephew and niece. Dr O'Donnell was told that Ratz had died and that Alma was now facing a murder charge. In the afternoon, he called at the Villa Madeira to find Irene alone. He wondered if Alma had really attacked Ratz. Irene replied, 'I know she did not!' O'Donnell told Irene that if she had further information, she must tell the police. She was conflicted but was persuaded that now Alma was facing a murder charge, they had to do anything they could to help her. O'Donnell called the police, who came to the house. At 2.35 p.m., they took a statement in which Irene confirmed what Stoner had told her. In an attempt to mitigate the damage to Alma, she lied to the police and said that Alma and Stoner had only been on 'very friendly terms' for the past two months and that she had only seen them kissing each other once. Searching Stoner's bedroom, the police found the bill for the stay at the Royal Palace Hotel made out to Stoner, but paid by Alma. They also found the receipt for the engagement ring made out to Mr G. Rattenbury.

The police then interviewed Stoner's grandparents and uncle at Bournemouth Police Station. Mrs Stevens confirmed that Stoner had visited them on the night of the murder and had taken away a mallet.[24] When the police presented it to him, Richard Stevens identified the mallet as his. He'd last used it just before Christmas.[25] Mrs Stevens confirmed that it was the mallet that her grandson had borrowed.

The Bournemouth Police contacted Scotland Yard by telephone and asked them to arrest Stoner at Holloway, but by the time Chief Inspectors Sharpe and Keech arrived there at 6 p.m., Stoner had left. Arriving at 11.30 a.m., he had not been permitted to see Alma, so he left the flowers and bobby pins for her and travelled back to Bournemouth.[26]

At 5 p.m., the police surgeon in Bournemouth, Harold Simmonds, conducted the post-mortem on Ratz's body in the presence of Dr O'Donnell and Alfred Rooke. Both eyes were bruised a deep purple colour. On removing the scalp, Simmonds uncovered the extent of Ratz's injuries, finding a considerable amount of blood and a 9-inch fracture across the skull. This wound, which must have been made with 'considerable force', had resulted in 'contra coup', where the brain had been bruised on the opposite side of the skull in the direction of the blow. The injuries indicated Ratz was sitting in the armchair with his head inclined to the right, so probably dozing, and that the assailant was above him when the blows were inflicted. There was no evidence of any struggle and the large quantity of urine Ratz had passed was evidence of a loss of consciousness. Simmonds removed a piece of Ratz's scalp and gave it to Inspector Carter as evidence.[27]

As Stoner's train drew into Bournemouth railway station at 6.35, Inspector Carter was waiting for him. As Stoner descended onto the platform, Carter approached him, saying, 'You know me to be a police officer?' Stoner confirmed that he did. Carter cautioned him before driving him to Madeira Road, where he was charged with murder. All he said was, 'I understand.'[28] When Stoner was searched, Carter found two photographs of Alma, one of the letters she had sent from prison, a letter from Lewis Manning to Alma referring to her forthcoming interview with the police[29] and her father's heavy hunter gold watch. Stoner warned the police to be careful: 'It was given to me by Mrs Rattenbury and is worth £20.'

The next day, Stoner appeared in Bournemouth Police Court, smartly dressed in the grey striped suit, blue tie and blue striped shirt that Alma had bought for him. He 'stepped lightly into the dock and smiled recognition to [his parents] in the public seats'.[30] When he was charged with murder, a voice from the back of the court shouted, 'It's a lie!' The only witness to be called was Carter, who reported that Rattenbury had died the previous day. He asked for a remand until the following Tuesday, when both Stoner and Alma would appear together. Stoner also made an application for legal aid under the Poor Prisoners' Defence Act, which had only been in practice since 1930.[31] Though Alma was assembling the best legal team that money could buy for her defence, Stoner's would be left to the state.

After the hearing, at about 11.10 a.m., Stoner was in DC Gates's custody in the detention room at the Police Court and asked him, 'You know Mrs Rattenbury, don't you?' Gates said that he did. Stoner went on, 'Do you know that Mrs Rattenbury had nothing to do with this affair?'[32] Gates immediately cautioned Stoner, who said, 'I don't care, if you know what I mean, yet I do care.' He then made a confession:

> When I did the job, I believed he was asleep. I hit him and then came upstairs and told Mrs Rattenbury, she rushed down then. You see I watched through the French window and saw her kiss him good-night then leave the room. I waited and crept in through the French Window, which was unlocked. I think he must have been asleep when I hit him. Still it ain't much use saying anything, I don't suppose they will let her out yet. You know there should be a doctor with her when they tell her I am arrested, because she will go out of her mind.[33]

Stoner was then transferred to Dorchester Prison, where in 1856 Thomas Hardy had witnessed the execution of Martha Brown, the abused wife turned murderess who many years later would inspire *Tess of the D'Urbervilles*. He would be accommodated at Dorchester until 14 May when he would be transferred to Brixton Prison in preparation for the trial.

Lewis Manning had arranged to meet Inspector Carter that evening at Holloway. At 5.40 p.m. Carter saw Alma and Lewis Manning, and informed them that Ratz had died that morning. Consequently Alma was now being charged with murder. A devastated Alma was silent. Sunday would be Mothering Sunday and she would not be permitted to see her children. That evening, the story of the drama at the Villa Madeira was the front-page headline of the *Bournemouth Echo*: 'Sensational East Cliff Tragedy Development'.[34]

Stoner was to be represented by E. W. Marshall Harvey, another esteemed Bournemouth solicitor. On 2 April, accompanied by John Bickford, a clerk from Marshall Harvey's office, the police made a search of the Villa Madeira for drugs, examining the contents of Alma's medicine cupboard – the sleeping draughts, sedatives and anti-depressants. At the back of the cupboard, they also came across a hypodermic syringe.

* * *

Meanwhile, Joshua Casswell had written to the attorney general, Lord Inskip, that there was a crucial point of law at stake and that Reginald Woolmington's case should to be taken to the House of Lords. Inskip agreed with Casswell and the case was to be heard by the Lords for the first time since the Court of Criminal Appeal had been set up in 1907. The Lord Chancellor Lord Sankey advised Casswell that the case should be defended by a King's Counsel, or KC. Casswell was disappointed as he had defended Woolmington from the start, but realised that a more senior lawyer might help the cause. The defence was to be led by Terence O'Connor KC with Casswell assisting.[35] The appeal was heard by the Lords from 4 April, with Woolmington looking down from the public gallery. O'Connor and Casswell argued their case before the Lord Chancellor and four Law Lords. After two days, the appeal was granted and the conviction quashed. Casswell and O'Connor had succeeded; after eighty-one days in custody, Woolmington was released.

The headline in the *Daily Express* was, 'Law Gives Man Back His Life; Peers Quash Death Sentence for First Time in History'.[36] Sir John Smith QC commented, 'Never, in my opinion, has the House of Lords done a more noble deed in the field of criminal law than on that day.' Lord Sankey then published a fourteen-page document that established that a defendant should be innocent until proven guilty, a directive that has shaped the law to this day: 'Throughout the web of the English criminal law one golden thread is always to be seen; and that is that it is the duty of the prosecution to prove the prisoner's guilt ... if at the end of, and on the whole of, the case, there is a reasonable doubt created by the evidence by either the prosecution of the prisoner, as to whether the prisoner killed the deceased with a malicious intention, the prosecution has not made out the case and the prisoner is entitled to acquittal.'[37]

Also on 4 April, now that Stoner had been charged, the police in Bournemouth took a statement from Frank Hobbs, the former chef at the Villa Madeira. He was now living in Blackfriars in London.

He had volunteered his evidence 'in fairness to the Chauffeur who is charged with Mrs Rattenbury: Had I fallen in with her suggestions, I might have become infatuated and easily agreed to do anything which she might have suggested.'[38]

* * *

On Sunday 7 April, Frank Titterton broadcast a radio concert with the BBC Orchestra, performing one of Alma's songs, 'Avelette'. Though it reported that Alma had not heard the broadcast, the *Daily Express* stated that 'thousands of listeners sitting by the fireside heard it. They knew nothing of the drama behind it.' After the broadcast Titterton spoke to the press:

> 'Avelette' is one of the last songs that Mrs Rattenbury composed. It is a beautiful song. Part of the words are: *My heart seeks your heart in the darkness, And whispers a tender goodnight.* I could not help thinking of the composer as I sang those words. I knew Mrs Rattenbury well and was at her house six weeks ago. She composed a special song for me and gave me several of her manuscripts. She has a flair for composing and sometimes had done two or three songs a week. Mrs Rattenbury is a talented pianist. She was playing with the Toronto Philharmonic Orchestra when she was only seventeen years old. I wish it could have been possible for her to listen in on Sunday.[39]

Shortly afterwards, Titterton and Beatrice Esmond were allowed a short visit with Alma in Holloway, ostensibly to discuss the publication of some of her songs. Alma was brought from the infirmary to the bare waiting room, her arms outstretched theatrically to greet her guests, but wasn't permitted to touch either of them. Beatrice had brought Alma some flowers, but was forbidden to give them to her. Alma apologised that they should have to meet in such conditions – 'How dreadful it is to meet like this!'[40] She told them that what she was particularly missing were cigarettes and music. The only way of passing the time was to recite her songs and poetry over and over again to herself. Titterton delighted in telling the *Express* all about the twenty-minute visit: 'She looked wan and was worried about the children. She spoke little about the charge against her, but from her conversation it was plain that she had not the slightest doubt what the outcome would be. She discussed plans for the publishing of her songs and again and again she spoke of what she would do "when it is all over and I am free again". Towards the end of the brief interview, she said to me wistfully, "Oh! I am so hungry for some music."'[41]

Titterton bent towards her and softly hummed a verse from one of her songs that he was to record the next day. Clearly, he regarded the visit as an unmissable opportunity to plug his new recordings in the press: 'Lozanne went into ecstasies. It was pathetic to see her. She told me she was sleeping badly and that it would help if she was allowed to compose songs while in prison.'[42]

Beatrice asked if there was anything she could send her and Alma requested some strongly perfumed soap, as she hated the overpowering prison smell of disinfectant. After the visit, Titterton sent Alma a bundle of lyrics so that she could occupy herself setting them to music. Sensing Titterton's commercial instincts, Dr Morton returned them to him saying that the prison commissioners had decided that Alma couldn't have them. Writing to a friend, she admitted that her songs gave her some comfort.

> *How extraordinary the words sound of 'By Some Mistake' – I spent last night repeating them over and over again – to help keep my mind sane & off this tragedy – God grant that it all ends soon.*[43]

Meanwhile, whenever Lewis Manning or his partner visited her in prison, Alma asked after her children and wrote to them often.[44]

> *Darling Little John,*
> *This picture reminded me of Dinah's puppies, so I cut it out for you. I suppose you are using your garden tools now, unless the weather is cold at Bournemouth – like it is here.*

> *By by for now, Chipmonk – soon we'll be together again.*
> *A big big kiss and hug from your old mummie who*
> *loves you,*
> *Lozanne*
> *'God keep you night and morning*
> *God keep you everywhere.'*[45]

On 10 April, the inquest into Ratz's death was formally opened by the Coroner F. G. Lefroy, with Manning appearing for Alma and Marshall Harvey appearing on Stoner's behalf. The body was identified by Keith Miller Jones and Lefroy invited the jury to view it. The inquest was adjourned until 27 June. The next day, an hour and a half before the court was due to sit, a small group of women had gathered outside the magistrates' courts in Stafford Road in their eagerness to secure seats. An hour later, the queue had grown to about 150. Some had brought food with them for the duration but were disappointed when the proceedings were over in four minutes.[46] Stoner seemed composed but Alma showed 'signs of languor and leant her head on an upraised hand during the proceedings'.[47] The clerk announced that he had been in touch with the director of public prosecutions and the case had been remanded until 11 April when Irene, Dr Rooke, Dr O'Donnell, Stoner's family, the police and the pathologist who had examined Ratz's body would all be called as witnesses.

On 11 April, the story was headline news again in the *Bournemouth Daily Echo*: 'Bournemouth East Cliff Murder Charge; Woman and Chauffeur in Court, Sensational Allegations by the prosecution'.[48] The Police Court was crowded with members of the public, as well as a knot of twenty-five journalists waiting to hear every salacious detail of the case. Four police officers and a police sergeant were called in to regulate the queue to get into the court. The function of these preliminary or committal hearings was to establish if there was sufficient evidence for Alma and Stoner to be tried by a judge and jury. This would be decided by a panel of lay magistrates, none with any legal training. Stoner was first to arrive just before eleven o'clock, then Alma was driven up in a large car accompanied by two wardresses who drew the blinds as they approached the rear entrance to the courts. In front of the magistrates' bench was Ratz's chair and some cushions. Laid out on a table were various exhibits including a folded pair of brown trousers, two suitcases, shirts, ties and crêpe de Chine pyjamas. There was also a stained pack of playing cards as well as the library book and the wooden mallet. Alma entered the dock first in a beige dress, wearing a large pink carnation. Though their eyes met, there was no sign of recognition between her and Stoner. As each of them was a self-confessed murderer, the director of public prosecutions, represented in the court by G. R. Paling, had no choice but to put both of them on trial. Significantly, he had not charged them with conspiracy to murder, which would have entailed the prosecution proving a plot or agreement between them. By charging them individually, the DPP would leave it to the jury to decide which of the two was telling the truth and by charging them in the same indictment, Alma and Stoner would be tried together, unless the judge decided otherwise. Lewis Manning requested that Stoner's name should appear on the indictment first. Alma had originally been charged with attempted murder. She was only charged with murder after Stoner had been arrested on the platform at Bournemouth railway station and subsequently charged at Madeira Road. There were, Lewis Manning believed, 'certain advantages accruing to the order in which the persons were charged'. But Marshal Harvey objected. Alma was charged with attempted murder first, so should appear first. The magistrates agreed: Alma's name would appear on the charge before Stoner's. A plan of the Villa Madeira was distributed. The events of 24 March were discussed, as was Alma's confession and arrest. Paling talked through Alma and Stoner's trip to London and suggested that the prosecution evidence would 'clearly show that the relations between the accused persons were not confined to those usually expected between a servant and the wife of his master'. With English understatement, he also guided the magistrates by saying that, in light of the evidence, they might think that the statement that Alma had made as to having struck the blows 'was not perhaps as strictly accurate, but that the statement made by Stoner that he was the person who struck the blows, may possibly be a little more accurate account'.[49]

The court heard evidence from the salesmen at Harrods and the desk clerk at the Royal Palace Hotel as well as from Irene and O'Donnell. When questioned about what he had been treating Alma for, O'Donnell seemed uncooperative and refused to say. Whether this was simply professional discretion or an indication that he didn't want to volunteer what drugs he might have been prescribing for her was unclear. As lay magistrates rarely sat day to day, there were often several adjournments, so the case was adjourned until 24 April.

During these preliminary hearings only the prosecution made their case and there was nothing said in defence of Alma and Stoner. Consequently, there was a frenzy in the press, which widely reported the most lurid, gruesome and sensational aspects of the case, as well as the bizarrely mundane: 'Sensational Allegations by Prosecution';[50] 'Mr Rattenbury's Head Wounds';[51] 'Mrs Rattenbury's Pink Carnation'; 'Alleged Purchases at London Store'. The display of the clothes Alma bought for Stoner in London, unnecessary in terms of real evidence, was emblematic of what the press already felt that Alma was guilty of: she had purchased the sexual services of a young working-class man by indulging him with luxurious gifts and money; she'd written twenty-four cheques to him between 1 September 1934 and 5 April 1935 amounting to £37 6s 5d.[52] By sleeping with another man she had betrayed her husband, but by sleeping with a servant she had betrayed her class. The story that now began to emerge seemed a classic farce scenario, or the subject of a saucy seaside postcard by Donald McGill – the elderly miser cuckolded by a randy young servant and his insatiable wife. She was 'an inhuman ghoul' who had seduced and incited Stoner to commit a 'peculiarly horrible murder', a seaside Lady Macbeth.[53]

Given the sensational revelations from the preliminary hearings, the story was now picked up internationally. The *Vancouver Sun* printed an interview with Frank Rattenbury, who had been estranged from his father and Alma for many years. He was by then divorced and working as a director of the Marquis Shipping Company, endeavouring to promote a shipping service between British Columbia and Mexico. He was proud, if perhaps resentful, that he had achieved this position with no help from his father. 'In none of my business ventures did my father assist me. He believed in letting me shift for myself.' He relished the opportunity to publicly stick a knife into his father's reputation and right into Alma's back.

In sweeps of lurid color the picture of the early romance of Francis Mawson Rattenbury with the woman now on trial as his slayer, was painted today by Francis Burgoyne Rattenbury, his 36-year-old son. It was the picture of an eccentric architectural genius falling under the spell of a talented but self-seeking enchantress and sacrificing home, friends and reputation at her bidding. Rattenbury, who is remarkably like his father in appearance and mannerisms, sketched his stepmother Alma Rattenbury, alleged mallet murderess, as a twentieth century Circe who changed her victims, not into swine, but into the slaves of her ambition.[54]

He ominously added that 'there will be a lot of mention of dope at this trial and it won't be any surprise to me. I prefer to say nothing more about that now.'[55] Touch paper lit, he retreated to allow the British press to speculate feverishly.

With the Easter holidays ahead, it was arranged that Keith Miller Jones would take care of his godson at his London flat in Halkin Place that he shared with his sister, Katharine. With no communication from Ratz's older children in British Columbia, Lewis Manning wrote a letter to Daphne Kingham who was Compton Pakenham's sister. Thirty-four-year-old Daphne, who was always known as 'Pinkie', had first been sent from Japan to boarding school in England in 1914 following the death of her mother. She had married

Geoffrey Kingham in 1926 and they lived in Berkshire with their seven-year-old son, Michael. Manning wanted to know if Pinkie would look after Christopher in the school holidays, and was there any other way she might be persuaded to help Alma? Pinkie duly collected Christopher and took him home. She was intrigued by the sister-in-law she had never met, so she made an appointment to visit her in Holloway. Both being mothers with young boys, Pinkie and Alma took to each other as soon as they met. Alma clearly 'adored her children and they in return were always asking about her and champing to be with her'.[56] The prison interview room was bare and they had to sit opposite each other across a long wooden counter that stretched from wall to wall. Pinkie put her handbag on the counter and invited Alma to use her make-up. Mrs Grieg the wardress turned a blind eye as Alma started to make up her face. She told Pinkie that she was convinced that Stoner would not be convicted of murder and that the worst that could happen would be a verdict of manslaughter.[57] Pinkie updated Alma on how Christopher was doing and then asked what she had been up to. 'I've been scrubbing floors,' Alma replied. 'I don't know whether I should have been made to do this as I am officially innocent unless and until found guilty, but it was easier to acquiesce than to have a row about it.'[58]

Immediately after she left the prison, Pinkie was stunned to be contacted by the press with a proposition. Alma Rattenbury was the most talked-about woman in the country in the most sensational story of the day. Would Pinkie sell her own story, and Alma's, for £500?[59]

* * *

Lewis Manning was convinced that Alma was innocent, but nothing he could say or do would induce her to say a word prejudicial to Stoner. Whenever his name was mentioned, she refused to talk.[60] Alma had been told by Manning to write to Irene if she needed anything from home in preparation for the trial and advised not to discuss the case, but on Maundy Thursday her emotions were running high and for the first time she implied that Stoner was responsible for the attack on Ratz.

S[toner's] feelings must take some weighing up, but he'll be the same and not allow himself to think. Should think his remorse at what he's brought down on my head, the children's etc – smashed lives – would drive him a raving lunatic – a frightful responsibility to hold in one person's hands. God deliver me from such a hellish responsibility. I couldn't have courage to bear that pain; my own is more than enough in a hundred lifetimes as it is.[61]

Knowing that this admission might help Alma's case, Irene volunteered the letter – and another nine Alma had written her – to the police.

As Alma was not allowed to fund her defence with money from Ratz's estate, Lewis Manning received £400 from Alma's mother and her family in British Columbia, who committed to financing all her legal costs. Curiously, despite her insistence that she wanted to protect Stoner, Alma made no offer to assist with any of his legal costs, though she may well have been advised against this by her own legal team.

When Pinkie Kingham next went to visit Alma in Holloway, she was asked by the governor, Dr Morton, to come and see him in his lodge by the main gates. He told her that he was very sorry for Alma. She should never have been pressed by the police to make statements when she was under the influence of alcohol and drugs. He and her lawyers all thought that she was innocent and believed that she would be cleared of the charge if she would only tell the truth. They had assured her that by shielding Stoner she could not save him, but would simply be putting a rope around her own neck. As Frank Titterton's visit to Alma had now been reported in the newspapers, Morton told Pinkie that he was not allowing Alma any more visitors apart from her. Pinkie admitted that she had been offered £500 for her story by the press, and Morton impressed upon her that, 'If you accept it, I'll have nothing more to do with you.'[62] Galvanised by her conversation with Dr Morton, Pinkie visited Alma again and tried her best to persuade her to tell the truth, but Alma was stubborn and Pinkie found herself resorting to brutal tactics: 'It's not fair on the children. They have all their lives before them – are they to be known as the sons of a woman who was hanged for murder? You have no right to blast their lives to shield Stoner. You owe it to them to tell the whole truth, hiding nothing – and if you won't do anything for your own children, why should anybody else? You needn't expect me to go on looking after Christopher for you.'[63]

This was food for thought for Alma. She loved Stoner. But she loved her sons. She faced a stark choice; she must sacrifice her lover or risk leaving her children as orphans. The prospect for Alma was agonising.

She continued to write to the boys, reassuring them that she would see them when she returned from her 'holiday':

Darling Little John,

I missed not hearing from my baby, this week, however, it will not be long before mummie is reading you stories again. 'Peter Pan and all the Fairies' – and oh! So many hugs and kisses first, my chipmonk. God bless you. Be a good little boy and do what you are told.

A big big kiss from your old mummie who loves you,

Lozanne

Finally, having anxiously waited for communication with the children, Alma received some letters from little John and wrote back, hopeful for the future.

Darling Little John,

I was very pleased to receive two letters from you this morning – and the little pictures that you had coloured.

Yes, it will be wonderful to see my baby again, you will have grown inches and inches by then, for it seems a very long time since I saw you, Chipmonk. However, in a short while, mummie will be with you again, and you'll have so

*much to tell me, and how your new teeth will have
grown!*

   Much love baby mine and God bless you,
   Your old mummie who loves you always and always,
   Lozanne[64]

                              * * *

The Police Court hearings concluded on 24 April. Some of the
crowd outside the court, many of them holidaymakers, had waited
for a glimpse of the protagonists for three hours. Despite the blaz-
ing sunshine and summerlike heat, Alma wore a large fur coat. In
the dock, 'with flashing dark eyes and intensely red lips',[65] she wore
another pink carnation. On behalf of the director of public prosecutions, Paling asked the magistrates to commit her and Stoner
for trial. During the reading of the charge, she adjusted the fur
collar of her coat and when asked if she had anything to say, she
said, 'I am not guilty. I reserve the right of cross-examination and
reserve my defence.' Stoner also said, 'I am not guilty and reserve
any defence.'[66] On Alma's behalf, Lewis Manning requested that
the case should be heard at the Central Criminal Court in London.
The assizes on the Western Circuit would next be heard in July
and he argued that it would be a 'great hardship' on Alma to wait
that length of time.[67] There was apparently no concern for how the
eighteen-year-old Stoner might be feeling, but Marshall Harvey
agreed. The trial would take place in Court Number One at the Old
Bailey, the most notorious courtroom in the greatest criminal court
in the world.

   On 1 May, Alma and Stoner were formally committed to trial.
The date for the next sitting of the Central Criminal Court was 21
May. Alma was also to be tried as being an accessory, having 'comforted, harboured and assisted' Stoner on the day of the murder. Her
solicitor now went about securing the best defence team that money
could buy. He was delighted to secure the services of Terence James
O'Connor, who had just successfully helped to change the law in

the case of Reginald Woolmington. He was a man of wit and charm as well as ambition, tall and well built with a ruddy complexion.[68] He was born in Shropshire in 1891 and at the time he represented Alma he was also the Conservative MP for Central Nottingham. He had fought in the First World War with the Highland Light Infantry and the Western African Frontier Force. He had been called to the Bar in 1919 and though he would have been the last to claim that he was a strikingly erudite lawyer, 'by his industry he paved the way to a presentation of his case which conveyed all that was necessary for a tribunal to consider'.[69] He was assisted by 34-year-old Ewen Montagu, the second son of Lord Swaythling. He had been educated at Westminster School and Oxford and had served with the Royal Naval Volunteer Reserve before being called to the Bar in 1924.[70]

Advised by Manning, despite the hugely negative press that had been aired since the preliminary hearings, O'Connor and Montagu were equally convinced that Alma wasn't guilty, but she still refused to cooperate. Time and again they pressed her to tell the truth, but whenever Stoner's name was mentioned she would refuse to talk. 'Oh, I cannot do anything to hurt him; I cannot sink so low as that.'[71] They were at an impasse; they couldn't help her if she refused to help herself.

As the weeks leading towards the trial passed, tensions increased at Holloway, particularly on the first floor landing where the condemned block was situated. Many years had passed since the execution of Edith Thompson, so the block was being redecorated. A new lavatory was installed for use in the three weeks Alma might spend between the passing of the death sentence and her execution.[72] Workmen passed up and down the passage with ladders and tools, the hammering was constant. The assistant housemistress at Holloway, Cicely McCall remembered,

I wished that some of the people in favour of capital punishment could experience the horror it generated among the women occupying the adjacent cells. The officers too were tense. They knew that if Mrs Rattenbury was convicted they would have to share

the duties of guarding her for those three weeks of waiting. Two
of them would have to lead her – or carry her – to the scaffold. I
was told that after the last hanging at Holloway, one of the officials present committed suicide, and two others left the service.
Certainly when I was there there was a deep dread among the
rank and file prison officers that they would be called upon to
participate.[73]

Meanwhile, unable to afford such esteemed counsel as Alma, and
with no offer of financial support forthcoming from her, Stoner was
reliant on whomever Marshall Harvey could secure under the Poor
Prisoners' Defence rules. The maximum fees for a capital offence
were 6 guineas for a solicitor, 11 guineas for junior counsel and
15 guineas for leading counsel. Consequently, this sort of work
was only taken on by inexperienced barristers and the less successful. For Stoner, it was to be the luck of the draw. Joshua Casswell,
who had assisted O'Connor in Reginald Woolmington's case in the
Court of Criminal Appeal, was not yet a KC. He had been working
as a barrister for twenty-five years and was forty-nine at the time
he defended Stoner. He had been educated at King's College School
and Pembroke College, Oxford, where he graduated in Classics in
1907 before taking an honours degree in jurisprudence in 1909.
After being called to the Bar, his first major case was the representation of some of the families of the 1,490 passengers who had been
lost on the *Titanic*, who sued the White Star Line for damages. At
the outbreak of war, Casswell went on to serve as a major in France
and had been mentioned in dispatches. He then went on to have a
varied career at the Bar and, of the forty murder cases he defended,
five ended in execution. Many of these cases Casswell accepted,
like Stoner's, as Poor Prisoners' Defences. The fees were so low that
they barely covered expenses, but Casswell claimed that he 'always
made a point of accepting these briefs whenever [he] was available,
not only because they provided [him] with a challenge of a stimu-
lating kind ... but because [he] considered them an essential part
of [his] professional duties'.[74] Tall with an angular, rugged face,

Casswell was a family man with three sons and a daughter. Though a man of great integrity, academic ability and modesty, Sir Bernard Napley was less than generous about Casswell's abilities as a barrister, feeling that he 'barely, if at all, knocked on the door of the middle grade'.[75]

*　*　*

Meanwhile, the news was dominated by the large-scale 'gas attack' at Chislehurst Caves in Kent as the Red Cross rehearsed their strategy in the event of chemical air raids. Women of the 60th Kent Voluntary Aid Detachment wore masks and protective rubber clothing. The disturbing front-page images were straight out of H. G. Wells.[76] In response to the expansion plans of the Luftwaffe, on 23 May Lord Londonderry announced that Britain's strength in the air was to be tripled by 1937; 22,500 men would be recruited and 920 extra machines manufactured.[77] But such ominous reports could not deflate the national mood of celebration at the beginning of May, when the whole country was overtaken with Jubilee fever. There was to be nearly a month of celebrations, starting with a royal procession through the city on Accession Day, 7 May, followed by a thanksgiving service at St Paul's.[78]

At Holloway, with two weeks to go before the trial, Alma was still refusing to tell her lawyers the truth and was determined to give evidence that might hang her. According to Manning, she would have done anything or everything – even risking the death sentence – to save Stoner.[79] So they were forced to confront her with 'callous directness';[80] if she persisted in shielding Stoner, she would hang. Nothing she could say or do would affect Stoner's position. But still Alma remained silent. With the greatest reluctance, Manning and O'Connor resorted to manipulative tactics to persuade Alma to save herself. Manning arranged with Pinkie Kingham to talk to Christopher. It was explained to him 'as gently and tenderly as possible'[81] that his mother was in great danger and that they needed him to persuade her to tell the truth. The lawyers' only hope was that 'mother love would be stronger than any other feeling'.[82] Meanwhile, the weather turned unseasonably wintry with snowstorms and blizzards across the country; it was the coldest May for ninety-four years.[83]

On 16 May, with only eleven days to go before the trial opened, Christopher was taken to Holloway by Pinkie to meet his mother. He saw her in the bare interview room. Alma had an eye infection so was wearing a bandage over her eye. She was delighted to see Christopher, but the effect of his visit on her was devastating. He begged her to tell all that she knew about the murder.[84] Finally, Alma broke down and, for the sake of her children, admitted that it was Stoner who had killed Ratz, not her.[85]

The lawyers quickly looked through the evidence and formulated a plan. With the story she had to tell, they decided that Alma must take the stand. She would be the star witness at her own trial. But it was a huge risk. O'Connor knew only too well that 'had Edith Thompson not gone into the witness box and given evidence on oath, the jury might have found a verdict other than the one they did find. Mrs Thompson insisted on doing so and in consequence, both she and her youthful lover, Frederick Bywaters, perished on the scaffold.'[86]

For Alma, it was a matter of life and death.[87]

* * *

Meanwhile, Stoner had been under observation at Dorchester, but on account of the suggestion of 'backwardness' and his youth, it had been recommended that he be transferred to Brixton prison to await his trial, where he could be observed by Dr Grierson and Dr Gillespie.[88] Brixton was 'dull and gloomy' with 'all the characteristics of a prison in the nineteenth century'. In 1902, it became the remand prison for male prisoners in the London area who could not afford or were not awarded bail, and in 1906 it had also become the main prison for debtors. Only the debtors were treated as prisoners and Stoner would not have had to work unless he chose to, but if he did he could earn 3s a week. Many prisoners awaiting trial chose to work making mailbags to make the days less monotonous. Stoner was allowed to wear his own clothes, read newspapers and even eat his own food. He could have had his own cell for 5s a week and this would be cleaned for a further 7s.[89] Though the doctors saw no signs of mental disorder or evidence of insanity, Dr Gillespie found Stoner tense, anxious and of a morbid disposition. When Grierson assessed him, Stoner claimed that he was backward at school, though reports from two of his teachers indicated that he was of average ability.[90] Despite never having mentioned it in his statements to the police, while at Brixton Stoner began to sketch out what would be the foundation of his defence – that he was a drug addict. He claimed that he had taken cocaine 'ten or eleven times' in the past few months.[91] Stoner had put on weight when he was in prison, and had slept and eaten well. He had given no indication that he might be experiencing withdrawal symptoms. He stated that on the afternoon of the murder he had taken two egg-spoonfuls of cocaine between slices of bread. The normal dose was from an eighth to a quarter of a grain; one heaped egg-spoon contained thirty-six grains. But when probed by Grierson about what cocaine looked like, Stoner told him that it was brown with black specks.[92] He'd obviously never even seen cocaine, let alone taken it.

The weekend before the trial was due to start, Saturday 25 May, Casswell visited Stoner at Brixton with John Bickford. Even before he arrived at the prison, Casswell had decided not to call Stoner as a witness, and this visit confirmed his instinct. In the barred conference room, Stoner sat 'silent and almost completely uncooperative',[93] insisting on a defence that in no way suggested that Alma was guilty. He was not interested in proving his own innocence but only in ensuring that Alma was not convicted. He insisted that he had committed the attack under the influence of cocaine. Casswell deliberately didn't encourage Stoner to give an account of what had happened on the night of 24 March. He knew that if he did, Stoner might easily insist on confessing to the murder. If that had been the case, by the rules of the legal profession, Casswell would not have been allowed to call any evidence to prove Stoner's innocence, but could only claim that the evidence brought against him was insufficient. Casswell genuinely wasn't sure if Stoner was guilty or not, but if he were to suggest in open court that Alma was guilty of murder, he was sure that Stoner would 'dramatically and emphatically deny'[94] that she had anything to do with it. He would declare that he was the killer and he alone. In his memoirs, Casswell felt that 'such loyalty may have been a loving demonstration of romantic passion, but it made the task of defending counsel extraordinarily difficult'.[95] It also meant that Casswell would not be able to cross-examine Alma at all forcefully. If he did so, Stoner might well interrupt him from the dock, swearing that he was guilty and the trial would be over. Essentially, Casswell would be entering the fray at the Old Bailey with his hands firmly tied behind his back.

ENTR'ACTE

SING SING, 12 JANUARY 1928

Mrs Snyder

This woman, this peculiar venomous species of humanity was
abnormal; possessed of an all-consuming, all-absorbing sexual
passion, animal lust, which seemingly was never satisfied.

– Trial of Snyder and Gray, 9 May 1927[1]

Ruth May Brown had been born to poor Scandinavian immigrants
in Hell's Kitchen in 1895. At the age of eighteen she joined the New
York Telephone Company and met her husband, Albert Schneider,
while working the telephone switchboard. A layout artist for *Motor
Boating* magazine, he was thirteen years Ruth's senior and had
yielded to anti-German sentiment when America entered the First
World War, changing his name to Snyder. He and Ruth married in
1915 and, despite his insistence that he didn't want children, Ruth
gave birth to a daughter, Lorraine, two years later. By 1923, the
Snyders had settled in the Queens district of New York City, 'that
Canaan of the white-collar worker, where addresses run dizzily into
five digits and uniform clapboard houses jammed cheek by jowl,
row upon row, block upon block ... into limitless monotony'.[2]

Like Edith Thompson, Ruth was stimulated largely by cheap
romances and detective stories, giving herself up to an inner life
of unachievable fantasy.[3] In 1925, by then a housewife, Ruth was

introduced to Henry Judd Gray, a salesman dealing in women's underwear. A God-fearing, timid and impressionable man, Gray was of Puritan stock and unhappily married to his wife Isabel ('a home girl'[4]), who was disinclined to join him at the Corset Salesmen's Conventions that frequently drew him away from home in New Jersey. Ruth represented a vigorous and colourful alternative. After several drinks one night, she complained that her neck and shoulders were sunburned 'almost raw', so Gray offered to rub them with some Vaseline he had at work. After hours in the offices of Benjamin and Johnes on 34th Street and 5th Avenue, Gray rubbed Ruth's shoulders. Both the alcohol and the intimacy made them bold and Gray offered Ruth a new corselet to try on. He never referred to his merchandise as 'corsets', insisting that they were 'intimate garments' or 'corselets'. With trembling fingers, Gray proceeded to fit it for her himself.[5]

Soon after Ruth and Gray had become lovers, Albert Snyder was plagued by a series of domestic accidents. A keen motoring enthusiast, one evening he had been changing a tyre on his Buick with the car jacked up. The jack slipped and the car lurched forward, and Snyder narrowly missed being crushed to death. Soon afterwards he was under the car, again tinkering with the undercarriage as the engine was left running. The night was cold and Ruth came out into the garage with a glass of whisky for him. After she had left, Snyder became drowsy and realised that the doors had closed shut and the garage was filling with carbon monoxide. It was a narrow escape. In July 1926, Snyder had been sleeping on the sitting-room sofa when he awoke gasping for air, to find that the gas tap directly behind the sofa had been turned on. In 1927, he suffered an attack of hiccups lasting several hours. Ruth treated him with a medicine that only seemed to make the condition worse and caused him to vomit. She later told Gray that she had administered bi-chloride. In all, newspapers at the time of the trial identified seven 'accidents' that had befallen Snyder in the two years before his eventual demise.[6] At the same time, Ruth tricked her husband into taking out life insurance policies for $1,000 and $5,000, and a third for $45,000 carrying a double indemnity clause.[7] In the event of Snyder's death by accident, Ruth would receive $96,000 in compensation.[8]

The affair between Ruth and Gray carried on for two years, with the lovers meeting in hotels and speakeasies around the city. Ruth played upon the trusting Gray's weaknesses, convincing him of her unhappy marriage. She relayed her revulsion at the sexual relations she was obliged to endure with her husband and started to suggest that they ought to 'do away with the governor'. She told Gray that Snyder was so violent towards her and their daughter that she had been forced to buy a gun. In time Gray found himself incited to hate a man he had never even met. When Gray was drunk or in bed with her during sex, Ruth begged him to help her kill her husband. In February 1927, while sleeping together at the Waldorf Astoria Hotel, they began to evolve a plan. They would drug Snyder senseless, then batter his head in.

Gray dutifully bought a phial of chloroform and a weight for a sash window weighing 5lbs. All he needed now was a rope. Unable to find anything suitable, he bought a coil of picture wire and gave the implements to Ruth to hide in the house. On Saturday 19 March, she arranged to be with her husband at a friend's party in Hollis Court Boulevard, a few minutes' drive from the Snyder home, leaving one of the doors at the house unlatched. Gray downed a large amount of whisky as he waited for Ruth and her doomed husband to return home and go to bed.

When Snyder was finally in bed sleeping, Ruth and Gray met in the bedroom to carry out their plan. Emboldened by alcohol, Gray brought the sash weight down onto Snyder's head, but this was just a glancing blow and only succeeded in alerting Snyder, who then grappled with his assailant as Gray tried to stifle his cries with the bedclothes. Gray struck again and hurled himself on top of Snyder's struggling body, dropping the sash weight, only for Snyder's desperate hands to find his tie and start strangling him. Gray screamed to Ruth for help – 'Momie, Momie, for God's sake, help me!' – before she brought the sash weight hard down on her husband's skull.

Gray straddled Snyder's dying body with his knees, squeezed his throat with his right hand and covered the weakening man's mouth with his left. Thinking Snyder now dead, Ruth and Gray then went about staging a burglary. They trussed up her husband's hands and feet with some neckties and picture wire, overturned the furniture and ransacked the drawers, throwing pillows about. Worried that Snyder might still be clinging on to life, Ruth was determined that Gray should make doubly sure. She found some more alcohol for Gray to steel his nerves and encouraged him to pull the picture wire taut around her husband's throat. Gray garrotted him.[9]

Certain that Snyder was now dead, Ruth placed her revolver in his hands in order to indicate an attempt to defend himself. She then asked Gray to tie her up and knock her unconscious so that it would appear that she had been attacked by a burglar. This is how she was found by a neighbour the next morning, who then called the police.

But the police were immediately suspicious of the inept attempts to make the crime look like a burglary gone wrong and suspected that Ruth was behind it. They quickly found Gray's name in her address book and one of her cheques made out to him. They duped her by saying that Gray had confessed to the murder. Enraged by his apparent betrayal, Ruth admitted that she had helped with the plan, but denied any active part in it. She also told them exactly where Gray could be found. Threatened with the prospect of the electric chair, Ruth and Gray turned on each other, each insisting that the other had struck the fatal blows. Ruth was arrested and sent to Sing Sing Prison. The courts denied them separate trials and, as a result, the trial at Long Island Courthouse evolved not so much as The State vs Ruth Snyder and Judd Gray, but as Ruth Snyder vs Judd Gray. Despite the joint accusation, as in the cases of Edith Thompson and Alma Rattenbury, it was Ruth who was the focus of the trial. For here was a heroine made for Hollywood, where the investigation of her appearance and sexuality seemed to be the primary concern of the press, if not the courtroom: 'Niagras of ink have flowed in appreciation of her blond hair, worn thick and coiled and high on her head, and of her shapely body. Her best features seem to have been her eyes. They held the deep intensity of blue ice.'[10]

Even before the trial opened, the press depicted Ruth as sexually voracious and deceitful; an aberrant, unnatural subspecies who preyed on weak men like Gray. The reporting of the case was salacious, racist and bordering on the pornographic:

A national-known reporter once told me, 'If she hadn't been on trial for her life, I would have made a pass at her myself.'[11]

Swedes are emotional and passionate. Norwegians are cold-blooded and deliberate. In this woman who was born of Swedish and Norwegian parents there was a strange mingling of the dominant characteristics of both races. She was passionate and she was cold-blooded, if anybody can imagine such a combination.[12]

For many, Ruth was the object of erotic fascination; while on remand she received 164 offers of marriage.[13]

The trial began on 18 April 1927 and lasted a monumental eighteen days, with fifty-eight witnesses giving their testimony. Three hundred and ninety potential jury members were examined before the final twelve men were sworn;[14] women would not serve on juries in New York until 1937.[15] The trial was the sensation of its day and inspired a flourishing business in counterfeit tickets to the courtroom, with spectators paying up to $50 for a seat. Hundreds of miniature sash weights mounted on stickpins were sold outside the courtroom as mementos for ten cents each. Justice Scudder had to remind the press and public that there were to be 'no photographers in the courtroom. No Minors or picnics.'[16] The trial, though, became a national circus and was attended by journalists, celebrities and Broadway playwrights in search of inspiration or titillation.[17] A journalist for the *New York World*, James M. Cain, who attended the trial, famously translated it into a new, hard-boiled style of fiction in *Double Indemnity* and *The Postman Always Rings Twice*. Perhaps most curiously of all, the trial was attended by Maurine Dallas

Watkins, a reporter on the *Chicago Tribune* who had covered the infamous Leopold and Loeb trial, which had taken place in Chicago in 1924. She had also written a play based on two other unrelated murder trials in Chicago the same year. Two married women, Beulah Annan[18] and Belva Gaertner,[19] were each accused of murdering their lovers. Both were ultimately acquitted but inspired Watkins's satire on the idea of American justice seen through the prism of the entertainment industry. This play, originally entitled *The Brave Little Woman*, went on to be a great success in the Broadway season of 1926, retitled *Chicago* and starring Francine Larrimore as the murderous heroine, Roxie Hart.[20] Belva Gaertner, by then a celebrity in her own right, attended the opening night, pretty much confirming Watkins's uncomfortable thesis that murder was box office and murderers were stars. In the play, Roxie observes, 'I'm so gentle I wouldn't harm a fly.' Before her trial opened, Ruth Snyder precipitated a near riot by announcing, 'Kill my husband? Why, I wouldn't hurt a fly.'[21] As if this blurring of fact and fiction weren't enough, Larrimore attended Ruth Snyder's trial together with Watkins, watching the latest instalment of real-life drama unfold before going on to play Roxie Hart that evening in the theatre.

Throughout the trial Judd Gray was depicted as an ordinary Joe seduced by a rapacious and immoral woman:

> That woman, that peculiar creature, like a poisonous snake, like a poisonous serpent, drew Judd Gray into her glistening coils, and there was no escape. That woman. Just as a piece of steel jumps and clings to the powerful magnet, so Judd Gray came within the powerful compelling force of that woman, and she held him fast gentlemen. This woman, this peculiar venomous species of humanity was abnormal; possessed of an all-consuming, all-absorbing sexual passion, animal lust, which seemingly was never satisfied.[22]

On 9 May, after deliberating for an hour and thirty-seven minutes, the jury found both Snyder and Gray guilty of murder; electrocution was mandatory. An hour after the death sentence was passed, on her way back to the jail, Ruth passed the prison chaplain and expressed her earnest desire to become a Roman Catholic; within moments, she was converted. When Ruth and Gray were hand-cuffed and driven to Sing Sing on 16 May, a raucous throng lined the route all the way from Long Island to the outskirts of New York shouting bawdy insults and jeering at the condemned pair.

Ruth's lawyers appealed. They insisted that the jury had been preju-diced by pre-trial newspaper judgements. They argued that the trial had been more like a circus sideshow than the execution of justice, with the proceedings compromised by the microphones, amplifiers and recording equipment in the courtroom, noisy crowds in the aisles and corridors, a press committee issuing ringside seats and spectators laughing, hissing and jeering throughout. Some indication of the public antipathy towards Ruth is apparent from an anonymous postcard that had been distributed to each of the judges of the Court of Appeals:

We will shoot you if you let that Snyder woman go free. She must be electrocuted. The public demands it. If she is not done away with other women will do the same thing. She must be made an example of. We are watching out.
THE PUBLIC[23]

Senator William Lathrop Love of Brooklyn dismissed any pos-sibility of clemency for Ruth based on her gender: 'Women should suffer the same penalties that are meted out to men for the crimes they commit. If a woman enters the competition with men, she has a chance to gain the same ends, and I see no reason why she should not suffer the same penalties.'[24]

If women were to embrace their new political freedoms and responsibilities, they must also accept the consequences of their actions, a belief that the *New York Times* delighted in supporting in an editorial: 'Equal suffrage has put women in a new position. If they are equal with men before the law, they must pay the same penalties as men for transgressing it.'

The execution was set for the night of 12 January 1928.

* * *

Shortly before her last evening meal, Ruth's lawyers paid her a visit, finding her a pitiful, terrified wreck: 'She was too far gone to know what she was doing. I never saw anything more terrible. I cannot describe her agony, her misery, her terror. I died a thousand times in the fifteen minutes we were with her. It was awful.'[25]

At eleven o'clock, with no reprieve from the governor, two matrons led Ruth out from her cell and through the green door into the death chamber. She walked unsupported. As guards adjusted the electrodes, Ruth gave her final words, 'Father, forgive them for they know not what they do.'[26] She was then fitted with the regulation football helmet that was wired to 2,000 volts. She would be the first woman to be electrocuted at Sing Sing since 1899 and only the third in American legal history.

But there was a last extraordinary twist to this already extraordinary tale of justice as popular entertainment. The moment of Ruth's death was infamously – and shockingly – captured on film. Among the twenty-four witnesses to the electrocution, all were men and twenty were journalists. One of them, Thomas Howard, was a young photographer on a special assignment for the *New York Daily News*. Posing as a reporter, he carried concealed in his trouser leg a tiny ankle camera. He secured a front seat in the death chamber, 12ft from the electric chair. As the state executioner shot the current through Ruth's body and it heaved against the leather straps, Howard clicked the shutter. The room was lit by indirect white frosted lamps, giving him excellent conditions to take the photograph. It took seven minutes for the current to extinguish Ruth's life. At 11.10 p.m., Judd Gray entered the death chamber. He made no speech and died within four minutes.

The next morning's front page of the *Daily News* carried a blurred picture of Ruth strapped in the electric chair in the midst of the electrocution, under the headline, 'Dead!' But if readers were appalled by this graphic image, it didn't stop them buying a copy of it; that day's sales of the *Daily News* increased by 750,000, temporarily giving the paper the highest circulation per head of population achieved anywhere in the world.[27] For his part in securing the scoop of the century, a 'nauseating violation of human decency', Howard received his boss's congratulations and a $100 bonus and his image became the 'most famous tabloid photo of the decade'. The *Washington Post* summed up the 'drama of violence':

> It was a grand show. It never failed once. It had no surprises, no Theatre Guild stuff, no modernisms. It was the good old stuff done well and fiercely. It was grim and grand. It moved slowly and inevitably like Dreiser. And it came at last, last night, to the magnificent, the tremendous, the incomparable curtain that the audience was counting on. Everybody walked out with a satisfied feeling. It was regular.[28]

Barely eight months after Ruth's execution, with unseemly haste, Sophie Treadwell's expressionist drama based on the murder, *Machinal*, opened in New York on 7 September 1928, starring Zita Johann with Clark Gable in his Broadway debut as her lover. The popular press had made Ruth Snyder a national celebrity. The trial had been dramatised in the tabloids as a real-life version of a hard-boiled Hollywood melodrama, with life-or-death stakes at their most heightened and their most cruel. But the image of an adulterous, unhappy wife caught in the moment of her death and plastered across the front page was more than the denouement of a national soap opera. For the women of the Jazz Age, on both sides of the Atlantic, it was a clear and savage warning.

RUTH SNYDER'S DEATH PICTURED!—This is perhaps the most remarkable exclusive picture in the history of criminology. It shows the actual scene in the Sing Sing death house as the lethal current surged through Ruth Snyder's body at 11:06 last night. Her helmeted head is stiffened in death, her face masked and an electrode strapped to her bare right leg. The autopsy table on which her body was removed is beside her. Judd Gray, mumbling a prayer, followed her down the narrow corridor at 11:14. "Father, forgive them, for they don't know what they are doing" were Ruth's last words. The picture is the first Sing Sing execution picture and the first of a woman's electrocution. *Story p. 3; other p'gs. 3, 28 and back page.*

Execution of Ruth Snyder

ACT THREE

Rattenbury's skull

CHAPTER FOURTEEN

THE OLD BAILEY

27–29 May 1935

A woman cannot be herself in the society of the present day, which is an exclusively masculine society, with laws framed by men and with a judicial system that judges feminine conduct from a masculine point of view.

– Henrik Ibsen, *Notes for the Modern Tragedy*[1]

At the heart of the City of London on the corner of Newgate Street and the street of Old Bailey stands the Central Criminal Court. It is built on the site of Newgate Prison, where English justice had been practised and retribution delivered for a thousand years. A 'bloody code' had prevailed in England between 1688 and 1815, when the number of capital crimes had grown to such an extent that by the end of the eighteenth century there were 220 crimes that were punishable by death.[2] Many of these related to property, but also included poaching, forgery, associating with gypsies and damaging Westminster Bridge.[3] Public executions took place outside the prison and over the centuries Newgate had become the site of popular, and ghoulish, entertainment. Local householders whose windows looked out over the gallows would rent out space at their windows on execution days for people to give parties, 'at which champagne flowed freely, immorality was rampant, and the writhings on the gallows of the dying prisoners were regarded as an enjoyable addition to the entertainment'.[4]

Public officials at the prison also gave what were known as 'hanging breakfasts',[5] when a feast would be served within the prison after the execution as the prisoner's body remained hanging at the scaffold, often pelted with rotten fruit or stones until the ritual cutting down of the body. So popular were these events that, in 1807, 80,000 people squeezed into the narrow street known as Old Bailey to see the execution of two murderers, but even before the arrival of the prisoners, several women were trampled to death, initiating a near riot.[6] Twenty-eight onlookers were killed that day and seventy sustained severe injuries. Concern over civic disorder at public executions, rather than any concern about the morality of the practice, resulted in public hangings being abolished in 1868, though private executions continued at the Old Bailey until 1902, when the gallows was relocated to Pentonville Prison.

The new building, designed by Edward Mountford, was opened by Edward VII in 1907. Parts of the frontage retained some of the stone from the original Newgate structure, with the remainder faced in Portland stone. Above the copper dome, which was designed to reflect nearby St Paul's, presided the bronze figure of Lady Justice, 16ft high, holding scales from her left hand to indicate the weighing of evidence, and a sword in her right promising that justice would be swift and final.[7] Uniquely, this figure of Justice was not blindfolded as she is usually depicted, as the Corporation of London were keen to stress that after many injustices and acts of cruelty on the Newgate site, justice in the twentieth century would no longer be blind, but clear-sighted.[8]

The weather was warm on Monday 27 May, with a light northeasterly wind.[9] Early that morning, Alma was driven from Holloway to the Old Bailey in a saloon car attended by two prison officers and assistant housemistress Cicely McCall who would sit with her in the dock throughout the trial. At the same time, Stoner was transported from Brixton in a Black Maria. They each waited in one of the ninety-six holding cells below the courtrooms, among a warren of dimly lit offices and tiled corridors, the women's cells being on a separate corridor to the men's. The cells were small and dark, little more than cubicles with weighty wooden doors and small windows protected by heavy iron bars. Each was tiled halfway up the wall, the rest distempered. On some of the walls, previous prisoners had written graffiti; others had carved their initials deep into the plaster. The only furniture was a wooden table and bench, both screwed into the floor. Alma and Stoner would wait in their respective cells until being called up to appear at 10.30 a.m.

The headline in that day's *Bournemouth Echo* declared there had been an 'All-night Queue for Villa Murder Trial'; 'amazing interest' had been taken in what had become known as 'the Bournemouth Villa Murder'.[10] F. Tennyson Jesse later revealed that an official engaged in the case was offered £500 from a newspaper as his 'rake off' if he could persuade Alma to sell her life story, such was the extraordinary interest in the trial.[11] On Saturday, the *Echo* had reported that there had a been a 'rush for seats' from well-known people who were keen to take up the 'privilege seats' behind the lawyers, as if trying to book the best seats in the stalls at a matinee.[12] There were few places among the fifty seats in the public gallery that morning as applications were oversubscribed, but most of those lucky enough to secure a seat were women.[13] Outside the building, unemployed men who had waited at the side entrance since eleven o'clock the night before headed the queue for seats, as they had done at the trial of Edith Thompson. A coffee-stall owner had supplied the queue with hot drinks and rolls throughout the night and one man had slept in the doorway until wakened by a policeman's flashlight.[14] At 1 a.m. he had offered to sell his seat for £2, but by the morning he was hoping to sell it for £10.[15] Pinkie Kingham had requested a place in the courtroom, but this hadn't materialised, so by 8 a.m. she had also joined the queue, which now numbered 100 people.

Above the pillared main doors of the Old Bailey was a quote from Psalm 72, 'Defend the Children of the Poor and Punish the Wrongdoer'.[16] Directly above the wrought-iron entrance gates was a sculpture of the recording angel supported by the figures of

Fortitude and Truth. Inside was a wide sweep of steps up a baroque staircase of marble and alabaster that led upwards to the majestic Upper Hall, the walls and floors of which were lined with Sicilian marble. The hall extended almost the whole length of the building and gave access to the four main courts. The 67ft-high domed ceiling above was supported by sculptures of Prudence, Charity, Mercy and Justice and painted with images of Art, Labour, Wisdom and Truth by Gerald Moira.

The trial of Rattenbury and Stoner was to take place in Court Number One, which had been the backdrop to some of the most celebrated trials in British criminal history, including those of Oscar Wilde, Crippen, Seddon, as well as Thompson and Bywaters, a 'roll-call of English murder which gave the Central Criminal Court as a whole its own peculiar mystique and global reputation'.[17] The square, panelled courtroom of Austrian oak was lit by a domed glass ceiling and dominated by the vast dock at the centre, where the two prisoners would face the judge's bench ahead, the sword of justice in its dark red sheath hanging on the wall behind him. The judge and the accused, the dock and the jury would be barely 30ft apart from each other. The body of the court that day was completely packed with the press and law students, and the public gallery overflowed with 'fashionably dressed' women. Once the Usher of the Court announced the start of proceedings, the court rose as the judge entered in his full wig, red gown and white gloves. He carried a nosegay of flowers, a tradition that went back to the times when judges carried herbs to counteract the stench of the foetid Newgate Prison.[18] He also held a neatly folded square of black cloth, which he would wear when passing sentence of death, the black cap.

Richard Somers Travers Humphreys was sixty-eight, born in London and educated at Shrewsbury School and Trinity Hall, Cambridge.[19] He had been called to the Bar in 1899 and had appeared as junior counsel on behalf of Oscar Wilde in his disastrous libel suit against the Marquis of Queensbury, as well as appearing for the prosecution against Crippen, Seddon, Roger

Casement and George Joseph Smith. In 1922, he had read out Edith Thompson's love letters in the same courtroom to deadly effect. Since then he had always been 'distressed by the morbid curiosity which [brought] crowds to a "spicy" murder trial'.[20] As a prosecutor it had been said of him that he was 'so damned fair that he [left] nothing for the defence to say'. As a judge he would go on to preside over the trials of James Camb, the 'porthole murderer', in 1948 and the Acid Bath Murderer John George Haigh a year later. His extraordinary career was considered to be 'the story of criminal law of his time'. He was known to be witty and clubbable, though from a distance could seem 'fierce and somewhat intimidating'. Humphreys was accompanied by the aldermen of the City of London, who took their seats beside him. There was great anticipation as the court waited for the arrival of the two prisoners.

Despite having never attended a trial before, Barbara Back, a fashionable writer of short stories ('pitched between Maugham and Michael Arlen'), had been sent by the *Daily Mirror* to cover it, examining the process of the law in England and how a trial was carried out: 'I was surprised when I got into my seat at the smallness of the court. I don't know why but I had always imagined the Old Bailey to be enormous. The kindness of the officials and of everybody present, and the dispassionate look of the faces of the jury, seemed as it should be. The human element was missing. But the moment the prisoners were brought into the dock, everything changed.'[21]

Alma was the first to walk up the stone steps from the holding cells to take her place at the right-hand side of the dock rail. She was wearing a fox fur over a dark blue coat and navy blue silk dress with a blue-and-white spotted scarf. Her hair was braided around her ears[22] under a blue straw hat, her elbow-length gloves of dark blue suede. Her face was lightly powdered and her lips reddened. Back was enthralled by Alma's looks and stylish clothes: 'She is more than a pretty woman; her face is attractive with its large, perfect eyes, short nose and thick-lipped mouth. She was said to be thirty-eight. She looked much younger.'[23]

For, despite the joint accusation, Alma was the star of the

show. As she waited for Stoner to join her from the cells below, she glanced around the court, her face half hidden by her fur. This would be the first time they would have seen each other since the night of the murder. Stoner joined her at the left of the rail, dressed in the light grey suit she had bought for him at Harrods. She gave him a fleeting glance, but he didn't return it. The clerk of the court rose; the five-day trial had started. 'Alma Victoria Rattenbury and George Percy Stoner, you are charged with the murder of Francis Mawson Rattenbury on 28th March last. Alma Victoria Rattenbury, are you guilty or not guilty?'

With a 'faint smile', Alma said, 'I plead not guilty.'

The clerk then addressed Stoner: 'George Percy Stoner, are you guilty or not guilty?'

In a clear voice, Stoner declared, 'I am not guilty.'

At this point, Alma's counsel, O'Connor, leant along the bench and told Casswell, 'Mrs Rattenbury is going to give evidence against your boy.' Casswell was staggered. It was the first indication he had had that Alma 'was going so far in her efforts to save her own neck as actually to give testimony' against his client.[24] Still recovering from the unwelcome news, Casswell asked Mr Humphreys if the jury might retire as they discussed Alma's letter to Irene of 18 April. He felt that it showed the 'distinct intention to throw the responsibility' onto Stoner and would have a 'very bad influence upon the minds of the jury'. He asked for the document to be excluded or to grant Alma and Stoner separate trials. But Humphreys didn't see the necessity – he would guide the jury as necessary and the trial would go ahead. The jury, ten men and two women, returned and were sworn in.

As was the form, the trial would start with the case for the prosecution. The crown's prosecuting counsel, Reginald Croom-Johnson KC, was born in 1879 and, after studying law at London University, was called to the Bar in 1907. He served as a lieutenant with the King's Own Yorkshire Light Infantry in the First World War, before returning to the law and developing a practice that specialised in tax and finance.[25] In 1929, he was elected as the Conservative MP for Bridgwater in Somerset where his speeches were 'competent rather than enlivening'.[26] His chief recreation, the *Daily Mail* yearbook for 1934 noted, was stamp collecting.[27] In court he was known to be 'dignified' but to have a 'slight pomposity of manner'.[28] On the other hand, his junior counsel, forty-year-old Edward Anthony Hawke, was a hugely popular figure with a wealth of experience in criminal trials, which Croom-Johnson lacked. He had been educated at Charterhouse School and Magdalen College, Oxford before being called to the Bar in 1920. He was regarded as a quiet, fair but very determined prosecutor. In his opening speech, Croom-Johnson stated:

> It is the submission of the prosecution in this case that the rela-
> tionship between Mrs Rattenbury and Stoner had ceased to be
> that of the wife of the employer and the man employed but had
> become an adulterous intercourse. On their going back to the
> Villa Madeira [after the trip to London], where Mr Rattenbury,
> the somewhat elderly husband, was residing, the situation was
> likely to be one of some difficulty, and the prosecution submits
> that Mr Rattenbury stood in the way of their indulgence in this
> guilty passion.[29]

Alma and Stoner had 'set out to get rid of Mr Rattenbury who ... stood in their way'.[30] They had only failed to kill Rattenbury out-right, he argued, because Alma had not the strength to do so. At one point in his speech, Croom-Johnson held up for the jury to see for the first time Exhibit No. 7, the deadly mallet. Barbara Back was enthralled by the way Croom-Johnson laid out the facts of the case: '[He] began to tell us the story of the lives of those people so simply and clearly, lives not unlike our own ... after sitting in the court for several hours, you become unconsciously part of the machine. Your heart stops aching for the prisoners. You can look at them without feeling cruel or inquisitive. You watch the judge, wondering if he will show by the flicker of an eyelid what he is feeling.'[31]

But the length of Croom-Johnson's hour-and-twenty-minute opening speech resulted in inertia as far as Back was concerned, as she felt 'lulled into a sort of coma by the droning of the KC's voice'.[32] After concluding his speech at 12.12, the first of the witnesses for the prosecution was summoned. The established procedure was that the witness would first be questioned by the counsel that had called them (that is, the defence or the prosecution). In this 'examination in chief', the witness was not allowed to be asked 'leading questions' (those that suggested the answer).[33] The opposing counsel had no such restrictions in their cross-examination that followed, having much more freedom to question the witness.

Stoner's grandmother confirmed his visit to collect the mallet on the day of the murder. During cross-examination by Casswell, she outlined her grandson's lonely childhood and his backwardness as a boy. She'd noticed that since he had started working at the Villa Madeira he'd been looking pale. She firmly declared that he was 'a good lad ... an extraordinarily good lad'.[34] This was echoed by Stoner's Uncle Richard's evidence – he was 'the best boy that I have ever seen in my life'[35] and he too had noticed how pale Stoner had become since Christmas. As soon as Casswell began to cross-examine the early witnesses, he too referred to Stoner as a 'boy', preparing the way for his defence of a guileless young man dominated by a sex-hungry vixen. 'He was a decent, respectable boy, was he not?'[36] 'Did this boy, Stoner, live with you?'[37]

This polarisation of the characters of Alma and Stoner would continue to develop throughout the trial, supported not only by the prosecution, but by Alma's defence as well, so that it became less an investigation of the facts and more a trial of character.

The most anticipated evidence of the opening day of the trial was that of Irene Riggs, the first witness who had intimate experience of daily life at the Villa Madeira. Smartly attired in a green dress and white hat,[38] she described the unusual scenario at the Villa Madeira, the events leading up to the crime and those that followed it. She was determinedly loyal to Alma, and would reiterate and clarify the points that she had come to make on her friend and employer's behalf. Casswell thought her ('this domestic servant') 'one of the strongest witnesses'[39] he had ever cross-examined. Essentially, she would attempt to paint Alma in a much more sympathetic light than she had hitherto been depicted in the press. But she was also keen to focus the blame for the murder firmly on Stoner. Crucially, despite Casswell's objections, Alma's letter to Irene was read out with the incriminating implications of Stoner's guilt:

> S.'s feelings must take some weighing up, but he'll be the same and not allow himself to think. Should think his remorse at what he's brought down on my head, the children's etc. – smashed lives would drive him a raving lunatic – a frightful responsibility to hold in one person's hands.[40]

Irene was cross-examined by O'Connor first as Alma's name was first on the indictment. It was soon apparent that both he and Irene had the same objective – to save Alma's neck. Stoner was depicted in a darker, more insidious light:[41] he carried a knife and, Irene testified, he had threatened Alma with violence, though it was revealed that the gun that Stoner had threatened Alma with wasn't dangerous at all – it was a child's toy.

Led by O'Connor, Irene talked about the drunken condition Alma was in when the police arrived at the Villa Madeira on the night of the attack, 'raving about the house', trying to kiss the police and barely able to hold a coffee cup, so hoping to undermine any of the statements she had made during that period claiming that she was responsible for the murder. Irene then proceeded to volunteer information that she had apparently not shared with the police. She stated that on the morning of 25 March, Alma had whispered to her, 'Tell Stoner he must give me the mallet', clearly implying that Stoner had hidden the murder weapon. At the same time, on that morning before Alma was taken away, Stoner had asked Irene in the kitchen, 'I suppose you know who did it?' Irene had answered, 'Well?' And nothing more was said. Having established this, and his cross-examination apparently finished, O'Connor was about to sit down when Irene carried on: 'There's something else on the Tuesday I remember. I asked Stoner *why* he had done it.'[42]

There was a 'perceptible raising of the tension'[43] in the court as Humphreys asked O'Connor if he'd like to continue questioning Irene. O'Connor accepted the gift horse offered, and Irene continued: Stoner 'had seen Mr Rattenbury living with Mrs Rattenbury in the afternoon', meaning that he had seen them making love. However unlikely it was that the Rattenburys would be having sex in the middle of the afternoon after tea, this is what Irene claimed that Stoner had said. Already on the first day of the trial, here was not just the identification of the murderer, but a motive as well. Casswell, who was about to cross-examine Irene, was shocked that these exchanges had not been raised by the prosecution, who 'would not have left so important a piece of testimony to be elicited by defending counsel'.[44] Irene had deliberately held back this evidence until the trial, when she knew it would have the most impact and possibly throw the prosecution off course.

Casswell attempted to cast doubt on Irene's integrity – or at least her partiality – as a witness. She was more of a friend to Alma than a companion-help, wasn't she? Alma had always taken Irene on trips with her, had she not? That was, until the arrival of Stoner. For the jury's benefit, Casswell began to hint at the possibility of another love triangle at the Villa Madeira.

'Did you know from that day onwards that they were sleeping together?'

'Yes, but they did not at the [Randolph Hotel in Oxford].'

'You were sleeping with Mrs Rattenbury at a hotel, were you?'

Understanding his implication, Irene was quick to clarify, 'I was in a communicating room to Mrs Rattenbury's.'

Casswell pursued the issue further. 'You did not mind him being in the house, but you knew he was always going into her bedroom, did you not?'

'Yes.'

'Did you approve of that?'

'Well, it was not my duty to approve or disapprove. It just hurt me.'[45]

This was exactly where Casswell had wanted to lead Irene, to admit that she was at least emotionally attached to Alma and therefore not an objective witness. And perhaps, if Irene had felt sidelined by Alma after Stoner's arrival, she might have a very good reason for wanting to confirm his guilt in her evidence. Humphreys, sensitive to the intention of Casswell's questioning, clarified the issue with Irene himself.

'How did it hurt you?'

'Well, just because Mrs Rattenbury, shall we say, hurt my feelings.'

Irene was a servant, not an intimate who might complain of 'hurt feelings'. With her now surely feeling very uncomfortable about the direction of the questioning, Casswell took up his cross-examination of her again.

'You were not pleased, were you – perhaps naturally – having been a close friend of Mrs Rattenbury's for about four years, that suddenly this lad of seventeen should come in?'

'No.'

'You were not pleased about it, were you?'

'Not very.'

'I mean before that you used to call her "Jack", did you not?'

'Call her what?'

'Jack?'

'Never.'

'What did you call her?'

'I had no special name for her. I used to call her "Darling".'[46]

Casswell had coaxed Irene to admit that her relationship with Alma was much warmer than that of mistress and servant. The only witness from the Villa Madeira who could have informed Casswell that Irene might have had an intimate, masculine name for Alma – and perhaps a special attachment to her too – was Stoner himself.

Questioned about Alma's unusual and erratic behaviour, Justice Humphreys wondered if Irene felt that Alma's unusual and erratic behaviour might have been related to alcohol? Irene admitted that she 'always thought so'.[47] She was then asked if she had ever known Alma take cocaine, morphia or heroin, to which she protected herself with a qualified negative, 'No, not to my knowledge.'[48] It was the first time that the possibility of heroin had been mentioned and suggests that it must have been raised among the lawyers in their preparations for the trial. Finally, at 4.40 p.m., the court adjourned until the next day. With huge relief, Irene, an inexperienced young woman from the suburbs of Bournemouth, left the witness box after three and a half gruelling hours, her own character and behaviour as much under scrutiny as Alma's.

On Tuesday morning, sensational newspaper headlines continued to whip up excitement about the trial. The queue for the public gallery was even longer than the day before and the scene outside the Old Bailey was one of intense activity: 'Many well-dressed women who arrived in cars were disappointed in their efforts to secure seats.'[49] One enterprising young man identified a romantic *and* a business opportunity:

> I have been here since before midnight. I'm hoping to get married and if I can sell my place in the queue I may get enough money to set myself up in a little business. I am unemployed and a man I met yesterday told me he sold his place for £2, and while I don't like doing this – my girl knows nothing about it – I am quite prepared to wait. I've been out of work, apart from odd jobs, for several months and I would probably be sleeping out during the night in any case. I intend to come each night while the trial lasts.

A group of about thirty enthusiastic people who had waited all night and failed to get seats were moved on 'time after time' by the police.[50]

Before the start of the day's proceedings at 10.30 a.m., the public gallery was already crowded with people eager to hear the next instalment of this popular melodrama. Some women 'with picnic baskets containing vacuum flasks and sandwiches picnicked in court. Others crowded into their seats at the last minute before the judge entered.'[51]

Casswell began by cross-examining George Budden, the police

officer who had discovered the hypodermic syringe and needles in the washstand cupboard in Alma's bedroom, together with several of Christopher's strange drawings. One of these was the sketch of a boy sitting up in bed holding a sixpence with a man leaning over and threatening him with a stick, as if the man had put a long hypodermic needle right through the boy's arm.[52] There had been no investigation by the police as to why a thirteen-year-old might be regularly drawing such pictures. Irene was re-called and explained that she had never seen the syringe used in the house, but imagined it was used on Christopher when he'd had a bad leg a year or two previously. Despite the debate about drugs in the press and at the trial, there had been no forensic examination of the syringe to see what drugs it had contained, if any. As to the drawings, Irene admitted that 'all the boy's drawings were weird'.[53]

The day's most significant witness was Dr O'Donnell, who described the events of the night of 24 March. He was keen to reiterate that Alma's statements that night were unreliable as she had been drinking and he had given her half a grain of morphia. Cross-examined by O'Connor, he explained how Rattenbury's frequent suicidal thoughts had led to the violent argument between him and Alma on 9 July, the only other occasion that O'Donnell administered morphia to her – or certainly the only time he admitted to doing so. After the altercation with her husband she had been given a quarter of a grain and subsequently slept for eight hours, waking peacefully and refreshed the next day. On 24 March, she had been given *double* that dose, but could still not settle. The next day, when O'Donnell saw her at the police station, he stated that she was unable to walk without assistance. Alma was, he admitted, an excitable woman and, though not a chronic drunkard, she did drink too much and he had warned her 'to lead a quiet life and not to drink' at all.[54] But he had never suspected her of being a drug addict; she was 'averse to any kind of dope', which is, of course, exactly what he would say if he had been supplying drugs to her himself.

In cross-examining O'Donnell, Casswell attempted to explore the nature of the relationship between him and Alma.[55] As with her relationships with Stoner and Irene, Alma had confused the bound-aries between mistress and servant, employer and employee, doctor and patient. Casswell was at pains to make clear that O'Donnell's opinions were not the objective views of a medic, but those of a close friend. From August 1932 to March 1935, O'Donnell had made 100 professional visits to the house, and, between March 1934 and February 1935, he had earned £50 in fees from his visits to the Rattenburys, a substantial sum, though he insisted that when he was summoned, it was not related to Alma's temperamental fits but to genuine illness. He was questioned about Alma's admission of her affair with Stoner on 12 February and about her concerns that Stoner had been taking cocaine. O'Donnell's response to Stoner's apparent drug-taking seemed to lack any curiosity: he did not look for symptoms of addiction in Stoner; he did not ask how long it had been going on; nor did he enquire what effect the drugs had on Stoner or how he funded his addiction. Casswell informed O'Donnell that Stoner had claimed that he first found cocaine 'at home'.[56] This was assumed to mean at his parents' house, but nobody thought to clarify what Stoner meant. 'At home' might equally have meant where he was living at the time: the Villa Madeira.

Meanwhile, Alma sat through the whole proceedings with her eyes intent on the witnesses, showing no emotion even when her own statements were being read out, a warder and a wardress separating herself and Stoner. All through the parade of witnesses, in his neat grey suit, with his hair brushed back, his long, fair eye-lashes and his frank, open face, Stoner looked like a 'graven image'. Throughout the long day he sat with his elbow on the corner of the dock with his eyes half closed, watching Croom-Johnson, Casswell, O'Connor and the judge as they asked questions, but with appar-ently no interest in the witnesses, least of all the woman in the dock with him.

Alfred Rooke was then called to give his graphic evidence about the night of the murder and the severity of the injuries that Rattenbury had sustained.[57] He was subsequently cross-examined by O'Connor on Alma's behalf, who tried to establish where the assailant might have been standing when the blows were struck. Rooke insisted that the perpetrator must have been behind Rattenbury's chair during the attack because of the internal damage to his skull. He was the only professional witness called to discuss the injuries. There was no evidence from the police of whether Stoner or Alma were left- or right-handed, which might have had a bearing on the case. Instead of exploring this fruitful area, for the rest of the day the police witnesses were questioned, with Bagwell confirming that Alma had tried to kiss him and Mills reiterating the confession she had made to him.

'What did she say?'

'She said, "I did it; he gave me the book."'

'Did you know what book she was referring to?'

'No.'

'What else did she say?'

'"He has lived too long. He said 'Dear, dear.'"'

'Did those two sentences follow one another?'

'Yes. "I will tell you in the morning where the mallet is."'

'Up to that time had anybody mentioned a mallet in your hearing?'

'No one at all.'[58]

O'Connor pressed Mills about Alma's statement about the whereabouts of the mallet. At the time, why did Mills not question her further about where it was? His point was that if she were unable to locate the mallet, this would be further proof of her lack of complicity in the death of her husband.

Inspector Carter was then called and confirmed the exchange he had overheard at the bottom of the stairs.

'Do not make fools of yourselves.'

'You have got yourself into this mess by talking too much.'[59]

Carter did not agree with Irene that Alma's hand was shaking so much that she could not hold a coffee cup. Nor did he agree with O'Donnell's recollection that in the police station the next day Alma was unable to walk without assistance – 'I say she was quite normal'[60] – and he wanted to clarify that this opinion was based on twenty-three years' experience in the police force.[61] Together the police witnesses insisted, contrary to O'Donnell and Irene's evidence, that Alma was 'not incapably drunk' and should therefore be held accountable for the statements she made on the night of the murder. As far as the police were concerned, when she had said she had hit her husband with the mallet, she was telling the truth.

* * *

The third day, Wednesday 29 May, was by far the most anticipated of the trial, when Alma herself would take the stand: 'Everybody's attitude seemed to be one of expectancy.'

> Inside the court while the sunlight shone through the round glass ceiling there was a hum of conversation as the spectators discussed the latest phases of the trial. Behind the front row of counsel engaged in the case sat three women barristers – behind them rows of women in fashionable clothes with furs around their necks. Suddenly a hush fell on the court, eyes were turned to the judge's door. White gloves and black cap in hand, Mr Justice Humphreys gravely judicial in his scarlet robes and wig entered the courtroom. A pause. A man and woman appeared in the dock.[62]

At this point in the trial, the press and the public were already convinced of Alma's immoral character and her guilt. Tennyson Jesse, who was in the courtroom every day taking notes for her edition of the *Notable British Trials*, was as sure of these widely held assumptions as everybody else: 'In everybody's minds ... there was a picture of Mrs Rattenbury as a coarse, brawling, drunken and callous woman.'[63]

All she would be doing by going into the witness box was to confirm the prejudices that had been growing around her for months: 'There was probably no one in England, and no one in the court when the trial opened save Mrs Rattenbury, her solicitor and counsel, and Miss Riggs, who did not think that Mrs Rattenbury was guilty of the crime of murder.'[64]

At the start of the session, the court was advised that Dr Morton, the governor of Holloway, was seriously ill and unable to attend the trial.[65] Though his statement that Alma was still in a state of confusion when she arrived at Holloway was read out in court, it was not possible to cross-examine him about it. Dr Roche Lynch, a senior Home Office analyst, had been called to give evidence about the mallet, but now found himself also answering questions about cocaine addiction: 'Have you any experience of cocaine addicts?' His reply was 'No.'[66] Having established the witness's lack of expertise, Casswell proceeded to ask him all about the subject. Lynch confirmed that cocaine addiction could bring about anaemia, emaciation, jealousy, feelings of persecution and, significantly, hallucinations. Dr Grierson, who had examined Stoner at Brixton on a number of occasions, was called and confirmed that his behaviour had been normal, his conversation rational and that he had eaten and slept normally; he had even put on 8lbs since he had entered the prison, hardly indicative of a man addicted to anything. Cross-examined by Casswell, Grierson confirmed that Stoner had told him that he had been taking cocaine between slices of bread and that, at 4.30 on the afternoon of 24 March, he had taken two egg-spoonfuls.[67] One heaped egg-spoon contained thirty-six grains; just ten grains could result in death in less than an hour. Stoner had claimed that cocaine made him feel excited and that it generally made him curse and swear. Casswell hinted that Stoner had taken a large dose of cocaine and then experienced some sort of hallucination in which he believed he saw Alma 'living with', or having sex with, Rattenbury, thus motivating him to fetch the mallet and make his attack. But Stoner had suggested to Dr Grierson that the drug was a brownish powder with black specks, and in cross-examination by Croom-Johnson, Grierson confirmed that cocaine was always white.[68] This evidence seemed to discredit Stoner's supposed addiction to cocaine and the entire basis of his defence.

Several witnesses were then called from the different men's departments at Harrods to describe the suits, pyjamas, shirts, handkerchiefs, mackintosh and underwear that Alma had bought for

Stoner. The scheduling of these witnesses was unfortunate, being immediately prior to Alma giving her own evidence. Even before she opened her mouth the jury had heard that she was a middle-aged woman who had indulged her young lover, dressing him in clothes he could never afford, like a hired male escort. These witnesses to what Humphreys insisted on describing as Alma and Stoner's 'orgy in London' brought an end to the prosecution's evidence.[69]

Now came the moment that everybody who was assembled in the courtroom had come to see, the highlight of the show trial: Alma Rattenbury's turn to take the stand. Dressed in blue, a fox fur around her shoulders and her face shaded by a wide-brimmed straw hat,[70] Alma left the dock. Suddenly the atmosphere in the court 'became electrical'. Watching her, the theatre reviewer James Agate, covering the trial for the *Daily Express*, felt that 'one had the same kind of exhilaration as when at Lord's in a test match, some great player goes in to bat'.[71] Every eye followed her as she moved slowly through the well of the court to the right-hand side of the judge's bench and just to the left of the jury. The moment she entered the witness box, a 'sudden tension swept over everybody. Mrs Rattenbury held the stage.'[72]

CHAPTER FIFTEEN

AS FOR THE WOMAN

29–31 May 1935

> You may think of Mrs Rattenbury as a woman, self-indulgent
> and wilful, who by her own acts and folly has erected in this
> poor young man a Frankenstein of jealousy, which she could
> not control. Frankenstein was too great for her, Frankenstein
> pursued her and Nemesis, I suggest, came on the night
> of March 24.
>
> – Defence counsel, closing speech, 30 May 1935[1]

At 12.15 p.m., Alma took the oath from the witness box in a voice
that was scarcely audible, so O'Connor, counsel for her defence,
asked her to speak up. Her 'soft, musical'[2] voice then became
firm and everything she subsequently said could be clearly heard,
at times charged with feeling. When offered a chair by Travers
Humphreys, Alma thanked him, but said she preferred to stand.
Journalist James Agate noted that 'emotion was plain for all to see
in the hollow eyes of a woman no longer young and in the full red
moist lips continually pouting and twitching'.[3]

As with the various contradictory interpretations of her character
and behaviour, there was no consensus about Alma's performance
in the witness box. Tennyson Jesse was hugely impressed, finding
her 'an excellent witness'[4] in her 'simple acceptance of the values of
life as she knew it'.[5] To her, Alma seemed terrified of what might

happen if she diverted from the truth, even if that meant making statements that might depict her in a negative light: she was 'perfectly calm, but it was a frozen and not an apathetic calm'.[6] 'Her voice was low and rich. She gave a great impression of truthfulness, and she was astonishingly self-controlled. Only a nervous tick in the side of her face, which jerked perpetually, betrayed the tension in her mind.'[7]

But Casswell, tasked with cross-examining Alma, completely disagreed: 'She seemed vague and unconvincing, at times almost inarticulate; to some questions she replied merely with a gesture of the hands. She made so profound an impression on me that I thought – almost certainly mistakenly – that she was under the influence of a drug.'[8]

This suggestion that she was drugged seems highly unlikely, given that she had been living in custody since March, unless she had been administered a sedative. Casswell aside, the majority of observers in the courtroom at the time agreed with Tennyson Jesse that Alma acquitted herself very well. She stood in the witness box, clasping and unclasping the edge of it with her gloved hands[9] as O'Connor posed his questions. As well as embellishing her answers with theatrical gestures, she would frequently use the word 'absolutely' in her statements – one of the fashionable catchwords of the day – as well as using it when she wanted to make emphatic agreement. Early in his examination, O'Connor wanted to establish the status of the Rattenburys' marriage before Stoner arrived at the Villa Madeira.

'Since the birth of your little boy, did you and Mr Rattenbury live together as man and wife?'

'No.'

'Did you occupy separate rooms?'

'Yes.'

'On what terms were you with your husband?'

'Quite friendly.'

'No marital intimacy, but you were quite cordial?'

'Absolutely.'

'Was your married life happy?'

'Like that.'[10]

At this point, Alma 'gave a shrug and a slight wave of her hands', which Agate felt 'perfectly conveyed timeless indifference'.[11] Barbara Back thought it a 'meaning shrug',[12] expressing nothing specific, but the gesture of a woman who was resigned to disappointment. Alma confirmed that, though he could be charming, Rattenbury was mean with money and often ill tempered. He frequently had suicidal thoughts and she had spent much of her married life trying to placate him. The marriage was stale and sexless, but apart from occasional rows or sulks, it remained steady.

'Were you fond of your husband?'

'I did not love him, no; I was more of a companion than anything.'

'If he had wanted his rights as a husband would you have been ready to grant them to him?'

'If he had wanted what? Oh no, I do not think so.'

'In March of 1935?'

'Oh no, I do not think so. Decidedly not.'

'Were you fond of this boy?'[13]

Alma fought to express herself, to answer this question truthfully, her mouth twitching with nervous strain. Over in the dock, for the first time in the trial, Stoner began to show signs of emotion. He became restless and began to fidget. Alma leaned over the witness box, her hands outstretched as she barely breathed the words, 'I loved him.'[14]

'I suppose you told him that you and your husband had not been living as husband and wife?'

'It was obvious to anyone living there. They would know it.'

'He would know it?'

'Naturally.'

'Did you tell him you were looking for sympathy?'

'No, most decidedly not.'

'You were looking for that, were you not, from someone?'

'No, I was certainly not.'

'It was just an infatuation, was it not?'

'I think it was more than that?'

'You fell in love with him?'

'Absolutely.'[15]

Again and again, despite his lower social status, despite his youth, Alma stated that she loved Stoner. Whatever the court or the press and public beyond the Old Bailey might think, for her it was not just physical infatuation, but something more substantial. As Tennyson Jesse later commented, she 'had created something that to her was beautiful'.[16] Though Alma now had the opportunity to lay the blame for the murder fully on Stoner, she used any way she could to show him in a more positive light. When Casswell attempted to cajole her to confirm Stoner's drug addiction, she was no help, her half-hearted corroboration of Stoner's predilection for cocaine convincing nobody. And despite the fact that Stoner had become so violent and jealous that she had had to consult Dr O'Donnell and admit her affair in order to get his help, she now protested that she did not take Stoner's threats seriously, attempting to mitigate the effect that Irene might have had by her focusing on Stoner's increasingly violent behaviour. Alma was so truthful in the witness box that many of the admissions she made seemed to pass by both defence and prosecution un-noted. On first hearing what Stoner had done, she told O'Connor, her immediate instinct, when she realised the gravity of the situation, was to protect him, even if it meant taking the blame herself, whatever the consequences.

'What was the thought uppermost in your mind when you heard the news from Stoner?'

'Upstairs?'

'Yes.'

'After he told me, he was about five minutes.'

'After he had told you in bed?'

'To try to protect him.'

Travers Humphreys then clarified her point:

'To protect?'

'To protect him – that is Stoner.'[17]

She had loved Stoner at the time, and as was clear from her evidence in the witness box, she still did.

The most damaging of the crown's questions were related to the location where Alma and Stoner had sex. She admitted that they would most often sleep together in her bedroom and in her bed. Croom-Johnson was aghast at the thought.

'Did John sleep in the same room?'

'Yes, but in another bed at the other side of the room.'

'It is not a very large room?'

'No, but little John was always asleep.'

'Are you suggesting to members of the jury that you, a mother fond of her little boy of six, were permitting this man to come into your bedroom with you, in the same room where your little innocent child was asleep?'

'I did not consider that was dreadful; I did not consider it an intrigue with Stoner.'[18]

None of Alma's protestations that her son was a heavy sleeper would soften the impact of this unpalatable fact. Not only was she a deceitful and adulterous wife, she was an immoral and depraved mother.

'You told me ... that on the Saturday night Stoner was intimate with you?'

'Yes.'

'In your room or in his room?'

'My room.'

'With little John in bed in the room?'

'But he was sound asleep.'

'With little John in bed in the room?'

'Yes; he was sound asleep.'[19]

Tennyson Jesse felt that this 'very shocking'[20] revelation was the thing that most damaged Alma's character in the courtroom and with the press, but the fact that she was prepared to be candid about a fact that might colour the jury's perception of her also convinced Tennyson Jesse of Alma's absolute reliability as a witness.

Throughout her evidence Alma rigorously stuck to the story that

she had decided to tell. For the sake of her children, she was determined to extricate herself from the confessions she had made on the
night of the murder but without giving the crown too much evidence
with which to hang Stoner. She did so by preserving, as Casswell
noted, 'this impenetrable barrier of loss of memory'.[21] She said that
she remembered seeing Ratz in the chair, the blood, treading on his
dentures. Then she had deliberately tried to make herself insensible,
so poured herself a glass of whisky, but after that she didn't remember anything; not the arrival of the police, not the statements she
made, nothing.

'I have tried in the last two months very, very hard to remember
with piecing together and still cannot.'[22]

'I felt as if I was the one who had been hit over the head.'[23]

'It is all absolute double-dutch to me.'[24]

'I cannot remember.'[25]

For the only time in her testimony, Alma struggled to control
her emotions as she admitted that the last thing she remembered of
Stoner that night was his kissing her goodnight: 'I remember Stoner
kissing me goodnight in my bedroom, and I cannot remember going
downstairs to the car, but I remember little John at the door, and
those are the only things at the Villa Madeira I remember after that
awful night.'[26]

Apart from what Croom-Johnson dismissed as these 'trifling
things' – the last image of her son, the last goodbye from her lover –
her mind was a complete blank.[27] As Dr Morton was too ill to be
cross-examined about her state of mind on the day after the murder,
the court had to accept his statement that she was 'very depressed
and seemed confused and kept repeating the same sentence over and
over again'. If Alma said she had lost her memory, then that was that.

Alma had been questioned for three long hours, her sincerity and
candour convincing many of her essential truthfulness and honesty.
She revealed herself as an unhappy woman, all too aware that she
had been foolish and had committed a great wrong, though she
didn't quite understand how or why it had led to her current position in the dock. Moreover, she seemed genuinely anxious to make

amends.[28] Alma left the witness box pale but composed, having altered the perceptions of many in the courtroom and the jury who had listened to her: 'The woman who at first had seemed so guilty, was seen to be undoubtedly innocent.'[29]

That night's *Evening Standard* covered the trial in six of its thirty-two pages, including the front page. Such was the interest in the case following her evidence that the £500 'rake off' that had been offered by the press on Monday to secure her life story was raised – in writing – to £3,500. If this was the commission alone, the sum to pay Alma would have been astronomical. But 'None of the offers were considered for a moment.'[30]

Alma's performance in the witness box that day had a profound effect on James Agate, who was covering the trial for the *Daily Express*, but now found himself 'immensely moved' by it. After watching her give evidence, he wrote about her at length in his diary, casting her as the contemporary successor to the French literary heroines, Madame Bovary, Cousin Bette and Therese Raquin:

It was all very like the three French major novelists. The way in which the woman debauched the boy so that he slept with her every night with her six-year-old son in the room, and the husband who had his own bedroom remaining cynically indifferent – all this was pure Balzac. In the box, Mrs Rattenbury looked and talked exactly as I have always imagined Emma Bovary looked and talked. Pure Flaubert. And last there was that part of her evidence in which she described how, trying to bring her husband round, she first accidentally trod on his false teeth and then tried to put them back into his mouth so that he could speak to her. This was pure Zola. The sordidness of the whole thing was relieved by one thing and one thing only. This was when Counsel asked Mrs Rattenbury what her first thought was when her lover got into bed that night and told her what he had done. She replied, 'My first thought was to protect him.' This is the kind of thing which Balzac would have called sublime, and it is odd, so far as I saw, not a single newspaper reported it.[31]

The next morning, he also wrote enthusiastically about Alma's performance in the *Daily Express*:

> [O]ver and over again she knocked two questions into one, like
> a skilful golfer with his approach shots. Asked whether she
> became Stoner's mistress, she replied 'In November.' Invited to
> say whether her banking account was overdrawn, she made the
> succinct answer, 'Always!' The facts of this case might be mate-
> rial for a great novelist. She had been Stoner's mistress as a result
> of her husband's consent that she should lead her own life. She
> thought the boy was four years older than he was. She had tried
> to end the affair through comparison in the matter of age. She
> had had no inkling of anything wrong until Stoner came into
> her bedroom and said he had hurt her husband. She had tried
> to revive her husband and had fallen into hysterics stepping on
> his false teeth which she had tried to put back so that he might
> speak to her! She remembered nothing further, except the face
> of her little boy standing in the doorway, until some days later
> in Holloway. She spent over three hours in the witness box. The
> sitting closed with Stoner's counsel insisting upon the difficulties
> of joint defence, and inviting the jury to disabuse their minds of
> the impression that there was any parallel between this case and
> that of Thompson and Bywaters.[32]

Tennyson Jesse believed that the courtroom was haunted by the
trial of Edith Thompson, 'an echo of that tragedy'.[33] But Travers
Humphreys, who was present at both trials, disagreed: 'I do not
believe that the jury were in the least influenced by what happened
some thirteen years earlier ... and I am certain I was not.'[34] But
the next day, in his opening speech for Stoner, Casswell conjured the ghost of Edith Thompson as a warning to both Travers
Humphreys and to the jury:

> Many years ago, in this very dock stood two defendants, Mrs
> Thompson and Bywaters, and they were accused together of

murder. You may remember that, and if you do, and if you have confused it with this in any way, think again, because in that case there was evidence beyond dispute that the two people before the jury were both there when the fatal blow was struck. You might have read about the case, since many doubts have been expressed as to whether one of those two people was righty convicted. That is the sort of thing you will be particularly careful to see does not happen here. There must be no mistake. Can you imagine any crime which bears less evidence of having been the result of two people working it out before?[35]

Stoner's parents were then called. His father was questioned about their son's background and poor schooling. He outlined how Stoner had changed in manner and appearance since he had started working for the Rattenburys. Mrs Stoner briefly confirmed the last time she had seen him on the afternoon of 24 March. To the *Daily Mirror*, the Stoners were tragic figures, traumatised by the ordeal that their only son was going through.

The tall man, tall, soldierly; the woman, frail, in tears ... they faced the most tragic moments of their lives, called as witnesses in the case in which their son is accused of murder ... In the dock, the pale, fair-haired lad watched them, heard his father tell in quiet, clear tones, of his weakness in childhood and then say, 'You couldn't wish for a better boy.' Soon the father left the box and passing the dock, he smiled. His smile bore a message of affection and encouragement to his son. Then the mother. Only for a little time was she in the box, her faltering sentences almost inaudible. To every mother her son remains a baby all his life and what must that poor woman have felt like! I had a lump in my throat and my heart ached as she answered the few questions that were put to her. She was crying when she stepped down from the witness-box. With lowered head she walked past the dock without a glance at the accused boy.[36]

Next Dr Lionel Weatherly was called from the Royal College of Surgeons. Weatherly was an elderly man who had been practising for sixty-two years. He had not worked in general practice since 1888 and had only known three cases of cocaine addiction, though several of addiction to other narcotics. He was so deaf that he used an ear trumpet, making his evidence painfully protracted as he struggled to hear and the rest of the court strained to understand him. Casswell began:

'It is said in this case that Stoner carried a small dagger. Do you place any reliance on that?'

'I cannot hear you.'

'It is said that Stoner carried, towards the end of his stay at the Villa Madeira, a small dagger.'

'I cannot hear that.'

An exasperated Humphreys then intervened. 'Cannot you hear?'

'I could not hear my Lord.'[37]

Weatherly told the court that cocaine addicts were prone to feelings of persecution and hallucinations and frequently resorted to carrying weapons to protect themselves. He had examined Stoner in prison and had noted that his pupils were dilated. He concluded that Stoner's paranoid behaviour and feelings of morbid jealousy on the afternoon before the murder were completely consistent with his having taken cocaine. However, another medical witness, Dr Robert Gillespie, a doctor of psycho-medicine at Guy's Hospital, was unable to confirm that Stoner was a drug addict. Humphreys clarified the medical evidence for the jury; Stoner's behaviour might not indicate an addiction at all, but something much more mundane, that he was 'very angry and very jealous of his mistress'. To make his point, the judge wondered if Dr Gillespie had ever read *Othello*?[38]

Because of the order of Alma and Stoner's names on the indictment, Casswell had the advantage of giving his closing speech on Stoner's behalf before O'Connor gave his in Alma's defence and before Croom-Johnson's on behalf of the crown. But Casswell was conscious, because of the restrictions Stoner had obliged him to adhere to in what amounted to a 'preposterous'[39] defence, that he was unable to make a really persuasive speech on his client's behalf. As he had done from the opening of the trial, he was determined to polarise the jury's perceptions of the two defendants, casting Stoner as a misguided innocent in contrast to the deceitful and dominating Alma. He admitted that Stoner had wielded the mallet ('he does not deny that it was his hand struck the blows'[40]), but argued that his mind was so disturbed by drugs that he could not be held responsible for what he had done: 'This cannot have been the actions of a sane boy?':[41] 'I shall ask you to say that this crime is, in my submission, almost inexplicable in a young Englishman – you might perhaps expect it in a sadist, a man who killed for the joy of killing, a man killer – you might expect it in a man of hot blood and of a Latin race, urged on perhaps by jealousy or some kindred emotion, but is it the sort of thing that one expects in a lad of seventeen or eighteen and an English lad?'[42]

Casswell argued that there was no motive for the crime other than to prevent the Rattenburys from going to Bridport. It was 'the clumsiest crime that could possibly be imagined': 'You get this clumsy crime committed in this clumsy manner with no chance of alibi, no attempt to escape, no chance of the defence of accident, no chance of a plea that it was suicide. Therefore [the jury] have a very exceptional case.'[43]

He went on to reiterate Stoner's unpromising background, the paltry education he'd had before he went to live at the Villa Madeira when he came under the 'domination of Mrs Rattenbury and became infatuated with her'.[44] Blithely ignoring the two women, he asked the gentlemen of the jury to look back to their own youth:

> [T]ry to put yourselves in the position of that boy who was a servant in the house, the house of a lady who is well known, a writer of music under the name Lozanne, a lady who provides him with more money than he ever had before, and finally offers herself to him ... Do you remember perhaps, the glamour of those days in the late teens – I feel sure that some of you do – the glamour of the older woman for a young man?[45]

Casswell insisted that it was the combination of Alma's louche example and Stoner's addiction to drugs that had brought about the change in his character. Why had he become to violently opposed to the trip to Bridport? 'It is suggested that that is the jealousy of a normal man. Do you think it is? In my submission it is not and it is not the sort of thing you expect to find in an English boy of eighteen.'[46]

Drawing his speech to a close, Casswell proposed to the jury that Stoner was guilty but insane because of the drugs that he was taking or that he was guilty of the lesser charge of manslaughter, not murder.[47]

After a short adjournment, Croom-Johnson began his closing speech for the prosecution. He apologised to the jury for having had to listen to a story 'of immorality and vice'.[48] He agreed with Casswell that Stoner had been dominated by Alma and that she had been responsible for transforming him from an inexperienced young virgin to a jealous and vengeful lover:

> Unfortunately, you may think in this case that what looked at one time to be not merely an ordinary English boy of eighteen, but an English boy of irreproachable character and manifestly, having seen his parents, of good upbringing, that this boy has done a great many things which possibly all of you would not expect a boy of those antecedents to do. It is no good trying to suggest otherwise to you; in all humility it is no good venturing to look at things through dark spectacles. Truth, it is said, is stranger than fiction. Cases that get into these Courts are not the ordinary cases of ordinary decent English life; we are dealing with exceptional circumstances and exceptional cases.[49]

Croom-Johnson argued that Alma and Stoner had planned the murder in order to remove Rattenbury as an impediment to their relationship and for Alma to inherit Rattenbury's substantial fortune. This was despite the fact that it was Alma's children and not Alma herself who would be the main beneficiaries in the event of

Rattenbury's death. Casswell felt this theory was as preposterous as the defence he had been obliged to present on behalf of his client:

> [Croom-Johnson] put to them the to me quite incredible suggestion that what had happened was that, in pursuance of a pre-arranged plan, Stoner had fetched the mallet and given it to Alma, who had then herself struck the fatal blows. I do not think Mr Justice Humphreys for one moment believed this fanciful prosecution theory.[50]

Finally, it was O'Connor's turn to speak in Alma's defence, which he did with great passion. But if she had expected that he would treat her more kindly than Casswell or Croom-Johnson had, she was in for an agonising shock. In defending Alma against the charge of murder, O'Connor felt it necessary to ally himself with what he assumed would be the same judgemental prejudices as the jury. Alma was not guilty of murder, but he admitted that she was guilty of adultery, deception and the corrosion of a youth; she might well be of evil character, but she was not a killer.

> Cases arise in which, through no fault of the prosecution, a person comes before you with a record and with a history which inspire you with revulsion. It is in those cases that the task for the jury is most difficult of all. They have to separate in their minds the natural revulsion which they feel against behaviour which nobody would seek to condone or commend, to dissociate in their minds evidence of evil character and evil behaviour, of ill or damage done to other people – to divide all these prejudicial elements and features of the case from the crime of which the person is being arraigned. I want you, in your approach to this case, in your consideration of it after I have sat down, and after my lord has summed up for you, to begin, each and all of you, by making quite certain that you have purged your minds of any feeling that this woman should suffer because of the woman she has been.[51]

O'Connor dismissed the prosecution's claim that the crime was in any way premeditated:

> If this woman had the foresight or cunning to make the prepa-
> rations of which you have heard on the fatal evening, is it
> conceivable that she should have been so clumsy as to bring home
> for the week-end her child who might have remained at school?
> Can you conceive that she would have ordered from Harrods for
> her lover, to be delivered on the Monday after the crime, those
> fatally incriminating tokens of her affection for Stoner? If the
> crime was pre-meditated, can you conceive of Mrs Rattenbury
> and Stoner sitting down and solemnly deciding upon a mallet
> for the execution of the act? Why a mallet? Why a mallet bor-
> rowed from Stoner's parents, the ownership of which could easily
> be traced? Why not a poker picked up from the fireplace if the
> impression to be conveyed that it was the act of an intruder? Why
> not one of the swords which were hanging above the fireplace?
> Members of the jury, I suggest that the very clumsiness of the
> crime brands it as a crime of impulse.[52]

O'Connor declared that based on the objective evidence, 'No jury in the world could convict this woman.' It was Stoner and Stoner alone who was responsible for Rattenbury's death.

> Stoner, as you know, is still a lad. His upbringing was simple.
> He had but few friends and no girlfriends. He is flung, at the age
> of eighteen, into the vortex of illicit love. The evidence shows
> him to have been an unbalanced, melodramatic boy, given to
> violent outbursts. The witnesses for the crown have proved that
> on previous occasions he assaulted Mrs Rattenbury. They have
> also proved that he used to go about with a dagger and with a
> toy revolver. An unbalanced, hysterical, melodramatic youth.
> Consider his first association with passionate womanhood. The
> natural reactions of a jealous youth, possibly, I do not know,
> accentuated by drug taking. He is taken away from his work as

a chauffeur, stays sumptuously in a west-end hotel for a week with his mistress, dressed in silk pyjamas from a west-end store, and then brought back to earth and to his drudging duties, and submitting to the orders of his mistress's husband. If you were judging of moral responsibility in this case, your task might be a light one, for you cannot resist nausea and disgust at the way in which this middle aged woman has ensnared and degraded this hapless youth. But that is not your task today. If you are tempted to cast moral reproach, I would say to you with reverence, 'Let him that is without sin cast the first stone'.[53]

At this point, Tennyson Jesse noted, the deathless New Testament reference sounded throughout the hushed court. O'Connor went on: 'Perhaps also you may think that during that fatal night there were indications of a belated nobility on Mrs Rattenbury's part in the way she sought to shield her lover and in the indications of her anxiety at all hazards to take the blame. Too late, like Frankenstein, she had discovered that she had created a monster that she could not control.'[54]

As he came to the end of his speech, he again begged the jury again not to confuse their attitude to Alma's character, her 'moral turpitude', with their task at hand, to convict or release her on the charge of murder:

I beg you ... to discount your horror at her moral failure and to remember that the worst misery which you could inflict upon this wretched youth would be to convict her for something for which he knows she is not responsible. Mercifully you may say to yourselves, 'She has been punished enough. Wherever she walks she will be a figure of shame.'[55]

The court adjourned until Friday, the final day of the trial and Judge Travers Humphreys's summing up. Stoner's guilt for the crime was firmly established, as was Alma's innocence. But her character and reputation had been annihilated in the unforgiving glare of the tabloid press.

* * *

On Friday, members of the public continued to queue outside the Old Bailey all through the night despite the steady rain. By now Alma was looking 'twenty years older' than she had when the trial had started. Even her hands had changed colour and were now a 'livid greenish white'.[56] Humphreys began his summing up at 10.37 a.m. Alma listened 'intensely and fixedly looked at the Judge. Stoner continued to bear his nonchalant demeanour, and for the most part sat immovable, the knuckles of his left hand pressed against his cheek.' As Humphreys addressed the jury, 'so hushed was the court that an occasional cough or a rustle of paper jarred vibrantly in the tense atmosphere' as he patiently and calmly advised the jury. He began by explaining the legalities regarding the charge of murder. If Alma had prompted, coerced or persuaded Stoner to attack her husband, she would be guilty of being an accessory before the fact, even if she were absent when the incident occurred. He then went on to discuss the characters of the main players in the drama at the Villa Madeira, noting that both Irene and Dr O'Donnell had regarded Rattenbury as a nice, quiet man, in contrast to Alma's depiction of him as mean and occasionally ill tempered. He had suggested, according to Alma at least, that she should live her own sexual life and she had taken him at his word. As such, Humphreys regretted that he was 'a *mari complaisant*, a man who knew that his wife was committing adultery and had no objection to it – not a nice character'.[57]

With regard to the suggestion that Alma had been taking drugs, Humphreys dismissed the idea. The syringe from her medicine cabinet was old and dirty and had clearly not been used for some time: 'There is really no evidence at all that this woman was addicted to drugs at any time.'[58] He also dismissed the suggestion that Stoner was a drug addict and had been under the influence of cocaine at the time of the murder. He had no knowledge of what cocaine actually looked like. Nor did he mention drugs when he confessed to Alma what he had done in her bedroom and he didn't display any of the characteristics of an addict when he was observed by the doctors in prison.

Humphreys implied that the whole cocaine defence had been conjured by Stoner in prison in conversations with Dr Grierson and that there was no evidence that he had acted under the influence of drugs and was insane at the time when he attacked Rattenbury whatsoever.

Humphreys then began to describe Alma's moral character and recognised that many of the things that even her own counsel had said about her the day before must have been 'very painful for her to hear, if indeed, she is a person who has any moral understanding at all'.[59]

It is the case for the prosecution that this woman is a woman so lost to all sense of decency, so entirely without any morals that she would stop at nothing to gain her ends, particularly her sexual gratification, and if that be true, then say the prosecution, do you think that woman would stop at the killing of her husband, particularly if she had not to do it herself, if she were once satisfied that would enable her to live the sort of life that she was living more comfortably or with less interference or prospect of interference. And so it is that it seems to me necessary that you should for yourselves have in your minds a picture of that woman, and there was one incident in this case which you may think is sufficient to show you the sort of degradation to which this wretched woman has sunk. You will remember that she gave evidence herself that she was committing adultery – she is an adulteress of course – regularly in bed with her husband's servant in her bedroom and that in that bedroom in a little bed there was her child of six, and counsel asked her: 'Do you really mean that you chose that room when if you wanted to gratify your passions you could have gone into the man's room which was just along the passage and done it there? Did you really choose the room where your child was asleep?' And you will remember that the woman, who was in the witness-box, seemed surprised that any one should put such a question to her and her answer was apparently given in perfect good faith, 'Why not? The little boy was asleep. He was a sound sleeper.' Well, there it is. That is the woman. A woman, who, having ceased, as she says, to have

ordinary relations with her husband, chose as a paramour a boy
of seventeen, almost young enough to be her son.[60]

As with the other lawyers in the trial, having attacked Alma's character, Humphreys sympathised with the situation that Stoner had
found himself in, which was due to the 'domination of that woman
over him. It is a pitiable thing that he should be in that position.'[61]
Tennyson Jesse noted the lawyers had simply articulated a deeply
held 'Anglo-Saxon' prejudice that they shared with 'the man in the
street' – 'that because of her greater age, Mrs Rattenbury dominated her younger lover. It was this same assumption which hanged
Mrs Thompson.'[62]

  Though, as Tennyson Jesse pointed out, a criminal court was
not supposed to be a court of morals, 'in this trial, it clearly was', as
Travers Humphreys continued to attack Alma's character:

> Members of the jury ... it may be that you will say that you
> cannot possibly feel any sympathy for that woman, you cannot
> have any feeling except disgust for her, but let me say this. That
> should not make you more ready to convict her of this crime;
> it should, if anything, make you less ready to accept evidence
> against her ... but beware you do not convict her because she
> is an adulteress, and an adulteress, you may think, of the most
> unpleasant type. Now that is Mrs Rattenbury.[63]

In a direct repetition of the trial of Edith Thompson and Frederick
Bywaters, Alma's character had been set in opposition to Stoner's in
the savage and uncompromising language of patriarchy. Stoner was
young, male, silent, inexperienced, straightforward, practical. Like
Bywaters, he was the epitome of young English manhood, whereas
Alma was a vamp who was older, foreign, divorced, artistic, sexually forthright – a self-confessed liar and adulteress. In 1935, the
Great War was still a recent trauma. Counsel on both sides as well
as Travers Humphreys and all of the jury had either served themselves or had fathers, brothers, husbands and sons who had fought

in the war. Stoner didn't speak throughout the trial, and the more the defence, the prosecution and Travers Humphreys spoke about him as an emblematic English boy, the more the jury and the wider public were drawn in sympathy with him and what he appeared to represent: the flower of young English manhood that had been sacrificed at Flanders. And now every day in the world outside, the tabloids carried stories about the developing RAF and the need for a new generation of young men to train and defend their country, young men just like Stoner and Freddy Bywaters, the coming generation of decent British lads that the empire would come to rely on, and, indeed, always had. Was it right or just that this promising young man should be sacrificed because of the machinations of a middle-aged nymphomaniac?

After an adjournment for lunch, Humphreys talked to the jury about the possibility of returning a verdict of manslaughter if they believed that the prosecution had failed to persuade them that Stoner had intended to kill Rattenbury or cause him grievous bodily harm. He pointed out that Stoner was an available and admissible witness: 'If he wishes to prove that he is or was addicted to drugs, is there any witness on earth who can do it as well as Stoner?'[64] But because Casswell had not dared to put Stoner in the witness box, Humphreys pointed out that this was 'a fact of the utmost significance'. After summing up for three and a half hours, he reminded the jury that, though O'Donnell had said Alma was unfit to answer questions the next day in the police station, she was still aware enough to organise and sign cheques for Irene and Stoner, with a very clear signature. Thus Alma's consistent claim that she remembered absolutely nothing about most of the events of the night was brought into question. He ended by reiterating what Alma had stated all along – 'My first thought on hearing Stoner's story was to protect him'[65] – a clear steer to the jury that Alma's only crime that night had been to protect the man she loved. The jury retired at 2.47 p.m. Alma and Stoner were taken below to await their fate. While the jury was considering the verdict, Alma waited below the dock with Cicely McCall. One of the court officials approached

McCall and asked her if she could enquire from Alma when she
had had her last period. If there was any chance of her being pregnant she could not be hanged. Alma was surprised by the question
but 'was too wrapped up in her own thoughts', to answer.[68]

* * *

Many of the barristers and members of the public who were waiting
in the corridors around the court assumed that in such a complex
case the jury would take hours to reach their verdict. So they were
surprised when it was announced that the jury had reached a decision in just forty-eight minutes and quickly rushed back to their
places for the verdict. The jury returned at 3.35 p.m. A double
knock on the door heralded the arrival of Travers Humphreys, who
was acknowledged by a bow from each of the four aldermen carrying bouquets of anemones and carnations. Humphreys returned
their greeting and strode towards his chair, carrying his white
gloves on the arm of his crimson robe. Beneath the white gloves was
the black cap.

The courtroom was hot, expectant and tense[66] as everyone waited
for Alma and Stoner to take their places in the dock. A weak Alma
was helped into the dock by the two wardresses; her face was pale
and her dark eyes so hollow and expressionless that it was 'impossible to tell whether she could see the court in front of her or not'.[67]
Stoner, his face as impassive and his movements as controlled as ever,
took his stand calmly in the dock and appeared to brace himself
for what he already seemed to know would be the outcome. Briefly,
'as if to spare all he could to the woman and the boy before him',[69]
the clerk of the court asked the foreman if the jury had reached
their verdict.

'Do you find the prisoner, Alma Victoria Rattenbury, guilty or
not guilty of murder?'

'Not guilty.'[70]

Alma showed no emotion when the foreman spoke the words as
she waited to hear what was so much more important to her – the fate
of Stoner. The clerk of the court now asked for the verdict on him.

'Do you find the prisoner, George Percy Stoner, guilty or not guilty?'

'Guilty, but we would like to add a rider to that; we recommend him to mercy.'[71]

The verdict had been quietly spoken. A devastated Alma took a step forward, seemed to stagger, then thrust out her hands as if by gesture alone she could somehow change what had been said, crying out quietly, 'Oh ... no.'[72] The wardresses grasped her and hurried her from the dock. Stoner was to face his sentence alone. His mother, inconsolable now, had to be escorted out of the court by his father.

For a whole minute, Stoner stood in silence as Humphreys entered the sentence in the court records, the scratching of his pen the only sound to be heard in the stunned and silent courtroom. In the public gallery, some women wept.[73] When the clerk asked Stoner whether he had anything to say before judgement of death was given, he replied, very quietly, 'Nothing at all.' It was the first time he had spoken throughout the long trial since pleading not guilty when the proceedings began.[74] The two female members of the jury averted their eyes[75] as the judge's clerk spread open the square foot of black cloth and placed it over Mr Humphreys's white wig in preparation for the sentencing: 'George Percy Stoner, you will be taken hence to the prison in which you were last confined and from there to a place of execution where you will be hanged by the neck until you are dead and thereafter your body will be buried within the precincts of the prison and may God have mercy upon your soul.'

The press was there to scrutinise exactly how Stoner accepted his fate, searching his face for vulnerability, for any weakness in his stiff upper lip.

Brave as the boy had been throughout the trial, so uncannily brave that it had been scarcely possible to guess what resolution lay behind that outwardly calm face, he could not quite control his emotion at hearing the verdict. His eyes dilated, staring at the Judge in a last supreme effort of self-control, his hands stirred vaguely from his sides and grasped the side of the dock, he swallowed painfully two or three times and the knuckles of one hand began to tap with gentle monotony against the dock until the judge's voice had ceased. Then he turned abruptly towards the stairway to the cells and was gone.[76]

Casswell asked permission for Stoner's father to see his son before he left the court. As Stoner was being led below, Humphreys recalled Alma to face the charge of being an accessory. In the small corridor beneath the court, she was being assisted towards the stairs when Stoner appeared. They met with the full knowledge that this would be the very last time they would see each other, but nothing was said. Alma looked hard at him as he was hurried past her between two burly warders. Her lips moved, but no sound came. Stoner, his arms held tightly to his sides by his escort, nodded at her and smiled. Alma was taken back up to the court, weeping and incoherent. She was found not guilty and discharged.

The ghost of Edith Thompson had been exorcised; however appalling the murder of a defenceless old man, the judicial murder of a foolish – but guiltless – woman was not to follow it. But though her life was saved, Alma's spirit had been crushed.

Her self-control gone, her eyes shadowed with exhaustion and her white face smudged with tears, this woman whom the judge had described in his summing up as a 'woman so lost to all decency, so entirely without any moral sense that she would stop at nothing to gain her ends', hung limp and weeping in the strong grasp of the two wardresses who supported her. On their strength only – for her own was utterly broken – was she able to leave the dock and pass, what is ironically called a 'free woman' for the last time down the steps of the Old Bailey.[77]

The unthinkable had happened. Alma was free. Stoner was to die. And it was all her fault.

Alma and her doctor, following the verdict

CHAPTER SIXTEEN

A WOMAN OF PRINCIPLE

31 May–4 June 1935

Even if she is free, she's got her punishment. All her life she'll
hear those things the judge said, ringing in her ears and know
that everyone in England read them in the papers, and there's
not a decent woman in the country would shake hands with
her, or even speak to her for what she is. Though I don't know
that she'd care – a woman like her.

– John Van Druten, *Leave Her to Heaven*[1]

If it was the women of England who hanged Mrs Thompson,
against all reason and all justice, then it was equally due to the
women of England that Mrs Rattenbury was saved from the
gallows: for surely if Mrs Thompson had not been hanged, Mrs
Rattenbury surely would have been.

– Francis Iles, *The Anatomy of Murder*[2]

Immediately following the verdict, Alma was in a state of collapse. A
doctor was called to attend to her in the basement of the Old Bailey
for a quarter of an hour before she felt strong enough to leave the
building. Outside, thousands of members of the public and dozens
of reporters and photographers had assembled to watch the final
moments of what had become a national drama. The main hall at

the Old Bailey gave access to all the courts, so it was cleared for Alma to leave the building unhindered, though she was supported by two police matrons.[3] Ever loyal, Irene appeared with a bouquet of flowers she had brought for her.[4] Pinkie Kingham was waiting in a taxi outside the eastern entrance to the public gallery in an attempt to avoid the expectant crowds. Just as she was about to leave, Alma turned to Cicely and said 'Thank you', pushing into her hand a bar of chocolate.[5] Five seconds later, the door was opened and Alma was smuggled out of the building accompanied by Dr O'Donnell. As they saw Alma's taxi depart, some of the waiting crowd booed her.[6]

As previously arranged, Pinkie took the traumatised Alma to Keith Miller Jones's house at Halkin Place in Belgravia, where they were to have tea. 'Rather a hostile crowd' of reporters and members of the public had followed them and proceeded to wait intimidatingly outside. Miller Jones could see that none of this was beneficial to Alma's fragile state of mind. He called the police, who arrived shortly afterwards to clear the street, but a stubborn group of reporters refused to leave. Concerned for Alma, Miller Jones called a friend, Dr Bathurst, who practised in Harley Street, to come and examine her.[7] Finding Alma in a state of hysteria, Bathurst recommended that she be sent to a nursing home straight away and arranged for her to be admitted to one in Bayswater. Miller Jones would drive Alma there himself. As they left the house, the reporters fired questions at them. Would Alma sell her story? Where was she going? What was she going to do now? But Miller Jones refused to answer. Just as he helped Alma into the car, one of the reporters shouted to him, 'If you take her to Bournemouth, we'll follow you there.'[8]

The Cleveland Nursing Home in Cleveland Gardens was a grand building typical of west London, with a pillared porch and white stucco exterior. As soon as Alma arrived, it was clear to the matron that she was in a 'very delicate state of health mentally'.[9] She was given a perfumed bath and then put to bed, where she had something to eat. Dr Bathurst felt that, though clearly in a highly nervous state, the only treatment she needed was rest and something to help her sleep. She would need to be carefully supervised, but in order to be sure she didn't feel watched or guarded, Bathurst avoided 24-hour observation. The matron and her staff knew that Alma's was a 'difficult case', but were surprised by her behaviour in the circumstances: 'She was charming to everyone – as nice as anyone could expect. She was a woman who had been through a terrible lot. You could see it in her eyes.'[10]

Aware of the various allegations at the trial, she observed that Alma showed no sign of drug dependency and didn't drink any alcohol at all, nor did she seem to crave it. That evening she was visited by Irene and talked continually about the trial, living through it over and over again, even re-enacting scenes from the courtroom. She was wracked with guilt that it was her evidence that had sent Stoner to the gallows. It was also clear to Irene that the judge's comments about her character had shocked and hurt Alma deeply. She insisted on giving instructions for her funeral, wanting to be dressed in pink in her coffin and to be surrounded by pink flowers.[11] Alma loathed white and hated traditional white funeral lilies. Irene felt that there was no indication in this conversation that Alma actually wanted to die; rather that she wanted her affairs in order. Alma then hurriedly wrote to Lewis Manning in Bournemouth:

I see by tonight's papers immediate steps are being taken
for Stoner's reprieve – also an appeal. Nothing must be left
undone – and I will get all the money that can possibly be
raised for this end. I think you understand this without my
writing but it relieves one's mind to say it.[12]

Alma continued to talk obsessively, incessantly, about Stoner. She insisted to the matron that as he was going to be executed, she was determined to die too. When he was hanged, she would kill herself. The matron tried to calm her patient as tactfully as she could, using a little emotional blackmail; she wouldn't want to kill herself at the nursing home, would she? Dr Bathurst and all the medical staff were doing everything they could to get her well. Alma promised, at least, not to kill herself while she was on the premises: 'You're all very kind to me. I'm sure I don't know why.'[13] The matron could see that she was suicidal, but felt that if Alma stayed under her care she'd be well enough physically and mentally to put things in perspective and give up the idea. In tears of despair, heartbreak, fear and guilt, Alma told the matron how much she loved Stoner and how she ached to see him: 'If I had just one word with him, even if I just had one look at his face again, he would understand. I must see him again. Can't anything be done?'[14]

The matron said that she would look into it. On Alma's behalf, she telephoned the governor at Pentonville Prison, Reginald Moliere Tabuteau, wondering if a visit would be possible?[15] The governor told her that it was unlikely that permission would be granted but that she could apply in writing. Encouraged, Alma wrote to Stoner via the prison:

> *29 Cleveland Gardens*
> *London W2*
> *Friday*

> *Darling – I wasn't allowed to see you. God Bless you – keep your courage up – Please write me I pray, and anything and everything will be done for your reprieve – sweet one – I love you always and always.*
> *Address me*
> *Mrs Radclyffe*[16]

An indication, perhaps, of her anguished state of her mind, she signed the letter with one of the names of her deceased first husband. Sending the letter seemed to give Alma some comfort, but she still had a restless, sleepless night.

The next day was Saturday. As the address of the nursing home had been published in the newspapers, there were reporters and members of the public outside, waiting for a glimpse of Alma, so she sent a nurse out for armfuls of back numbers of newspapers that had covered the trial.[17] She read them voraciously, chain-smoking as she did so. It was only now that it became apparent to Alma what had been said about her in the press, including the banner headline in the *Evening Standard* from the previous night: 'You Cannot Have Any Feeling Except Disgust for Mrs Rattenbury'.[18] Otherwise she did nothing but talk of Stoner and how she planned to help him. She intended to devote her life to doing everything she could to make his easier.[19] No money was to be spared on his behalf either for an appeal or a reprieve. Alma seemed to be recovering and facing the challenges of the future. Since she had arrived at the nursing home, she had even tried to write a song, humming or singing the melody, then repeating the same lines, trying to put them to the music. She tried many variations of the words, but, to the matron's concern, they were all concentrated on the same themes – love and death.

> *We have lived together,*
> *We two:*
> *We have loved together,*
> *I and you:*
> *We will die together,*
> *You and I –*
> *We will swing together.*[20]

Saturday afternoon's newspaper reported that Stoner had been moved the night before to Brixton Prison. Alma broke down; he wouldn't have received her letter. The matron telephoned both prisons,[21] but they refused to confirm where Stoner was until she insisted that Alma was heading for a complete mental breakdown if she felt that Stoner had not received her letter. At last the prison officials informed her that Stoner was still held at Pentonville. This reassured Alma, who took it for granted that Stoner would get the letter, whereas in fact this was at the discretion of the prison officials. The matron again requested if Alma might see Stoner, but to no avail.

While at Cleveland Gardens that weekend, Alma was visited by various friends including Keith Miller Jones, his sister Katharine, Daphne Kingham and Irene. At some point on Saturday Irene arrived with a bouquet of sweet peas and roses. She stayed chatting with Alma for a long time, but got upset and teary. The matron felt this display of emotion wasn't good for Alma, so she asked if Irene could make her visits a little shorter in the future as Alma's health was so delicate.[22]

Sunday 1 June was Alma's forty-third birthday, and even if she registered it, there must have seemed little for her to celebrate. She talked 'a little wildly'[23] again of suicide, of Stoner, and of leaving the home. The matron advised her that she was getting stronger every day. She was much better than when she had arrived, wasn't she? Alma agreed that she was. But throughout the day, the nursing home was haunted by curious crowds and reporters, so it was impossible for her to go out, even for a breath of air.

On Monday morning, Alma reiterated to the matron that she wanted to see Stoner and that she wanted to leave the nursing home. The matron thought Alma was in need of some sort of distraction, so she was pleased when Alma agreed to the hairdresser coming in: 'A woman can be an almost different person when her hair is permed and her face made up.'[24] The hairdresser shampooed her hair and gave her a permanent wave. Then a manicurist arrived to do her hands and nails, and she was given a massage. The treatments seem to have perked Alma up, and by the time Dr Bathurst saw her at five o'clock on Monday afternoon she seemed significantly better than she had been when she'd first arrived at Cleveland Gardens. She was sleeping, and even eating a little. Bathurst recommended that she should stay in the nursing home for a month so that she could completely recover from her ordeal and Alma seemed happy to comply. Bathurst thought it a good sign that she was talking about the future, which included her plans to help Stoner: 'He is so young. I am sure he will be reprieved.' She had investigated how long he might spend in prison if the death sentence was commuted to penal servitude for life. A life sentence was twenty years and the maximum remission for good behaviour was five, so Stoner would still be quite a young man when he was released. She'd been reading the day's newspapers with great interest as she had done every day, reports of her own progress and the plans for Stoner's reprieve. She will have read that day's *Daily Sketch*, which carried a blistering editorial by the anonymous 'Candidus', one of many who resented the fact that Stoner had taken the blame and would pay the penalty for the murder, while Alma had got off scot-free. 'Legal Innocence', he stated, 'is not the same as Moral Innocence':

> It does not seem right that the woman who is morally the more guilty should go free and a morally less guilty boy lie under sentence of death ... The judge, very properly told the jury that they must not let their moral indignation with the woman's conduct influence their verdict. Yet many reading the case must have wished that there were such an offence in law as being a moral accessory to a crime.[25]

Candidus believed that, despite being acquitted of the crime of which she was accused, Alma should be still punished, and it is telling that he assumed that Stoner's passion for her was 'genuine', whereas Alma's for him was mere 'appetite'.

Alma confided to Dr Bathurst that she was keen to get on with publishing her songs. With all the publicity she'd had, she was convinced they would be successful: 'Now is the time for the rest of my songs to be published; they'll sell like hot cakes now.'[26] She hardly spoke of her two children, though she did mention again – twice – the memory of her son at the front door when she was arrested and taken away to Bournemouth Police Station, so that image was clearly playing on her mind. But it was Stoner who continued to preoccupy her; 'she was obsessed by him'.[27] Leaving her that evening, Bathurst was much happier. There had been no discussion about leaving the nursing home and no talk of suicide for some time. As Alma prepared to go to bed on Monday evening, the matron remarked that she looked so much better, even cheerful. Alma agreed: 'Yes, I am much better, aren't I?'[28]

But that night, when the nine o'clock post was delivered and the matron took Alma's letters up to her room, she found that

Alma had a female visitor she didn't recognise. This woman was neither Irene nor Pinkie Kingham, both of whom the matron had met before. She may well have been Keith Miller Jones's sister Katharine, who had visited Alma in prison. Later, at about ten o'clock, Katharine sought out the matron to tell her that Alma was leaving. 'No, she's not,' said the astonished matron. 'She can't be. She's going to sleep for the night.'[29] She explained that it would be very dangerous for Alma to leave in her condition. She was improving, but she certainly wasn't well enough to leave. Trying another tactic, the matron told Katharine that it would be a great responsibility to take Alma on without professional care. Katharine nervously agreed, but this was Alma's decision, not hers: 'She's going. And no one can stop her.'[30] She and Alma had discussed taking a service flat together, or maybe moving into a hotel. The matron thought this plan completely ridiculous and decided to have it out with Alma herself. Upstairs she found Alma not only out of bed, but dressed and her packing almost finished. One glance at Alma's face told the matron that nothing she or anyone else said would prevent her from going: 'She was that kind of woman.' The matron tried to reason with Alma – it was late, it would be impossible to get a service flat at such short notice, and too late to get a room in a hotel. 'Just go back to bed tonight and have a nice long sleep,' she urged her, 'and you'll feel much better in the morning. Then you can move in comfort. I can't do anything to stop you if your mind is made up, but that is a much better plan.'[31] But Alma's mind was made up: 'You can't compel me to stay here, can you? I'm a free agent. I can leave when I want to.'[32] She wouldn't even allow Dr Bathurst to be telephoned. With her hands tied, the matron reluctantly carried one of Alma's bags down to a car that was waiting outside. Before they left, Katharine reassured the matron that there would be a trained nurse with Alma at all times.[33] But the matron insisted that this wasn't a good idea either as it would only result in Alma feeling trapped. Alma got into the car and was driven away into the night.[34]

This sense of being under constant scrutiny had been depressing

Alma since her arrival at Holloway. Every movement she made seemed to be a story; even the fact that she had left the Cleveland Nursing Home made the front pages of several newspapers the next day. That night she went with Katharine to consult another doctor, who could see that she was in a state of 'great nervous distress'.[35] She told him she had had to leave the Cleveland Nursing Home because 'I could not put my nose outside the door without being stared at.'[36] She wanted to lose her identity, escape from the horrors of the previous week and make a new start. With some peace and rest she could gather her strength to look after her children and would do everything possible to save Stoner's life. The doctor advised her to go to another nursing home under an assumed name. After checking that there was a back door she could use, Alma agreed to go to the Elizabeth Fulcher Home at Devonshire Street in Marylebone. She was checked in by the manager as 'Mrs Martin', a patient suffering from a nervous breakdown. The only people who knew her real identity were him and the matron, Maude McClellan, who noted immediately that 'Mrs Martin' seemed to want to hide away from everyone.[37] Alma told her that she just wanted to be allowed to forget her ordeal and make a fresh start. She took a sleeping draught and went to bed.

Next morning, Alma claimed to have had the best night's sleep since the death of her husband in March.[38] She ate a good breakfast and seemed more placid and peaceful than when she had arrived. But this new calm was deceptive. By now she had fully absorbed the extent and severity of what the press had written about her throughout the trial and this may have deflated any plans she had of making a fresh start. Crucially, she continued to be denied any communication with Stoner. Whatever the trigger, by Tuesday morning, Alma had decided that she wanted to die.

She had been organised enough to take some writing paper with her from the Cleveland Nursing Home and, sitting in bed with a cup of coffee, she wrote her farewell letter to the world. Significantly, it was addressed to nobody in particular, an anguished cry from the heart of guilt and despair to anybody who cared:

Tuesday Morning, June 4th

I am afraid force of circumstances have made it imperative I get off quickly. Reporters calamering for one's 'life storey' [sic] & my mind on nothing but Stoner, Stoner, Stoner. And that boy's face on the stairway looking up – with his sweet smile – & then standing there on that awful Friday. They wouldn't let me stand whilst he was sentenced – I was pulled below – down those awful stairs again, & I clung to the bars – pleading to just see him for only one second – oh! Just one more look – just one more look. Would someone be kind enough to tell Stoner or get the message through to him – that I would never have given evidence against him, had I known. I had made my mind up to say everything was blotted from my memory from 9 o'clock that Sunday night – & THEN – let the Judge and Jury fight it out amongst themselves as to who did kill Ratz.

But, my lawyer informed me at our last interview, that if I spoke the truth, it would clear Stoner. I went into that box feeling confident and strong – that the evidence I was giving would clear the boy.

However –

This woman – that woman that appallingly degraded woman who is now free – has wished a million times since – I had stuck to my first stories that night – that I did kill Ratz – for I remember quite well what I was doing until I drank too much – but only after 3 in the morning.

I went downstairs twice that night – after Stoner told me. And always – 'oh! God oh! God how can I help this boy!' That was the only thought in my bewildered mind, and the whole of England knows the muddle I made of it! This woman – so low – so degraded (I can still hear the Judge's words) really loved Stoner, we both loved each other – make [of] the difference in age what you will. And lies have been told – lies & more lies – & mud slung to right & left – but our love was not a filthy thing – it was beautiful – and we loved

*each other from the moment we met, we just came together
because it was fate.*

*I was not looking for a man to sleep with, that would have
made matters simple if it were so – & God knows Ratz suspected dozens of times – to make up to his men friends for
money – To cheer him up & pull his leg (the contempt I felt
one would have thought EVEN he could have seen) I agreed
to make myself attractive to his various friends that Sunday
afternoon. 'A kind man – a charming man' – & always
agreeing to everything with a smile, 'Yes, darling, no darling
etc' – always trying to cheer him up – so that the atmosphere
would be pleasant at home. I dont [sic] think I ever spoke
one word of truth to Ratz. He knew as much about me as I
know about Timbucktoo. All he saw was a smile, all he heard
was the 'yes darling – no darling' – a mask that agreed with
his every mood. And heaven help one if they did otherwise!*

*Am writing this in bed – having coffee. Slept last night –
thank God for sleeping draughts – & my beloved had been
up two hrs. I wonder whether he was allowed the 2 letters I
wrote? So many Regulations to prison life. This is the only
reason I thanked God [I] was not back in Holloway – I am at
least free – free to a sense – that is I hope so – when I take (I
hope) my last walk this morning. Had it been possible to have
made a home for my beloved children I would have stuck it –
but what help to boys – having a mother who would always be
pointed at as – 'That woman'. Never to go to a cricket match
again to see Christopher play or Little John when he grows
up. Never to have any of their friends at the house – I had
looked forward – just to see their dear little faces again – but
as this would be too unkind for them – to rekindle memories
of the mother they loved and were proud of. It is better I just
fade from the picture. Kinder for them. The pain in my heart
is so intense, it is almost not a pain. I can't look back on
memories, I have no future. And the present is Hell.*

God Bless Stoner – God bless my children. When we meet

*again, may it be under happier circumstances. Stoner used to
say, 'I feel I have not earned this love, it has dropped into my
hands too easily & I must surely have to pay the price for it
someday, somehow.' I tried to think that perhaps the price I
had paid for life – the unhappiness – the previous marriages
that I wished to heaven had never happened – might atone
for him & spare him unhappiness – but oh, it didn't. When
we are born again, surely our love will be happy then. How
many times we have talked of this. We didn't row – 'quarrel'
as it was said. We were too happy for that. Stoner used to ask
me to write a 'love song' to us. I said that was the one song I
would never really write. 'How write a love song whilst one
was living it?'*

   *Stoner would never say 'goodbye'. He said that was one
word he couldn't say. I have thought of that thousands of times.
So we have not said goodbye. And will never say goodbye.*
   Alma Rattenbury[39]
   *By some mistake, by some divine mistake,
   I dreamed awhile, but now I wake! I wake!*[40]

Having written the letter and put it in her snakeskin handbag, Alma
told the doctor that she would like to go out shopping. She asked Mrs
McClellan if she could possibly borrow £2 as she wanted to buy some
toys for the children.[41] Mrs McClellan lent her the money, Alma put
on her fur coat and a fawn-coloured hat and left Devonshire Street
heading for nearby Oxford Circus Tube station.

   Alma went down the escalator and onto the platform, waiting
for a train to rush through. She was determined to throw herself
under one, but at mid-morning the Tube was busy and there were
too many people about. She needed to rethink her plans, so retraced
her steps back up to street level at Oxford Circus, a frantic traffic
hub of bicycles, cars, buses, trams and pedestrians. Perhaps she
could throw herself in the path of an oncoming bus? But the West
End was packed with shoppers and commuters. There were still too
many people about. It wasn't the pain or fear of death that made her

hesitate, but the worry that she would be prevented from achieving her aim. 'One must be bold,' she later observed, 'to do a thing like this.'[42] She needed an alternative strategy to end her life, and to do it, she must be alone.

Surrounded by West End stores, Alma went to make some final purchases with the £2 that Mrs McClellan had lent her. In one ladies' clothes shop she bought herself a pink crêpe de Chine night-dress. But this was not for her to sleep in, nor was she imagining another romantic night with Stoner; it was to be her shroud. Next, she went into a hardware shop and made another purchase – a brand new knife in a sheath, with a sharp, 8-inch blade. It was wrapped for her in a paper bag.

She returned to the Elizabeth Fulcher Home at midday for lunch and perhaps for her own clarification wrote down her thoughts again, but this time it was more of a diary note than a letter:

> *June 4th*
> *I want to make it perfectly clear, that no one is responsible for what actions I may take regarding my life – I quite made up my mind at Holloway to finish things – should Stoner be sentenced – & it would only be a matter of time – & opportunity – And every day night & minute is only prolonging the appalling agony of my mind. They say I dominated Stoner – am afraid I have never met the person who could dominate that boy. He had colossal strength. Never have I known any one with so much determination & strength of opinion, & character. 'Weakness & Stoner' could never be associated in the same breath. He should make a wonderful man – if he uses that strength the right way.*
> *Alma Rattenbury*[43]

After having lunch at 2.30 p.m. Alma told Mrs McClellan, 'Now I am going out again. Don't be worried if I am later than nine o'clock. It will be quite all right.'[44] She picked up her umbrella, left the nursing home and headed for Waterloo station, the gateway to southwest

England and home. She had no intention of returning to the nursing home or to London ever again.

At Waterloo, she considered her final destination. Perhaps Bournemouth to see Irene or the Villa Madeira again? Or maybe one of the places where she had taken the children on picnics near Christchurch, when she had played the violin while they swam in the river? Christopher was at school near Christchurch now, and hadn't Stoner once told her that he had nearly jumped out of a train across the bridge just outside the town? A rash, foolish act, by a rash, foolish boy. She couldn't decide, so, as she had often seen Stoner do, she tossed a coin: Christchurch it was. She bought a single ticket for the 4.30 p.m. express – she would have no need of a return.

On the train she settled into a compartment and was recognised by a member of the public; there was nowhere that she could be anonymous. Avoiding their glances, she went to the buffet car and ordered a cup of tea, looking pensively out of the window; another fellow passenger noticed that 'her face was white and drawn and her eyes gave her a haunted expression'.[45] As the train travelled west, she began writing with a pencil on the envelope in which she'd put her suicide notes, a further stream of consciousness, writing slowly and thoughtfully:[46]

> *Diary*
>
> *Please do not bury me near R[atz].*
>
> *Surely my death can wipe out a little – the appalling things said – its [sic] so awful – those two children thinking through their lives – Their mother was worse than Mary Magdalene. To know all – is to understand and forgive all. I did think that by my saying 'I did it' & being arrested, it would help Stoner, but oh God I made such a muddle of everything – & never helped him at all. If only my lawyer had not told me to speak the truth, at our last interview, that boy might be free by now.*[47]

With more to say, but no paper to write on, she now took out an empty envelope addressed to the governor of Pentonville Prison to add an afterthought:

> *If I only thought it would help Stoner, I'd stay on but it has been pointed out to me too vividly I cannot help him and that is my death sentence.*

She put the papers back in her handbag as the train hurried down to the coast.

Shortly before they reached Christchurch, Alma left the compartment, stood in the corridor and looked out of the window as the train passed Three Arches Bend, where the track crossed the River Avon overlooking the meadows around Christchurch. Returning to the compartment, she now wrote 'feverishly' on another empty envelope that had been addressed to her:

> *It must be easier to be hanged than to have to do the job oneself, especially in these circumstances of being watched all the while. Pray God nothing stops me tonight. Am within five minutes of Christchurch now. God bless my children and look after them.*[48]

She arrived at Christchurch at 8 p.m., where once again she was recognised, this time by the bookstall clerk, who noticed that she walked slowly, 'as though she had nowhere particular to go'.[49] She then made her way out of the station and towards the marshes, a hard walk in Alma's state of health and in unsuitable shoes across uneven, sodden fields. Finally, she arrived at the remote riverbank where the railway line crossed the river over three solid, red-brick arches. She would wait for the evening darkness to fall for the last act of her extraordinary life of love, loss, sorrow, disappointment, joy and, now, so it seemed, more loss.

She watched the swans floating across the water, then reread a letter Christopher had sent her that had given her the determination to fight for her life in the courtroom. Then she wrote on the back page of Christopher's letter:

One has to be so blastedly careful – it's awful having to wait
until its dark – I do hope it gets dark soon – the smell of the
grass is marvellous. I wonder how deep the water is? Pray
God it's deep enough.[50]

On the back of an envelope on which she had already written, she
added more thoughts. As with the other notes she had been writing
all afternoon, they were fragmentary afterthoughts to the suicide
letter she had written that morning.

8 o'clock. And after so much walking, I have got here – and
oh! To see the swans and spring flowers – to just smell them.
And how singular I should have chosen the spot where Stoner
said he nearly jumped out of the train. It was not intentional
my coming here. I tossed a coin, like Stoner always did, and
it came down Christchurch. It is beautiful here. What a lovely
world really.[51]

Alma had a letter from Victoria in her handbag, a place that seemed
a world away now; her parents, her music, Dolling, Pakenham, Ratz.
She scribbled a few more words on the back of it:

I tried this morning to throw myself under a train at Oxford
Circus. Too many people about. Then a bus. Still too many
people about. One must be bold to do a thing like this.

A chain-smoker for much of her adult life, she took a cigarette out
of a big box she had brought with her and lit it, her heart aching
with regret, despair and guilt. She made one final addition to the
note she'd been writing:

It is beautiful here and I am alone.
Thank God for peace at last.[52]

Then she took the knife from its sheath.

At 8.30 p.m., local cowman William Mitchell was walking across the meadow adjoining Stoney Lane to see to some of his heifers. As he approached the railway line, he caught sight of a woman's hat above the tall grass. When he first saw Alma, he thought it was 'some lovers sweethearting'.[53] She was sitting on the bank of the stream that passed under the railway, smoking. Mitchell crossed the stream by the bridge and went down the embankment on the other side. As he did so he looked through the rails of the bridge and saw that Alma had now taken off her hat and fur coat and laid them on the riverbank. She stood at the water's edge then walked down into the water. Mitchell thought she might have been picking some marsh flowers until he noticed the ominous knife in her right hand. As she half-walked, half-slid into the water, she took the knife and stabbed herself in the left breast. She then stabbed herself again, deeper this time, piercing her heart. Once more she stabbed herself. Again and again – five savage inward wounds. A sixth puncture was slighter as she weakened and her life drained away.[54]

Mitchell ran up the bank, over the bridge, and down the other side towards the edge of the river. When he reached the water Alma was lying on her back, face upwards in the stream, a few feet from the bank. Mitchell entered the water and tried to grab Alma's feet but was unable to reach her. He was also concerned for his own safety for, tragically, Alma's potential saviour couldn't swim. He grabbed her fur coat from the bank and, taking one end, threw the other end to her and shouted, 'Catch hold of this!' Alma didn't speak. Mitchell nearly lost his footing and grabbed the grass to save himself, for the water in the pond was 15ft deep. Alma made no attempt to take hold of the coat. Mitchell then saw blood rising to the surface of the water.[55] Alma floated, staring silently at the sky above. Realising that she may already be dead, Mitchell ran to a nearby cottage and raised the alarm. He told James Penny, a local labourer, that he had found a woman in the stream and had been unable to save her. Penny raced to the riverbank and tried to reach Alma with a pole, but it wasn't long enough. He returned to his cottage for a longer one and with this they recovered Alma's body. They laid her on the riverbank among the pathetic props of her final scene – the handbag, umbrella, fountain pen and the paper bag containing the sheath of the knife. The melodrama that had been Alma Rattenbury's life had ended with the bleak finality of a Roman tragedy.

CHAPTER SEVENTEEN

THE SON OF ANY ONE OF US

31 May–10 June 1935

For Stoner, there is not very much to be said.

– Francis Iles, *The Anatomy of Murder*[1]

When the death sentence was passed at the Old Bailey, Stoner 'remained absolutely unmoved'. Taking his lead from the admiring tributes to him in the closing speeches, Geraint Goodwin praised Stoner in the *Daily Sketch* for his stiff upper lip, his *Boy's Own* composure and his boy scout bravery:

> He bit his lip. He steeled himself by an effort of will, clearly obvious to those who were a few yards away. 'A mere boy' ... a phrase used more than once in this trial; a mere boy he stood there. A mere boy, but it may be that he behaves as a man behaves. He bit his lip; he was in common parlance, to 'take it.' But with the dread words of the judge ... 'body buried in the precincts of the prison', his eyes shut, he reeled, he staggered. Two burly warders stood beside him in case he was to fall. He did not fall. But as this dread sentence of death was passed he seemed incapable of thought, or act or speech. He was capable, in his manliness, of summoning up the will power to stand upright; that was all.[2]

As he was taken below, his father, whose eyes were tear-dimmed and full of pent-up emotion, asked permission to go down and see his son before he was taken away to Pentonville. They met in a 'visiting box' beneath the court, a converted cell equipped with a steel grille where convicted prisoners were permitted to see friends or relatives. They were allowed to converse but not to touch. Stoner told his father, 'I am content. They have set her free. What happens to me does not matter. I am glad that she had been spared.'[3]

Stoner left the Old Bailey before Alma, transported in a Black Maria with dark blinds, which swung through the great wooden and iron-bound gates where scores of police had been placed in case there was any demonstration from the large crowds that had assembled outside the court. He was transferred to Pentonville Prison, which in 1902 had taken over the responsibility from Newgate for the execution of male prisoners.[4] The governor, Reginald Tabuteau, was an ex-naval officer who ran the prison with firm but intelligent discipline. He had also supervised Edith Thompson during her trial at the Old Bailey in 1922 and had been witness to her execution.[5] Stoner would be accommodated at Pentonville in the condemned cell away from the other prisoners. The cell would be lit twenty-four hours a day and he would be supervised by teams of two or three warders in eight-hour shifts. Their primary roles would be to prevent Stoner from committing suicide and to offer emotional support, but they would also record everything he said in case he confessed or volunteered new evidence. He would be weighed at regular intervals so that the executioner could calculate the correct length of drop for when he was hanged.[6]

That evening, the officials at Pentonville received a phone call from the matron at the Cleveland Nursing Home on Alma's behalf asking if she could visit Stoner. She was told that this was unlikely but she could apply in writing. However, the Prison Commission immediately advised Pentonville that it would be 'undesirable' for Alma to visit or even communicate with Stoner. If she did write, the governor should return her letter, at the same time informing her that she was not permitted to write to him again.[14] The letter that

Alma was so desperate for Stoner to receive was returned to the Home Office.

After Stoner had left for Pentonville, his father spoke to the press: 'What can I say now that this terrible blow has fallen? He is my only son. My boy seemed glad that the jury had found Mrs Rattenbury not guilty.'[7] Meanwhile, in Bournemouth, Stoner's grandfather called a family conference and said to the press, 'We would not have the matter as it stands. We must do everything for an appeal.'[8] Stoner's Uncle Richard stated that he would be willing to sell one of the properties he owned in order to get the money together for an appeal. Local people from Bournemouth, led by an accountant and business consultant, F. W. Thistleton, decided to form a committee to mobilise support on Stoner's behalf. They would organise a petition and would submit it to the home secretary. When Stoner's parents arrived back in Bournemouth that night, his father revealed to the press that they had received shoals of letters:

> They came from all parts and said that everything possible should be done to get a reprieve. Some of the letters are very touching. It will not be possible to answer all the letters, but I should like the senders to know how much my wife and I are comforted by them. We feel the weight of public opinion is with our son and will welcome any effort to help him. Quite a number of writers speak of the brave way in which the boy behaved throughout the trial. Requests for petition forms as soon as they are ready have been made to us and the boy's grandparents and uncle, who live nearby. We are willing to do everything we can for our son, even to sacrificing ourselves.[9]

Joshua Casswell felt that after the verdict Stoner remained 'as closed as an oyster'.[10] If he was to make an appeal against the verdict, his legal team would have to do so by 10 June. Casswell, though, was confident that Stoner would be reprieved, so held back from making an appeal immediately. On Saturday 1 June, Travers Humphreys sent a personal note to Casswell telling him that he had 'made a good fight' and advising him that he had added a strong recommendation to mercy of his own to that of the jury and hoped that it would be 'all right'. He supposed that Casswell hadn't been able to call Stoner as a witness because he was 'probably too honest'.[11] Although Travers Humphreys had been obliged to pass the mandatory death sentence as the jury had found Stoner guilty, he was able to make this recommendation to the home secretary. When a trial judge recommended mercy, it was rarely ignored by the Home Office. Between 1900 and 1949, 1,210 death sentences were passed with the jury recommending mercy in 460 of them and only 112 of these defendants were ultimately executed. In the same period, there were only six occasions when a judge's recommendation to mercy was overruled.[12]

Condemned prisoners had had the right of appeal against their conviction for murder since 1907, but not against their death sentence. Stoner's appeal would run in parallel to the reprieve process. The Home Office would receive the trial papers, together with the recommendation from Travers Humphreys. Then a report would be prepared for consideration by the permanent secretary and the home secretary. Stoner would be examined by a panel of three Home Office psychiatrists to determine if he was legally sane and fit to hang. All the discussions relating to the reprieve and any recommendations to the home secretary were kept completely secret. If there was to be no reprieve, the home secretary would write 'the Law must take its course' on Stoner's file and the execution would go ahead.[13]

Over the weekend, the campaign for Stoner's reprieve, now based in Thistleton's offices in St Peter's Road in Bournemouth, was bolstered by the addition of the mayor, Alderman John Robert Edgecombe, whose signature headed the first sheet of the petition. He was joined by Brigadier-General Sir Henry Page-Croft, MP for Bournemouth, and Gordon Hall Caine, who was the MP for East Dorset. Support for the campaign came from many other influential people across the country, including the novelist Clemence Dane, who asked in Tuesday's *Daily Mail*, 'Is a boy of 18 a grown-up person? Public opinion denies this when it denies him a vote, but if such a boy is not old enough to be entrusted with the responsibilities of an adult, is it right to punish him as if he were an adult?'[15]

On Thursday, Stoner was visited in his cell at Pentonville by the governor, Mr Tabuteau, accompanied by his solicitor, Marshall Harvey, and the chaplain.[16] It was the only visit Stoner had had since he had been convicted. The governor informed him of the date of his execution. He was to hang at 9 a.m. on 18 June, less than two weeks away.[17] But before Stoner had a moment to absorb the information, Tabuteau told him that Alma was dead.

Stoner nearly fainted. He was given some water but was dazed and only seemed able to mumble from then on. When the governor left, Marshall Harvey talked with Stoner further. He knew that he had been keeping things back from him. He wanted to know the source of the cocaine and repeatedly asked if he could tell him anything else. Was everything that he told him previously true? But Stoner had nothing to add. After his interview with Stoner, Marshall Harvey suggested to the governor that now Alma was dead, Stoner might have more to say about the murder. He also informed him about the petition that was being organised on his behalf. Marshall Harvey was keen to know if Stoner had been allowed to read the last letter Alma had sent and if it had any bearing at all on the case, but Tabuteau confirmed that it was 'purely a love letter'. Marshall Harvey then informed the governor 'in the strictest confidence'[18] that the press knew about the existence of the letter and were desperate to get hold of it and were prepared to pay £1,000.[19] Stoner would have had to work for twenty years to earn that sum on the wages he'd been earning at the Villa Madeira and it would have represented a year's housekeeping money for Alma.

The announcement of the execution date and that of Alma's suicide galvanised support for the campaign for Stoner's reprieve. Thistleton stressed the urgency of the matter to the press, asking for volunteers to arrange tables for people to sign the petition forms in public places – cinemas, shops, in the streets, on the beaches and across Bournemouth, Poole and Christchurch, as well as the local villages.[20] He was also keen to raise funds to support the petition and to help with expenses for Stoner's parents, who had little money. The committee proceeded to argue their support for the reprieve across the press, based on nine points:

- George Percy Stoner is a boy
- He was subjected to undue influence
- He was a victim of drugs
- He was probably under their influence when the crime was committed
- He shows by his behaviour at the trial that he is capable of better things
- His execution, while strictly legal, benefits the community in no respect
- He might, if reprieved, turn out to be a respectable member of society, and be an asset to the state
- He was temporarily insane when the crime was committed; though not legally so
- He might have been the son of any one of us[21]

Motorists driving around Bournemouth with petitions on their windscreens stopped in busy streets to get more signatures and hundreds of local people volunteered to take the petition from house to house. There had now been requests for 700 petition forms from around the country. These forms could take 100 names each and it was anticipated that there would be 70,000 names collected by the end of the week. They planned to submit the petition to the Home Office on 14 June. Meanwhile, as there was no news of a reprieve, on Saturday 8 June, with only two days to lodge an appeal, Marshall Harvey's managing clerk, 36-year-old John Bickford, visited Stoner at Pentonville and handed him the notice of appeal.[22] Stoner read it and only remarked, 'Yes but they don't know about the mallet.' As Stoner clearly had more to say, Bickford told him that if he was finally prepared to make a statement, he had to do it by Monday, or it would be too late.

Bickford waited anxiously all over the Whitsun weekend for a communication from Stoner. On the morning of Bank Holiday Monday, Stoner handed him a handwritten letter for Casswell. This statement was to further confuse what had already been an extraordinarily confused and muddled case. After keeping silent for four months, Stoner admitted that his defence had been a lie. There had been no cocaine. He was entirely innocent. It was Alma who was guilty of murder.

Alma's body recovered from the Clockhouse Stream

CHAPTER EIGHTEEN

LEAVE HER TO HEAVEN

Behind the corpse in the reservoir, behind the ghost on the links,
Behind the lady who dances and the man who madly drinks,
Under the look of fatigue, the attack of migraine and the sigh
There is always another story, there is more than meets the eye.

– W. H. Auden, 'At Last the Secret is Out'[1]

Alma had been determined to die. Despite access to sleeping draughts and over-the-counter poisons routinely available at the time, she had decided to end her dramatic life in a fierce, perhaps operatic way. Stabbing herself six times, piercing her broken heart, would have been physically difficult – and extremely painful. As soon as it was announced publicly, the news of her suicide was a sensation. Once again, she was front-page news, the *Evening Standard* announcing, 'Mrs Rattenbury Stabs Herself to Death'.[2] James Agate recorded in his diary that the headline was the 'most dramatic thing he had seen in the streets since "Titanic Sinking"'.[3] The playwright Terence Rattigan also saw the *Standard* headline while he was on a bus in Park Lane: 'My God, what a revenge on her detractors, of whom, God knows, I was one. I was with everybody else in thinking she was the bitch of all time. My dramatic instinct was inspired at once by this and I thought what a superb end ... but it was almost too corny, you know? I couldn't use it then, but I thought one day I would have a shot at it.'[4]

The diverse opinions about Alma that had raged since she was arrested continued after her death, with some seeing her tragic end as just deserts, while others read her life as a morality tale about the dangers of embracing individualism over the binding strictures of the tribe.[5] There seemed to be no consensus about what sort of woman Alma Rattenbury had been. Though he sympathised with the pain she had suffered, J. H. Campbell in the *Sunday Post* wanted to have it both ways, praising her character on the one hand – 'Mrs Rattenbury deserves more of our pity than our scorn or condemnation. Here was a woman, educated, kind-hearted, clever, original with wealth and children – a woman, who despite ill-health, might have radiated sunshine all along her path.'[6] – and yet attacking it on the other in the same judgmental language that Travers Humphreys had used in his summing up: 'What she felt impelled to do she would do – and neither convention nor the moral code would stand in her way. Unlike her more conventional friends and neighbours, she permitted the primitive to control the rational. Her tragic downfall, the public exposure of her wantonness and weakness, brought her at last to a sense of her own unworthiness.'[7]

In the *Daily Sketch*, the lethal Candidus slightly, if smugly, revised his opinion, admitting even to a grudging admiration of her:

In one respect I was unjust to Mrs Rattenbury in my comments on the murder trial. Like nearly everyone else ... She too, seems to have felt that it was wrong that the boy should die and she go on living and though the law had acquitted her, she carried out a sentence of death on herself ... It is now possible to think that her infatuation for the boy was more than a mere appetite. The sense of honour was certainly not dead in her for it seems to have been the point of honour and of moral justice that pricked her conscience, and so severely that she sought death ... It was a Roman or a Japanese suicide to save honour, and though it is not countenanced by the ethics of Christianity, it is one that human nature everywhere can at least respect. Suicide can be the most cowardly and contemptible of crimes; this suicide was not.[8]

* * *

Irene Riggs was staying with her parents in Holdenhurst Road and had not seen Alma since Saturday. On the morning of Wednesday 4 June she was called to Bournemouth Police Station and informed about Alma's death. Broken-hearted, she was driven to the mortuary in Christchurch to identify Alma's body. She left in tears, leaving her father to speak to the press: 'My daughter is in a terrible state. She has been unable to speak to me. We have had to put her to bed and call a doctor to attend to her. The case has upset her terribly and this has just broken her up entirely.'⁹

When Alma's solicitor Robert Lewis Manning heard about Alma's death, he couldn't believe it: 'I had a letter from her yesterday morning from the nursing home in London the day before. The tenor of the letter was that no money should be spared on behalf of Stoner either for an appeal or a reprieve.'¹⁰

He allowed the letter she had sent him to be printed in the *Daily Sketch* as he hoped that it would mitigate public feeling about Alma's character. He also revealed that he was sending a letter to Stoner's solicitor offering money towards an appeal or a reprieve. He stressed that all Alma's statements had been directed towards exonerating Stoner from any participation in the murder of her husband:¹¹ 'She was convinced that Stoner would never be convicted of murder, and thought that the worst that could happen would be a verdict of manslaughter. Every time I or my partner visited her in prison, Mrs Rattenbury asked anxiously after her two boys. In many ways, indeed Mrs Rattenbury was a noble woman. I think she would have been a far finer woman had it not been for the series of tragedies that had marred her life.'¹²

But as soon as Stoner was condemned to death and Alma realised that there was nothing she could do to save him, Lewis Manning felt that 'life meant nothing to her'.¹³

Keith Miller Jones was stunned and spoke of his own shock as well as the distress of Pinkie Kingham. They had only visited her at the weekend: 'You will understand how distressing this has been for her and indeed all of us. I went to see Mrs Rattenbury at the nursing home, but the last I saw of her was on the Saturday before she died. I had no idea she would leave the home as she did. It has all been a great shock.'[14]

The Elizabeth Fulcher Nursing Home published a press release in response to 'many inaccurate statements' about Alma's death.[15] The matron had warned Alma and Katharine Miller Jones of the dangers of leaving the home, but they could not keep any patient against her will,[16] thus absolving themselves of any responsibility. When questioned about why Alma might have killed herself, Dr Bathurst was also quick to state that as far as he was concerned there had been no signs that she might take her own life and he was reluctant to lay the blame anywhere specific: 'Mrs Rattenbury was not in a suicidal frame of mind when I saw her on Monday afternoon. On the contrary she was anxious to assist in recovering her health as much as possible. I can only suggest that returning to Bournemouth brought back the events of the past so strongly that it upset her balance.'[17]

Bathurst also reported that when Katharine Miller Jones heard the news she had collapsed in the street and had to be taken in an ambulance to a nursing home. Maude McClellan, who had only known Alma for twenty-four hours, commented that 'it never struck [her] in the slightest as being likely to do what she did'. The reasons for Alma's suicide might be more complex than simply the state of her mental health: 'I cannot help feeling sorry for her. The world has judged her on what evidence it has. I think it has judged her a little harshly.'[18]

A witness from the trial who didn't want to be identified – but most likely to be the ever-discreet Dr O'Donnell – lamented her death, but knowing her personality and the stress she had been under, was not surprised by it: 'I knew Mrs Rattenbury as a nervous, highly-strung and excitable woman. In view of all that has happened, and of her nature, I am not surprised at the tragic end to the awful business. The strain of her ordeal at the trial and her feeling that she would have to face the opprobrium of the world, would all tend to upset her mind and to drive her to desperation.'

On the morning of 4 June, police divers and half a dozen officers waded through the waters at Three Arches Bend in thigh boots, while others raked through the long grass searching for the knife. Electric magnets were also dropped into the stream at various points in the hope of finding the weapon. Despite drenching rain, many 'morbid-minded persons' crowded down to the riverbank to see the place where Alma had taken her life.[19] The knife was never recovered and to this day lies somewhere beneath the water. Her funeral was planned for that Saturday and the inquest would take place at 3 p.m. the day before in the Old Board Room of the Public Assistance Guardians at Fairmile House, where her body lay in the mortuary.

With both their parents now dead, it was imperative to formulate a plan regarding Alma's children, who were both still at school. Who would tell them the tragic news? And what should be organised about their future? Keith Miller Jones was concerned, but had no idea what to do for the best: 'This is all going to make things difficult for them. No one knows what will happen to them. Something will have to be done. I am so sorry for them. Neither of them as far as I know saw their mother after her acquittal. None of my uncle's other relatives has taken any interest so far ... This has been a terrible thing. I don't know what will be done next. If something can be done for the children, I shall be happier.'[20]

Rattenbury's adult children by his previous marriage, Frank and Mary, felt no obligation towards the two orphaned children. Their antipathy towards Alma remained resolute and unforgiving. In the end, Daphne Kingham would take responsibility for her nephew Christopher, and Keith Miller Jones would do the same for his godson, John. There seemed to be no discussion that the two boys who had just lost both parents in traumatic circumstances might be better off together. As for breaking the news to them, despite the continued press interest in the story and the likelihood that the boys might find out what had happened to their parents in a casual manner at school, Pinkie and Miller Jones decided not to tell them about their parents' deaths; the two boys were told that their mother and father had gone away on holiday.

* * *

The narrow road that passed Fairmile House that Friday afternoon was crowded with cars half an hour before the inquest was due to start, many of them belonging to holidaymakers from Bournemouth. About a dozen members of the public were scattered around the Board Room, sitting in yellow armchairs. Just before the court opened, a police officer carried in a bedraggled brown umbrella and parcel containing Alma's pathetic belongings: a handbag, a fawn hat, a large box of cigarettes, the crumpled scraps of paper on which she had written her last words and a paper bag containing the sheath of the knife she had driven into her heart.[21] The coroner, Percy Ingoldby, sat on a raised platform under a wooden canopy. There would be no jury, but six witnesses would be called – the pathologist Dr Jones, William Mitchell, James Penny, Maude McClellan, Irene and PC King, the first police officer at the scene. Lewis Manning represented Alma's family and Marshall Harvey represented Stoner. Dr Jones confirmed that Alma had stabbed herself six times and had died from the severe loss of blood. Death had been almost instantaneous and she may even have been dead before she hit the water. An emotional Irene, dressed in grey with a wide-brimmed straw hat, was called to identify Alma's handbag and her handwriting. Looking very pale and sobbing, she had to be supported by a police officer and her shoulders shook as she struggled through the oath. Ingoldby upbraided her, 'Pull yourself together. I won't distress you more than necessary.'[22] He saw no necessity for kindness. After all, Irene was only Mrs Rattenbury's servant.

He then proceeded to quote excerpts from Alma's last letters, 'vivid with a sense of doom', choosing not to read from the considered suicide letter that she had been at pains to finish. 'Then', he remarked, 'she goes into quite a lot of neurotic statements which I do not propose to read',[23] concerned that making the full text of the letters public might cause distress to those remaining. Alma's last statement, her own reasoning for her suicide, was never made public. Ingoldby judged that Alma had committed suicide while of unsound mind. Just before the 29-minute procedure was over, he asked Lewis Manning how old Alma had been when she died and, loyal confidante to the last, Irene volunteered that Alma was thirty-seven. What good would the truth do now? Irene was given her witness's fee and waited with Manning for some considerable time before leaving to avoid a crowd of people who were waiting outside in the road to get a glimpse of her. In that evening's *Bournemouth Echo*, the campaign for Stoner's reprieve made the front page, while the report of Alma's inquest only made page twelve. Her brief moment of celebrity was already waning, even before she was buried.

The formalities over, Alma's funeral would go ahead as planned at noon the next day. It was supposed to have been a simple, private affair, but like so much of Alma's life, events took their own course and the whole day descended into unseemly and undignified chaos. The date coincided with the Whitsun weekend and thousands of holidaymakers descended upon Bournemouth in search of fun and sunshine by the sea. But the funeral of the woman at the heart of a tabloid sensation was an added attraction that few tourists could resist. Throughout that Saturday there was a constant procession of visitors to the various sites associated with the case. Crowds of sightseers flocked to the Villa Madeira and a few visitors took wreaths to the cemetery. But at the cemetery many openly proclaimed that they did not feel charitably towards Alma and argued fiercely with anyone who disagreed. Some abused Irene, too, with suggestions that she and Alma had also been conducting an improper relationship. For a long time before midday, hundreds of people started arriving, gathering around the plot in which Alma was to be buried, leaning against gravestones and chatting as they waited for the arrival of her coffin.

The coffin was of polished oak and simply inscribed, 'Alma Rattenbury, Widow of Francis Rattenbury'.[24] There was an abundance of colourful flowers, blue irises, pink carnations, cornflowers and yellow roses, but pink flowers dominated, just

as Alma had wanted, and there were none of the white flowers
that she despised. Several wreaths bore inscriptions; on one
'ATONEMENT' was written in capital letters, and above it 'Judge
not lest ye too be judged'. A card attached to another wreath said
'Rest in Peace' with 'As we forgive those that trespass against us'
written underneath. Other inscriptions read, 'Thoughts as sweet
as the flowers you loved' and 'To love is to suffer – from one who
knows'. There was a wreath from British Columbia, 'With deepest sympathy from Auntie Florrie', and a bunch of roses inscribed
with 'Mother's love'. A large cushion of pink carnations stated
simply, 'All my love, darling – Irene'.[25]

A short private service was held in the cemetery chapel by
Reverend W. L. Freeman, the assistant priest at St Peter's Church. It
was attended by Keith Miller Jones, Irene, her parents, sister and her
little niece. Weeping throughout the service, Irene wore a long fur
coat, perhaps one that had belonged to Alma, and a brown straw
hat. The chapel doors had to be locked to keep out the crowds. By
now as many as 3,000 people[26] had swarmed into the cemetery, the
majority of them women, many with babes in arms, trampling on
graves and climbing on gravestones to get a better view.[27] Special
police detachments were hastily summoned to control the growing
number of spectators.[28]

After the service in the chapel, Reverend Freeman led the coffin
to the burial plot, fighting his way through the mob that now surrounded the graveside. He was appalled at the behaviour of the
crowd, which had turned an intimate, private service into a bank
holiday sideshow. 'If the police had not been telephoned for, I do not
know how we would have reached the graveside. The crowd filled
the pathways.' Finally, at the graveside for the internment, Freeman
read two extra prayers not usually heard at funerals, which had a
special reference to absolution. Then he recited Psalm 130:[29]

> Out of the depths have I cried unto thee, O Lord.
> Oh Lord, hear my voice: let thine ears be attentive to the
>   voice of my supplications.

Irene's father, who was a gravedigger at the cemetery, supported her as she was overcome with grief while Alma's coffin was gently lowered into the grave lined with moss, pink pyrethrum and mauve rhododendrons.[30] Reverend Freeman then had to push his way back through the crowds. 'It was a crowd whose curiosity seemed to be entirely without restraint ... Such a scene for Bournemouth was surprising. It would have made me happier if there had been some show of respect or sorrow but it was a gathering without devotion and without sympathy and only moved apparently by morbid curiosity.'[31]

During the funeral, alive to the potential of such a large and interested crowd, one of the committee organisers had copies of the petition to hand and asked for signatures to secure Stoner's reprieve.[32]

That day's *Daily Mirror* published an extraordinarily acerbic piece boxed within a black border, hinting at the press's sense of responsibility – and their own guilt – about what had happened to Alma:

Funny Story for Today!
   So they are burying Mrs Rattenbury today.
   I was in a lift when I heard she'd killed herself. The liftman told me and laughed. His laughing shocked me.
   I can see most jokes, but this one got by me. I couldn't get that last journey of hers out of my head – the journey down to the Sunny South Coast.

* * *

The cruel, monstrous apparatus of publicity had done its best. The poor, half-crazed woman (are you smiling?) wanted to get away from it all.
   The only point was, that there wasn't anywhere to get away to (the liftman would have laughed at this).
   Well, as you know, she got to Bournemouth all right. God knows what happened there.

Then on to Christchurch.

At this stage a knife comes into the picture.

'A long thin knife,' says one paper: 'a stiletto,' 'a dagger,' 'a bread knife,' 'a sort of bowie' – the horrible, gloating chorus is a bit out of harmony. (Funny story, eh?)

* * *

Then out into the quiet fields.

Now she sits and the pathetic last letters are scrawled down.

Is she thinking of Stoner? What is he doing? How are they treating him?

What'll he say when he hears this …

* * *

You know the rest.

The clumsy stabbing, and the attempted drowning just to make sure.

Make sure of what?

To make sure of getting away, not from the law that says she's an innocent woman, but from you and me. And millions like us.

And, of course, from the liftman who laughed.[33]

Irene had arranged for most of Alma's furniture to be put into storage and the majority of her clothes had been sent for safekeeping to Holdenhurst Road.[34] But though the Villa Madeira lay empty following the funeral, it had not remained unoccupied. There had been a series of breaks-ins by sightseers and ghoulish souvenir hunters intent on having mementos of the tragedy that had taken place there; even the garden had been stripped of flowers.[35] A break-in on the evening of 16 June was particularly invasive. The kitchen door had been broken open and a pane of glass near the window catch smashed.[36] After being alerted by the police, the landlady, Mrs Price, arrived to see what damage had been done and was shocked to find the state the house was in. Somebody had scrawled graffiti on the wooden 'rising sun' gate: 'Who did the murder?'[37]

In the drawing room, there were crumbs and spillages all over the sofa, indicating that people had been eating and drinking there. Alma's prized signed photograph of Frank Titterton had been stolen from above the fireplace, her black fox fur was missing, as was the hearth brush, some kitchen knives and Wedgwood ornaments from her bedroom. Two of Ratz's pipes had gone and even John's toy wooden house had been stolen. A cache of letters addressed to Mr Rattenbury, which Mrs Price had packed up to send to his executors, was taken, as well as three letters that were written to her by authors who wanted to stay in the house, hoping that sitting in the room where the murder had been committed might give them some 'inspiration'. Nothing was too small or insignificant to be looted; even a packet of tea from the shelves in the kitchen was taken. Mrs Price was appalled:

> For many days past people have been visiting the premises and going into the garden but they have never before gone so far as this. They have removed plants and flowers from the garden and they were found during the Whitsun holiday having picnics in the garden. Recently there was a party of four men and six women in the garden and one day a group were discovered sitting around eating ice creams there.[38]

Some looters had even taken the screws from Mrs Price's car as it was sitting in the driveway, believing that it belonged to the Rattenburys. She had also received many letters from people requesting that she might let the house or even sell it to them. One woman claiming to be a clergyman's daughter offered 10s a week to move into the house so it might 'recover its prestige'. Another threatened to burn the house down.[39] In order to put a stop to the looting and an end to the morbid interest in the property, Mrs Price decided to redecorate and live in it herself. But she would take down the nameplate from the gate. 5 Manor Road would never be known as the Villa Madeira again.[40]

* * *

Alma died owing £873 7s 10d to the various Bournemouth department stores, chemists, grocers, merchants, schools and hardware
stores that she had struggled to pay while she was alive.[41] £43 7s 2d
was owed to Wheeler's the wine merchant alone.[42] Even the bill
from her spree with Stoner at Harrods pursued her beyond the
grave. The Rattenburys' furniture and household goods were sold
for £531. Their remaining personal possessions, Alma's furs and
jewellery, including the ring that Stoner had bought for her in
London, were sold off for £400 25s. Their unusual left-hand drive
car was sold for a bargain £72.[43]

Intent on escaping the traumatic events in Bournemouth, Irene
moved to London, living quietly in Paddington and working in
anonymity as a bookkeeper. Knowing how much Alma loved her
little dog, it is comforting to think that perhaps Irene took Dinah in.
Irene never married and before the end of her life she moved back
to Holdenhurst Road to live with her sister. On 22 September 1964,
she died from breast cancer, aged fifty-five.

Having played one of the central roles in the most dramatic
murder trial of the 1930s, and before slipping into the background
of history, discreet and ever faithful, Irene gave her only interview
to the press after Alma's funeral:

I would have stayed by her no matter what happened. I spent a
long time with Mrs Rattenbury after the trial and her distress
was pitiful. In her more hopeful moments Mrs Rattenbury was
determined to live the scandal down. We had planned to go away
somewhere far away until people had begun to forget. But she
was always thinking of Stoner and all the terrible things people
were saying about herself. She was so sensitive to criticism. When
I took her to the nursing home after the trial she told me that as
long as she lived she would remember what the judge at the Old
Bailey had said about her. I think his words hurt her more than
anything else. I did think, now that Mrs Rattenbury is dead,

people who did not know her – how kind and generous and good to others she was – would be more charitable. Their evil tongues are pursuing her to the grave. It was shocking to hear some of the things that were said at the funeral and again by the crowds at the graveside today. They say the most scandalous and untrue things about Mrs Rattenbury, and now about me as well. I simply cannot bear it any longer. I am going away where no one knows me so that I can get rest and peace. I am sorry now that I was not able to stay with Mrs Rattenbury in the nursing home. Perhaps I might have been able to save her life, but I was too ill. My nerves have gone. I had no idea when Mrs Rattenbury told me what she would like to have done when she died that she had any thought of suicide in her mind. I am happy now to think I have been able to carry out her last wishes. I dressed her all in pink – the colour she loved – before she was buried and I saw that there were plenty of pink flowers at the funeral. She had a horror of white. I say, in spite of everything and everybody, that Mrs Rattenbury was a wonderful woman. No one knows what an agony it was for her to give the evidence she did at the trial. Few other women would have had such supreme courage.[44]

Campaign to save Stoner

CHAPTER NINETEEN

STAY OF EXECUTION

10 June 1935–24 March 2000

Years from now – when you talk about this –
and you will – be kind.

– Robert Anderson, *Tea and Sympathy*[1]

The holiday weather over the Whitsun weekend was poor.[2] There were thunderstorms and rain over much of the country. In some areas great hailstones fell and streets were flooded. But despite the weather, Bournemouth was packed with holidaymakers and the reprieve campaign organisers continued to collect signatures in pubs, restaurants and churches. There were queues to sign across the whole area – at railway stations, bus stops and on Bournemouth Pier. Mrs Price prominently displayed a petition form outside her tobacconist's shop in Old Christchurch Road.[3] The mayor told the *Daily Mirror* that the petition had now been signed by hundreds of thousands of people: 'everybody in Bournemouth wants to sign. Never has a reprieve been more popular.' But the campaign had now taken on an energy beyond Bournemouth and the demand to save Stoner started to grow nationwide. The petition organisers worked all over the weekend, dealing with the huge number of requests for forms pouring in from all over the country. Thousands of completed forms lay on the floor at the campaign office in St Peter's Road, with Thistleton estimating that they had at least 50,000 signatures in front of them alone. He was amazed at the support they were getting from all over the United Kingdom: 'Everyday our correspondence shows the nationwide sympathy that is felt for Stoner, and the number of people who want to sign the petition is astonishing. There seems to be no end to the requests for petition forms.'[4]

Indeed, forms were so much in demand that people wanting to sign were advised to head sheets of ordinary foolscap paper with 'Petition for the Reprieve of George Percy Stoner'.[5]

* * *

On Bank Holiday Monday, Stoner's handwritten confession, demonstrating in his poor grammar and spelling the limited education he had received, was rushed to Casswell by John Bickford.

> *Dear Sir,*
>
> *I sincerely hope that my writing to you will be of great use. In the first place I wish to state that you have been mislead in my case. My reasons for this of course was to be the greates [sic] benfit [sic] to Mrs Rattenbury to whom I'm in love. I may state that you would not have the real story, had it been that Mrs Rattenbury was still alive. I will start of [sic] by saying that I am perfectly inncent [sic] of this crime. On Sunday evening the day of the crime, I fetch the mallet for a perfectly inncent [sic] reason, that was to erect a tent on the following Monday. I did this because Mr Rattenbury said, he would be using the car on Monday, by this I knew I would not be able to get home so quick and back again on the Monday. When I came back with the mallet I put it in the coal seller [sic] and, went up to my bedroom. I undressed, and got into bed. I also went to sleep, this is the front bedroom. When I awoke I found I had been asleep just over an hour. I judge by this time that Mrs Rattenbury was in bed, so I got out of my bed, came out of my bedroom on to the landing. I stopped for a second and lean over the bannister, at this moment, Mis [sic] Riggs appeared at her door, she ask me what was the matter. I replied. Just looking to see if the lights*

were out. Which was perfectly trues [sic] because sometimes
they are out when I go into other bedroom, she appeared to be
satisfied and withdrue [sic] in her room. I continued on my way
into Mrs Rattenbury's bedroom. There I found her in bed, she
seem to be in the most terrified state, she said two words, 'hear
him' at that moment I heard a loud groan. At this she got out
of bed and ran down stairs. I immediately redressed excpting
[sic] for my coat and waistcoat, because I gain the impression
that somthing [sic] was wrong down stairs. I came down stairs
and went into the drawing room, there I found Mr Rattenbury
in the arm chair with severe head injuris [sic], quit by axident
[sic] I found my mallet beside the settee. I kicked it behind the
settee. Apparently Mis Riggs had not notice it, so when she
went to telephone, I hid the mallet out side the house. When
Mis [sic] Riggs came back from the phone, we, that is all three
of us, carried Mr Rattenbury into his bedroom and laid him
on his bed. I then went out and got the car out and went round
for D.c. O.Donald, who had left befor [sic] I got there, he had
arrived back on the premises befor [sic] me. When the ambulance arrived back on the scenes [sic] Mr Rattenbury was taken
to the nursing home. Under the direction of Mrs Rattenbury I
follow the ambulance so as to bring D.c. O.Donald back. When
we arrived back the police were there. Mrs Rattenbury was
under the infuence [sic] of drink. D.c. O.Donald seeing her in
this condition gave her morphine and put her to bed, but when
he had gon [sic] she came down stairs, this time I carried her up
stairs and put her to bed. In the morning inspector carter asked
for a statement, had I known Mrs Rattenbury had made any
statements, I would have placed myself in her position there and
then. When Mrs Rattenbury was arrested I was terribly upset.
I did everthing [sic] I thought would get sufficient evidence
against me. I showed Mis Riggs were I fetch the mallet from
because I knew she would have to give evidence.

    Yours Faithfully

    George Percy Stoner[6]

It's unlikely that Casswell entirely believed Stoner's confession, which required him to accept that Alma happened on the mallet that evening while she was for some reason in the coal cellar on the warmest night of the year. It's more likely that he assumed it was a reasonable attempt to save his neck in the wake of Alma's death. But at least he now had the statement he had wanted from Stoner all along. But he couldn't refer to it in the Court of Appeal on Stoner's behalf unless the court permitted him to call Stoner as a witness, so they had to move quickly. Casswell immediately made an official application to call Stoner to give evidence outlining the reason he had not wanted to give evidence before 'for fear that under cross examination I might say something which would incriminate Mrs Rattenbury'.[7] He insisted that he was not present when the blows were struck and he knew nothing about it 'until after it had been done'.

The next day, Stoner's solicitor Marshall Harvey announced that the notice of appeal had been lodged but that he was unable to give any more details about the grounds for the appeal. Thistleton advised the *Daily Sketch* that he understood that the home secretary was 'willing to accept the petition, but now the notice of appeal has been lodged he will probably not give an answer until after the decision of the appeal court has been announced'.[8]

The reprieve committee raced to submit the petition by the end of the week as planned. Just before 11 a.m. on Friday 14 June, Sir Henry Page-Croft and Gordon Caine Hall arrived at the Home Office by car accompanied by Mr Thistleton in order to deliver the petition to the home secretary personally. They got out of the vehicle and carried four huge brown-paper parcels into the building, each labelled 'Stoner Petition'. In an age before social media, they had mobilised support across the whole country, collecting 321,000 signatures in just fourteen days.[9]

As Stoner and the rest of the nation counted the days to the appeal, the issue continued to be furiously debated in the letters columns of the press, the Twitter of its day:

Why all this maddening sympathy for Mrs Rattenbury? What would have been her attitude and Stoner's, if both had been acquitted? What of the generous and indulgent husband? Has no one a word of sympathy for him?
  – A native of Bournemouth[10]

The manner in which Stoner conducted himself throughout the ordeal is surely a magnificent example of the courage of a British lad.
  – Hereford Youth[11]

The sentiment displayed by some of your correspondents is nauseating. Life and not death is the acid test. Mrs Rattenbury would have been worthier of respect had she lived to make some reparation.
  – P. J. Piggott, Derby[12]

The people who are shrieking for the abolition of capital punishment should pay a little attention to those who view with alarm the increase in juvenile crime. The extent of 'slop' and 'sob' over each case has been so curiously similar that it could well be taken for an organized system of propaganda.
  – Arnold Harley, Newcastle[13]

Then, after weeks of dismal cold, on Midsummer Day there was a sudden heatwave across Britain, with cloudless skies and fourteen hours of unbroken sunshine. In the cities, commuters unseasonably dressed in overcoats sweltered on trains, trams, tubes and buses. Holidaymakers on the crowded Bournemouth beaches had to be treated for sunstroke as temperatures reached 28°C in the shade. On Monday 24 June, the tennis championships at Wimbledon opened in the glorious weather, though for some spectators the sun was too hot and there were many empty seats, even when star player Bunny Austin appeared on Centre Court.

Outside the entrance to the gothic Royal Courts of Justice in the

Strand, sandwich men paraded with boards saying, 'Stoner Must be Reprieved' and 'Stop Illegal Killing'. One poster had an image of the gallows and bore the words, 'End Capital Punishment'.[14] These sandwich men had been stationed outside the courts by the eccentric millionairess Violet Van der Elst. Mrs Van der Elst had built her own business selling cosmetics and Shavex, the first brushless shaving cream. When her second husband had died in 1934, she had resolved to redirect her grief – and invest much of her fortune – into a populist campaign to abolish the death penalty. She arrived for Stoner's appeal in her white Rolls-Royce and as she stepped onto the pavement a woman approached her with a bouquet of roses. She accepted them with a smile and walked into the main hall, accompanied by a barrister.

The court was oppressively hot that day and people crowded into the gangways to witness the next twist in the Bournemouth Triangle Murder. Stoner would be appearing before Mr Justice Swift, Mr Justice Lawrence and the Lord Chief Justice, Lord Hewart. Hewart had sat on the appeal of Edith Thompson in 1922, a case he had dismissed at the time as a 'squalid and indecent one of lust and adultery'.[15] It was unlikely that his feelings had mellowed.

Casswell argued that the court of appeal had said in a number of cases that separate trials should always be granted where there was a likelihood of a miscarriage of justice. During the trial, he argued, the defence were faced with two individuals who each claimed, 'I did it and I did it alone.' Stoner was deeply in love with and completely dominated by Alma, which put him in a terrible position. In effect, the prosecution had said, 'We say that one of you is guilty. Now, Stoner, if you want to clear yourself, your counsel must cross examine this woman, and every time he makes a point in your favour, he makes a point against her. If you go into the witness-box and give evidence on your own behalf, you will help to convict her.'[16]

If Stoner had given his word to Alma that he would take the blame for the murder, could anyone blame him as an honourable man for keeping his word and not going into the witness box? He had only not done so for fear of incriminating Alma. So Casswell requested that Stoner should be allowed to give his evidence now. At the same time, he proposed that Travers Humphreys had 'slurred over' some of the evidence and had failed to suggest the option of manslaughter as a possible verdict to the jury.[17] Stoner rose from his seat with a warder on each side of him and grew paler as Hewart proceeded to respond to Casswell. Mrs Van der Elst was moved by the composure of the young man whose fate was about to be decided: 'I have never in my life seen anyone's face so completely grey looking. He did not care if they condemned him to death or what happened to him. A newspaper stated that he looked around the Court: this was not true. He showed no fear; he stood there, immovable. He has a strong face for such a young man. His hands were clasped behind him and he stood facing the judge unflinchingly, but with a look of terrible despair in his eyes.'[18]

Hewart indignantly refused Casswell's application. He dismissed the suggestion of Stoner offering himself as a witness now, 'swearing what he would not swear, and was not prepared to swear' was 'almost sinister'.[19] Casswell was also refused permission to refer to the letter that Stoner had written. Hewart bristled at the implied criticism of Travers Humphreys, 'a Judge of great experience in the criminal law'. The issue of whether trials were separate or not was down to the discretion of the judge alone and the suggestion that Travers Humphreys did not quite appreciate the evidence was absurd; 'a man who was capable of believing that was capable of believing anything'. There was no need, Hewart declared, to review the evidence in this 'sordid and squalid case':[20]

There is nothing at all in this appeal except that it arises out of a charge of murder. It is a mere waste of time. The fact, if it be a fact, that a lad of good character had been corrupted by an abandoned woman old enough to be his mother raises no question of law, nor can it be employed as a ground of appeal to this Court. We have no power, nor have we the inclination, to alter the law relating to murder in this respect. The appeal is dismissed.[21]

Stoner seemed dazed and did not appear to realise that the appeal was over until one of the warders touched him on the shoulder.[22]

The whole procedure had taken just fifteen minutes. The sentence stood; Stoner's execution would go ahead.

A journalist from the *Bournemouth Echo* promptly visited the Stoners' home in Redhill Drive to get their reaction to the failure of the appeal. Everything now depended on the king's prerogative of mercy. Despite the worry that had riven both their faces, Stoner's parents put up a brave front: 'We can only wait and hope for the best. There is nothing more to be done.'[23]

That night was the hottest Britain had experienced in twenty-four years. Hundreds of people fainted and four died from the intense heatwave.[24]

* * *

The responsibility for advising the king of his prerogative was held by one man. He had been in office for just two weeks. Sir John Simon had been a successful barrister before entering politics as a Liberal MP. Over his long career he would hold many of the great offices of state, and is one of only three people in British history to have served as home secretary, foreign secretary and chancellor of the Exchequer. But he was possessed of a chilly manner and lacked the ability to create political allies or warm friendships; 'God, what a toad and a worm Simon is,'[25] wrote Harold Nicolson in his diary. Simon had headed the public inquiry into the sinking of the *Titanic* in 1912 and had first served unsuccessfully as home secretary in Asquith's government during the First World War. He is remembered today for having initiated the least auspicious decade in the history of British foreign policy. His tenure at the Foreign Office was the start of 'a disastrous era in which ... British power and influence steadily declined and Britain was fatuously conducted towards the Second World War'.[26]

Simon left the Foreign Office, Lloyd George observed, 'an acknowledged failure'.[27] During the Second World War, he would become an associate of Chamberlain and named as one of the 'Guilty Men' who sought appeasement with the Germans in 1940 and was regarded by some as 'the snakiest of the lot'.[28] In the

Evening Standard Howard Spring lamented his appointment as home secretary: 'To me his smile is the most terrible thing about him. It is the sad, understanding smile of a janitor at a crematorium accustomed to the bonfire of daily hopes and coloured dreams ... No, Sir John is not a crusader, he is a coroner.'[29]

On Simon's new desk at the Home Office was a framed card listing the names of convicted murderers, including Stoner, who had been sentenced to death and were awaiting execution. Stoner's case was the first capital charge that he would deal with in his new role in June 1935. The dates of each step in the procedure were laid out on the card, with an ominous blank column that was to contain the final decision as to reprieve or hanging. On the frame enclosing the list of impending executions, Simon had had inscribed a line from Juvenal, *Nulla unquam de morte hominis cunctatio longa est*, translated by Dryden as, 'When a man's life is in debate, the judge can ne'er too long deliberate.'[30]

After the extraordinarily hot night following the appeal, a series of torrential storms left a trail of havoc across Britain the next day, with buildings struck by lightning, roads flooded, cars marooned and railways brought to a halt by landslides. Among the chaos, six people died.[31] That evening, as twenty storms ringed around London before spreading north, there was, at last, an announcement from the Home Office: 'In the case of George Percy Stoner, convicted of murder and sentenced to death, the Home Secretary has recommended a reprieve with a view to the commutation of the capital sentence to one of penal servitude for life.'[32]

Both the judge and jury had recommended mercy and the Home Office had received close to 350,000 signatures pleading for a reprieve, so there was little doubt as to what Sir John Simon's decision would have been. But now the reprieve was official; Stoner would live. The governor at Pentonville, Commander Tabuteau, went to the condemned cell to give Stoner the news: 'Stoner's strange self-possession deserted him. He listened almost unbelieving, to the governor's words, and the long tension of weeks broken, sobbed unrestrainedly. He sat down and buried his pale face in trembling hands, muttering a broken, "Thank you, Sir."'[33]

'The final curtain [had] fallen on one of the most remarkable dramas in modern times.'[34] The news was issued to the press and was immediately posted on the windows of the *Bournemouth Echo* offices before it would be communicated to Stoner's family. An *Echo* journalist went directly to Redhill Drive to give Stoner's parents the good news and, of course, to record their exclusive reactions for his newspaper. The Stoners ushered the journalist into their small front parlour. At first they seemed stunned, 'so heavy was the burden of anxiety which had settled upon them',[35] but as they began to realise the full meaning of what was happening, 'their faces brightened as the shadow of a great dread fell away and relief and gratitude took its place'. Stoner's mother was thankful: 'I wish I had some wine to offer you. This news is so good, so great, after all we have been through. I am very grateful for all that has been done to save my boy. Everybody has been so good.'[36] As tears threatened to overwhelm her, Stoner's father gripped the reporter's hand in thanks as his wife continued to speak as if she had been relieved of a great weight:

> This trouble has been hanging over us for so long that the burden of it was becoming intolerable. There have been so many disappointments that sometimes we have not known what to think and although we have never given up hope, we could not help wondering, sometimes, what would come next. There was the terrible shock of the verdict, and then the still greater blow when the appeal was dismissed on Monday. Our only hope was that the pleas for mercy would prevail. Now the dreadful suspense is over and I shall be able to rest.[37]

She admitted that it was going to be hard getting used to the idea of their son's imprisonment, but she was assured by the reporter that they would be able to see him regularly and that he'd be well looked after. There was also the possibility of remission for good conduct and a reduction in the sentence. One day Mrs Stoner hoped that he would write and tell his parents 'what happened at that house on that terrible night'. As the reporter left, Stoner's father assured his wife that time would soften the blow of having their son taken from them: 'Let us be glad, at least, that he will not hang and that he is spared to us. Who knows but that we may live to welcome him home one day.' Tears came to Mrs Stoner's eyes again as she spoke of the many friends who had rallied round them in their time of trouble: 'I never knew until this blow fell there were so many people who thought so kindly about us.'[38]

Nowhere was the news received with greater satisfaction than among the organisers of the reprieve committee at St Peter's Road. Mr Thistleton was jubilant: 'This is a great day for us,' he said, 'a day of triumph.'[39] The news spread quickly throughout Bournemouth, a moment for local pride and celebration. Soon local people were flocking to the Stoners' bungalow to offer their congratulations.

Stoner was officially pardoned by George V on 30 June 1935, the twenty-sixth year of his reign. After the extensive and warm Jubilee celebrations that year, this would be the last but one royal pardon that the king would issue before his death early in 1936. The next would be granted by his son, Edward VIII, in a year when another alluring divorcée was to dominate the British tabloids.

On 3 July, Stoner asked if he could see the letter he had been sent by Alma before she died. The next day, the prison commissioners wrote to the governor at Pentonville permitting Stoner to receive the letter on condition that he did not communicate it or its contents to anybody or for it to appear in the press. After he had had it a reasonable time, it should be placed 'under seal' with the rest of his property. On 11 July, he was transferred to Maidstone Prison[40] and was given the letter from Alma the same day. He reassured the prison authorities that he had no intention of making its contents public.[41]

Finally, he read Alma's last words to him: 'Sweet one – I love you always and always.'[42]

* * *

Maidstone had been opened by Winston Churchill in 1912 and had formerly been a mixed prison. There were now two main wings at right angles to each other, each 230ft long and 36ft wide. B Wing housed adult male prisoners in 128 cells and A Wing housed young offenders in 127 cells. A kitchen, laundry, baths and chapel were housed in a separate building. For young offenders there were courses in carpentry, metalwork and crafts in addition to classes in bricklaying, plastering, painting and general labouring. As well as offering something to focus on during their sentence, these schemes provided experience and a qualification when the prisoner was released: 'It will keep him fresh in mind and spirit and do something to mitigate the monotony of a long sentence in a confined prison. He will be provided with something to learn and something to achieve and will feel that he is making progress and not standing still.'

Worrying that he was young and good-looking, the authorities at Maidstone placed Stoner with the younger offenders so that he could be protected from predatory older prisoners. One ex-prisoner wrote of his experiences of Maidstone Prison in the *Sunday Dispatch*, observing that 'it is not difficult to imagine that the eyes of Mrs Rattenbury might rest on [Stoner] with interest, and then with desire.'

I watched him at parades, at work, and in the blue and grey chapel. He rarely spoke at all, but when he did it was with a quiet, pleasant voice and a clean tongue – in itself a rare distinction in Maidstone. For weeks he looked and behaved like a man in a trance, as though still in that state in which I have observed many new-comers to be, a sort of twilight sleep, which seems mercifully to be induced by the bludgeoning and cruelty of the trial. He was confined in a part of the prison set apart for those of tender years, who, it is deemed, should be segregated from the older prisoners – in an attempt, and in my opinion an unsuccessful attempt – to deal with those acute problems of sex and perversion in the unnatural conditions of prison life. His features may lose their clear, open lines and his tongue may become furred with the filth that he hears. He is young and impressionable, and these things are all about him, despite the care and vigilance of prison officials. They will creep upon him unless the resistance is exceptional, and if he remains there long enough they will leave their indelible mark upon him. In the name of commonsense, what else is to be expected?[43]

On 14 July 1941, Casswell wrote to the home secretary suggesting that Stoner be released.[44] In August the secretary of state issued instructions that Stoner was to be released after he had served seven years of his sentence, 'subject to good behaviour and industry'.[45] He was transferred to Camp Hill Prison on the Isle of Wight, where prisoners had greater access to the outside world. His 'conduct and industry were most satisfactory', according to the governor at Camp Hill, though on 3 March 1942 he left the group he was working with without permission and posted a letter in a pillar box on the main road. He was punished with three days' close confinement, three days' basic diet and his release would be delayed by seven days.[46]

Stoner was finally released from prison on 27 May 1942, though he would be on licence for life.[47] Since he began his sentence, a war had started, a king had died, another had abdicated and a third had taken his place. Having left Camp Hill, he found work as a mechanic and tractor driver. On 18 November 1943, he joined the Royal Army Service Corps and went to train at Hadrian's Camp in Carlisle as a lorry driver.[48]

After training, Stoner joined 755 Bulk Petrol Transport Company.[49] Originally based in the north of England, the company was responsible for the transportation of tankers, tanker vehicles, tractors and trailers. One of the towns in which 755 Company had temporary headquarters was Elland, a mill town in West Yorkshire, just south of Halifax.

Christine Scholey had grown up in Elland and during the war she was working in a grocer's shop. She first met Stoner, now a soldier and 'quite a good-looking young man', on a bus coming home from night school.[50] She introduced him to her parents and they took to him right away. After a year of courting they started to discuss getting married. It was then that he said there was something she ought to know, before telling her that in his past he had been tried and convicted for murder. At first Christine was 'dumbfounded'. She had never even heard of the Rattenburys. Then, after a few minutes, she said, 'It was all a long time ago and was best forgotten.' She loved him and 'had the measure of the man'. Whatever he had done, they would put it behind them. It seemed as if Stoner had paid his dues to society and was to have a second chance. They didn't say anything at all about her fiancé's past to her parents, but she thought that they probably knew; the mores of another generation, it was never discussed.[51] On 17 May, Stoner and his unit were warned that they were to be deployed overseas, so on 24 May he married Christine at Elland, but there was no time for a honeymoon or settling down to married life; 'We had a quick cup of tea with some family and friends after the wedding and then caught the train to Bournemouth to see the in-laws.' Like many whirlwind courtships at the time, Stoner and Christine may have married quickly because it had become increasingly clear that the war was coming to a decisive moment. 755 Company were mobilised to Bognor Regis where there was a high concentration of American and Canadian troops.[52] 'By early June,' one veteran remembered, 'the whole of the south of England was one big camp.'[53] These were the preparations for D-Day. Stoner's unit subsequently embarked to France. Like millions of young men and women of his generation, he would play a crucial role in the liberation of Europe, his past forgotten in the urgency of the national emergency.

* * *

Stoner's mother died in January 1945, so he and Christine moved into Redhill Drive with his father. On demobilisation in 1947, he was awarded the 1939–45 War Medal and praised by his commanding officer as 'an excellent soldier, a capable driver and thoroughly recommendable at all times'.[54] When Christine was expecting their first child in 1948, she developed a kidney infection and the baby had to be induced. They had a daughter, Yvonne. Stoner was 'a good father and husband. Nothing fazed him. He went the same gentle pace all the time.'[55]

In March 1949, Stoner's father died, leaving the house and his estate of £1,650 to his only son. Though inheriting a home of their own may have seemed a dream come true for many couples of their age and class, providing them great security, settling in Bournemouth was a risk for the Stoners, who hoped that the events of the past would stay there. And perhaps this was their biggest error. They stayed in Bournemouth in a property where the family were very well known. Consequently, Stoner was easy to locate, easy to identify and easy to contact. Meanwhile, by 1951 Christine was pregnant again, but the child was stillborn. She remembered that 'it affected us very much at the time. It was a wanted baby, but my blood wasn't compatible with my husband's. After losing the second baby, they told me I couldn't have any more children.'[56]

Yvonne was to be their only child.

In a world before the internet, the young Yvonne Stoner wasn't aware of the Rattenbury murder, her father being a 'very private person in that way'.[57] She was brought up by her parents with strong values and a sense of justice and fairness, always listening to both sides of any story. She later learned about her father's history from friends who didn't want her to come across it in articles or books about the murder without having been prepared for it.[58] The Stoners stayed in Bournemouth but would visit Yorkshire for holidays. Stoner was working and they 'didn't do too bad'. There were some neighbours, though, who never forgot the Rattenbury scandal. Christine remembered: 'Some were supportive, but some didn't want to know us, although I made a lot of friends through the Salvation Army and Townswomen's Guild. We wanted to forget all about what happened and we just didn't discuss it after we moved down to Bournemouth. We thought we'd let sleeping dogs lie but we weren't allowed to.'[59]

* * *

The events at the heart of the Rattenbury story and what they revealed about attitudes towards class and sexuality in Britain had gripped the nation in March 1935; a love triangle, adultery, murder, a beautiful, passionate woman and a red-blooded young servant. It was *Arden of Faversham*, *Lady Chatterley* or *Miss Julie* transposed to the English seaside. Just after the trial ended, the *Daily Express* had observed that they had previously serialised Francis Iles's *Malice Aforethought*, which was also based on a real trial, but felt that 'the case of Mrs Rattenbury contains the material for a story that would eclipse all'.[60] Quick to exploit the public interest in the story, Tennyson Jesse's edition of *The Trial of Alma Rattenbury and George Percy Stoner* was published just in time for Christmas 1935, Compton Mackenzie in the *Daily Mail* remarking that 'this sad story is more absorbing than 99 per cent of our detective novels'.[61] And it wasn't only criminologists like Tennyson Jesse who were drawn to the case. Like the lives and deaths of Edith Thompson and Ruth Snyder, Alma's story was to inspire novelists and even poets. During the original run of *Night Must Fall*, the actor and playwright Emlyn Williams suggested the Rattenbury murder as the subject of a film to the producer Alexander Korda to star Merle Oberon and Laurence Olivier. But the project stalled when Williams transferred with *Night Must Fall* to Broadway and he and Oberon signed up to Korda's ill-fated film version of *I, Claudius*.[62]

In 1936, the surrealist poet David Gascoyne conjured images of the murder and the circumstances of Alma's suicide in his prose poem, *Lozanne*.

The panelling of the room where they asked you questions was made of exactly the same wood as the mallet which you had to hate.

The dusty and ashen residue of a passion that now raged elsewhere, but still raged, rose slowly upwards to the surface of the lake as your blood sank slowly through it.[63]

Writing around the same time, W. H. Auden must surely have had the case in mind when writing 'At Last the Secret is Out' ('Behind the lady who dances and the man who madly drinks ...').[64]

In 1939, Francis Iles published *As For the Woman*, the first of a projected three-novel sequence that merged aspects of the Thompson/Bywaters and Rattenbury/Stoner cases. At a crucial point in the story, in an extraordinary collision of fact and fiction, the Edith/Alma character Evelyn Pawle reads aloud to her young lover Alan from a transcription of the Thompson and Bywaters trial:

'She loved this man just like I love you, Alan. Why is one to feel nothing but contempt for her? She couldn't help it could she?'

'I think the theory is she should have helped it.'

'Well, she couldn't – any more than I could help loving you.'

'You mustn't take seriously what they say in court.' Alan smiled.

'But I do, dearest. Don't you see? It might be us.'[65]

In 1948, Shelley Smith published *The Woman in the Sea* inspired by the case and Tennyson Jesse's introduction to it. Though set in the 1940s at 'Villa Arcadia', it closely follows the details of the story, even down to fictional versions of Alma's suicide letters,

I have made a mess of everything ... My world is in ruins. I am tortured by it all and I can't stand it any more. The best thing I can do now is to get out before I cause any more harm. I don't want my kiddy to suffer for having a mother like me.[66]

Much anthologised in popular studies of crime, in 1943 the *Strand Magazine* observed that the Rattenbury case was an 'extraordinary hotch-potch of the probable and the incredible, the human [and] the inhuman', citing it as 'the crime writer's favourite murder'.[67] In less than a decade, the story had taken its place as one of Orwell's classic English murders, 'a crime [which] can have dramatic and even tragic qualities [and] excite pity for both victim and murderer'.[68] But it is in dramatic form that the story would find lasting fame.

In 1937, an application had been made to produce *Villa Mimosa*, a play based on events leading up to the trial by an actor called Francis James, who had played Laertes to Gielgud's celebrated Hamlet at the Queen's Theatre in 1930. However, the Lord Chamberlain, who regulated and censored plays at the time, refused it a licence as the dramatisation of recent murder cases was forbidden in deference to the feelings of surviving relations. Subsequently, in 1940 a rewritten and still uncensored version of the play opened in March at the Chanticleer Theatre in South Kensington under the name *Belle View* and starring Beatrix Thomson, the third Mrs Claude Rains. Though the script was praised ('certainly a play worth seeing'[69]), *The Times* felt the Alma character had 'that fatality about her which finds itself at home both in reports of murder trials and in the less successful pages of D. H. Lawrence'.[70]

In 1940, the prolific Anglo-American dramatist John Van Druten – who later penned *Bell, Book and Candle* and the Isherwood-inspired *I am a Camera* – wrote *Leave Her to Heaven*, largely based on Tennyson Jesse's edition of the trial, the title a quotation from *Hamlet*. Van Druten dedicated the published version of the play to Tennyson Jesse, 'most indebtedly'. The production[71] marked the return to Broadway of the film star Ruth Chatterton, but was not a success, with *Time* magazine dismissing it; 'some distinctly unattractive people who do decidedly unsavoury things and come to extremely unpleasant ends.'[72] Chatterton 'had a field day running the gamut, but the play was too weak to sustain her'.[73] The play closed after only fifteen performances, did not transfer to the UK and has never been performed here, or indeed anywhere else, since its Broadway premiere.

By the 1960s, just as the anxieties of the 1930s were starting to look prehistoric in the context of the *Lady Chatterley* trial and the Profumo affair, the young Simon Gray came across a green penguin paperback of Tennyson Jesse's study of the case, which had been discarded in a railway compartment. 'I left the book where I'd found it, but for the rest of that day, and for many subsequent days and (especially) nights, I was haunted by Mrs Rattenbury's story – or what of it I could perceive behind the dozen pages or so in which her trial had been described.'[74]

In 1967, Gray was commissioned to write his first piece for television, *Death of a Teddy Bear*, as a BBC Wednesday Play starring Brenda Bruce in the Alma Rattenbury role. It went on to win that year's Writers' Guild Award for best new play. The play resurfaced ten years later at the Palace Theatre Watford, retitled *Molly* and starring Mary Miller.

The best-remembered dramatisation of the story, however, was the final play by the great British writer of repression and reticence, Sir Terence Rattigan. Theatrically and commercially astute, Rattigan must have been aware of *Villa Mimosa* and may even have seen the premiere. He would certainly have known about the failure of *Leave Her to Heaven* on Broadway. So he may have been deterred from writing about the Rattenburys in the 1930s because he'd been beaten to it by other writers. Though he'd been drawn to the story at the time of the trial, he'd also struggled to find a way of dramatising it, so put aside the idea for over forty years, when James and Van Druten's plays – and the real events behind them – had been forgotten. In 1964, Rattigan invested in the first production of a new play by a rising young playwright, Joe Orton. *Entertaining Mr Sloane* depicts an older woman infatuated with a sexually provocative young stranger who moves into the house she shares with her brother and elderly father. The play ends with Sloane killing the old man in a psychedelic re-visioning of the Rattenbury ménage, which perhaps subconsciously reignited Rattigan's interest in the material. In the end, he was invited by the BBC to explore the story as a radio drama.

Rattigan, who knew he was dying when he was writing the play, didn't interview any of the surviving protagonists in the case, nor did he consult any sources other than Tennyson Jesse's forty-page introduction to *Notable British Trials*. Rattigan dramatised Tennyson Jesse's key arguments in his play, railing, as she did, against the chauvinism that dominated the trial. As well as the Rattenbury story, Rattigan added the contrasting autobiographical subplot of Mrs Davenport, a repressed female juror based on Rattigan's mother. Interviewed by the *Radio Times*, Rattigan said, 'I believe the audience will cry at Mrs Rattenbury's fate. I know I did.'[75] He remembered the huge impact the trial had at the time: 'Nobody talked about anything else.' Something of a coup, the BBC secured former '50s sex kitten Diana Dors to play Alma.

It was only when the play had been recorded that the Stoners in Bournemouth heard about it. *The Observer* announced 'BBC finds murderer in Rattigan play alive' and reported that despite 'extensive BBC researches' they had failed to establish that Stoner was living with the same name in the same house in which he had lived as a young man. A BBC press statement was clearly intent on using this last-minute off-stage drama as way of promoting the broadcast of the play. They made an agreement with Stoner's lawyers to change the name of his character to spare him, they claimed, any unwanted publicity: 'Our chief concern is to protect the man. Both sides are happy with what has been done.' The production underwent a last-minute change as the Stoner character was renamed George Alfred Wood.[76]

Cause Célèbre or *A Woman of Principle* was broadcast on 27 October 1975 and was politely received, though Paul Ferris in *The Observer* felt that, though it was 'polished', it was an 'old fashioned piece': 'As for the radio technique, a clock tick-tocked to show time passing, and a newsboy was heard shouting, "'Orrible murder latest … thank you Guv." (*ITMA* was poking fun at that sort of cliché 30 years ago.)'[77]

Rattigan subsequently adapted the play for the stage, which opened in the West End on 4 July 1977. As it was now a star vehicle for Glynis Johns, the story was concentrated on the character of the tragic heroine, Alma. Johns's presence ensured that the production was a popular success, and her performance as Alma, 'of much fun and great dignity',[78] was much admired, John Barber writing in the *Telegraph* of her 'profound study of a woman in torment'.[79]

Reactions to Rattigan's play were less enthusiastic, with Herbert Kretzmer in the *Express* dismissing it as 'little more than an over-cluttered pot-boiler'[80] and the *Evening Standard* agreeing that 'Johns had some excellent moments of hysteria and brooding regret as she tries to interpret a woman who was much too complex for Mr Rattigan's pen'.[81]

The next year, on 25 October, Simon Gray's *Molly* opened at the Comedy Theatre, by then starring Billie Whitelaw, meaning the middle of the punk era saw two different plays in the West End inspired by the same antique murder case. Benedict Nightingale observed that it was 'Gray's version of the Rattenbury myth that repays the more careful examination ... it has a resonance that makes Rattigan's timbre sound just a little woolly.'[82]

These stage productions inspired a new wave of press intrusion for the Stoners. Even though Stoner's name had been changed in the play, however hard he tried to forget or escape it, the murder at the Villa Madeira just wouldn't go away. Christine Stoner remembered:

> We were bombarded with calls night and day, forcing us to change our phone number several times. The papers just wouldn't leave us alone. But we wouldn't speak to them. George asked me a couple of times if I wanted to move and start a new life somewhere else, but I said, 'Do you want to move?', and he said no, and I said, 'Well, we won't, I don't see why we should let them turn us out of our home.'[83]

Already beleaguered by the press, in 1987, ten years after the West End premiere, the Stoners heard that Anglia Television were planning to produce a TV film of *Cause Célèbre* starring Helen Mirren. The producer John Rosenberg had been 'obsessed' by the story for years as it 'had everything'.[84] He didn't approach Stoner before production because he 'felt that he may have suffered enough and to a certain extent', he claimed, 'we wanted to protect him'.[85] In this version of the play, Anglia almost completely cut the parallel story of Mrs Davenport, the repressed juror. It was the real-life drama of Alma

Rattenbury that made *Cause Célèbre*, not Rattigan's autobiographical subplot. In a bid to protect themselves against any potential libel action, ITV changed Stoner's name to 'Bowman', but the facts of the case remained the same. The Stoners protested that the project should be abandoned. By then seventy-one, Stoner attacked Anglia for tormenting him and his family with painful memories: 'These TV people can't possibly know anything about the case. It was so long ago there was no other person to witness the actual event.'[86]

As filming went ahead, the Stoners, both very distressed, continued to protest, but ITV disregarded their appeals. Finally, for the first time, they tried to make their feelings heard in the local Bournemouth press, with Stoner granting David Kavanagh an interview.

> We feel it is not necessary at all and their knowledge will be far from the truth. The whole crime was committed on an emotional basis. Both I and the lady concerned were in a highly emotional state. Our emotions were completely out of control. But there was no money involved, or jealousy. Alma was very uptight about being married to this man. He was previously married with four children and left them [*sic*]. Alma didn't want to marry him in the first place but pressure was put on her by her parents. I got in such a state I didn't know what to do. I'm very ashamed at what I did, but I was young and youngsters can get into a high pitch of emotion.[87]

They simply wanted to be allowed to get on with their lives without discussing the circumstances of the murder. But the tabloids insisted on squeezing any sensational headlines they could out of the story:

The Murderer who'll see himself killing again, 50 years on

> This man cheated the hangman ... He was sentenced to the gallows after battering his mistress's husband to death ... now he faces trial again ... this time by television.[88]

Christine wept with anger at 'the lies' printed about them in the newspapers:[89] 'For God's sake, all we want to do is live in peace and forget everything that happened before. It's haunted us all our lives. It's cruel to keep it going ... We have been offered the earth, considerable sums of money, to talk. One man from America wanted to write a book about it all but we turned him down, too. It should be left where it belongs, in the past.'[90]

Though there's no evidence that he ever saw or read *Cause Célèbre*, a frustrated Stoner advised readers to take the TV film with 'a pinch of salt'.[91] He and his wife would not be watching the programme. But the broadcast incited even more interest in the story and, ironically, by protesting about it Stoner provoked even more sensational headlines, such as 'Murderer Hits Out Over Film; Tangled Web of Love and Death 50 Years Ago'.[92] The Stoners were once again harassed by phone and at their doorstep by the media, just as they had hounded Alma years before, all the way to the river at Christchurch. Stoner was despairing. 'Not now, or anytime in the future do we want anyone to call at our home. After half a century we feel it should remain where it belongs, buried in the past. I just wish they'd forget everything.'

By the late 1980s, Stoner had developed symptoms of Alzheimer's disease. His condition deteriorated and Christine began to worry about his erratic behaviour: 'He used to get aggressive. You couldn't have a proper conversation with him. His brain just didn't seem to work like it had.'[93]

* * *

Anne Griffiths, the daughter of Robert Lewis Manning, the local solicitor who had represented Alma, was four at the time of the murder. She inherited her father's copy of the Rattenbury and Stoner *Notable British Trials* edition, which Tennyson Jesse had signed, 'For R. Lewis Manning, who says he dislikes most women, with thanks from the Editor.' Years later, Mrs Griffiths served as a magistrate in Bournemouth and one day, in conversation with a fellow magistrate, she happened to mention her father's connection to the Rattenbury case. Her colleague told her that, by coincidence, he attended a men's club where Stoner was a member, and he knew him well. He wondered if she'd like him to ask Stoner to sign her father's copy of the book, as Tennyson Jesse had done? As Stoner reportedly never spoke publicly about the murder, she was surprised when Stoner added his signature beneath a photograph of himself that was one of the illustrations in the book. Some years later, she was to come face to face with Stoner in difficult circumstances.[94]

On 13 August 1990, a twelve-year-old boy had stopped to use a public toilet in Bournemouth. He walked in on the 73-year-old Stoner masturbating naked in a cubicle. Stoner beckoned the boy, who went over to him. He kissed the boy on the lips, took his trousers down and fondled him. After the incident the boy ran off and alerted the police. The next day, the police kept watch on the toilet. Sure enough, Stoner arrived in the late afternoon. When the police followed him into the toilet, they found him in a cubicle, naked, apart from his shoes, socks and a hat. He was arrested and charged with indecent assault.[95] He appeared at the magistrates' court before Lewis Manning's daughter, Anne. The case was adjourned as Stoner's solicitor asked for an opportunity for Stoner to undergo a medical assessment. At the next hearing, Stoner's solicitor Michael Skinner gave no defence but submitted psychiatric and probation reports. The presiding magistrate warned, 'You came very close to going to prison but we believe that in these circumstances it would have served no purpose at all.'[96]

He was ordered to pay £30 costs and put on probation for two years. But the incident reached the newspapers and the whole story of the murder at the Villa Madeira once again made headlines in the local news: 'Naked assault on boy in toilet'; 'Scandal followed him through life';[97] 'Killer admits charge'.[98] It even made a small, lurid feature in *The Guardian*: 'Sex attacker sentenced.'[99] Loyal as ever, Christine couldn't believe what had happened: 'I didn't know what to think at the time, but I just can't imagine anything happening because he loved children. George was always a good husband to me. I wonder if the brain tumour that eventually killed him was already coming along. That could have affected him, you see.'[100]

Soon after his conviction, Stoner began to attend a day-care unit. Christine struggled to care for him for as long as she could, but in 1996, old and ill, he went to live in a nursing home. In 1998, when the first major revival of *Cause Célèbre* opened at the Lyric Hammersmith in London, the press began to pester Christine, now living alone in Redhill Drive, with her husband in care:

> [Stoner's] wife peers out through the net curtains of the bungalow where they spent most of their lives together and beckons visitors to the side door ... She is small and vulnerable, there are tears in her eyes and her voice cracks with the weight of emotion, but she comes from a generation where it was not done to be rude, even to prying strangers.[101]

But still the journalist Kevin Nash probed the elderly Christine with questions, hoping for a late scoop about the murder at the Villa Madeira. Exhausted by the questioning, she begged for some privacy and some peace. She had nothing to say and nothing to add: 'Please, I don't want to talk about it. It was all so long ago, over sixty years now. He's old and sick. Why do they have to drag it all up again? I really think they should let it drop.'[102]

George Percy Stoner died of a brain tumour and dementia on 24 March 2000, at the age of eighty-three. It was sixty-five years to the day that he had struck another frail old man in the head three times with a mallet and left him for dead. For him and for the other occupants of the Villa Madeira, life was never the same again. Each of their lives would be defined by what happened that night in March of 1935. Stoner died in Christchurch Hospital, which overlooks the marshes and the railway line that crosses the stream where Alma had taken her own life. Her penance for the role she played in her husband's death had been painful but swift. Without the money to threaten injunctions or the powerful connections to pull the right strings on their behalf, the Stoners were left vulnerable and exposed, relentlessly pursued for over half a century by a press determined not to let a good story die, even if many of the main players involved in it had.

Two years after his death, Christine Stoner spoke about her husband for the first and only time to the journalist York Membery. At seventy-nine, frail and vulnerable-looking, she lived alone in the house she had shared with Stoner for nearly fifty years. Membery noted that the house was cosy, 'in an old fashioned way', although money was obviously tight: 'The wallpaper is fading, damp patches stain the ceiling and the kitchen is a throwback to a post-war world of austerity. She sits in her lounge surrounded by pictures of her daughter and her grandchildren – although, bizarrely, there are no pictures of her husband.'[103]

She believed that as a child Stoner 'didn't really have a very happy home life', and that his 'upbringing may have had something to do with what happened', cut off from children of his own age by his mother.[104] She claimed that she had never broached the subject of the murder with him and felt that he must have been 'overcome by a moment of madness'. Though he had never actually expressed remorse for what had happened 'in so many words', she knew that he regretted what had happened: 'Sometimes he'd go very quiet and you'd see tears rolling down his cheeks. You just wanted to leave him alone and get over it. I didn't like to keep going on about it.'[105]

Loyal to the last, Christine Stoner never spoke again about the night Rattenbury was attacked. Whatever she knew or suspected about the murder at the Villa Madeira, she took to her grave. She died on 4 April 2010. It's hard not to think that, though she offered Stoner a second chance, by marrying him she condemned herself to become another casualty of the Rattenbury case, her own life haunted by the ghost of a woman she had never even met.

Stoner during the Second World War

John Rattenbury, 1950

EPILOGUE

TALIESIN, 15 AUGUST 1914

Almost invariably it is the woman who breaks out of the
cage, or the ark, or the dollhouse. And [Ibsen] believes that
she, without the barriers, will find her right road, led by a
surer instinct than the man. For Ibsen, there is no higher moral
law than the devotion of the personality to its ideal ... to
make his own choice; in action to write anew his own
law, choose his own sacrifices, run his own dangers, win
his own freedom, venture his own destruction, choose his
own happiness

– Ellen Key, *The Torpedo Under the Ark, Ibsen and Women*
(trans. Mamah Borthwick)[1]

Following the murder of Ratz and the subsequent suicide of Alma,
Keith Miller Jones administered the family estate and acted as
John Rattenbury's guardian. Christopher was still at school and
though his natural father had become a successful journalist, helping to found the magazine *Newsweek*, he had as little interest in
Christopher as he had had in his daughter Simona. Christopher
would be cared for by his Pakenham relatives before being sent to
Vancouver to live with Alma's mother, who had, by then, been mellowed by 'two religious conversions'.[2]

In adulthood, John Rattenbury found it completely understand-
able that Miller Jones should have told him that his parents had
gone away on holiday, rather than admit that they were both dead:
'How do you break that kind of news to a six-year-old? I was

too young to know and everybody was afraid to tell me.'[3] A year after the deaths of his parents, a boy at school 'rather cruelly' told him that his father had been murdered and his mother had killed herself. Eighty years later he still remembers that 'it was such a shock'.[4] He carried on boarding at Cliff House and in the holidays was farmed out to various relatives, spending Christmas with a great aunt and uncle and other holidays elsewhere. Keith Miller Jones, who had no children of his own, always arranged for him to be doing something interesting in the holidays and one summer he spent with the Sea Scouts. In 1939, he joined the choir school at King's College, Cambridge, where, again, he boarded. The years following his parents' violent deaths were hard: 'I'd sit in class and suddenly burst into tears. Some of the teachers used to give me hell. On one level it was very painful. But at that age you're pretty resilient.'[5]

In the summer of 1940, with the Battle of Britain raging and German forces threatening invasion from across the Channel, the government set up the Children's Overseas Reception Board (CORB) to evacuate British children to the safety of the four Dominion countries: South Africa, New Zealand, Australia and Canada. Within two weeks of the announcement of the scheme there were 200,000 applications from parents for 20,000 places. Not all members of the government supported the programme, with Churchill implacably opposed to the scheme as it seemed an inherently defeatist policy. By the end of 1941, though, some 14,000 children would be evacuated, 6,000 of these to Canada. Douglas Hogg, the former lord chancellor, even suggested that the Princesses Elizabeth and Margaret Rose would be safer in Canada, inspiring one of their mother's most celebrated wartime remarks: 'The children won't go without me. I won't leave the king. And the king will never leave.' Keith Miller Jones decided that John Rattenbury should go to Canada to live with his brother Christopher and maternal grandmother, Frances, though she was still mourning the death of her second husband, Russell Melville Smith, who had died just before the outbreak of war. All the children sailed alone, though accompanied by teachers or escorts, one to every fifteen children. There were no passports; instead each child was identified by a luggage label with their CORB number written on it and an identity disc. John departed from Liverpool for Montreal on the *Duchess of Bedford* on 16 July 1940.[6] This was to be one of the last evacuations of British children to the colonies and Churchill's opposition to the scheme was proved, tragically, to be well founded. The *City of Benares* was torpedoed on 17 September with the loss of 121 crew and 134 passengers. Of the ninety CORB children on board, only thirteen survived and the wartime evacuation of British children abroad was abandoned.

When John arrived in Montreal, there was nobody to meet him. 'When we disembarked I sat on my trunk and waited because I didn't know how I was going to get to Vancouver.' His train didn't leave for another two days and he knew nobody in the city. He sat on his trunk for hours until a kindly couple approached the lone traveller from England and offered to look after him until his departure. He was eleven.[7]

Finally, he arrived in Vancouver and moved into 3661 Cameron Street with his grandmother, where the atmosphere of mourning can't have been conducive to the raising of a traumatised young boy. He settled down to school at St George's in Vancouver, which had small classes and good teachers. He threw himself into his studies as well as playing rugby and cricket 'in an attempt to block out [his] parents' death'.[8] But on 17 January 1941, when John had barely settled into life in Canada, his grandmother died, so he was then sent to live with her youngest sister, Amy Snider. Meanwhile, his brother Christopher had found it hard to settle in Canada and had become a troubled young man, drawn to delinquency. During the war, he returned to England and, as he had dual nationality, joined the US Army. In a desire to put the past behind him, he changed his name from Christopher Rattenbury to Christopher Compton Pakenham. When the war was over, he returned to America, settling in Orange County, New Jersey, where he married and had a family, working as a commercial artist, living quietly and avoiding any public discussion of the case. In the 1970s, when Anthony Barrett contacted him about the circumstances of his mother and stepfather's deaths, Barrett was surprised when Christopher wrote back. They enjoyed a long correspondence during which Christopher shared family memories and photographs. He admitted to Barrett that his parents' tragedy had had a deep effect on him. He died in 1995, having led an unhappy life, unable to fully recover from the trauma of the murder at the Villa Madeira.[9]

John Rattenbury remembers that he was barely a teenager when he instinctively felt that 'in return for the gift of life on this earth [he] should strive to give something back' and, as he grew up, this feeling evolved from an instinct into a 'conscious recognition'.[10] It was while he was at St George's that he began to develop a real interest in architecture. Since the school was in poor repair, the headmaster proposed a student competition to design a new campus. John submitted an inventive and ambitious design that was completely tailored to the needs of the students. The main focus of the plan was a large gymnasium featuring a floor that slid back to reveal a swimming pool. Despite the impracticality of the design, John was awarded the first prize of $5. His fate was sealed – he must become an architect, just like his father. At the time, he wasn't really aware that he was following in Ratz's footsteps, but later he recognised that it was 'in [his] blood'. As a four-year-old, he had started a 'love affair with the beauty of pencil lines on paper'[11] when he had seen his father's work one day at the Villa Madeira; 'The beautiful image was etched so sharply in my mind that I can recall it clearly to this day.'[12]

On leaving school, he enrolled at the University of British Columbia with the intention of becoming an architect, but was disappointed to learn that he was required to take a year of arts study and two years of engineering before he could start to design buildings. After two unhappy years struggling with endless structural equations and having exhausted his inheritance, he went to work for a logging company in northern British Columbia, where he learned many practical skills such as operating a bulldozer and firing a steam locomotive. Eventually, having grown in experience and self-confidence, John had earned enough money to continue his education. He was keen to attend a smaller establishment that offered a more direct route to becoming an architect. Oregon State College had recently established a new Department of Architecture where there were only twenty-five students and two professors. It was the perfect course and the perfect environment, so he began to study in earnest. As he matured, he began to sense 'the quiet sound of an intriguing inner voice. Gradually [he] became aware that it was telling [him] that [he] should search for some meaning in life.'[13]

One evening, he was in the college library when he picked up a book, *In the Nature of Materials: The Buildings of Frank Lloyd Wright* by Henry-Russell Hitchcock, which had been published in 1942. The first illustration in the book was a bright colour photograph of Taliesin West, Wright's winter home and studio in the Arizona desert. John had never heard of Wright before and until looking at his body of work in the book had had no idea that architecture could be 'so beautiful, so exciting, so different'.[14] Wright's designs, sympathetic to their settings and made of local materials, were the antithesis of his father's bombastic classical style. He stayed up all night reading the book and was 'blown away'[15] by what he read. It was a 'defining moment' in his life.[16]

That summer, John returned to Vancouver and secured a job in an architectural practice with a friend of his father, William Frederick Gardiner. He was paid $50 a week and was finally designing buildings. Two other young architects in the practice, Larry Bruin and Jackson Wong, were great admirers of Frank Lloyd Wright and had a copy of *Architectural Forum* from 1948, which mentioned that Wright had a group of apprentices called the Taliesin Fellowship that he had been nurturing since 1932. Applicants came from all over the world and were required to send $200 in advance of a personal interview with Mr Wright. Wong was planning to join them.

In the summer of 1950, Bruin was driving to Detroit and

was planning to drop Wong off on the way at Wright's summer residence in Wisconsin, Taliesin East. 'Acting on blind faith' that he'd be accepted, 21-year-old John packed a small suitcase and asked if he could accompany his friends on their journey; he wanted to join Wright's fellowship too. They left Vancouver and crossed into the United States, driving for several days to Wisconsin. Until this point, John had never actually seen a Frank Lloyd Wright building, but, looking out of the car window as they drove through the town of Richland Center, Wright's birthplace, he saw a building that he was convinced must be by Wright. He asked Bruin to stop the car and jumped out. He was mesmerised by the building – red-brick walls, topped with a buff-coloured concrete frieze with a geometric pattern. Suddenly a very stylish woman passed him on the pavement. 'You must be one of the boys from Taliesin?' she asked. John said he wasn't, but 'that is where I want to go'. The woman replied, 'Well, when you do you will meet my daughter, Kay.' The boys got back in the car and made the uphill drive to Taliesin.

Taliesin was a large, beautiful house built into the Wisconsin hills, designed along the principles of Wright's 'organic architecture'. As soon as he saw it, John felt like he was 'in a dream', and had the feeling of 'coming home', the building and the gardens around it were so beautiful. The three students asked for Mr Wright and were told to wait outside in the garden for him.

The buildings and landscape seemed to grow out of the hills, as though they had been there forever. An enormous oak tree spread out its green canopy above us. The gardens were filled with color – scarlet cardinal flowers, magenta phlox, orange day lilies, pink and ivory hollyhocks. The rough texture of golden-buff limestone walls and chimneys contrasted with sand-colored stucco. The window sash was painted a rust-red color. Gently sloping cedar-shingle roofs extended into space and created deep shadows. It was a poem, a world of magic. It had a spiritual quality that moved me very deeply.[17]

A door opened and an older woman in a white dress and wearing a wide-brimmed summer hat stepped out, accompanied by a younger woman. The two women were to change the whole direction of John's life and career. They were Lloyd Wright's wife, Olgivanna, and Kay Schneider, who was indeed the stepdaughter of the woman John had met at Richland Center. Finally, he met the man himself, Frank Lloyd Wright. At their first meeting John was drawn by Wright's magnetic presence. He was eighty-two at the time, sixty-one years older than the aspiring architect, but John found him 'spellbinding'. Wright would certainly have been aware of John's father's architectural achievements as well as the nature of his death. But he had another reason to find a unique empathy with this rootless young man. He instinctively understood how an act of violence could affect and define a life, how the trauma of murder continued to affect the families left behind. After only a few minutes, John Rattenbury felt that Frank Lloyd Wright 'saw into my soul'.[18] And there was a very good reason why.

In 1903, Wright had been commissioned to design a house in Oak Park for the Chicago businessman Edwin Cheney and his wife, the feminist Mamah Borthwick. The Cheneys had a son, John, born in 1902, and a daughter, Martha, born two years later. It may even have been before the birth of young Martha that Wright and Mamah began an affair, and by 1909 they informed their respective spouses that they had fallen in love. Wright then abandoned both his business and his family to build a studio and self-sustaining farm as well as a home for himself and Mamah in Spring Green, Wisconsin. The house, named 'Taliesin', was a bold public statement, symbolic of his union with Mamah. The neighbouring community and the local press, however, made clear their contempt for Wright's brazen flaunting of his adulterous relationship with Mamah and their 'love bungalow': 'Any man and wife should be legally married ... otherwise they are a menace to the morals of a community and an insult to every family therein.'

In the summer of 1914, Mamah's children were staying at Taliesin for the school holidays. In addition to the family, there were six workmen lodging at Taliesin while Wright was working away in Chicago.

The staff who looked after the household were a black couple from Barbados, a butler-cum-handyman called Julian Carlton and his wife Gertrude, who did the cooking. They had only arrived at Taliesin in mid-June, highly recommended by one of Wright's friends.[19]

On 4 August, Britain had declared war on Germany and, three days later, Carlton had bought a bottle of hydrochloric acid from the pharmacy in Spring Green, apparently for domestic use. The next day he had an altercation with a draughtsman called Emil Brodelle, refusing to saddle his horse. Brodelle retorted by calling Carlton a 'black son of a bitch'. Carlton had developed an increasing paranoia since he had arrived at Taliesin and this incident with Brodelle came to a head on 15 August. That morning was blazingly hot and the daily routine began as normal. Gertrude was preparing lunch in the kitchen just north of the staff dining room. About 80ft away, the family had their own dining room. At midday, Carlton took the soup from the kitchen and went to serve it to Mamah and the children, who were lunching on the screened terrace outside the dining room. Having served them, he then took an axe – a shingling hatchet – and struck Mamah in the back of the skull. With 'one swift and horrific blow to the forehead', he then killed her son. Traumatised, eight-year-old Martha ran from the terrace back into the dining room and out into the grounds. Carlton caught up with her and hammered her repeatedly in the head with the hatchet. Assuming the girl to be dead, he went to the staff dining room and, again, served the soup. As the workmen started to eat, Carlton bolted the door from the outside, poured petrol under the door, lit his pipe and then dropped the match onto the petrol. The dining room burst into flames. The men rushed to the door only to find it bolted. They were trapped. Outside the door, Carlton was ready with his axe and proceeded to attack the workers as they escaped from the inferno. With all the inhabitants of Taliesin now apparently dispatched, Carlton grabbed some more petrol and returned to the terrace outside the family dining room where Mamah's body lay on the floor and her son's remained in his chair. He doused the bodies with petrol and then set them alight. Taliesin was engulfed in flames.

When the alarm was raised, hundreds of local people helped to stop the spreading fire. At about 5.30 p.m., Julian Carlton was found half conscious, having drunk the hydrochloric acid he had purchased. The next morning Wright visited Taliesin to survey the devastation by daylight. Seven people were dead and two-thirds of the house lay smouldering in ruins. Mute for much of the visit, a defiant Wright stated, 'I will rebuild it all, every line of it, as it was before she ... this is home.'[20] To Wright's disgust, some in the press and local community saw the tragic events at Taleisein as a judgement on his and Mamah's unconventional lives, a 'brazen violation of both moral and statute law'. Carlton died without ever explaining the reasons for the murders. Mamah was buried in Wright's family plot in Spring Green. And, true to his word, Wright re-built Taliesin in her memory.

It is to Taliesin that John Rattenbury, a young man traumatised by the violent death of both his parents, had come into Frank Lloyd Wright's life in 1950. He became one of Wright's associates and married fellow student Kay Schneider, the young woman he had been introduced to there on his first day. Frank Lloyd Wright died in 1959 and was buried next to Mamah Borthwick.[21]

John became a key member of Wright's architectural practice, working on iconic buildings like the Guggenheim Museum in New York and the Price Tower Oklahoma, Wright's only skyscraper. In 1997, he designed *Life* magazine's Dream House, reminiscent of one of Wright's Prairie Houses. Looking back, he is struck by the strange coincidences that drew him to the Wrights. Rattenbury and Wright were both called Frank, both were architects and both had been born in 1867. Alma was a composer and pianist, many years younger than Rattenbury; Olgivanna Wright was thirty years younger than her husband and also composed music. Olgivanna and John shared a birthday and she and Wright married on the day John was born. Wright had also caused a scandal in his home neighbourhood of Oak Park, just as Rattenbury and Alma did in the similarly conservative district in 1920s Victoria. John firmly believes that Providence has guided his life: 'How else can I explain finding mentors and spiritual parents to replace the ones I lost when I was five?' Both John

Rattenbury and Frank Lloyd Wright lost women close to them who had challenged the conventions of their time, and paid for it, undermined and attacked by the popular press. And each of their lives had been devastated by the murderous rage of a resentful servant.

In the 1980s, John and his wife Kay travelled to British Columbia and visited Iechinihl – the place where a good thing happened – by then a school. Kay Rattenbury died in 1996. Two years later, John was invited to Victoria for the 100th anniversary of the opening of his father's parliament buildings. For him, it felt like the 'closing of a circle and the highlight of my life'.[22] He speaks with a complete lack of anger about the events in Bournemouth in 1935. His life following the deaths of his parents gave him, he feels, 'an understanding from an early age of other people's pain and sorrow. And that's a quality I possibly wouldn't otherwise have possessed.'[23] Today only John Rattenbury survives of the five people that were present at the Villa Madeira on 24 March 1935. Remarkably, he feels nothing but pity for the man who killed his father and prompted the death of his mother: 'He was so young, so impressionable and he had this older, beautiful woman doting on him. I've never felt any animosity towards him. I just felt he was a terrible victim of circumstance. And of course, he went to prison. I am sure that he suffered great guilt. It must have been a terrible life.'[24]

Over ninety years old, John has had a very successful career as an architect and a full, rewarding life; 'I think my father and mother would have been proud of me.'[25] He continues to live at Taliesin West, the same seductive building he had first caught sight of in a photograph in a library book when he was a young man, seventy years ago.

For him, the murder at the Villa Madeira was a 'sad business' and he sees his parents as 'tragic figures in their own way'. He regrets that the drama of the end of their lives has eclipsed their achievements when they were living: 'Very few people mention … my parents' good qualities – my father's architecture and my mother's musicianship. That's how I prefer to remember them. And whatever anyone says, I know my mother was a good woman.'[26]

5 Manor Road, Bournemouth, 2019

Alma Rattenbury

Afterword

We all imagine we can mould our own lives – we seldom
can, they are moulded for us – just by the laws and rules and
conventions of this world, and if we break any of these, we
only have to look forward to a formidable and unattractive
wilderness.

– Edith Thompson[1]

Leave her to heaven
And to those thorns that in her bosom lodge
To prick and sting her.

– Shakespeare, *Hamlet*

On 5 November 1935, months after the drama of that summer, the
Daily Mail reported a seasonal ghost story from the Bournemouth
area. Local people were frightened to pass the place where Alma
had killed herself and would make wide detours to avoid it, especially at night. A local publican, Samuel Barber, reported that 'out
of the river mist appears a wraith in the shape of a woman, an eerie
light is said to gleam on the waters and at other times a ghostly
hand is said to float on the surface'.[2]

The rumour was that Alma's spirit haunted the area at night,
her hand clasping for the knife that had been lost deep in the

riverbed. A Mr F. Day of Christchurch decided to investigate. One night he lay in wait until he saw a strange figure walking towards him along the railway track on the embankment. In its hand was a knife. Mr Day flashed his torch at the figure and when it came closer he rushed forward and tried to engage with it. He was able to hit it on the head, which, he said, 'did not feel a bit ghostly. It was on the contrary, very hard and very human.'[3] The draped figure did not hesitate but tumbled down the embankment and, clutching what was clearly a sheet, made off across the marshland. 'Alma's ghost' was just a Halloween hoax.

In the spring of 1940, a Jewish doctor and his wife, Aurel and Antonia Landstein, who had fled from the Nazi-dominated Continent, had driven down from London to Bournemouth, looking for a house on the south coast to help improve Dr Landstein's health. As it was April, the rhododendrons were in bloom and they found themselves strolling down Manor Road. Mrs Landstein thought it was the loveliest road she had ever seen. She particularly liked the little white house peeping through the pine trees. One day, they thought, they would settle there. They then returned to London so that Dr Landstein could carry on with his war work. In 1955, they returned to Bournemouth, this time in search of a place to retire. Driving down Manor Road, they saw number five 'looking sad and neglected'.[4] And it was for sale. The estate agent 'was not anxious to mention the murder' and it was only when they moved in and an electrician 'hoped that they had mopped up all the blood' that they first heard about the house and its sensational history.[5] Once they moved in, Antonia Landstein felt a strong connection to Alma and had the garden planted as she might have had it, with pink flowers.[6]

In 1984, by then a widow, Mrs Landstein was interviewed by Roger Wilkes for a BBC radio series about locations at which historical murders had taken place and whether any trace of the drama that occurred there remained. In the case of the Villa Madeira, Mrs Landstein was convinced it did:

If I feel that Alma herself is somehow here, it's only in a vague way. I think about that poor woman, not as a person, but as the architect of all those tragic happenings here. Even after all these years they are almost tangible. And when the evening comes, many a shadow has its fear. And when the wind howls about the house, I seem to hear a sort of moaning noise, and I imagine poor Mr Rattenbury, sitting mortally injured in this very room.[7]

Every year, on the anniversary of the attack on Rattenbury, Mrs Landstein lit a candle in the house. She told Roger Wilkes she was convinced she wasn't the only Bournemouth resident to mark the date. Year after year, 'an elderly man walks slowly past the house, first on one side of the road, then the other. He just walks along very slowly and looks at the house. Not knowing really who he is, I cannot say for certain, but I think it is George Stoner. Every year he is drawn to the same place and remembers. I feel very sorry for him. It must be a terrible thing to live with a thing like that. Poor man. His whole life was ruined.'[8]

Mrs Landstein died in 1992, leaving the house to her niece Valerie, who continues to live there with her husband David. While I was on a research trip to Bournemouth, I visited them. Over tea in Alma's old drawing room, the sunlight filtering through the French windows, they were happy to talk about the history of the house, the occasional break-ins by trophy hunters over the years and the mournful way the coastal winds sigh down the chimneys and through the attic, giving it an uncanny atmosphere in the dark autumn and winter nights.

It's strange to sit in that room today and think of the events that took place there – not only the murder but the extraordinary messiness of ordinary lives. But the days when the Villa Madeira was part of the national consciousness have passed, the events that took place there far away, in an almost unrecognisably foreign country where people did things so very differently. Few visitors walk down Manor Road now in search of the little house that was once the most notorious address in Britain.

While researching this book, I contacted newspaper libraries for any photographs they might have associated with the case. Even John Rattenbury has few photographs of his mother after another fire at Taliesin in 1951 destroyed most of the family archive that he had possessed.[9] While I was in Bournemouth visiting Manor Road, one of the photo libraries I had been in contact with sent an excited email. They had delved into their pre-digital files and discovered some photographs they thought I would be interested in.

It was quite a shock to see it for the first time, but here was a photograph of Alma's body just as it had been removed from the water and laid on the riverbank. The photograph hadn't been published before, perhaps considered too indelicate to print at the time of her death. But it isn't a graphic port-mortem image. Her face averted from the camera, Alma lies still among the reeds, her clothing fully covering her, like a latter-day Ophelia. Having spent so much time investigating her life, I thought I'd try to locate where she had died – a sort pilgrimage, if you like. But though there are several newspaper photographs from the time of her suicide, I found it impossible to find Three Arches Bend. Peter Kazmierczak at Bournemouth Library helped me to check and cross-reference local guidebooks and ordnance survey maps from the 1930s, but to no avail.

After visiting Bournemouth Library, I had an appointment to meet the new owner of 104 Redhill Drive, where Stoner had spent most of his life. I'd been warned that the house had changed some-what since the Stoners had lived there, but I wanted to see what it looked like, how it felt, if there was any vestige of Stoner's life there. Arriving at Redhill Drive, I was dismayed to find that the house had not just changed, it had been completely obliterated, demolished, clearly in the past couple of years; and a smart new property had been built in its place. There'd be no trace of Stoner here, no sense of the past.

The new owner, Ian, told me that there was an old suitcase in the shed that had been left by a former owner. Perhaps there would be some clues in it? So we looked in the shed and found the suitcase, but there was nothing much in it, just some old newspaper cuttings and a programme for a production of *Cause Célèbre*. I was disappointed, but as I chatted to Ian over a cup of tea, he asked about the book I was writing and I mentioned my earlier study of Neville Heath, the ex-RAF pilot turned killer, who had murdered a woman in Bournemouth in 1946.[10] Ian was interested in this; he was currently on leave from the army and had personal experience of dealing with modern soldiers with PTSD. He wondered where I'd be going next in my search? I told him I was heading back to London as I couldn't find the place where Alma had killed herself. Not a man to be defeated, in seconds he was on Google Maps, scrutinising information I had from Bournemouth Library and checking a compass. And then, there it was. He wondered if I'd like a lift?

Three Arches Bend is situated nearer to Purewell than it is Sopley, which was where the local newspapers had stated it to be at the time. The three red-brick arches, a solid Victorian structure, support the railway above the Clockhouse Stream, a tributary of the River Avon. The embankment carries the South Western rail line from Waterloo to Weymouth, passing through Christchurch, where Alma left the train, nearing the end of her journey. The meadows that she walked through to reach her final destination still flood regularly, so the area retains a sense of peaceful desolation, despite the constant hum of the twenty-first century from the nearby A35 – the Christchurch bypass that didn't exist in the 1930s. There are no footpaths, the ground is marshy and only populated by a few indifferent cows. Down by the waterside it's overgrown, with the two outer arches now inaccessible with brambles and shrubs, the water almost still beneath the centre arch. You can hear the marsh birds and insects that prosper here and it's possible to imagine Alma reaching some sort of peace. I dropped some marsh marigolds in the water and watched as they gently floated downriver.

* * *

Writing in his memoirs in 1961, Joshua Casswell admitted that he was plagued with doubt about the Rattenbury case: 'The murder at the Villa Madeira will continue a mystery to the end.'[11] He believed that Stoner 'was so infatuated with [Alma] that even if she had killed her husband and he knew it I feel sure he would still have continued to take the blame'.[12]

Casswell's doubts are shared by Stoner's daughter, Yvonne: '[My feelings] come from small things my father said to us at different times, never with any direct reference to the case because he never discussed it with me. He seemed to be the kind of person who would keep a secret to the end if he considered it important. As I have no proof one way or the other I can only rely upon my feelings and my knowledge of the man he became.'[13]

This suspicion that the trial had not revealed the whole truth of the story was echoed by Michael Havers, who, having studied the case in the late 1970s, shared his thoughts with his co-author, Anthony Barrett: '[Havers] was convinced that Alma was far more deeply and directly involved in the murder than she claimed by the end. This was not because of any secret archive of material which could not be brought up at the trial, it was just his lawyer's instinct. He didn't expand, he just felt that things didn't add up.'[14]

In 1988, Bernard Napley questioned the verdict of the trial and proposed that Stoner's confession to Casswell might have been true, or at least contained elements of truth within it; Alma could feasibly have attacked Ratz in a drug-fuelled haze.[15] In an interview at the time of the TV broadcast of *Cause Célèbre*, he criticised the production, which he felt was 'riddled with mistakes' and 'even more slanted against George Stoner': 'I'm not saying that Stoner was innocent ... But to find him guilty and Alma Rattenbury innocent could only have come about after a totally inadequate trial.'[16]

Napley made the significant point that, though Alma had financial support from her family, she left Stoner to be represented by a legal aid team until her own life was safe and only then volunteered to finance his defence. Was this the strategy of a guiltless woman? At the same time, following his release, Stoner had many opportunities to fully clear either his name or Alma's, but didn't. Between 1935 and his death in 2000 he never clarified his guilt or Alma's innocence at any time. The little he did say was intriguingly ambiguous: 'The whole crime was committed on an emotional basis. Both I and the lady concerned were in a highly emotional state. Our emotions were completely out of control.'[17]

Our emotions, not *my* emotions.

When the police first arrived on the scene at the Villa Madeira, Alma told them a series of half-truths and lies: '[Ratz] dared me to kill him as he wanted to die. I picked up the mallet. He then said, "You have not the guts to do it."'

She repeated this phrase to the police twice that morning, at 6.15 a.m. and at 8.15 a.m. But was it actually *Ratz* she had said it to?

That afternoon, Ratz had spoken of suicide, inspired by the book he was reading. Then in Alma's altercation with Stoner after she'd telephoned Jenks, he had intimidated her with a gun and threatened to kill her with it. This was only later revealed to be a toy. So that afternoon, murder was already in the seaside air at the Villa Madeira, as well as suicide.

Behind the cosy façade of the house, there had been much theatrical posturing. Ratz frequently threatened to kill himself and, with much bravado, Stoner had declared himself a drug addict. Now he was threatening to shoot his mistress as he sulked for being asked to drive her to Bridport, which was, after all, what he was employed to do. When the argument relocated to the dining room at the front of the house, did Alma share with Stoner that she was as affronted as he was that her husband had proposed that she prostitute herself in order to secure his building project? Had Stoner in turn suggested that they do away with Ratz? And did she imply or hint that she wanted to be rid of Ratz once and for all, just as much as he did? She may have done so only to appease him at that moment, but had Alma challenged or even dared Stoner to kill Ratz in the same way that she had goaded Ratz the previous July? Had the exasperated Alma chided Stoner dismissively, 'You have not the guts to do it'? Unbeknown to her, Stoner had subsequently 'got in such a state [he] didn't know what to do'.[18] Alma had released a genie out of a bottle that would result in murder.

On the night of the murder, Alma admitted in her hysterical, drunken haze, 'I made a proper muddle of it.' Was she simply speaking the truth? When she saw that Stoner had acted on what she'd suggested or implied, she would have immediately recognised her responsibility for what he'd done. She may even have asked him to put up the sun shelter in the garden and suggested that, as the guy ropes were always falling out, what they needed was a mallet. So not only had she incited him, she might also have led him to the murder weapon. She would be as culpable as Stoner, just as Edith Thompson was deemed as culpable as Bywaters. Alma didn't need to wield the mallet herself to be guilty of murder and she knew it. Her first thought on hearing Stoner's story 'was to protect him': 'I did think that by my saying "I did it" & being arrested, it would help Stoner, but oh God I made such a muddle of everything – & never helped him at all.'[19]

Stoner was a boy and she was an adult. He was a servant and she was his mistress. She had told him what to do and he had done it. Was the motivation for her suicide, then, not only shame but also guilt? Feeling responsible for the death of her husband, the execution of her lover, the ruin of her reputation and the 'smashed lives' of her children, is it any wonder that Alma wanted to bring an end to the muddle she had made of her life?

* * *

The roads outside Wimborne Road Cemetery are known by locals as 'Cemetery Junction'. It's a busy crossroads, overcomplicated by traffic lights and barriers intent on protecting pedestrians and regulating traffic, a civic mess intruding on the once-graceful approach to a classic Victorian cemetery with a chapel in the middle and the graves radiating from it. There are mature pine trees here, as there are all across Bournemouth – in shaded suburban avenues like Manor Road, if not in less elegant addresses such as Redhill Drive.

There are so many graves here that I approach a gardener, Glenn, to ask for assistance. He is so used to the silence in the cemetery that he's surprised to meet somebody there who is actually alive and is happy to help me find what I'm looking for. He works at the cemetery throughout the year, but not so often as he used to, thirty-five years ago when he started. Many of the generation who used to tend graves regularly have also died. Graves are forgotten, weeds prosper. In 1985, there were eighteen gardeners here. Now there are only two to tidy up and keep things neat. Staying on top of it is like painting the Forth Bridge, says Glenn.

In 1935, Francis Rattenbury was buried between two ancient yew trees. After the suicide of his wife, the departure of their children from England and then a long war, his grave was forgotten. It accumulated memorials around it, engraved with the comforting sentiments of succeeding generations – 'dear husband, brave, unselfish, loving', from desolate wives celebrating much-missed husbands and fathers, many of whom in this part of the cemetery were killed in action in the 1940s. Some years ago, John Motherwell, a civil engineer and amateur historian from British Columbia, had visited Rattenbury's grave on a trip to England and was surprised that there was no headstone. Feeling that it was 'important that such an influential character should have a memorial',[20] in 2007 he had a granite headstone erected with Rattenbury modestly remembered as 'a British Columbia Architect'. An engraved image of the parliament buildings dominates the headstone, as they dominated Rattenbury's career. It is a fitting tribute to a man who had achieved many great things.

Some 20ft away to the southeast of his grave, beside memorials proclaiming more sentiments of undying love in the next world, there is another plot. Difficult to distinguish now, overgrown with tussocky grass, weeds and a few wild flowers, is the final resting place of Francis Rattenbury's second wife. She lies just 5ft beneath us, Glenn tells me.

On the morning she killed herself, Alma had specifically requested, 'please do not bury me near R[atz]'.[21] But even in death her wishes were ignored and now she lies a few feet away from a man she hadn't loved and whom she felt didn't know or understand her at all – 'He knew as much about me as I know about Timbucktoo.'[22] Unlike his grave, hers has no memorial.[23] There is not even a marker to distinguish the last remains of Alma Rattenbury, the beautiful, flawed soul who was in thrall to historical forces as much to her own desires and, for a few months in the spring of 1935, was one of the most famous, infamous women in the world.

APPENDIX OF SONGS BY LOZANNE[1]

'You Brought My Heart the Sunshine'[2]

Lyrics by Rex Gilmour

Night lay deep around my way,
Sadly the hours wandered past,
Then through the shadows you came,
Bringing the dawn at last!

You brought my heart the sunshine,
And day once more was mine,
Hours that were weary and lonely
Were filled with a song divine!
A world of joy and glory
Within your eyes I see,
You brought my heart the sunshine forever
When you gave your love to me!

Now no moment is sad,
Ever your voice I can hear,
Life is a wonderful dream,
Your heart is always near!

You brought my heart the sunshine,
And day once more was mine,
Hours that were weary and lonely
Were filled with a song divine!
A world of joy and glory

Within your eyes I see,
You brought my heart the sunshine forever
When you gave your love to me!

'Night Brings Me You'[3]

Lyrics by Edward Lockton

Day with her hopes and fears,
Fades when the light is done,
Breezes that sang in the trees,
Sleep at the set of the sun.
Flowers their weary eyes,
Kissed by the falling dew,
While in the dusk fondly I dream,
Love of my heart, of you.

Night brings me stars
Above this dark world softly beaming,
Night brings the moon
Across the blue hills gleaming!
Night brings me you,
And then all my heart is dreaming
Dreaming of love,
Your love that is mine alone!

Far though you wander now,
Oft in the silent night,
Back to your heart I return,
Singing dear songs of delight.
So thro' each lonely day,
Through hours of sun and rain,
Longing I wait till shadows fall,
Till you are mine again!

'Deep in My Heart'[4]

Lyrics by Edward Lockton

There comes a dream at the dawning,
Speaking of rapture to be;
There comes a song full of gladness,
Calling to me!

Deep in my heart love is waking,
Steadfast and tender and true
Deep in my heart light is breaking,
Leading me ever to you!
When you are far, I am lonely,
Sadly I wander apart,
But with you near love lives only
Deep in my heart!

Dark are the years as they wander,
But in the skies there will shine
Bright stars of wonder and glory,
If you are mine!

Deep in my heart love is waking,
Steadfast and tender and true
Deep in my heart light is breaking,
Leading me ever to you!
When you are far, I am lonely,
Sadly I wander apart,
But with you near love lives only
Deep in my heart!

'Dark-Haired Marie'[5]

Lyrics by Edward Lockton

Are you waiting in your garden
By the deep wide azure sea?
Are you waiting for your loveship,
Dark-haired Marie?

Through the flowery golden springtime,
When the summer winds blow free,
Through the lonely days of autumn,
Dark-haired Marie?

I am far across the waters,
But I hear you call to me,
In my dreams your eyes are shining,
Dark-haired Marie!

I shall come to claim you someday,
In my arms at last you'll be,
I shall kiss your lips and love you,
Dark-haired Marie!

'Loretta'[6]

Lyrics by Edward Lockton

The birds are singing round your eaves
A light wind whispers through the leaves,
The mist a web of crimson weaves,
Loretta! Loretta!

The curtains of the night are drawn,
Come down and tread the shining lawn,
Come down and let us greet the dawn,
Loretta! Loretta!

I know a little sanctuary,
By bab'ling brook, 'neath arching tree,
Oh! Come and journey there with me,
Loretta! Loretta!

There where the sunbeams peep between
cove boughs, and mosses soft and green,
There will I crown you love, my Queen,
Loretta! Loretta!

'Rose of Havana'[7]

Lyrics by Edward Lockton

I hear the sigh of the wind among the trees,
A happy song is floating on the ev'ning breeze,
And far away sounds the music of guitars
Waking sweet thoughts of love and rapture
as here my heart is waiting beneath the silver stars!

Your window gleams, are you listening to me now?
My grief is yours beloved, evermore I vow!
Oh! crown with perfect bliss that golden hour divine!
Come, I implore you,
Say you adore me,
Say that your heart is mine!

Rose of Havana,
Hark to my song!

Here do I wait where dark shadows throng,
For your sweet kisses sadly I long,
My arms are yearning to hold you fast!
Come while the moon is gleaming above,
Whisper to me of love,
For the night will only seem an idle broken dream,
Till you come to me at last!

Through all the day I've been longing for the night,
Just yearning for the time of shadow and delight,
I wandered sadly for you were far from me,
Slowly the moments passed,
I listened to her your voice come floating across the
    southern sea!

O magic flower when you lie upon my breast,
My grief will banish and my soul will be at rest,
Oh! crown with perfect bliss this golden hour divine!
Come, I implore you,
Say you adore me,
Say that your heart is mine!

Rose of Havana,
Hark to my song!
Here do I wait where dark shadows throng,
For your sweet kisses sadly I long,
My arms are yearning to hold you fast!
Come while the moon is gleaming above,
Whisper to me of love,
For the night will only seem an idle broken dream,
Till you come to me at last!

'Avelette'[8]

Lyrics by Edward Lockton

Avelette, the night is slowly falling,
On your garden sinks the twilight dew.
Now the last sweet bird of day is calling
Singing through this happy hour to you!
Far o'er the mountain the morn appears
And lays down her mantle of white
The world seems a garden of heaven
I whisper again my good-night.

Avelette, rest on till dawn,
Through the hours of sleep.
May the breezes sing to you all night long
For the sweetness of the flow'rs
They will waft unto you
And murmur from the trees in a song.
Your dreams shall be dreams of love's delight;
My heart all the while will linger near,
For angels from above
Will guard you with their love
Avelette, sleep on till dawn is here.

'By Some Mistake'[9]

Lyrics by E. Rutter Leatham

By some mistake my spirit held you dear,
But now I wake to agony and fear
To fading hope and thought distressed and grey
With outstretched hands I turn your face away.
With outstretched hands I turn your face away.

By some mistake you filled my empty days
But now I wake to face the parting ways
I see you smile, I hear the words you say
With no reply I hush your voice away.

By some mistake, by some divine mistake
I dreamed awhile, but now I wake, I wake,
Yet dying dream you keep my vision true,
I seemed to climb to Heav'n in loving you.

ACKNOWLEDGEMENTS

I'd like to thank the staff at the London Library, the British Library, the Imperial War Museum and the former British Newspaper Library at Colindale. The Lambeth Archives at the Minet Library in Camberwell and the Southwark Council Archives at the John Harvard Library in Borough offered valuable background about the life of the Wolff family in late nineteenth-century London. Barbara McLean at the Mitchell Library in Glasgow was hugely helpful as a guide to the extensive archive relating to the Scottish Women's Hospitals. Alan Cumming, who has valiantly promoted the story of Elise Inglis and the Scottish Women's Hospitals, assisted in researching Alma's war service in France.

In British Columbia, the BC Archives at the BC Museum and the City of Victoria Archives were invaluable resources regarding Francis Rattenbury's career and family life. Helen Edwards carefully combed the Rattenbury archives in Victoria on my behalf and Jaimie Fedorak and her colleagues at the Kamloops Museum and Archives also helped to research Alma's childhood in Kamloops. John Motherwell has also been very generous with his research about Rattenbury's business ventures in the Yukon.

I'm grateful to Dr Hwyel Maslen and Dr Stuart C. Blank for their excellent research into the experiences of Caldeon Dolling and Compton Pakenham during the First World War. The archivists at the British Red Cross and the *Croix-Rouge* kindly investigated the decorations awarded to Alma for her war work.

In Bournemouth, I'm grateful to the editor of the *Bournemouth Echo*, Andy Martin, and his staff, who provided material from their archive as well as offering practical help in trying to trace the relatives of individuals involved in the case. Peter Kazmierczak, Michael Stead and the Heritage team at Bournemouth Library have been a particularly informative resource. Roger Shore at the Moordown Local History Society gave me some helpful background to Stoner's school years. I'm also grateful to Ian Wilson, the current owner of 104 Redhill Drive, who identified the location of Alma's suicide and even drove me there. Thanks also to the administrative staff at Bournemouth Cemeteries, who identified Alma's grave, and to Glenn the gardener, who kindly led me to it.

Valerie and David Goldsmith welcomed me into 5 Manor Road and have been a fount of knowledge about the case and the history of the Villa Madeira. They have been extraordinarily generous with their time and insights and I'm hugely appreciative of their kindness.

Many thanks are due to Frank Ahern, the archivist at Canford School, who investigated Christopher and John Rattenbury's school days, and to Maddy Bowman at Tonbridge School for providing information about the Dolling brothers. Criminologist Keith Skinner has been, as ever, very generous with his insights, instincts and contacts. I'm very grateful to Francis James's daughter, Julia Jamett, for bringing her father's dramatisation of the story, *Villa Mimosa*, to my attention, which has effectively been lost since the 1930s and anticipated Terence Rattigan's *Cause Célèbre* by forty years. Michael Darlow kindly shared his memories of the final days of Terence Rattigan and the writing of *Cause Célèbre*. Rattigan's agent, Alan Brodie, also provided an introduction to John Rattenbury at Taliesin. Celeste Davison, Margo Stipe and the staff at Taliesin have been very patient answering my queries about Mr Rattenbury's life and his career with the Frank Lloyd Wright Foundation. York Membrey shared memories of his interview with Christine Stoner, and Michael Bully shared the archive of his father, Peter Shankland.

I'm indebted to James Ford, head of security at the Central Criminal Court, who provided a fascinating tour of the Old Bailey and access to

Court Number One. I'm also grateful to Kevin Eyles and Phil Taylor of the City of London Police for their insights into the backstage world of the Old Bailey. Professor John Moxham and Mr Michael Savvas at King's College Hospital advised about Alma's tuberculosis and the health and fertility of women in the days before the advent of the National Health Service. Simon Chaplin at the Wellcome Trust provided introductions to an invaluable number of experts in the field of middle-class women and narcotics in the 1930s and I'm particularly grateful to Lesley Hall, Mike Jay and Professor Jim Mills for their expert insights. Dr Christopher Hallam of the International Drug Policy Consortium provided excellent archive material relating to illicit drug use among GPs and nurses following the First World War. Dr Victoria Stewart at the University of Leicester generously shared her research relating to the archive of F. Tennyson Jesse as well as insights into the publication of the *Notable British Trials* series. Having investigated the trials of Edith Thompson and Alma Rattenbury while researching her excellent evocation of the period, *The Paying Guests*, Sarah Waters generously shared invaluable sources relating to contraception in the 1930s.

I'm grateful for the help and support of surviving protagonists related to the case and their relatives. Garth Manning and Anne Griffiths shared memories of their father, Robert Lewis Manning. Compton Pakenham's daughter-in-law, Rosalie Pakenham, kindly shared her family history with me. I am very grateful to Stoner's daughter Yvonne for her memories of her parents. I'm aware how painful examining this area of her family's past must have been. I hope she feels that her father's story has been told with fairness and sensitivity. It has been a particular privilege to talk to John Rattenbury and to discuss his parents, the life that they led at the Villa Madeira and what his mother called 'that awful night'.

I'd like to thank my agent, Judith Murray at Greene & Heaton, for championing this book from its inception. At Simon & Schuster, I'm grateful to Mike Jones, who first commissioned the book and later returned to help me shape it for publication. Melissa Bond has been thorough and patient throughout the edit, and Craig Fraser has created an arresting and elegant design for the book jacket and endpapers. I'm particularly grateful to Suzanne Baboneau for her patience in waiting some years for the delivery of this book when I was distracted by the demands of Ambridge and then Walford. I hope she feels that *The Fatal Passion of Alma Rattenbury* is worth the wait. I'm also grateful to readers of an early draft of this book for their encouragement: Emma Davie, Jackie Malton, Jane Villiers and Donna Wiffen. Paul Marquess offered some excellent advice about the structure of the narrative.

Professor Anthony Barrett has collaborated on two books about the Rattenburys. I'm grateful to him for reading a draft of this book and for sharing previously unpublished material from his personal archive. I'm most thankful for his generosity in sharing the privately held thoughts of Daphne Kingham and Lord Havers, as well as his own reflections of many decades about the case.

In the mid-1980s I was an undergraduate in the English Department at University College London. I was fortunate to have had René Weis as my tutor. At the time, René was writing his first book, *Criminal Justice*, about the life and death of Edith Thompson, still the definitive text on that case. René's painstaking depiction of Mrs Thompson's story made a deep impression on me at the time, so it was with some trepidation that I approached writing a book that was to be haunted by her. After thirty years of petitioning the Ministry of Justice, René successfully secured permission for Edith's body to be exhumed from the mass grave in which she had been buried at Brookwood Cemetery. On 22 November 2018, she was finally laid to rest in her parents' grave at the City of London Cemetery, ninety-five years after her execution. It was a privilege to be invited by René to read at the ceremony. One day I hope that Alma Rattenbury's grave will similarly be marked with a permanent memorial.

Finally, I must thank Rob Haywood for his patience and support and for sharing the house with the Rattenburys for far longer than I ever anticipated.

Sean O'Connor
London, 2019

NOTES

The police, prison and Home Office records relating to the Rattenbury murder and trial are held at the National Archives in Kew. Despite the vintage of the case and the fact that only one of the main players still survives, requests for all the information relating to the case to be released for study have been repeatedly denied by the Home Office. Some 1,257 pages of records and witness statements are restricted until 2043.

Records held at the National Archives (NA):

CRIM 1/778
CRIM 1/585/111
DPP 2/263
HO 144/21613
HO 144/21614
HO 144/21615
PCOM 9/2028

The archives relating to Francis Rattenbury, his family and his architectural achievements in British Columbia, are held in the British Columbia Archives and the Royal British Columbia Museum in Victoria. Many of Rattenbury's letters and all of Alma's, which had been available in the 1970s and '80s, have since been lost. The only surviving records of these letters are quotations from them in *Tragedy in Three Voices* by Sir Michael Havers, Peter Shankland and Anthony Barrett, *Francis Rattenbury and British Columbia* by Anthony Barrett and Rhodri Windsor-Liscombe, and *Rattenbury* by Terry Reksten.

Foreword

1   George Orwell, *Decline of the English Murder*, in *The Collected Essays, Journalism and Letters of George Orwell, Vol. IV: In Front of Your Nose 1945–50* (London: Secker & Warburg, 1968), p. 98, originally printed in *Tribune*, 15 February 1946

2   *Daily Mail*, 6 June 1935, p. 13

3   William Bixley, *The Guilty and the Innocent: My Fifty Years at the Old Bailey* (London: The Souvenir Press, 1957), p. 103

4   Orwell, *The Collected Essays, Journalism and Letters of George Orwell, Vol. IV: In Front of Your Nose 1945–50*, op. cit., p. 98

5   F. Tennyson Jesse, *The Trial of Alma Victoria Rattenbury and George Percy Stoner (Notable British Trials)* (London: Hodge, 1935), p. 241

6   Ibid., p. 242

7   Ibid., p. 4

8   See Appendix

9   Francis Iles, 'The Rattenbury Case', in *Anatomy of Murder: Famous Crimes Considered by Members of the Detection Club* (New York: The Macmillan Company, 1937), p. 220

10 Kevin Williams, *Get Me a Murder a Day! A History of Mass Communication in Britain* (London: Arnold, 2002), p. 56

11 See J. Sadie Clifford, *Expressions of Blame: Narratives of Battered Women Who Kill in the Twentieth Century Daily Express* (Riga: VDM Verlag, 2009). Whatever the picture of 1930s Britain that the popular press projected, in reality, the crime rate dropped significantly in the 1930s, particularly for murder. In 1935, there were 312 homicides in England and Wales, including infanticide (www.gov.uk/government/statistics/historical-crime-data). By comparison, in 2017, there were 709 homicides in England and Wales (www.ons.gov.uk/peoplepopulationandcommunity/crimeandjustice/articles/homicideinenglandandwales/yearendingmarch2017). Between 1920 and 1929, 141 men and women were hanged for murder. Between 1930 and 1939, the number dropped to 83. This was partly due to the unease surrounding the execution of Edith Thompson in 1923, which was to cast a long, dark shadow over capital crimes, even at the trial of Ruth Ellis in 1955.

12   Chris Horrie, *Tabloid Nation: The Birth of the Daily Mirror to the Death of the Tabloid* (London: Andre Deutsch, 2003), p. 51

13   Tennyson Jesse, *The Trial of Alma Victoria Rattenbury and George Percy Stoner*, op. cit., p. 12; 'There has been a growing consensus of public opinion ever since the Thompson–Bywaters trial, that the female prisoner was wrongly convicted and the memory of the earlier trial haunted the Courtroom like a ghost. The Rattenbury case seemed like an echo of that tragedy.'

14   'Murder, suicide and the pain of a surviving son', John Rattenbury interviewed by York Membery, *The Times*, 29 November 2007

Prologue

1   *Bournemouth Echo*, 23 March 1935, p. 8
2   Ibid.
3   Ibid., 22 March 1935, p. 6
4   Ibid.
5   William O'Donnell's statement, 26 March 1935, DPP 2/263 Part 4
6   Thomas Plumer's statement, 28 March 1935, DPP 2/263 Part 4
7   *A Pictorial and Descriptive Guide to Bournemouth, Poole and District* (London: Ward Lock & Co. Ltd, 16th edition, revised, 1936), p. 26
8   See Appendix. Echoing prevailing attitudes in the press and courtroom, Tennyson Jesse also accepted that the 'highly sexed' Alma was on 'the verge of nymphomania. Nymphomania is not admirable, but neither is it blameworthy. It is a disease.' (F. Tennyson Jesse, op. cit., p. 5) Tennyson Jesse and later writers on the case, such as Terry Reksten, equally accepted the unfounded myth that sufferers of tuberculosis were prone to an increased libido. See Terry Reksten, *Rattenbury* (Victoria, BC: Sono Nis Press, 1978), p. 145.
9   Ibid., p. 26
10   O'Donnell's statement, op. cit.
11   St Swithun's was built in 1876 as a chapel-of-ease to St Peter's, which was known as the 'mother church of Bournemouth' (*A Pictorial and Descriptive Guide to Bournemouth, Poole and District*, op. cit., p. 53)
12   Tennyson Jesse, *The Trial of Alma Victoria Rattenbury and George Percy Stoner*, op. cit., p. 11
13   Plumer's statement, op. cit.
14   O'Donnell's statement, op. cit.
15   Plumer's statement, op. cit.
16   Ibid.
17   Ibid.
18   O'Donnell's statement, op. cit.

19 'I Knew Mrs Rattenbury', *Strand* magazine, Vol. CV, No. 269, May 1943, p. 78

20 Carter's statement, 11 April 1935, DPP 2/263 Part 3

21 A plan and photographs of the house, the drawing room and the armchair are held in DPP 2/263 Part 3

22 O'Donnell's statement, op. cit. The detail of the dentures was 'pure Zola', as James Agate later noted in his diary (James Agate, *Ego* 2 (London, Victor Gollanz, 1936), p. 187).

23 O'Donnell's statement, op. cit.

24 Alfred Basil Rooke's statement, 26 March 1935, DPP 2/263 Part 4

25 Ibid.

26 Henry William Hoare's statement, 7 April 1935, DPP 2/263 Part 4

27 Rooke's statement, op. cit.

28 PC Arthur Ernest Bagwell's statement, 28 March 1935, DPP 2/263 Part 4

29 Ibid.

30 William James Mills's statement, 29 March 1935, DPP 2/263 Part 4

31 Ibid.

32 Ibid. Here he differs from O'Donnell, who remembered leaving the book on the piano.

33 All quotes from Bagwell's statement, op. cit.

34 Ibid.

35 Mills's statement, op. cit.

36 O'Donnell's statement, op. cit.

37 Mills's statement, op. cit.

38 Ibid.

39 O'Donnell's statement, op. cit.

40 Ibid. There are slight discrepancies between O'Donnell's and Mills's statements at this point. O'Donnell recalls Mills questioning a confused Alma for information. Mills suggests that she volunteered the information, perhaps suggesting, as was the police's case in court, that she was in full control of her faculties:

> 'I can tell you who did it.'
> 'His son.'
> 'How old is he?'
> 'Thirty-two. I don't know where he is.'

41 Ibid.

42 Mills's statement, op. cit.

43 William Goldsworthy Carter's statement, 30 March 1935, DPP 2/263 Part 4

44 Carter's statement, op. cit.

45 Bagwell's statement, op. cit.

46 Carter's statement, op. cit.

47 Ibid., also confirmed by Sydney George Bright's statement, 29 March 1935, DPP 2/263 Part 4
48 Carter's statement, op. cit.
49 Ibid.
50 Ibid.

1. From London to Victoria

1   *Friends' Intelligencer and Journal*, Society of Friends, Vol. XLV, 1888, p. 624
2   Stephen Inwood, *A History of London* (London: Macmillan, 1998), p. 411
3   Panikos Panayi, *German Immigrants in Nineteenth-Century Britain 1815–1914* (London: Bloomsbury, London, 1995), pp. 42–3
4   Ibid., p. 120
5   Ibid., p. 124
6   Inwood, *History of London*, op. cit., p. 449
7   L. B. C. Seaman, *Life in Victorian London* (London: B. T. Batsford, 1973), pp. 13–14
8   Panayi, op. cit., p. 125
9   There were the *Deutscher Turnvein* (the German Gymnasium Society), the *Deutscher Gewerbe und Theatr Verein* (the German Industrial and Theatre Club) and various clubs that provided for the sick, the unemployed and the burial of the dead. See Panayi, op. cit., p. 184.
10 Panayi, op. cit., pp. 183–4
11 Quoted in Panayi, op. cit., p. 184
12 Panayi, op. cit., p. 190
13 Charles Booth, *Life and Labour of the London Poor, Vol. I: Poverty* (London: Macmillan, 1892), p. 271
14 Stephen Inwood, *City of Cities* (London: Macmillan, 2004), pp. 59–60
15 Charles Dickens, *Bleak House*, Charles Dickens Library, Vol. XI (London: The Educational Book Co. Ltd, 1910), p. 386
16 Stephen Humphrey, *Elephant and Castle: A History*, Amberley Publishing, Stroud, 2013, p. 5
17 Advertisement in the *South London Press*, 17 September 1887, p. 13. See also W. J. Gordon, *The Horse-World of London* (London: The Religious Tract Society, 1893).
18 *South London Press*, 1 March 1884, p. 6
19 *Kilburn Times*, 4 April 1884, p. 5
20 Alma was later to sit London College of Music and Royal College of Music examinations at Zetland House School in Kamloops, which is where the confusion may stem from
21 *South London Press*, 12 July 1884, p. 7

22 D'Oyly Carte Opera Company Archive, gsarchive.net

23 Ibid.

24 Twenty thousand copies of the vocal score had been sold on publication and over 70,000 copies of various arrangements were sold within days

25 Rowlands had toured with the production to New York in the spring of 1890 where it was received much less enthusiastically than it had been in London. But despite the failure of the American production, he proceeded to perform in the British cast at the same time as Tilly Wolff.

26 See Charles Booth, *Life and Labour of the People in London, Vol. II: Industry* (New York: Macmillan & Co., 1903), p. 141. First-class theatres offered between 42s and 50s – for seven performances, but second-class houses could pay as little as 25s for the same engagement. Musicians could also supplement their earnings with music lessons and music copying for between 3d and 6d a page.

27 A young musician like Ernest Wolff Jr would be expected to work his way up to playing in the larger theatres and better-class music halls until he was engaged in concert work. Performers who became sufficiently well-known would be able to make a good living entirely from concerts and giving music lessons. See Charles Booth, *Life and Labour of the People in London, Vol. II: Industry*, op. cit., p. 142.

28 The Canterbury, the Borough in Union Street, the Surrey Theatre at the junction of Waterloo and Blackfriars Roads and the South London Palace of Varieties on London Road were all situated near to the Wolffs' home

29 Francis Sheppard, *London: A History* (Oxford: Oxford University Press, 1998), p. 301

30 W. J. Macqueen-Pope, *The Melodies Linger On: The Story of Music Hall 1888–1960* (London: W. H. Allen, 1950), p. 7

31 Charles Booth, *Life and Labour of the People in London, Vol. III: Religious Influences*, p. 173–85. Quoted in Inwood, *City of Cities*, op. cit.

32 The previous year, a nineteen-year-old music hall performer called Hannah Hill married the son of a butcher at St. John's. Charles Chaplin also earned his living as a middle-ranking music hall performer and would father one of southeast London's most famous sons, the silent movie star Charlie Chaplin.

33 Before Sir John Lubbock promoted his Bank Holidays Bill in 1871, Christmas Day and Good Friday had been the only bank holidays. Other than Sundays, for working people they were the only days off in the year. Lubbock's Act added Boxing Day, Easter Monday and Whit Monday, and created an entirely new holiday on the first Monday in August. For tactical reasons he limited his Bill to bank clerks but always expected that these new holidays would eventually become

general. However, the idea of statutory holidays for working people was opposed by many who believed that workers would spend their leisure hours drinking.

34 See Charles Booth, Jess Steele (ed.), *The Streets of London, The Booth Notebooks: South East* (London: Deptford Forum Publishing, 1997), p. 43. The street was 'wood paved', full of 'old-fashioned houses' and had once been home to the poet William Blake.

35 R. C. K. Ensor, *England, 1870–1914* (Oxford: Clarendon Press, 1936), pp. 111–12

36 *South London Press*, 13 February 1886, p. 4

37 Paul Begg, *Jack the Ripper: The Definitive History* (London: Routledge, 2004), p. 181

38 'Wanted: An Efficient Police Force', *South London Press*, 6 October 1888, p. 9

39 Richard Cavendish, *History Today*, Vol. LVII, Issue 12, December 2007

40 Quoted in Terry Reksten, *The Illustrated History of British Columbia* (Vancouver: Douglas & McIntyre, 2001), p. 127

41 Norman Macdonald, *Canada: Immigration and Colonisation, 1841–1903* (Aberdeen: Aberdeen University Press, 1966), p. 7

42 Frances Mcnab, *British Columbia for Settlers: Its Trade, Mines and Agriculture* (London: Chapman & Hall, 1898), p. 1

43 Ibid., p. 104

44 Børge Solem, 'The Transatlantic Crossing – Chapter 2: Steerage Passengers – Emigrants Between Decks', www.norwayheritage.com/steerage.htm

45 An information booklet published by the Allan Line warned intermediate passengers not to expect too much: 'The attention of passengers is directed to the fact that the Intermediate is only an improved Steerage, and that it in no way resembles a Cabin Passage. The Intermediate Passengers are subject to the same Rules and Regulations as the Steerage.' *Information and Advice for Emigrants*, Liverpool, 1883.

46 Mcnab, op. cit., p. 107

47 Ibid.

48 Ibid.

49 Ibid.

50 Don MacGillivray, *Captain Alex MacLean: Jack London's Sea Wolf* (Seattle: University of Washington Press, 2008), p. 29

51 Rudyard Kipling, *Letters of Travel* (New York: Doubleday, Page & Co., 1920), p. 210

52 Ibid.

53 Terry Reksten, *More English than the English: A Very Social History of Victoria* (Victoria, BC: Orea Book Publishers, 1986)

54 Ibid.

55　Harry Gregson, *A History of Victoria 1842–1970* (Victoria, BC: Victoria Observer Publishing, 1970), p. 121

56　Ibid.

57　Ibid.

58　Ibid., p. 137

2. Miss Clarke

1　Terence Rattigan, *Cause Célèbre* or *A Woman of Principle* (London: Hamish Hamilton, 1978), p. 10

2　Tennessee Williams, *Summer and Smoke* (London: John Lehman, 1952), p. 14

3　D. H. Stewart, *Kipling's America: Travel Letters, 1889–1895* (University of North Carolina, Greensboro: ELT Press, 2003), p. 81

4　Marian Wilson Kimber, *The Elocutionists: Women, Music, and the Spoken Word* (Urbana, Chicago and Springfield: University of Illinois Press, 2017), p. 21

5　Ella Wheeler Wilcox was a popular American poet of the time. There is no evidence that Frances had performed the poem in London, successfully or not, but her recital was a piece of lurid gothic, the story of the guilt of a psychopathic woman scorned.

6　Ella Wheeler Wilcox, *Maurine* (Milwaukee: Cramer, Aikens & Cramer, 1876), p. 167

7　*Victoria Daily Colonist*, 21 July 1891, p. 5

8　Ibid.

9　Frances was now billed under her married name or as the more exotic-sounding 'Miss Franceska Wolff'. 'Mrs W. W. Clarke will give, by special request a character recital, "The Maniac", which she has performed so successfully, in London, Eng. and which will be quite a feature of the evening. Mr Clement Rowlands, the popular baritone, is already too well known to need any special comment, and those who wish to spend a really enjoyable evening will avail themselves of the opportunity to hear this talented family.' *Victoria Daily Colonist*, 27 September 1891.

10　See *Victoria Daily Colonist*, 15 October 1891, p. 8

11　Passport held in DPP 2/263 Part 3

12　*Victoria Daily Colonist*, 29 May 1897, p. 1

13　Ibid., 15 August 1897, p. 2

14　The early history of Kamloops is described in Ron Hatch, Elizabeth Duckworth, Sylvia Grupp and Sherry Bennett, *Kamloops: Trading Post to Tournament Capital* (Kamloops, BC: Thompson Rivers History and Heritage Society, 2012)

15　*Kamloops Inland Sentinel*, 5 March 1897, p. 8

16 *Kamloops Standard*, 21 April 1898

17 Anthony Barrett and Rhodri Windsor-Liscombe, *Francis Rattenbury and British Columbia: Architecture and Challenge in the Imperial Age* (Vancouver: University of British Columbia Press, 1983), p. 373

18 Sir Michael Havers, Peter Shankland and Anthony Barrett, *Tragedy in Three Voices: The Rattenbury Murder* (London: William Kimber, 1980), p. 20

19 *Kamloops Standard*, 1 February 1900, p. 1

20 'Western Canada's Musical Prodigy', interview with Mary Lomas in *Westward Ho!*, February 1910, p. 89

21 Ibid.

22 Ibid.

23 *Kamloops Standard*, 27 June 1901, p. 1; Urso performed Mendelssohn's Violin Concerto, Chopin's *Variations brillantes* and Paganini's *Witches' Dance* (see *Victoria Daily Colonist*, 25 June 1901, p. 1)

24 'Western Canada's Musical Prodigy', interview with Mary Lomas in *Westward Ho!*, February 1910, p. 88

25 Ibid.

26 Ibid.

27 The concert, however, was 'miserably attended', prompting the *Colonist* to censure the Victorians: 'One had but to scan the small handful present to discover that even those who pose as musicians were conspicuous by their absence. What encouragement is held out to a really good concert company to give Victoria a visit when they receive such scant courtesy at the hands of local musicians. Female violinists of note are somewhat rare, which is an astonishing fact when it is considered that there exists in the female character the distinguishing charm of what may be styled an exquisite sensibility, which has its fittest musical exponent in the powers of the violin. Madame Urso's art is audible rather than visible, if such a distinction may be made. That is to say, her playing is magnificent, but not graceful. Her delicacy is astonishing and her general technique a poser for the aspiring amateur, and her tone – well, it is remarkable for a woman.' *Victoria Daily Colonist*, 25 June 1901, p. 1.

28 *Victoria Daily Colonist*, 26 November 1898, p. 7

29 Ibid., 1 May 1907, p. 6

30 Raymond Massey, *When I Was Young* (London: Robson Books, 1977), pp. 21–2; Massey was one of only two boys taught at the school at the time he and Alma attended it

31 Ellen Mary Knox, *The Girl of the New Day* (Toronto: McClelland & Stewart, 1919), p. 141

32 Ibid., p. 151

33 *Sunday Dispatch*, 9 June 1935, p. 9

34   Ibid.

35   Torrington was also a composer of the popular patriotic songs
     'Canada, The Gem in the Crown' and 'Our Country and King'

36   *Victoria Daily Colonist*, 11 July 1906, p. 6

37   There were four terms a year – fall (1 September–6 November 1909),
     winter (8 November–29 January 1910), spring (31 January–16 April) and
     summer (18 April–25 June). Examinations were held in February and
     June. See *Toronto College of Music Calendar and Syllabus, 1909–10*.

38   John George Hopkins, *The Establishment of Schools and Colleges in
     Ontario, 1792–1910*, Vol. III (Toronto: L. K. Cameron, 1910), p. 398

39   *Victoria Daily Colonist*, 10 August 1907, p. 6

40   Ibid., 1 May 1907, p. 6

41   'Western Canada's Musical Prodigy', interview with Mary Lomas in
     Westward Ho!, February 1910, p. 88

42   Ibid., p. 89

43   Havers, Shankland and Barrett, op. cit., p. 45

44   'Western Canada's Musical Prodigy', interview with Mary Lomas in
     Westward Ho!, February 1910, p. 89

45   *Kamloops Standard*, 25 July 1908, p. 5

46   'Western Canada's Musical Prodigy', interview with Mary Lomas in
     Westward Ho!, February 1910, p. 88

47   Ibid., p. 87

48   Ibid., p. 89

49   Ibid., p. 89–90

50   'Victoria Birthplace of Great Pianist', *Victoria Daily Colonist*, 30
     April 1911

51   See Olga Samaroff Stokowski, *An American Musician's Story* (New
     York: W. W. Norton & Co., 1939)

52   Ernest Wolff had died in San Francisco the year before. He had lived
     there for many years, still working as a tailor, with his wife Elizabeth,
     trusting that the southern climate would be good for his health.

53   J. C. Dunn, *The War the Infantry Knew: 1914–1919* (London: Abacus,
     1987), p. 170. See also Havers, Shankland and Barrett, op. cit., p. 21.

54   'Four Years' Friendship', interview with Frank Titterton, *Daily
     Express*, 1 June 1935, p. 3

55   Alma's father didn't attend the wedding and shortly before the war
     would return to England

56   'Miss Victoria Clarke, daughter of Mr and Mrs W. W. Clarke and
     Caledon R. J. R. Dolling, son of Caledon RJR Dolling of Dublin,
     Ireland were married Wednesday afternoon July 23 at 5 o'clock, in St
     Mark's Episcopal Church. Rev. E. V. Shalyer officiating. The bride,
     gowned in travelling suit and hat, was given in marriage by her mother.
     She carried a cluster of lilies of the valley. The couple left for a trip

through British Colombia and after August 1 they will be at home in Vancouver B.C.', *Seattle Times*, 27 July 1913.

57   Quoted in Havers, Shankland and Barrett, op. cit., p. 21
58   *Victoria Daily Colonist*, 23 July 1913, p. 1
59   Winston S. Churchill, *The World Crisis 1911–1914, Vol. V: The Eastern Front* (London: Thornton Butterworth, 1923), p. 1178

3. Mrs Dolling

1   Winston S. Churchill, *The World Crisis 1918–1928, Vol. IV: The Aftermath* (London: Bloomsbury, 2015), p. 313
2   Quoted in Martin Thornton, *Churchill, Borden and Anglo-Canadian Naval Relations, 1911–14* (London: Palgrave Macmillan, 2013), p. 17
3   *Vancouver Province*, 30 July 1914, quoted in Reksten, *The Illustrated History of British Columbia*, op. cit., p. 166
4   *Victoria Daily Colonist*, 5 August 1914, p. 1
5   Ibid.
6   Reksten, *The Illustrated History of British Columbia*, op. cit., p. 167
7   *Victoria British Daily Colonist*, 11 August 1914, p. 1
8   C. L. Flick, *Just What Happened: A Diary of the Mobilization of the Canadian Militia* (London: Chiswick Press, 1917)
9   The National Archives (NA) WO 339/42143. In his declaration for his commission, 28 August 1915, Dolling states, 'I wear glasses.'
10   The 2nd Battalion of the Fusiliers was considered to be one of the elite corps of the army
11   Dunn, op. cit., p. 2
12   Ibid., pp. 166–7
13   Robert Graves, *Goodbye to All That* (London: Octagon Books, 1980), p. 137
14   Llewelyn Wyn Griffith, *Up to Mametz and Beyond* (Barnsley: Pen and Sword Military, 2010), p. 73
15   This incident is recorded in the War Diary for the RWF 2nd Battalion, (NA) WO 95/2423/1
16   See J. Macartney-Filgate, *The History of the 33rd Divisional Artillery in the War, 1914–1918* (Uckfield: The Naval and Military Press, 1921)
17   Post Office Telegram, 9 February 1916, (NA) WO 339/42143
18   Post Office Telegram, 13 February 1916, (NA) WO 339/42143
19   *The Gazette*, 13 March 1916
20   Vera Brittain, *Testament of Youth: An Autobiographical Study of the Years 1900–1925* (London: Virago, 2014), p. 258
21   Post Office Telegram, 28 April 1916, (NA) WO 339/42143
22   *Belfast News Letter*, 30 May 1916, p. 8
23   It was common for soldiers to be given an acting rank, which was

essentially a promotion. A temporary rank was officially published in *The Gazette* – the official public record – while an acting role was not. An acting rank was generally given 'temporary' status after thirty days' service in the field and was then published in *The Gazette*.

24 As the months wore on, men like Dolling at the front became inured to the conditions they were living in, harrowingly remembered by Stuart Cloete in *A Victorian Son: An Autobiography, 1897–1912* (London: Collins, 1972), pp. 236–7: 'The sun swelled up the dead with gas and often turned them blue, almost navy blue. Then, when the gas escaped from their bodies, they dried up like mummies and were frozen in death positions. There were sitting bodies, kneeling bodies, bodies in almost every position, though naturally most of them lay on their bellies or backs. The crows had pecked out the eyes of some, and rats lived on the bodies that lay in the abandoned dugouts or half buried in the crumbled trenches ... Burial was impossible. In ordinary warfare the bodies went down with the limbers who brought up the rations. But then there were seldom more than three or four in a day. Now there were hundreds, thousands, not merely ours, but German as well. And where we fought several times over the same ground, bodies became incorporated in the material of the trenches themselves. In one place, we had to dig through corpses of Frenchmen who had been killed and buried [previously]. These bodies were putrid, of the consistency of Camembert cheese. I once fell and put my hand right through the belly of a man. It was days before I got the smell out of my nails.'

25 Post Office Telegram, 26 August 1916, (NA) WO 339/42143

26 War Diary for the RWF 2nd Battalion, (NA) WO 95/2423/1

27 List of Fallen Officers, *The Times*, 31 August 1916, p. 9

28 *Sunday Dispatch*, 9 June 1935, p. 9

29 Note from Alma Dolling to the War Office, 7 August 1916, (NA) WO 339/42143. Though Alma wrote from Chislehurst, she requested that her husband's possessions be sent to Warrington Crescent, Maida Vale, where she may have been lodging while she worked in Whitehall.

30 Brittain, op. cit., p. 235

31 Letter from Alma's solicitor to the War Office, 2 October 1916, (NA) WO 339/42143

32 Letter from assistant Financial Secretary, War Office, to Alma's solicitor, 2 October 1916, (NA) WO 339/42143

33 Letter from McBride to Alma, 2 November 1916, (NA) WO 339/42143

34 Letter from Alma's solicitor to the War Office, 6 November 1916, (NA) WO 339/42143,

35 Ibid.

36 Dolling's possessions were sent from France via Cox's Shipping Agency

(Report of the Standing Committee of Adjustment, 28 October 1916, (NA) WO 339/42143)

37   Letter from H. R. H. Dolling to Havers, Shankland and Barrett, quoted in *Tragedy in Three Voices*, op. cit., p. 22; 'I was with there when my brother's sleeping bag came from France. I helped her to unroll it, and the first item we got out were his glasses in broken pieces.'

38   Kitchener had established mobile units for dealing with the dead and, in 1915, the French government allocated the land for the burial of British soldiers. Sir Fabian Ware was part of a mobile Red Cross unit who began recording where some of the dead were buried and began to maintain the graves. Official recognition was given to his unit by the War Office and it was incorporated into the British Army as the Graves Registration Commission in 1915. By summer 1919 the Commission announced that half a million bodies could not all be brought back to England and the principle of equality suggested that, if all the dead could not be brought back to England, none should be. See Denis Winter, *Death's Men: Soldiers of the Great War* (London: Penguin, 1979), p. 156.

39   Letter from the War Office to Mrs C. R. J. R. Dolling, 23 November 1916, (NA) WO 339/42143

40   Letter from the War Office to Alma's solicitor confirming her pension entitlement, 18 December 1916, (NA) WO 339/42143

4.   France

1   Leah Leneman, *In the Service of Life: The Story of Elsie Inglis and the Scottish Women's Hospitals* (Edinburgh: Mercat Press, 1994), epigraph. Butler was a member of the London Unit and the Elsie Inglis Unit of the Scottish Women's Hospitals.

2   Letter from Elsie Inglis to Millicent Fawcett, 9 October 1914, quoted in Lady Frances Balfour, *Dr Elsie Inglis* (London: Hodder & Stoughton, 1919)

3   Margot Lawrence, *Shadow of Swords: A Biography of Elsie Inglis* (London: Michael Joseph, 1971), p. 98

4   Ibid., pp. 99–100

5   Eileen Crofton, *Angels of Mercy: A Women's Hospital of the Western Front 1914–1918* (Edinburgh: Birlinn Ltd, 2013), p. 11

6   Ibid., p. 35

7   Ibid., p. 13

8   Two of the chauffeurs were men, as it was thought that the French authorities would not permit women to drive in the war zone

9   Crofton, op. cit., p. 20

10   Ibid., p. 36

11 Ibid., p. 21

12 Antonio Navárro, *The Scottish Women's Hospital at the French Abbey of Royaumont* (London: G. Allen & Unwin Ltd, 1917), p. 143

13 Crofton, op. cit., pp. 224–8

14 Ibid., p. 277

15 TD 1734/20/4/2/3, Scottish Women's Hospital Archive, Mitchell Library

16 Crofton, op. cit., p. 275

17 Leneman, op. cit., p. 116

18 Crofton, op. cit., p. 31

19 Leneman, op. cit., p. 219

20 Ibid.

21 Vera Colum, quoted in Crofton, op. cit., p. 274

22 Leneman, op. cit., p. 219

23 See Imperial War Museum Archive, Evelyn Hope Proctor's letter to her mother, 27 July 1917, quoted in Crofton, op. cit., p. 141–2: 'I've completely lost track of the days but I believe today is Friday, for which I am very glad as our washing comes back – By the way we have a clean sheet once a fortnight ditto towel, so we have to be careful! Did I tell you that the sole furniture consists of converted packing cases but we do get a bed and a mattress – I share a cubicle with a girl called Parkinson whom I met at the London office of the SWH before I left. She is quite nice – for which I am glad. I also have a window my side of the cubicle – my dressing table is quite smart as it consists of an old door that has been put on top of an old bagatelle table – and I have bought some stuff which I am going to hang round it. You will send me a bath as soon as possible, won't you? The country round here is perfectly lovely – I wish I had brought my bicycle with me, a lot of girls have them, it is the only method of propulsion to the nearest village, 2 miles, Viarmes – I wish we were not quite so cut off. I am in the ward called Blanche de Castille. It is a lovely ward with all latticed windows with creepers round and a vaulted roof. This is a *lovely* old place. Breakfast at 7.30 consists of bread and butter or jam, and coffee. Then lunch [*sic*] at 10, the same, sometimes cheese instead. Lunch at 12.30, meat and generally fresh fruit or milk pudding. Tea – bread and jam – Dinner at 7.30, meat and fruit. It sounds more than it is and I am working as I have never worked in my life before and generally to be put to bed absolutely dead to the world. – We never wear sleeves – which is nice in the summer only our arms and our hands are absolutely *disgraceful* to look at – We eat off enamel plates or the table (generally the table) and we drink out of enamel cups.'

24 For heavy patients, four orderlies were deputed for each stretcher (Navárro, op. cit., p. 142)

25   This main body of this letter is quoted in Havers, Shankland and
     Barrett, op. cit., pp. 22–3, with additions available in Barrett and
     Windsor-Liscombe, op. cit., p. 264

26   Cicely Hamilton, *Life Errant* (London: J. M. Dent & Sons Ltd,
     1935), p. 108

27   This did happen in Serbia to four of the units of the Scottish
     Women's Hospital

28   Crofton, op. cit., p. 142

29   Havers, Shankland and Barrett, op. cit., p. 23

30   Crofton, op. cit., p. 143. Villers-Cotterêts was situated 50 miles north-
     east of Paris and 40 miles from Royaumont.

31   Orderly Grace Summerhayes (later Dr MacRae) letter to Eileen
     Crofton, July 1993, quoted in Crofton, op. cit., p. 146

32   Crofton, op. cit., pp. 143–4

33   Ibid., p. 145

34   Ibid., p. 147

35   Ibid., p. 5

36   Society, *Vancouver Daily World*, 19 December 1921

37   Ibid., 4 March 1922

38   Quoted in Havers, Shankland and Barrett, op. cit., p. 23

39   Rudyard Kipling, 'The Gardener', in *Debits and Credits* (London:
     Macmillan, 1926), p. 413

40   For details of Flatiron Cemetery and its location, see the
     Commonwealth War Graves website: www.cwgc.org/find-a-cemetery/
     cemetery/61700/flatiron-copse-cemetery/mametz

5. Mrs Pakenham

1   Brittain, op. cit., p. 448

2   F. W. Memory, 'Alma Rattenbury's Exotic Life Story; Genius who
     turned Cynic', *Daily Mail*, 6 June 1935, p. 18. Also quoted in *Sunday
     Dispatch*, 9 June 1935, p. 9

3   Gordon Martin, *Chefoo School 1881–1951* (Devon: Merlin Books Ltd,
     1990), p. 21

4   T. Compton Pakenham, *Rearguard* (London: Alfred A. Knopf,
     1931), p. 161

5   On 20 November 1915 at Christ Church, Mayfair. See marriage licence
     in (NA) J 77/1440/4339.

6   Simona Pakenham, *Pigtails and Pernod* (London: Macmillan, 1961), p. 44

7   Ibid.

8   For Pakenham's war service, see (NA) WO 339/45457

9   *The Gazette*, Issue 30287, 17 September 1917, recorded in Peter
     Warrington, *For Distinguished & Meritorious Services in Time of*

    *War – The Great War Recipients of the Military Cross 1914–1920: A
    Register British and Empire*, p. 519

10 This letter was sent from Phyllis's address, 21 Emperor's Gate, SW
    (NA) J 77/1388/2584, Divorce Court File: 2584. Appellant: Phyllis
    Mona Pakenham. Respondent: Thomas Compton Pakenham. Wife's
    petition for restitution of conjugal rights.

11 Ibid.

12 Lawrence Stone, *Road to Divorce: England, 1530–1987* (Oxford:
    Oxford University Press, 1990), p. 394

13 *Daily Telegraph*, 12 November 1918, p. 9

14 Ibid.

15 Brittain, op. cit., p. 424

16 For the notion of 'superfluous women', see Virginia Nicolson, *Singled
    Out: How Two Million Women Survived Without Men After the First
    World War* (Oxford: Oxford University Press, 2008)

17 Nicolson, op. cit., p. 28

18 Ibid., p. 29

19 Ibid.

20 A petition to the divorce court on 24 March 1919 stated that Pakenham
    had 'frequently committed adultery with Alma Victoria Radcliffe
    Dolling' at various addresses and hotels in Grantham and Chiselhurst.
    (NA) J77/1440/3449.

21 (NA) J 77/1440/4339, Divorce Court File: 4339. Appellant: Phyllis
    Mona Pakenham. Respondent: Thomas Compton Pakenham. Wife's
    petition for divorce.

22 *Victoria Daily Colonist*, 6 December 1923, p. 9

23 Ibid.

24 *Daily Express*, 6 June 1935, p. 8

25 Ibid.

26 Ibid.

27 Letter from Rattenbury to Kate Miller Jones, quoted in Barrett and
    Windsor-Liscombe, op. cit., p. 262–3

28 *Daily Express*, 6 June 1935, p. 8

6. Mr Rattenbury

 1 Letter from Rattenbury to his daughter Mary, 1920, quoted in Barrett
    and Windsor-Liscombe, op. cit., p. 4

 2 After reading W. B. Bridge's *Some Account of the Barony and Town of
    Okehampton* (1899), Rattenbury wrote to his mother on 1 June 1903
    that 'I did not know the Rats were such an old and very respectable
    family, nearly all leaders'. (See Barrett and Windsor-Liscombe, op.
    cit., p. 9)

3   For Rattenbury's early life and career in England, see Barrett and
     Windsor-Liscombe, op. cit., Chapter 1, and Terry Reksten, *Rattenbury*
     (Victoria, BC: Soni Nis Press, 1978), Chapter 1

4   See Barrett and Windsor-Liscombe, op. cit., p. 164

5   Ibid., p. 164

6   Ibid., p. 17

7   Reksten, *Rattenbury*, op. cit., p. 15

8   Barrett and Windsor-Liscombe, op. cit., p. 31

9   Ibid., p. 33

10 Ibid., p. 51

11 *Victoria Daily Colonist* quoted in Reksten, *Rattenbury*, op. cit., p. 36

12 Reksten, *Rattenbury*, op. cit., p. 38

13 *Victoria Times*, February 1898, quoted in Barrett Windsor-Liscombe,
     op. cit., p. 60

14 See Barrett and Windsor-Liscombe, op. cit., p. 51

15 See Barrett and Windsor-Liscombe, op. cit., p. 59, and Reksten,
     Rattenbury, op. cit., pp. 117–8

16 The wedding photographs held in the BC Archives showing Florrie in a
     traditional veil and white dress must have been taken on their return to
     Victoria. On the marriage certificate, which she would have supervised,
     Florrie stated that she was Mrs Howard's adopted daughter and recorded
     her father as George *Elphinstone* Nunn of the 47th Regiment. This little
     deceit implied a patrician connection with Mountstuart Elphinstone, who
     had been lieutenant-governor of Bombay where the Nunns had once lived.
     It may be that, with a lowly pedigree and having been abandoned by both
     parents, Florrie inflated her family connections in order to make her
     more marriageable or to endear her to Rattenbury's relations. Whether
     Rattenbury was aware of her actual family history or not is unclear.

17 See Barrett and Windsor-Liscombe, op. cit., Chapter 3

18 Reksten, *Rattenbury*, op. cit., p. 119

19 Barrett and Windsor-Liscombe, op. cit., p. 93

20 Ibid., p. 351

21 Ibid., p. 70

22 Ibid., p. 71

23 Havers, Shankland and Barrett, op. cit., p. 33

24 Letter from Rattenbury, 30 May 1900, quoted in Barrett and
     Windsor-Liscombe, op. cit., p. 72

25 Barrett and Windsor-Liscombe, op. cit., p. 121

26 Ibid., p. 122

27 Havers, Shankland and Barrett, op. cit., p. 34

28 Barrett and Windsor-Liscombe, op. cit., p. 118

29 Letter from Rattenbury to his mother, 13 May 1904, quoted in Barrett
     and Windsor-Liscombe, op. cit., p. 156

30   The first large shipment of Chinese had reached the city in 1878 when they had been pelted and jeered at on arrival, the *Daily Colonist* observing that 'as their presence in our midst is not desired, the welcome they received was not of the most flattering nature'. But by 1884, the number of Chinese had equalled the number of white settlers in Victoria, many having been brought to Canada to build the transcontinental railway and then abandoned as soon as construction was completed. The Chinese started businesses of their own and soon developed a thriving community to rival San Francisco's Chinatown, with shops, schools, churches, a newspaper and a hospital.

31   Reksten, *Rattenbury*, op. cit., p. 120

32   Ibid.

33   Letter from Rattenbury to his mother, 10 September 1905, quoted in Barrett and Windsor-Liscombe, op. cit., pp. 164–5

34   Havers, Shankland and Barrett, op. cit., p. 27

35   Reksten, *Rattenbury*, op. cit., p. 119

36   Ibid., p. 121; Terry Reksten interviewed Mary Burton (née Rattenbury) about the decline of her parents' marriage on 9 November 1974

37   Ibid., p. 122

38   Ibid.

39   Ibid.

40   Advertisement quoted in Pierre Berton, *The Crystal Gardens: West Coast Pleasure Palace* (Victoria, BC: Crystal Garden Preservation Society, 1977), p. 118

41   Barrett and Windsor-Liscombe, op. cit., p. 262

42   Ibid., p. 372

43   Ibid.

7.   The Second Mrs Rattenbury

1   Tennessee Williams, *A Streetcar Named Desire* (London: John Lehman, 1949), p. 75

2   Reksten, *Rattenbury*, op. cit., p. 131

3   Ibid., p. 132

4   *Daily Mail*, 6 June 1935, p. 18

5   See Barrett and Windsor-Liscombe, op. cit., p. 282

6   Ibid.

7   Reksten, *Rattenbury*, op. cit., p. 131

8   Ibid.

9   Ibid., p. 133

10   Ibid., p. 135, interview with Mary Burton (née Rattenbury), 9 November 1974

11   Reksten, *Rattenbury*, op. cit., p. 135

12   Havers, Shankland and Barrett, op. cit., p. 11

13   Ibid., p. 37

14   *Daily Mail,* 6 June 1935, p. 18

15   Ibid.

16   Ibid.

17   Ibid.

18   Ibid.

19   'Mrs Rattenbury's Tragic Life', *Vancouver Sun,* 17 May 1935

20   Letter from Rattenbury to Mary Rattenbury, 16 October 1925, quoted in Barrett and Windsor-Liscombe, op. cit., pp. 282–3. This letter from Mary Burton's archive has a later handwritten addition from Mary: 'My father's letter to me. Alma's influence I would think.'

21   Havers, Shankland and Barrett, op. cit., p. 37

22   Barrett and Windsor-Liscombe, op. cit., p. 280

23   This exchange between Alma and Mrs McClure was recalled by Frank Rattenbury in an interview with Terry Reksten, August 1974 (Reksten, *Rattenbury,* op. cit., p. 137)

24   *Vancouver Sun,* 17 April 1935, p. 1

25   City of Victoria Archives, letter from Rattenbury to F. E. Winslow, 27 January 1935. This business letter also includes a longer, typed addition headed, 'Personal'.

26   Barrett and Windsor-Liscombe, op. cit., p. 283

27   Havers, Shankland and Barrett, op. cit., p. 3

28   Barrett and Windsor-Liscombe, op. cit., p. 10

29   Terry Retsken, op. cit., p. 138. Interview with Mary Rattenbury, 9 November 1974

30   Ibid.

31   'Son says Rattenbury "Enslaved"', *Vancouver Sun,* 17 April 1935, p. 1

32   *A Pictorial and Descriptive Guide to Dartmoor* (London: Ward Lock & Co. Ltd, 1934), p. 82

33   Victoria City Archives, Last Will and Testament of Francis Mawson Rattenbury, 18 December 1929

34   *Vancouver Sun,* 17 April 1935, p. 1

35   Havers, Shankland and Barrett, op. cit., p. 38

ENTR'ACTE: Holloway, 9 January 1923

1   Virginia B. Morris, *Double Jeopardy: Women Who Kill in Victorian Fiction* (Kentucky: Kentucky University Press, 1990), p. 131

2   This reconstruction of the last hours of Edith Thompson is based on the investigation into the affair in 1956 based on prison files and remembered testimony of the individuals who still survived, including

the two warders who supported her from the condemned cell to the gallows (NA 1125/232; PCOM 9 1983)

3   Letter from June Akram, 21 March 1956, former principal officer at Holloway and present on the day of Edith Thompson's execution. The statements of the prison officers made in their retirement offer an alternative reading of Edith Thompson's execution as a miscarriage of justice. Akram supervised Mrs Thompson for nine weeks at Holloway and 'her cold calm attitude was not one of innocence, I feel very sure'. Another female officer, Cater, concurred. After the execution they washed her body; Cater felt that 'from my first contact with her to that last moment my whole impression was that she was undoubtedly guilty because she was so calm, so guarded, and so careful in her manner and speech as if to make certain she did not give herself away.' (Both in (NA) PCOM 9/1983)

4   Thomas Hardy, 'On the Portrait of a Woman about to be Hanged', 6 January 1923, *The Collected Poems of Thomas Hardy* (London: Macmillan, 1930), p. 741

5   *Daily Express*, 7 December 1922, p. 1

6   Quoted in Enid Huws Jones, *Margery Fry: The Essential Amateur* (London: Oxford University Press, 1966), p. 124

7   Morton was a 51-year-old Irishman who would still be governor when Alma Rattenbury was held at Holloway in 1935.

8   F. Tennyson Jesse, *A Pin to See the Peepshow* (London: William Heinemann, 1934), p. 462

9   René J. A. Weis, *Criminal Justice: The True Story of Edith Thompson* (London: Hamish Hamilton, 1988), p. 301

10 Letter from William Henry Young to the Home Office, 3 August 1948, 438,338/260 in HO 144 2685 Part 2. Young was one of the prison officers present at Edith Thompson's execution and it was he who told her, 'Come on, mate, it'll soon be over'. After the Criminal Justice Bill was before parliament discussing the abolition of the death penalty, he wrote to the press questioning stories that had appeared about the nature of the execution: 'It was as clean an execution as I've seen and when we brought her up, there was not a mark on her. During my service I have attended 17 executions. There was nothing whatever to distinguish Mrs Thompson's case from the other executions.'

11 Margaret Fry quoted by Arthur Koestler in *The Observer*, 11 March 1956 (also quoted in Weis, op. cit., p. 302)

12 (NA) PCOM 9/1983, letter from G. A. Woods, chief officer, HMP, to Mr Harris, governor, Exeter Prison, 22 March 1956

13 (NA) PCOM 9/1983. For the moments leading to Edith Thompson's execution, see Prison Commission Review 1125/232, 1956.

14 Weis, op. cit., p. 304

15 Ibid., p. 305

16 Margaret Fry quoted by Arthur Koestler in *The Observer*, 11 March 1956

17 *Daily Express*, 21 September 1932. However, in the *Sunday Observer* (25 March 1956), Bernard O'Donnell, a crime reporter acquainted with Ellis, claimed that Ellis 'was more disturbed by the hanging of the boy Jacoby than by the execution of Mrs Thompson'. The second woman Ellis had hanged in Scotland. In December 1927, Ellis appeared at the Grand Theatre in Gravesend as the Victorian hangman William Marwood in *Charles Peace*, a play about the infamous murderer and burglar. As Lizzie Seal notes in *Capital Punishment in Twentieth-Century Britain: Audience, Justice, Memory* (London: Routledge, 2014), ''Ellis' presence made the hanging scene uncomfortably realistic – and was also the reason to go and see the play', pp. 70–71. Ellis's appearance was 'the signal for a burst of applause from the audience'. And 'the whole attraction of the melodrama is obviously the hanging, with Ellis taking the part as hangman. The people who came to the theatre tonight wanted to see Ellis and the way he did his work', 'Hangman Acts in Play', *Daily Express*, 13 December 1927; *Daily Mirror*, 16 December 1927. In 1932, Ellis toured fairgrounds 'with a show demonstrating an actual hanging', 'The Fun of the Fair', *Western Daily Press*, 20 April 1932.

18 *Empire News*, 28 January 1923

19 *Daily Express* 24 November 1922, p. 5

20 Filson Young, *The Trial of Frederick Bywaters and Edith Thompson (Notable British Trials)* (London and Edinburgh: William Hodge & Co., second edition, 1951), p. 135

21 *Daily Express*, 7 December 1922, p. 1. Though Beverly Nichols, who attended the trial, thought Bywaters an 'amiable ape ... rigid with sex'. Beverly Nichols, *The Sweet and Twenties* (London: Weidenfeld & Nicolson, 1958), p. 67

22 *Daily Mail*, 18 October 1922, p. 13

23 The word 'Flapper' was defined by *Punch* in 1927: 'Flapper is a popular press catchword for an adult woman worker aged 21 to 30 when it is a question of giving her the vote under the same conditions as men.' Robert Graves and Alan Hodge, *The Long Weekend: A Social History of Great Britain, 1918–1939* (London: Faber & Faber, 1940), p. 44

24 *Illustrated Sunday Herald*, 22 April 1922

25 Dorothy Beddoe, *Back to Home and Duty: Women Between the Wars 1918–1939* (London: Pandora, 1989), p. 48

26 During the war, munitions factory workers, or 'munitionettes', had gained a reputation for promiscuity. Contraceptives, almost unknown

before the war, could by 1919 be purchased in every village chemist. 'Morality-mongers', wrote Sylvia Pankhurst 'conceived monstrous visions of girls and women, freed from the control of fathers and husbands, who had hitherto compelled them to industry, chastity and sobriety, now neglecting their homes, plunging into excess and burdening the country with swarms of illegitimate children.' Sylvia Pankhurst, *The Home Front: A Mirror to Life in England During the World War* (London: Hutchinson, 1987), p. 98.

27 Beddoe, op. cit., p. 48
28 Martin Pugh, *We Danced All Night: A Social History of Britain Between the Wars* (London: Vintage, 2009), p. 125
29 *Reynolds News*, 17 December 1922, p. 9
30 Bernard O'Donnell, *Should Women Hang?* (London: W. H. Allen, 1956), p. 53
31 Ibid., p. 52
32 Ibid.
33 Iles, 'The Rattenbury Case', in *The Anatomy of Murder*, op. cit., p. 215
34 Young, op. cit., p. 251
35 Letter from Edith Thompson to Bessie Aitken, 26 December 1922, quoted in Weis, op. cit., p. 269
36 *Evening Standard*, 9 January 1923
37 *Daily Mirror*, 10 January 1923, p. 2
38 *Daily Herald*, 10 January 1923
39 Ibid., 11 January 1923
40 *News of the World*, 14 January 1923
41 Violet Van der Elst, *On the Gallows* (London: Doge Press, 1937), p. 152
42 The sensational press reports of Edith Thompson's death continued over subsequent decades. In 1948, in a debate in the House of Commons about capital punishment, the MP Beverly Baxter stated that Mrs Thompson 'disintegrated as a human creature' before she was executed and that her 'insides fell out' when she was hanged. In 1956, Arthur Koestler, the anti-capital punishment campaigner, wrote *Reflections on Hanging*, which referred to confidential Home Office documents concerning the execution. On publication, the book inspired a debate in the Sunday press that re-ignited the controversy and led to debate in both Houses of Parliament and in the press. This initiated a flurry of letters to the press from former prison staff who refuted claims made in Koestler's book. The Home Office then initiated a thorough inquiry involving many of the former prison staff and doctors, since retired, who had been present at the execution. Among others, G. A. Woods, the former chief officer with HMP, answered a series of questions about the morning of the execution. 'Nothing unusual or dreadful happened at all, her

insides did not fall out.' They also disputed claims that Margery Fry had made concerning the governor and chaplain's reactions to the execution. It seems that the sensation surrounding Edith's death had been initiated – and inflated – by the press. Despite the refutation of the circumstances of Mrs Thompson's death, the story of a young woman dragged to her death in horrific circumstances still holds currency in popular culture.

43 For a fascinating examination of petty treason, see Frances E. Dolan, *Dangerous Familiars: Representations of Domestic Crime in England, 1550–1700* (Ithaca and London: Cornell University Press, 1994)

44 Helena Kennedy, *Eve Was Framed* (London: Vintage, 1992), p. 68

45 Ann Jones, *Women Who Kill* (New York: The Feminist Press, 2009), p. 24

46 Tennyson Jesse, *The Trial of Alma Victoria Rattenbury and George Percy Stoner*, op. cit., p. 13

8. A Third England

1 George Orwell, *The Lion and the Unicorn: Socialism and the English Genius*, 19 February 1941, in *The Collected Essays, Journalism and Letters of George Orwell, Vol. II: My Country Right or Left 1940–1943* (London: Secker & Warburg, 1968), p. 87

2 The Journey from British Columbia to England was related to Anthony Barrett in an interview with Christopher Pakenham (see Barrett and Windsor-Liscombe, op. cit., p. 286)

3 J. B. Priestley, *English Journey* (London: William Heinemann, 1934), p. 401

4 W. H. Auden, 'I September 1939', *Selected Poems* (London: Faber & Faber, 2009), p. 95

5 Ronald Blythe, *The Age of Illusion: England in the Twenties and Thirties, 1919–1940* (London: Phoenix Press, 2001)

6 William McElwee, *Britain's Locust Years 1918–1940* (London: Faber & Faber, 1962)

7 Juliet Gardiner, *The Thirties: An Intimate History* (London: Harper Press, 2010), p. 322. The development Gardiner discusses is the Cutteslowe estate in north Oxford.

8 Ibid., p. 323

9 *Western Morning News*, 8 September, 1930, p. 5

10 *Sunday Dispatch*, 9 June 1935, p. 8. Miller Jones worked for Braby and Waller, Arundel Street, Strand.

11 Reksten, *Rattenbury*, op. cit., p. 141

12 *A Pictorial and Descriptive Guide to Bournemouth, Poole and District*, op. cit., p. 23

13   S. Watson Smith (ed.), *The Book of Bournemouth* (Bournemouth: Pardy & Son, 1934), p. 48

14   Ibid., p. 51

15   *A Pictorial and Descriptive Guide to Bournemouth, Poole and District*, op. cit., pp. 16–48

16   *Paton's List of Schools and Tutors* (London: J & J Paton, 1926), pp. 210–11

17   See Louise Maud Price's statement, 5 April 1935, DPP 2/263 Part 4. Hankinsons of West Southbourne were an estate agency based at 50 Southbourne Grove, West Southbourne. See advertisement, *Bournemouth Echo*, 9 November 1934, p. 3.

18   Louise Maud Price's statement, 5 April 1935, DPP 2/263 Part 4

19   Leslie Randall, 'I Knew Mrs Rattenbury', *Strand Magazine*, May 1943, Vol. CV, No. 269, p. 78

20   Gardiner, op. cit., p. 315

21   *Daily Sketch*, 5 March 1935, p. 12. In 1935, the Post-Master General, Sir Kingsley-Wood, outlined his vision for the future with a £34,000,000 three-year investment in telecommunications: 'Perhaps well before 1960 we shall have a telephone in every home; television so advanced that we shall have the actual presentment of scenes and events, not only in our own country, but in many parts of the world, within a few seconds of their actual occurrence; and our mails will be delivered daily by aeroplane to most parts of the world.' *Bournemouth Daily Echo*, 30 May 1935, p. 10.

22   J. Burnett, *A Social History of Housing, 1815–1870* (Newton Abbott, David & Charles, 1978), p. 246

23   T. Jeffrey, 'A Place in the Nation: The Lower Middle Classes in England', in R. Kashar (ed.), *Splintered Classes: Politics and the Lower Middle Classes in Interwar Europe* (New York: Holmes & Meir, 1990), p. 75

24   *The Home of Today* (Daily Express Publications, 1935), p. 7

25   Gardiner, op. cit., p. 531

26   See Adrian Forty, *Objects of Desire: Design and Society 1750–1980* (London: Thames & Hudson, 1986), pp. 187–95

27   Ibid., p. 200

28   Ibid., p. 202

29   E. M. Delafield, *Ladies and Gentlemen in Victorian Fiction* (London: The Hogarth Press, 1937), p. 12

30   Blythe, op. cit., p. 47

31   J. Reith, *Broadcasting Over Britain* (1924), cited in J. McDonnell, *Public Service Broadcasting: A Reader* (London: Routledge, 1991), pp. 11–12

32   Blythe, op. cit., p. 57

33   Quoted in Blythe, op. cit., p. 52–3

34   Kevin Williams, op. cit., p. 97. The press was also determined to prevent the BBC from publishing listings of any of its programmes. This dispute had led to the BBC setting up its own publication in 1923, the *Radio Times*.

35   Television was still very much in its infancy, though the 1933 Christmas edition of *Punch* depicted the Christmas of the future with a family staring at a screen while Father Christmas, a Christmas tree and a pantomime were all broadcast to them from a TV studio

36   In Rose Macaulay's *Crewe Train*, published in 1926 (Collins), the protagonist is advised by her mother about a middle-class lady's daily schedule; '10–11 read the papers and write one's letters: 11–1 serious reading' (p. 305).

37   Jan Struther, *Mrs Miniver* (London: Chatto & Windus, 1939), p. 21

38   Jackie Winter, *Lipsticks and Library Books: The Story of Boots Booklovers Library* (Dorset: Chantries Press, 2016), p. 11

39   Nicola Beauman, *A Very Great Profession: The Woman's Novel 1914–1939* (London: Persephone Books, 2008), p. 14

40   Winter, op. cit., p. 10

41   Beauman, op. cit., p. 15

42   Ibid., p. 14

43   Winter, op. cit., p. 17

44   Beauman, op. cit., p. 245

45   Ibid.

46   Michael Joseph, *The Commercial Side of Literature* (London: Hutchinson, 1925), p. 9

47   See Beddoe, op. cit., p. 14

48   Ibid., p. 19

49   *My Weekly*, 25 January 1919

50   *Everywoman's*, 8 February 1919

51   Winifred Holtby, 'The Wearer and the Shoe', *Manchester Guardian*, 31 January 1930, in Lisa Regan (ed.), *Winifred Holtby: A Woman in Her Time: Critical Essays* (Newcastle: Cambridge Scholars Publishing, 2010), p. xiv

52   Gardiner, op. cit., p. 526

53   *Daily Sketch*, 17 September 1934, p. 14

54   C. Breward, *The Culture of Fashion: A New History of Fashionable Dress* (Manchester, Manchester University Press, 1995), p. 183

55   Catherine Horwood, *Keeping Up Appearances: Fashion and Class Between the Wars* (Stroud: The History Press, 2011), pp. 59–60

56   Ibid., p. 61

57   Gardiner, op. cit., p. 527

58   Ibid.

59   Horwood, op. cit., p. 19

60   *The Lady*, 9 January 1936, p. 72

61   Ibid., 9 July 1936, p. 93

62   *Miss Modern*, September 1932, p. 50

63   *Good Housekeeping*, February 1931, p. 18

64   *Sunday Dispatch*, 5 May 1935, p. 3

65   *Miss Modern*, January 1932, p. 9

66   *Good Housekeeping*, March 1930, p. 222

67   *Daily Sketch*, 13 November 1934, p. 19

68   Marie Stopes, 'The Unsuspected Future of the Cinema', *The New East*, 3:1 (1918): pp. 26–8, cited in Lisa Stead, *Off to the Pictures: Cinema-Going, Women's Writing and Movie Culture in Interwar Britain* (Edinburgh: Edinburgh University Press, 2016), p. 13

69   Stead, op. cit., p. 1

70   Pugh, op. cit., p. 221

71   *Daily Express*, 16 April 1935, p. 1

72   Quoted in Matthew Hilton, *Smoking in British Popular Culture 1800–2000* (Manchester: Manchester University Press, 2000), p. 99

73   Gardiner, op. cit., p. 536

74   Ibid., p. 538

75   See Horwood, op. cit., p. 11

76   Pugh, op. cit., p. 29

9. Villa Madeira

1   D. H. Lawrence, *Lady Chatterley's Lover* (Surrey: The Windmill Press, 1942), p. 9

2   Barrett and Windsor-Liscombe, op. cit., p. 308

3   Ibid.

4   Ibid., p. 287. See also Havers, Shankland and Barrett, op. cit., p. 43

5   See Louise Maud Price's statement, 5 April 1935, DPP 2/263 Part 4

6   John Rattenbury, *A House for Life: Bringing the Spirit of Frank Lloyd Wright into Your Home* (Toronto: Warwick Publishing, 2006), p. 20

7   Barrett and Windsor-Liscombe, op. cit., p. 287

8   Alma opened her Harrods account on 27 November 1933, Thomas Hall's statement (enquiry officer, Harrods), 5 April 1935, DPP 2/263 Part 4

9   Havers, Shankland and Barrett, op. cit., p. 45

10   Alma's 1934–35 statements at Barclays Bank, 61 Old Christchurch Road, Bournemouth are held in DPP 2/263 Part 4. She was continually overdrawn, sometimes by over £120 – a significant sum, given that the average wage at the time was £150 a year.

11   Under cross-examination by Casswell, Irene was asked if she remembered 'a chef named Davis'. Irene claimed he had left before she arrived

at the Villa Madeira. Raising the issue of Davis may well have been an attempt by Casswell to colour the jury's attitude to Alma by hinting that she regularly conducted inappropriate relations with male servants. (Tennyson Jesse, *The Trial of Alma Victoria Rattenbury and George Percy Stoner*, op. cit., p. 85)

12   Various nurses are mentioned in the electoral register and census for the Villa Madeira, including Nora White and Joyce Ypres Francis. Mrs Almond was the last nurse to be employed by the Rattenburys and left their service only days before Stoner started work.

13   Margaret Powell, *Climbing the Stairs* (London: Peter Davies, 1970), p. 1

14   Irene Riggs's evidence, 27 May 1935, quoted in Tennyson Jesse, *The Trial of Alma Victoria Rattenbury and George Percy Stoner*, op. cit., p. 81

15   Regular payments to Irene are recorded in Alma's Barclays accounts in DPP 2/263 Part 3

16   Irene Riggs's evidence, 27 May 1935, quoted in Tennyson Jesse, *The Trial of Alma Victoria Rattenbury and George Percy Stoner*, op. cit., p. 84

17   Leslie Randall, 'I Knew Mrs Rattenbury', op. cit. See also Irene Riggs's statement, 11 April 1935, DPP 2/263 Part 3. Irene stated that in terms of money Alma had given her 'no more than £5'.

18   Croom-Johnson's summing up, DPP 2/263 Part 5

19   Irene Riggs's evidence, 27 May 1935, quoted in Tennyson Jesse, *The Trial of Alma Victoria Rattenbury and George Percy Stoner*, op. cit., p. 83

20   Wood seems to have worked regularly for Rattenbury. When he died, Ratz owed Wood £230 for work done on his behalf, perhaps for the flats he was trying to finance. See Victoria Archives, Rattenbury Probate File, Supreme Court, Victoria Probate/Estate Files, 1859–1941.

21   Letter from D. A. Wood to the public prosecutor, 24 May 1935, DPP 2/263 Part 1

22   Dr William O'Donnell's evidence, 28 May 1935, quoted in Tennyson Jesse, *The Trial of Alma Victoria Rattenbury and George Percy Stoner*, op. cit., p. 105

23   Ibid.

24   Jonathan Gaythorne-Hardy, *Doctors: The Life and Work of GPs* (London: Weidenfeld & Nicolson, 1984), p. 19

25   Ibid., p. 19

26   For the work of GPs between the wars, see Anne Digby, *The Evolution of General Practice 1850–1948* (Oxford: Oxford University Press, 1999)

27   The contents of the medicine chest were recorded by PC W. G. Budden in a Hants police report, 4 April 1935, DPP 2/263 Part 1

28 *Daily Express*, 8 December 1933, p. 7

29 *The Citizen*, 25 October 1934, p. 1

30 *Daily Express*, 25 October 1934. Between 1927 and 1942, thirty-eight GPs and eight pharmacists were struck off for providing illegal narcotics to patients. See (NA) MH 135/157.

31 *The Times*, 17 December 1937, p. 9

32 Barrett and Windsor-Liscombe, op. cit., p. 373

33 Barbara Anne Pinder (Inexpensive Dresses Department Harrods), DPP 2/263 Part 4. When interviewed, Pinder remembered Alma well: 'The woman was plumpish.'

34 Knox, op. cit., p. 141

35 Letter from Rattenbury to Kate Miller Jones, 12 December 1931, quoted in Havers, Shankland and Barrett, op. cit., pp. 40–41

36 Irene Riggs's evidence, 28 May 1935, quoted in Tennyson Jesse, *The Trial of Alma Victoria Rattenbury and George Percy Stoner*, op. cit., p. 93

37 *Sunday Dispatch*, 9 June 1935, p. 9

38 Ibid.

39 All quotes from Frank Archibald Hobbs's statement, 4 April 1935, DPP 2/263 Part 4. Hobbs was not called as a witness at the trial. This was presumably because all he would have been able to confirm is that Alma proposed illicit relations with her staff, which was already clear from the indictment.

40 See Hobbs's statement, DPP 2/263 Part 4

41 October 1933, Irene Riggs's evidence, 27 May 1935, quoted in Tennyson Jesse, *The Trial of Alma Victoria Rattenbury and George Percy Stoner*, op. cit., pp. 83–4

42 See Hobbs's statement, op. cit.

43 The visit to Van Lier is quoted at length in a letter from Rattenbury to Kate Miller Jones, 12 December 1931, quoted in Havers, Shankland and Barrett, op. cit., pp. 40–41

44 Ibid.

45 *Daily Mail*, 1 June 1935, p. 7

46 Letter from Rattenbury to Kate Miller Jones, 12 December 1931, quoted in Havers, Shankland and Barrett, op. cit., p. 41

47 Ibid.

48 Ibid.

49 Ibid., p. 42

50 The pseudonym of the veteran American lyricist Edward Teschemacher

51 'Woman of Moods Who Compelled Attention,' *Daily Express*, 1 June 1935, p. 3

52 Ibid.

53 A YouTube video of a 1932 Pathetone recording has Titterton singing

'Dark-Haired Marie' accompanied by Alma at the piano: https://youtube/Or3bo2NhLU4

54   Frank Montague Allen's statement (Royalty Department, Keith Prowse), 4 April 1935, DPP 2/263 Part 4

55   *Daily Express*, 1 June 1935, p. 3

56   Ibid.

57   Alma's earnings in 1933–34 from her songwriting were £56 19s 3d, broken down as follows:
      September 1933: £47 9s 2d
      December 1933: £2 9s 6d
      March 1934: £5 12s 8d
      September 1934: £1 7s 11d

58   *Daily Express*, 6 June 1935, p. 8

59   York Membery, 'Murder, suicide and the pain of a surviving son', *The Times*, 29 November 2007, p. 10

60   Alma Rattenbury's evidence, 29 May 1935, quoted in Tennyson Jesse, *The Trial of Alma Victoria Rattenbury and George Percy Stoner*, op. cit., p. 179

61   Ibid., p. 165

62   Alma Rattenbury's evidence, 29 May 1935, quoted in Tennyson Jesse, *The Trial of Alma Victoria Rattenbury and George Percy Stoner*, op. cit., p. 164, and Dr William O'Donnell's evidence, 28 May, op. cit., pp. 8, 105

63   And it was only after 1934 that a divorced woman guilty of adultery was allowed access to her children as a right.

64   The fees of 40 guineas a term for John would be paid directly by Ratz. Alma would pay for Christopher's education out of the £50 a month she was given for running the house.

65   *Bournemouth Daily Echo*, 8 September 1934

66   Ibid., 5 September 1934, p. 1

67   *Daily Sketch*, 9 October 1934, p. 3

68   City of Victoria Archives, letter from Rattenbury to F. E. Winslow, 27 January 1935. This business letter also includes a longer, typed addition headed, 'Personal'.

69   Ibid.

70   Ibid.

71   *Bournemouth Daily Echo*, 26 September 1934, p. 1

72   Ibid., p. 2. On 7 June 1975, Terry Reksten interviewed Bert Parsons, who claimed to have seen the advertisement and applied for the job. He called at Manor Road and remembered being interviewed by a beautiful blonde woman who reminded him of the actress Madeleine Carroll. He was keen to take the position but disappointed when he was told that his duties would involve driving; he didn't know how

to drive. Alma reassured him: 'We'll soon teach you. The job is yours if you want it.' Parsons went home to tell his family the good news. But his sister felt that there was something too good to be true about the job and advised him not to take it. (See Reksten, *Rattenbury*, op. cit., p. 145.) Though it's clear from the advertisement that she placed in the *Bournemouth Echo* that Alma was looking for a houseboy, when asked in court by O'Connor, 'Was Stoner engaged as a house-boy or a chauffeur?', Alma answered, 'A chauffeur mainly.' (Alma Rattenbury's evidence, 29 May 1935, quoted in Tennyson Jesse, *The Trial of Alma Victoria Rattenbury and George Percy Stoner*, op. cit., p. 64.) Alma also stated in court that, 'I always put the advertisement like that, but I would not take any notice of the age. I have often had people come and call themselves seventeen when they had been a little older. I would not take any notice of that.' (Alma Rattenbury's evidence, quoted in Tennyson Jesse, *The Trial of Alma Victoria Rattenbury and George Percy Stoner*, op. cit., p. 181)

10. Stoner

1   Francis Iles, *As for the Woman: A Love Story* (London: Jarrolds, 1939), p. 243

2   *News of the World*, 2 June 1935, p. 13

3   Alma Rattenbury letter, 4 June 1935, DPP 2/263 Part 2

4   Alma Rattenbury's evidence, 29 May 1935, quoted in Tennyson Jesse, *The Trial of Alma Victoria Rattenbury and George Percy Stoner*, op. cit., p. 181

5   For motoring in Britain in the 1930s, see Peter Thorold, *The Motoring Age: The Automobile and Britain 1896–1939* (London: Profile Books, 2003)

6   Pugh, op. cit., pp. 257–9

7   George Stoner Senior's evidence, 30 May 1935, quoted in Tennyson Jesse, *The Trial of Alma Victoria Rattenbury and George Percy Stoner*, op. cit., p. 206

8   Ruth Adam, *A Woman's Place: 1910–1975* (London: Persephone Books 2011), p. 76

9   Ibid.

10 Ibid., pp. 80–81

11 Summary of Recorded Crime Statistics for England and Wales, 1898–2001/2 (Home Office)

12 Elizabeth A. Stevens's evidence, 27 May 1935, quoted in Tennyson Jesse, *The Trial of Alma Victoria Rattenbury and George Percy Stoner*, op. cit., p. 56

13 George Stoner Senior's evidence, 30 May 1935, quoted in Tennyson

Jesse, *The Trial of Alma Victoria Rattenbury and George Percy Stoner*, op. cit., p. 206

14 Ibid.

15 Elizabeth A. Stevens's evidence, 27 May 1935, quoted in Tennyson Jesse, *The Trial of Alma Victoria Rattenbury and George Percy Stoner*, op. cit., p. 56

16 See *A Century of Winton School 1877–1977* at the website of the Moordown Local History Society: www.jp137.com. The school had been set up in 1911 to accommodate 1,250 boys and girls in separate schools from the ages of five to fourteen.

17 York Membery, *National Post*, 30 November 2002

18 Casswell's examination of George Stoner Senior, 30 May 1935, quoted in Tennyson Jesse, *The Trial of Alma Victoria Rattenbury and George Percy Stoner*, op. cit., p. 207

19 Richard Edward Stevens's evidence, 27 May 1935, quoted in Tennyson Jesse, *The Trial of Alma Victoria Rattenbury and George Percy Stoner*, op. cit., p. 57–8

20 Police report, W. G. Carter, 5 April 1935, DPP 2/263 Part 1

21 Letter from D. A. Wood to the public prosecutor, 24 May 1935, DPP 2/263 Part 1

22 *Bournemouth Daily Echo*, 17 November 1934, p. 9

23 Irene Riggs's evidence, 27 May 1935, quoted in Tennyson Jesse, *The Trial of Alma Victoria Rattenbury and George Percy Stoner*, op. cit., p. 82

24 Gardiner, op. cit., p. 569

25 Marie Stopes's *Married Love* became a bestseller, with over 400,000 hardback copies sold between 1918 and 1923. Stopes's books were followed by *The Sex Factor in Marriage* by Helena Wright (1930) and Leonora's Eyles's *Commonsense about Sex* (1933).

26 For birth control in the 1930s, see Gardiner, op. cit., pp. 560–5

27 *Bournemouth Echo*, 26 June 1935, p. 1

28 This illness might have been related to the fainting fits that Stoner's father claimed his son suffered from, or the brainstorms that he himself experienced

29 Alma Rattenbury letter, 4 June 1935, DPP 2/263 Part 2

30 Ibid.

31 Ibid.

32 Ibid.

33 The trial documents of Rex *v*. Reginald Woolmington are held in (NA) HO 144/19946

34 Richard Edward Stevens's statement, 28 March 1935, DPP 2/263 Part 4

35 *Bournemouth Daily Echo*, 19 December 1934, p. 9

36 Points of View, *Bournemouth Daily Echo*, 18 December 1934, p. 4

37 'Bournemouth Expecting a "Capacity Christmas"', *Bournemouth Daily Echo*, 22 December 1935, p. 1

38 Ibid.

39 *Bournemouth Daily Echo*, 19 December, 1934, p. 9

40 Ibid., 24 December 1934, p. 7

41 Ibid., p. 9. 'The Empire Exchange' started at 1.55 p.m. with a Prologue, followed by the 'Bells of Bethlehem echoed by Bells of the British Commonwealth'. From 2 p.m., before the king's address at 3 p.m., there was a 'Programme of greetings and sound pictures depicting Christmas in all parts of the British Commonwealth including relays from Australia, New Zealand, Canada, India, South Africa, Southern Rhodesia, Irish Free State and United Kingdom'.

42 *Bournemouth Daily Echo*, 27 December 1934, p. 4

43 Alma Rattenbury's evidence, 29 May 1935, quoted in Tennyson Jesse, *The Trial of Alma Victoria Rattenbury and George Percy Stoner*, op. cit., p. 165

44 Alma Rattenbury letter, 4 June 1935, DPP 2/263 Part 2

45 Elizabeth A. Stevens's evidence, 27 May 1935, quoted in Tennyson Jesse, *The Trial of Alma Victoria Rattenbury and George Percy Stoner*, op. cit., p. 56

46 Richard Edward Stevens's evidence, 27 May 1935, quoted in Tennyson Jesse, *The Trial of Alma Victoria Rattenbury and George Percy Stoner*, op. cit., p. 58

11. Night Brings Me You

1 Terence Rattigan, *The Deep Blue Sea* (London: Hamish Hamilton, 1952), p. 33

2 Firearms were relatively common before the First World War with approximately 250,000 gun owners in Britain. The Firearms Act of 1920 was a response to the large number of service guns in circulation following the war, and further restrictions in 1937 effectively banned automatic weapons. At his trial in 1922, Frederick Bywaters had admitted that he was 'in the habit of carrying either a knife or a revolver'. He made this admission in an impassioned appeal to the Home Office to save Edith Thompson's life, following their conviction for murder (HO 144/2685).

3 All quotes in letter from Rattenbury to F. E. Winslow, 27 January 1935 (City of Victoria Archives). This business letter also includes a longer, typed addition headed, 'Personal'.

4 Ibid.

5 Letter from D. A. Wood to the public prosecutor, 24 May 1935, DPP 2/263 Part 1

6   Irene Riggs's evidence, 27 May 1935, quoted in Tennyson Jesse, *The Trial of Alma Victoria Rattenbury and George Percy Stoner*, op. cit., pp. 70–71

7   Alma Rattenbury's evidence, 29 May 1935, quoted in Tennyson Jesse, *The Trial of Alma Victoria Rattenbury and George Percy Stoner*, op. cit., p. 180

8   Dr William O'Donnell's evidence, 28 May 1935, quoted in Tennyson Jesse, *The Trial of Alma Victoria Rattenbury and George Percy Stoner*, op. cit., pp. 105–7

9   Alma Rattenbury's evidence, quoted in Tennyson Jesse, *The Trial of Alma Victoria Rattenbury and George Percy Stoner*, op. cit., p. 180

10 For the story of Billie Carleton and drug use by women in the West End in the 1920s and '30s, see Marek Kohn, *Dope Girls: The Birth of the British Drug Underground*, (London: Granta Books, 2001)

11 Terry M. Parssinen, *Secret Passions, Secret Remedies: Narcotic Drugs in British Society 1829–1930* (Manchester: Manchester University Press, 1983), p. 125

12 Tennyson Jesse, *The Trial of Alma Victoria Rattenbury and George Percy Stoner*, op. cit., p. 33

13 Maude Price's statement, DPP 2/263 Part 5

14 Alma Rattenbury letter, 4 June 1935, DPP 2/263 Part 2

15 The two women met alone on this occasion because Frank Titterton was going through a very public financial embarrassment at the time. He had speculated on the stock exchange in the early 1930s and in 1932 had become a sleeping partner in a firm of garage proprietors, part of the new motor industry boom. But the venture was a disaster and had left Titterton £2,000 in debt. He reassured the press – and his public – that his financial situation was not the result of a failing career: 'I am the victim of circumstances. My financial troubles are due entirely to a motor business. They are nothing to do with my profession. As a matter of fact, I have a large number of engagements to fulfil.' On 21 March, he would be meeting his creditors for the first time in London.

16 'I think this was because Mr Rattenbury was kindly disposed towards [Stoner] and regarded him as an object of sympathetic charity more than as a servant. Stoner was not of bright intellect and he had difficulty in obtaining employment. Mr Rattenbury was asked to do something for him, and therefore took him into his house and treated him in the most considerate way. I firmly believe that the first time Mr Rattenbury knew anything of the affair between his wife and Stoner was on the night of the murder.' *Sunday Dispatch*, 9 June 1935, p. 9. This uncredited interview is most likely to be Mr D. A. Wood, who was Rattenbury's only close friend who visited the Villa Madeira regularly.

17 Alma Rattenbury's evidence, 29 May 1935, quoted in Tennyson Jesse, *The Trial of Alma Victoria Rattenbury and George Percy Stoner*, op. cit., pp. 181–2

18 After this payment to Alma, the balance of Ratz's current account dropped from £491 6s 7d to £241 6s 7d, DPP 2/263 Part 3

19 Alma Rattenbury's evidence, 29 May 1935, quoted in Tennyson Jesse, *The Trial of Alma Victoria Rattenbury and George Percy Stoner*, op. cit., p. 185

20 Eliot Crawshay-Williams, *Stay of Execution* (London: Jarrolds, 1933), p. 13

21 *Evening Standard*, 19 March 1935, p. 6

22 Alec Arthur Assirelli's statement (receptionist at the Royal Palace Hotel), DPP 2/263 Part 4

23 *The Sketch*, 6 June 1894

24 Barbara Anne Pinder's statement (Inexpensive Dresses Department, Harrods), 4 April 1935, DPP 2/263 Part 4

25 The shopping card is held in DPP 2/263 Part 5. The police went to exhaustive lengths interviewing eight members of staff at Harrods during this shopping trip, later dubbed the 'orgy in London' by Travers Humphreys at the trial and later quoted as such in the press.

26 Alma was size 'N'. Exhibit 19, Memorandum of Purchase, 19 March 1935, Kirby and Bunn, 44 Old Bond Street, W1, (NA) DPP 2/263 Part 3.

27 Alma Rattenbury letter, 4 June 1935, DPP 2/263 Part 2

28 *Evening Standard*, 21 March 1934, p. 3

29 Ibid., p. 6

30 Letter from Alma to Christopher Rattenbury, 22 March 1935, written on Royal Palace Hotel notepaper, Anthony Barrett's archive

31 Crawshay-Williams, op. cit., pp. 30–31

12. The Place Where a Bad Thing Happened

1 *The Tragedy of Master Arden of Faversham*, in *A Woman Killed with Kindness and Other Domestic Plays* (Oxford: Oxford University Press, 2008), p. 60

2 *Daily Mirror*, 20 March 1935, p. 3. For Churchill's speech of 19 March 1935, see Parliamentary Debates, Official Report, Vol. CCXCIX, H.M. Stationary Office 1935.

3 *Bournemouth Daily Echo*, 23 March 1935, p. 1

4 Document 681193/2 in (NA) HO 144/19946

5 This would be the first time that a murder case had come before the Lords since the Court of Criminal Appeal had been set up in 1907.

6   Though this is not mentioned in any of the witness statements or in evidence, it must have been Alma or Irene who suggested that they should put up the tent and needed a mallet. When questioned at the trial, Alma denied that she had suggested it. It would be imperative that she didn't admit this (effectively suggesting the murder weapon) and as he was intent on protecting her, Stoner would have been highly aware that he must take sole responsibility for collecting the mallet.

7   Louise Maud Price's statement, 5 April 1935, DPP 2/263 Part 4. Mrs Price presumed that the Rattenburys had bought the tent themselves as it hadn't been in the garage when she vacated the house. A keen-eyed landlady, she had particularly noted the holes the pegs had made in the lawn.

8   Letter to the public prosecutor from D. A. Wood, 24 May 1935, DPP 2/263 Part 1

9   *Radio Times*, 18–24 March 1935, p. 864

10   Alma Rattenbury's evidence, 29 May 1935, quoted in Tennyson Jesse, *The Trial of Alma Victoria Rattenbury and George Percy Stoner*, op. cit., p. 185

11   Though it's not stated exactly when, Dinah must have returned quickly from the kennels after giving birth as she was an essential witness to the events of the night of 24 March

12   Crawshay-Williams, op. cit., p. 296. Rattenbury was very near the end of the book, it being 318 pages long.

13   Alma Rattenbury's evidence, quoted in Tennyson Jesse, *The Trial of Alma Victoria Rattenbury and George Percy Stoner*, op. cit., pp. 170–71

14   Ibid., p. 171

15   Terry Reksten, *Rattenbury*, op. cit., p. 151

16   The fact that Rattenbury had effectively asked Alma to sleep with Jenks in order to secure the money to finance his building project was relayed to Anthony Barrett in an interview with Daphne Kingham, 26 September 1978. Barrett felt ambivalent about making this public at the time he was collaborating on *Tragedy in Three Voices* (op. cit.), as all of Rattenbury's and Alma's children were still living. In an interview with the present author on 27 November 2017, Professor Barrett felt that with only John Rattenbury surviving, it was appropriate to reveal the motive that provoked Stoner to attack his employer.

17   Alma Rattenbury's evidence, 29 May 1935, quoted in Tennyson Jesse, *The Trial of Alma Victoria Rattenbury and George Percy Stoner*, op. cit., pp. 171–2

18   Violet Firth, *The Psychology of the Servant Problem: A Study in Social Relationships* (London: C. W. Daniel, 1925), pp. 19–20

19 Alma Rattenbury's evidence, 29 May 1935, quoted in Tennyson Jesse, *The Trial of Alma Victoria Rattenbury and George Percy Stoner*, op. cit., p. 172

20 Ibid., p. 174

21 Ibid., p. 173

22 The mallet was 4 inches in diameter and 6.5 inches in length, weighing 39 ounces (Gerald Roche Lynch's statement, DPP 2/263 Part 3)

23 Elizabeth Augusta Stevens's statement, 28 March 1935, DPP 2/263 Part 4

24 Stoner's statement, 30 March 1935, DPP 2/263. See also the letter from Stoner to Caswell, 9 June 1935, DPP 2/263 Part 2.

25 Irene Riggs's evidence, 27 May 1935, quoted in Tennyson Jesse, *The Trial of Alma Victoria Rattenbury and George Percy Stoner*, op. cit., p. 59

26 Ibid.

27 Irene Riggs's statement, DPP 2/263 Part 4

28 Irene Riggs's evidence, 27 May 1935, quoted in Tennyson Jesse, *The Trial of Alma Victoria Rattenbury and George Percy Stoner*, op. cit., p. 61

29 Alma Rattenbury's evidence, 29 May 1935, quoted in Tennyson Jesse, *The Trial of Alma Victoria Rattenbury and George Percy Stoner*, op. cit., p. 175

30 Ibid.

31 Though she did not admit it at the trial, Alma later confirmed that she had gone downstairs twice after Stoner had told her that he had attacked Ratz. She would have been stunned by the condition Ratz was in and then must have returned to the bedroom to discuss with Stoner what they should do. Letter from Alma Rattenbury, 4 June 1935, DPP 2/263 Part 2.

32 Alma Rattenbury's evidence, 29 May 1935, quoted in Tennyson Jesse, *The Trial of Alma Victoria Rattenbury and George Percy Stoner*, op. cit., p. 187

33 Irene Riggs's evidence, 27 May 1935, quoted in Tennyson Jesse, *The Trial of Alma Victoria Rattenbury and George Percy Stoner*, op. cit., p. 61

34 Irene Riggs's statement, 6 April 1935, DPP 2/263 Part 4

35 Irene Riggs's evidence, 27 May 1935, quoted in Tennyson Jesse, *The Trial of Alma Victoria Rattenbury and George Percy Stoner*, op. cit., p. 74

36 Dr William O'Donnell's evidence, 27 May 1935, quoted in Tennyson Jesse, *The Trial of Alma Victoria Rattenbury and George Percy Stoner*, op. cit., pp. 94–6

37 Arthur Bagwell's evidence, 28 May 1935, quoted in Tennyson Jesse, *The Trial of Alma Victoria Rattenbury and George Percy Stoner*, op. cit., p. 121

38 Ibid., p. 119

39 Ibid.

40 Irene's Riggs's evidence, 27 May 1935, quoted in Tennyson Jesse, *The Trial of Alma Victoria Rattenbury and George Percy Stoner*, op. cit., p. 76

41 William J. Mills's evidence, 28 May 1935, quoted in Tennyson Jesse, *The Trial of Alma Victoria Rattenbury and George Percy Stoner*, op. cit., p. 124

42 Alma Rattenbury's statements relayed in William J. Mills's evidence, 28 May 1935, quoted in Tennyson Jesse, *The Trial of Alma Victoria Rattenbury and George Percy Stoner*, op. cit., p. 125

43 York Membrey, *The Times*, 29 November 2002

44 Dr William O'Donnell's evidence, 28 May 1935, quoted in Tennyson Jesse, *The Trial of Alma Victoria Rattenbury and George Percy Stoner*, op. cit., p. 102

45 This was disputed in Carter's evidence, 28 May 1935, quoted in Tennyson Jesse, *The Trial of Alma Victoria Rattenbury and George Percy Stoner*, op. cit., p. 135

46 Irene Riggs's evidence, 27 May 1935, quoted in Tennyson Jesse, *The Trial of Alma Victoria Rattenbury and George Percy Stoner*, op. cit., pp. 80–81

47 Stoner's statement, taken at 7.30 a.m. on 25 March 1935 by Inspector W. G. Carter, DPP 2/263 Part 5

48 Alma Rattenbury's statement, taken at 8.15 a.m. on 25 March 1935 by Inspector W. G. Carter, CRIM 1/778

49 Irene Riggs's evidence, 27 May 1935, quoted in Tennyson Jesse, *The Trial of Alma Victoria Rattenbury and George Percy Stoner*, op. cit., p. 79

50 This exchange was also witnessed by DC Bright and Detective Inspector Carter (Sydney Bright, Carter, DPP 2/263 Part 4)

13. *Cause Célèbre*

1 *Bournemouth Daily Echo*, 25 March 1935, p. 1

2 Email from Garth Manning to Sean O'Connor, 9 July 2013

3 *Bournemouth Daily Echo*, 25 March 1935, p. 1

4 Dr William O'Donnell's evidence, 28 May 1935, quoted in Tennyson Jesse, *The Trial of Alma Victoria Rattenbury and George Percy Stoner*, op. cit., p. 102. Carter disputed Alma's behaviour in his evidence of 28 May 1935, quoted in Tennyson Jesse, *The Trial of Alma Victoria Rattenbury and George Percy Stoner*, op. cit., pp. 134–5.

5 John Camp, *Holloway Prison: The Place and the People* (London: David & Charles, 1974), p. 21

6 The following description of the first few hours of a new prisoner's arrival is described in Stella St John, *A Prisoner's Log: Holloway Prison in 1943* (London: Howard League for Penal Reform, 1943)

7   'When she exercised in the prison yard with the other prisoners await-
    ing trial, she wore her own clothes, including a fur coat, which made
    her easily recognizable from a distance. Convicted prisoners, if they
    got the chance, would peer out of the corridor windows and whisper,
    "That's 'er".' McCall p. 61

8   Albert Crew, *London Prisons of Yesterday and Today* (London: Ivor
    Nicholson & Watson, 1933), pp. 138–9

9   See St John, op. cit.

10 Ibid.

11 Joan Henry, *Women in Prison* (London: White Lion, 1973), p. 22

12 Letter from Alma Rattenbury to Stoner, 26 March 1935, DPP 2/263
    Part 2. This was never sent and Alma was advised to re-write it by
    the governor.

13 Letter from J. H. Morton, governor and medical officer, HMP
    Holloway, to clerk of courts, Central Criminal Court, 18 May 1935

14 Havers, Shankland and Barrett, op. cit., p. 52

15 Minutes from the governor to Head Office from HMP Holloway, 2
    April 1935, DPP 2/263 Part 3

16 Letter from Alma Rattenbury to Stoner, 27 March 1935, DPP
    2/263 Part 2

17 Letter from Alma Rattenbury to Stoner, 28 March 1935, DPP
    2/263 Part 2

18 Police report, W. G. Carter, 31 March 1935, DPP 2/263 Part 1:
    'List of articles taken possession of by police from 5 Manor Road,
    Bournemouth: One wooden mallet, one cretonne chair cover, one gents
    jacket, one gents waistcoat, one short collar, one pair braces, one pair
    trousers, two cushions, two swab cloths, one book, one lady's pyjama
    suit, one pair lady's red shoes, one kimono, one glass containing
    whisky, one armchair, one carpet, six cheque books.'

19 Henry William Hoare's statement, 7 April 1935, DPP 2/263 Part 4

20 See Irene Riggs's statement, 28 March 1935, DPP 2/263 Part 4 and Irene
    Riggs's evidence, 27 May 1935, quoted in Tennyson Jesse, *The Trial of
    Alma Victoria Rattenbury and George Percy Stoner*, op. cit., p. 88

21 Irene Riggs's statement, 28 March 1935, DPP 2/263 Part 4

22 Police report, G. H. Gates, 4 April 1935, DPP 2/263 Part 1

23 Irene Riggs's statement, 28 March 1935, DPP 2/263 Part 4

24 Elizabeth A. Stevens's statement, 5.15 p.m. on 28 March 1935, DPP
    2/263 Part 4

25 Richard Stevens's statement, 5.30 p.m. on 28 March 1935, DPP
    2/263 Part 4

26 This communication between the Bournemouth Police and Scotland
    Yard was leaked to the *Daily Mail* and caused, much to the chagrin of
    Major Cockburn the chief constable of Hampshire Police, 'the usual

flapdoodle', inflating the case into a 'Seaside Mystery' in which his hapless and hopeless provincial bobbies had to appeal to Scotland Yard for help. (NA) MEPO 3/736.

27 Dr Harold Simmons statement, 29 March 1935, DPP 2/263 Part 4

28 Police report by W. G. Carter, 31 March 1935, DPP 2/263 Part 1

29 'Police v. Yourself'; letter to Alma Rattenbury, HMP Holloway from Other, Manning and Boileau-Tredinnick, 118 Old Christchurch Road, Bournemouth, 26 March 1935, DPP 2/63 Part 1

30 *Bournemouth Daily Echo*, 29 March 1935, p. 1

31 Letter from E. W. Marshall Harvey to director of public prosecutions accepting Stoner's defence under legal aid, 8 April 1935, DPP 2/263 Part 1

32 George Henry Gates, 29 March 1935, DPP 2/263 Part 4

33 Ibid.

34 *Bournemouth Daily Echo*, 29 March 1935, p. 1

35 Casswell, *A Lance for Liberty* (London: George G. Harrap & Co. Ltd, 1961), p. 96

36 *Daily Express*, 6 April 1935, p. 1

37 Quoted in Casswell, op. cit., p. 98

38 Frank Archibald Hobbs's statement, 4 April 1935, DPP 2/263 Part 4

39 *Daily Express*, 11 April 1935, p. 3

40 Ibid., 1 June 1935, p. 3

41 Ibid.

42 Ibid.

43 Letter from Alma Rattenbury to unidentified correspondent, quoted in *Daily Express*, 6 June 1935, p. 1

44 *Daily Sketch*, 7 June 1935, p. 2

45 Letter from Alma Rattenbury, copy in Anthony Barrett's archive

46 The magistrates were Mr G. J. Lawson (chair), Mr E. L. Lane, Mr A. E. Kitcher, Mr W. Troath, Alderman D. E. Hillier, Councillor W. Wilkinson and Councillor A. Cull.

47 *Bournemouth Daily Echo*, 11 April 1935, p. 1

48 Ibid.

49 The proceedings at the police court are reported in the *Bournemouth Daily Echo*, 11 April 1935, p. 3

50 *Bournemouth Daily Echo*, 11 April 1935, p. 1

51 Ibid., 28 May 1935, p. 1

52 Ewart Morris Treggunnin's statement, 16 April 1935, DPP 2/263

53 *Strand Magazine*, May 1943, p. 79

54 *Vancouver Sun*, 17 April 1935, p. 1

55 Ibid.

56 Havers, Shankland and Barrett, op. cit., p. 61

57 *Daily Sketch*, 7 June, p. 2

58 Havers, Shankland and Barrett, op. cit., p. 59

59   Ibid., p. 61

60   *News of the World*, 9 June 1935, p. 11

61   Extract from Alma Rattenbury's letter to Irene Riggs, 18 April 1935, DPP 2/263 Part 3

62   Havers, Shankland and Barrett, op. cit., p. 60

63   Ibid., pp. 60–61

64   Alma Rattenbury's handwritten letters from Holloway in Anthony Barrett's archive

65   *Daily Express*, 25 April 1935, p. 2

66   *Bournemouth Daily Echo*, 24 April 1935, p. 3

67   Ibid.

68   Bernard O'Donnell, 'A Champion of Justice, Sincere and Convincing, T. J. O'Connor KC', *Sunday Graphic*, 16 June 1935, p. 19

69   Ibid.

70   Montagu is chiefly remembered today as the man who led the plan to dupe German Intelligence in the Second World War by dressing a dead tramp as a major in Combined Operations, whose body was then washed ashore, the supposed victim of an accident at sea. The body carried false documents to deceive the Germans about an Allied invasion of Greece as opposed to the invasion of Sicily they were planning in reality. The plan was successful and Montagu would receive an OBE for his part in it. In 1953, he wrote about the strategy in *The Man Who Never Was*.

71   *Daily Express*, 4 June 1935, p. 2

72   *Looking Back from the Nineties*, Cicely McCall, Gliddon Books, Norwich, 1992, p. 61

73   ibid p. 62-3

74   Casswell, op. cit., p. 62

75   Sir Bernard Napley, *Murder at the Villa Madeira: The Rattenbury Case* (London: Weidenfeld & Nicolson, 1988), p. 86

76   *Daily Mirror*, 10 April 1935, p. 32

77   Ibid., 23 May 1935, p. 1

78   Ibid., 4 May 1935, p. 1

79   *Daily Sketch*, 6 June 1935, p. 2

80   *Daily Express*, 6 June 1935, p. 2

81   Ibid.

82   Ibid.

83   *Daily Sketch*, 18 May 1935, p. 3

84   Havers, Shankland and Barrett, op. cit., p. 61

85   *News of the World*, 9 June 1935, p. 11

86   O'Donnell, 'A Champion of Justice . . .', op. cit., p. 19

87   Daphne Kingham later told Anthony Barrett that, 'I wish I had brought Christopher to her sooner.' (Havers, Shankland and Barrett, op. cit.,

p. 61) After the visit to Holloway, she took Christopher back to school and wrote gratefully to him: 'I saw your mother yesterday and she seemed very pleased to have seen you and also to know I had taken you back to school. I told her how we spent our time before returning to the school. Work hard and try to pass well into your next school as it is very important. With love from us all, Yours affectionately, P. Keep an eye on John, Love P.' (Anthony Barrett archive)

88   Note from the medical officer, E. W. Mann, Dorchester Prison, 2 May 1935, recommending transferral to Dr Grierson at Brixton Prison, CRIM 1/778

89   Crew, op. cit.

90   Report from Hugh A. Grierson, senior medical officer, HMP Brixton, 20 May 1935, CRIM 1/778

91   Letter from Dr Grierson to director of public prosecutions, 20 May 1935, CRIM 1/778

92   Report from Hugh A. Grierson, senior medical officer, HMP Brixton, 20 May 1935, CRIM 1/778

93   Casswell, op. cit., p. 109

94   Ibid.

95   Ibid.

ENTR'ACTE: Sing Sing, 12 January 1928

1   The transcript of the trial and definitive text on the case is John Kobler, *The Trial of Ruth Snyder and Judd Gray: Edited with a History of the Case* (New York: Doubleday, Doran and Co., 1938). Quote from 9 May 1927, William J. Millard, defending Counsel for Henry Judd Gray (Kobler, op. cit., p. 302).

2   Kobler, op. cit., p. 9

3   Ibid., p. 5

4   Quoted in Kobler, op. cit., p. 15

5   Kobler, op. cit., p. 17

6   Ibid., pp. 19–20

7   Ibid., p. 22

8   This aspect of the case inspired the 1943 novel by James M. Cain, *Double Indemnity*, and the 1944 film based on it. Ruth may have been inspired by *The Three Musketeers* (1921) starring Douglas Fairbanks, where Cardinal Richelieu tricks the queen into signing a document in the same manner (see Kobler, p. 22). Ruth covered the larger policies with the $1,000 one allowing only the space for the signatures to appear, telling her husband that they were the same policy to be signed in triplicate. The circumstances of the killing of Albert Snyder also inspired Cain's *The Postman Always Rings Twice* (1934).

9   Kobler, op. cit., pp. 28–39

10   Ibid., p. 7

11   Ibid.

12   Peggy Hopkins Joyce, *New York Daily Mirror*, quoted by Kobler, op. cit., p. 55

13   Kobler, op. cit., p. 60

14   Ibid., p. 50

15   One journalist described how 'grave essays were written at the time of women's alleged tenderheartedness knocking the scales of justice out of kilter. Tales of the feminine invasion of the jury box were related with glee. One new woman juror added to the critics' delight by an unfortunately timed display of her prerogative of changing her find – after signing the verdict. Male jurors complained that they couldn't see around the feathers adorning ladies' hats.' (*Milwaukee Journal*, 6 July 1947)

16   Kobler, op. cit., p. 56

17   Ibid., p. 50

18   Douglas Perry, *The Girls of Murder City: Fame, Lust and the Beautiful Killers who Inspired 'Chicago'* (London: Penguin, 2008), pp. 160–174

19   Ibid., pp. 39–57

20   Kobler, op. cit., pp. 230–39

21   Ibid., p. 51

22   Ibid., p. 302

23   Ibid., p. 58

24   Ann Jones, op. cit., p. 296

25   Kobler, op. cit., p. 63

26   Ibid.

27   Horrie, op. cit., p. 50

28   Ann Jones, op. cit., p. 299

14.   The Old Bailey

1   Henrik Ibsen, *The Collected Works of Henrik Ibsen, Vol. XII, From Ibsen's Workshop; notes, scenarios, and drafts of the modern plays* (London: William Heinemann, 1912), p. 91

2   Stephen Wade, *Britain's Most Notorious Hangmen* (Barnsley: Wharncliffe Local History, 2009), p. 9

3   Julian B. Knowles, QC, *The Abolition of the Death Penalty in the United Kingdom: How it Happened and Why it Still Matters*, 2015, www.deathpenaltyproject.org

4   Bernard O'Donnell, *The Old Bailey and its Trials* (London: Theodore Brun Ltd, 1950), p. 16

5   Ibid., p. 17

6   Ibid., p. 134

7   Clive Emsley, Tim Hitchcock and Robert Shoemaker, *History of The Old Bailey Courthouse*, www.oldbaileyonline.org

8   O'Donnell, *The Old Bailey and its Trials*, op. cit., p. 14

9   *The Times*, 'Forecast for Today', 27 May 1935, p. 16

10 *Bournemouth Daily Echo*, 27 May 1935, p. 1

11 Tennyson Jesse, *The Trial of Alma Victoria Rattenbury and George Percy Stoner*, op. cit., p. 34

12 *Bournemouth Daily Echo*, 25 May 1935, p. 1

13 Ibid., 27 May 1935, p. 1

14 *Evening Standard*, 27 May 1935, p. 12

15 Ibid.

16 Donald Rumbelow, *The Triple Tree: Newgate, Tyburn and Old Bailey* (London: Harrap, 1982), p. 211

17 Ibid.

18 *Daily Express*, 29 March 1935, p. 2

19 For Travers Humphreys's biography, see Napley, op. cit., pp. 93–4, and Stanley Jackson, *The Life and Cases of Mr Justice Humphreys* (London: Odhams Press Ltd, 1951)

20 Jackson, op. cit., p. 153

21 Barbara Back, *Daily Mirror*, 28 May 1935, p. 3

22 *Daily Express*, 29 May 1935, p. 2

23 Ibid.

24 Casswell, op. cit., p. 109

25 For Croom-Johnson's biography, see Napley, op. cit., pp. 88–9

26 Napley, op. cit., p. 89

27 *Daily Mail Yearbook* (London: Associated Newspapers Ltd, 1934), p. 115

28 See Napley, op. cit., pp. 88–9

29 Croom-Johnson, opening speech for the crown, 27 May 1935, quoted in Tennyson Jesse, *The Trial of Alma Victoria Rattenbury and George Percy Stoner*, op. cit., p. 50

30 Ibid., p. 53

31 Barbara Back, *Daily Mirror*, 28 May 1935, p. 3

32 Ibid.

33 For example, 'What were you doing yesterday?' is not a leading question, but 'What were you doing in your car at 10 p.m. yesterday?' is

34 Elizabeth Augusta Stevens's evidence, 27 May 1935, quoted in Tennyson Jesse, *The Trial of Alma Victoria Rattenbury and George Percy Stoner*, op. cit., p. 56

35 Richard Edward Stevens's evidence, 27 May 1935, quoted in Tennyson Jesse, *The Trial of Alma Victoria Rattenbury and George Percy Stoner*, op. cit., p. 57

36 Casswell's cross-examination of Frederick Clements, 27 March 1935,

quoted in Tennyson Jesse, *The Trial of Alma Victoria Rattenbury and George Percy Stoner*, op. cit., p. 54

37 Casswell's cross-examination of Elizabeth Augusta Stevens, 27 March 1935, quoted in Tennyson Jesse, *The Trial of Alma Victoria Rattenbury and George Percy Stoner*, op. cit., p. 55

38 *Daily Express*, 28 May 1935, p. 4

39 Casswell, op. cit., p. 111

40 Quoted in Croom-Johnson's examination of Irene Riggs, 27 May 1935, quoted in Tennyson Jesse, *The Trial of Alma Victoria Rattenbury and George Percy Stoner*, op. cit., pp. 68–9

41 O'Connor's cross-examination of Irene Riggs, 27 May 1935, quoted in Tennyson Jesse, *The Trial of Alma Victoria Rattenbury and George Percy Stoner*, op. cit., p. 71

42 Ibid., p. 81

43 Casswell, op. cit., p. 110

44 Ibid.

45 Casswell's cross-examination of Irene Riggs, 27 May 1935, quoted in Tennyson Jesse, *The Trial of Alma Victoria Rattenbury and George Percy Stoner*, op. cit., pp. 82–3

46 Ibid.

47 Ibid., p. 91

48 Travers Humphreys's questions to Irene Riggs, 27 March 1935, quoted in Tennyson Jesse, *The Trial of Alma Victoria Rattenbury and George Percy Stoner*, op. cit., pp. 90–91

49 *Daily Express*, 29 May 1935, p. 8

50 *Bournemouth Daily Echo*, 28 May 1935, p. 5

51 Molly Castle, 'Women Picnic at Old Bailey', *Daily Express*, 29 May 1935, p. 1

52 Croom-Johnson's examination of William George Budden, 28 May 1935, quoted in Tennyson Jesse, *The Trial of Alma Victoria Rattenbury and George Percy Stoner*, op. cit., p. 93

53 Casswell's cross-examination of Irene Riggs, 27 March 1935, quoted in Tennyson Jesse, *The Trial of Alma Victoria Rattenbury and George Percy Stoner*, op. cit., p. 94

54 Casswell's cross-examination of Dr O'Donnell, 28 May 1935, quoted in Tennyson Jesse, *The Trial of Alma Victoria Rattenbury and George Percy Stoner*, op. cit., p. 105

55 Ibid., p. 103

56 Ibid., p. 99

57 Alfred B. Rooke's evidence, quoted in Tennyson Jesse, *The Trial of Alma Victoria Rattenbury and George Percy Stoner*, op. cit., pp. 112–18

58 Croom-Johnson's examination of William James Mills, 28 May 1935,

quoted in Tennyson Jesse, *The Trial of Alma Victoria Rattenbury and George Percy Stoner*, op. cit., p. 125

59 Croom-Johnson's examination of William G. Carter, 28 May 1935, quoted in Tennyson Jesse, *The Trial of Alma Victoria Rattenbury and George Percy Stoner*, op. cit., p. 131

60 O'Connor's cross-examination of William G. Carter, 28 May 1935, quoted in Tennyson Jesse, *The Trial of Alma Victoria Rattenbury and George Percy Stoner*, op. cit., p. 135

61 Croom-Johnson's examination of William G. Carter, 27 May 1935, quoted in Tennyson Jesse, *The Trial of Alma Victoria Rattenbury and George Percy Stoner*, op. cit., p. 131

62 'Mrs Rattenbury and "That Awful Night", Her Ordeal in the Witness Box,' *Bournemouth Daily Echo*, 29 May 1935, p. 12

63 Tennyson Jesse, *The Trial of Alma Victoria Rattenbury and George Percy Stoner*, op. cit., p. 3

64 Ibid.

65 Morton subsequently died in his quarters at Holloway on 6 June 1935 (*British Medical Journal*, 15 June 1935, p. 1241)

66 Casswell's cross-examination of Dr Roche Lynch, 29 May 1935, quoted in Tennyson Jesse, *The Trial of Alma Victoria Rattenbury and George Percy Stoner*, op. cit., p. 150

67 Casswell's cross-examination of Dr Hugh A. Grierson, 29 May 1935, quoted in Tennyson Jesse, *The Trial of Alma Victoria Rattenbury and George Percy Stoner*, op. cit., p. 157

68 Sir Bernard Napley suggested in 1988 that what Stoner had described was heroin, not cocaine, but in the 1930s the heroin Stoner would have had access to would also have been a white powder

69 Tennyson Jesse took particular issue with Travers Humphreys about his description of the trip to London as an 'orgy': 'It is difficult to imagine an orgy at the Royal Palace Hotel at Kensington, and, indeed, this Editor has never been able to discover of what an "orgy" consists. It is associated, more or less vaguely, in the popular mind with the "historical" productions of Mr C. de Mille; glasses of wine, dancing girls, tiger skins and cushions are some of its component parts. The private coming together of pair of lovers and their normal physical ecstasies, however reprehensible these may be morally, do not seem well described by the word "orgy". Even shopping at Harrods does not quite come under this heading.' Tennyson Jesse, *The Trial of Alma Victoria Rattenbury and George Percy Stoner*, op. cit., p. 18.

70 *Bournemouth Daily Echo*, 29 May 1935, p. 12

71 James Agate, *Daily Express*, 30 May 1935, p. 2

72 Barbara Back, *Daily Mirror*, 30 May 1935, p. 2

15. As for the Woman

1   *News of the World*, 2 June 1935, p. 13 and *Evening Standard*, 31 May 1935, p. 8. James Whale's cinematic version of *Frankenstein* (1931) further popularised the confusion about whether the creature or the scientist who created him was the title character of the story. A sequel, *Bride of Frankenstein*, was released in 1935, which may have inspired the dramatic imagery in O'Connor's speech.

2   Barbara Back, *Daily Mirror*, 30 May 1935, p. 2

3   James Agate, *Daily Express*, 30 May 1935, p. 2. Agate was not the only writer to enhance their pen portraits of Alma as both vulnerable and alluring, with Tennyson Jesse observing that 'she had a pale face, with a beautiful egg-like line of the jaw, dark grey eyes and a mouth with a very full lower lip'. (Tennyson Jesse, *The Trial of Alma Victoria Rattenbury and George Percy Stoner*, op. cit., p. 4)

4   Tennyson Jesse, *The Trial of Alma Victoria Rattenbury and George Percy Stoner*, op. cit., p. 33

5   Ibid., p. 16

6   Ibid., p. 33

7   Ibid.

8   Casswell, op. cit., p. 111. Alma's theatrical hand gestures, which Casswell dismissed, some commentators found expressive and characterful: 'When she speaks her face lights up. She is unquestionably attractive. She leans forward in the witness-box as she talks in an ingratiating way. She uses her hands a great deal to express her feelings.' Barbara Back, *Daily Express,* 30 May 1935, p. 2.

9   *Bournemouth Daily Echo*, 29 May 1935, p. 12

10 Alma Rattenbury's evidence, 29 May 1935, quoted in Tennyson Jesse, *The Trial of Alma Victoria Rattenbury and George Percy Stoner*, op. cit., p. 164

11 James Agate, *Daily Express*, 30 May 1935, p. 2

12 Barbara Back, *Daily Mirror*, 30 May 1935, p. 2

13 Alma Rattenbury's evidence, 29 May 1935, quoted in Tennyson Jesse, *The Trial of Alma Victoria Rattenbury and George Percy Stoner*, op. cit., p. 191

14 *News of the World*, 2 June 1935, p. 13

15 Alma Rattenbury's evidence, 29 May 1935, quoted in Tennyson Jesse, *The Trial of Alma Victoria Rattenbury and George Percy Stoner*, op. cit., p. 178

16 Tennyson Jesse, *The Trial of Alma Victoria Rattenbury and George Percy Stoner*, op. cit., p. 40

17 O'Connor's examination of Alma Rattenbury, 29 May 1935, DPP 2/263. The trial transcript slightly differs from Tennyson Jesse here, which does not include the interruption of Travers Humphreys.

18 Croom-Johnson's cross-examination of Alma Rattenbury, 29 May 1935, quoted in Tennyson Jesse, *The Trial of Alma Victoria Rattenbury and George Percy Stoner*, op. cit., pp. 185–6

19 Ibid., p. 192

20 Tennyson Jesse, *The Trial of Alma Victoria Rattenbury and George Percy Stoner*, op. cit., p. 9; According to Tennyson Jesse, Alma was later to claim, 'I can't think what made me say that in the witness-box about Stoner making love to me when Little John was in the room. He didn't. I got bewildered and lost my head, and found myself saying it.' Tennyson Jesse, however, felt that what Alma said in the witness box was true.

21 Casswell, op. cit., p. 112

22 Alma Rattenbury to Croom-Johnson, 29 May 1935, quoted in Tennyson Jesse, *The Trial of Alma Victoria Rattenbury and George Percy Stoner*, op. cit., p. 188

23 Alma Rattenbury to Travers Humphreys, 29 May 1935, quoted in Tennyson Jesse, *The Trial of Alma Victoria Rattenbury and George Percy Stoner*, op. cit., p. 197

24 Alma Rattenbury to Croom-Johnson, 29 May 1935, quoted in Tennyson Jesse, *The Trial of Alma Victoria Rattenbury and George Percy Stoner*, op. cit., p. 193

25 Alma Rattenbury to Travers Humphreys, 29 May 1935, quoted in Tennyson Jesse, *The Trial of Alma Victoria Rattenbury and George Percy Stoner*, op. cit., p. 186

26 Croom-Johnson's cross-examination of Alma Rattenbury, 29 May 1935, quoted in Tennyson Jesse, *The Trial of Alma Victoria Rattenbury and George Percy Stoner*, op. cit., p. 188

27 Ibid., p. 197

28 *Strand Magazine*, May 1943, p. 79

29 Tennyson Jesse, *The Trial of Alma Victoria Rattenbury and George Percy Stoner*, op. cit., p. 3

30 Ibid., p. 34

31 Diary entry for 29 May 1935 (Agate, *Ego 2*, op. cit., p. 187)

32 James Agate, *Daily Express*, 30 May 1935, p. 2

33 Tennyson Jesse, *The Trial of Alma Victoria Rattenbury and George Percy Stoner*, op. cit., p. 12

34 Sir Travers Humphreys, *A Book of Trials* (London: Heinemann, 1953), p. 153

35 *Daily Sketch*, 30 May 1935, p. 3

36 *Daily Mirror*, 31 May 1935, p. 2

37 Transcripts of shorthand trial notes in DPP 2/263

38 Travers Humphreys's question to Dr Robert A. Gillespie, 30 May 1935, quoted in Tennyson Jesse, *The Trial of Alma Victoria Rattenbury and George Percy Stoner*, op. cit., p. 217

39   Casswell, op. cit., p. 114

40   Casswell's closing speech on behalf of Stoner, 30 May 1935, quoted in Tennyson Jesse, *The Trial of Alma Victoria Rattenbury and George Percy Stoner*, op. cit., p. 221

41   Ibid., p. 222

42   Ibid., p. 223

43   Ibid., p. 225

44   Ibid., p. 226

45   Ibid., p. 227

46   Ibid., p. 229

47   Ibid., p. 232

48   Croom-Johnson's closing speech for the crown, 30 May 1935, quoted in Tennyson Jesse, *The Trial of Alma Victoria Rattenbury and George Percy Stoner*, op. cit., p. 232

49   Ibid., p. 238

50   Casswell, op. cit., p. 114

51   O'Connor's closing speech for Alma Rattenbury, 30 May 1935, quoted in Tennyson Jesse, *The Trial of Alma Victoria Rattenbury and George Percy Stoner*, op. cit., p. 241

52   Ibid., p. 245

53   Ibid., pp. 245–6

54   Ibid., p. 246

55   Ibid.

56   Tennyson Jesse, *The Trial of Alma Victoria Rattenbury and George Percy Stoner*, op. cit., p. 33

57   Travers Humphreys's summing up, 30 May 1935, quoted in Tennyson Jesse, *The Trial of Alma Victoria Rattenbury and George Percy Stoner*, op. cit., p. 251

58   Travers Humphreys's summing up, 31 May 1935, quoted in Tennyson Jesse, *The Trial of Alma Victoria Rattenbury and George Percy Stoner*, op. cit., p. 262

59   Ibid., p. 252

60   Ibid.

61   Ibid., p. 254

62   Tennyson Jesse, *The Trial of Alma Victoria Rattenbury and George Percy Stoner*, op. cit., p. 12

63   Travers Humphreys's summing up, 30 May 1935, quoted in Tennyson Jesse, *The Trial of Alma Victoria Rattenbury and George Percy Stoner*, op. cit., p. 253

64   Travers Humphreys's summing up, 31 May 1935, quoted in Tennyson Jesse, *The Trial of Alma Victoria Rattenbury and George Percy Stoner*, op. cit., p. 270

65   Ibid., p. 287

66 Margaret Lane, 'Mrs Rattenbury cries "Oh No!"', *Daily Mail*, 1 June
    1935, p. 12
67 Ibid.
68   McCall p. 63
69 Ibid
70 Ibid.
71 Ibid.
72 Ibid.
73 *Daily Express*, 1 June 1935, p. 3
74 *Daily Mail*, 1 June 1935, p. 12
75 *Daily Express*, 1 June 1935, p. 3
76 *Daily Mail*, 1 June 1935, p. 12
77 Ibid.

16. A Woman of Principle

1 John Van Druten, *Leave Her to Heaven* (New York: Samuel French,
    1941), p. 106
2 Iles, 'The Rattenbury Case', in *The Anatomy of Murder*, op. cit., p. 215
3 *Daily Mail*, 1 June 1935, p. 11
4 Ibid.
5 McCall, p. 63
6 'Acquitted Woman Booed as she left Nursing Home', quoted in *Daily
    Mail*, 19 August 1987, p. 18
7 *Sunday Dispatch*, 9 June 1935, p. 9
8 Havers, Shankland and Barrett, op. cit., p. 217. The behaviour of the
    press at Halkin Place was relayed to Anthony Barrett by Keith Miller
    Jones in an interview on 6 June 1978.
9 *Sunday Dispatch*, 9 June 1935, p. 8
10 Ibid.
11 Ibid., p. 9
12 Letter from Alma Rattenbury to Lewis Manning, 1 June 1935, printed
    in *Daily Sketch*, 7 June 1935
13 *Sunday Dispatch*, 9 June 1935, p. 8
14 Ibid.
15 Ibid.
16 Letter from Alma Rattenbury, 4 Halkin Place, SW1, to Stoner, HMP
    Pentonville, Friday 31 May 1935, CRIM 1/778
17 *Daily Sketch*, 6 June 1935, p. 22
18 *Evening Standard*, 31 May 1935, p. 13
19 *Daily Express*, 6 June 1935, p. 8
20 *Sunday Dispatch*, 9 June 1935, p. 8
21 Minutes, HMP Pentonville, 1 June 1935, CRIM 1/778. A memo on 2

June commented that, 'It seems very undesirable that Mrs R. should be allowed to visit or to communicate with Stoner, and you may consider it desirable that the governor should return the letter and inform her that she will not be permitted to write to this prisoner.'

22 *Sunday Dispatch*, 9 June 1935, p. 8

23 Ibid.

24 *Sunday Dispatch*, 9 June 1935, p. 8

25 *Daily Sketch*, 3 June 1935, p. 7

26 *Sunday Dispatch*, 9 June 1935, p. 8; At some point she contacted Frank Titterton: 'She told me she wanted to get well as quickly as possible so that she could attend to the publication of her songs. She said she would use all the money she could find to help Stoner get a reprieve.'

27 *Daily Express*, 6 June 1935, p. 8

28 *Sunday Dispatch*, 9 June 1935, p. 8

29 Ibid.

30 Ibid.

31 Ibid.

32 Ibid.

33 *Daily Mail*, 6 June 1935, p. 14

34 *Sunday Dispatch*, 9 June 1935, p. 8

35 *Daily Express*, 7 June 1935, p. 2

36 Ibid.

37 Ibid.

38 *Daily Mail*, 7 June 1935, p. 13

39 Alma was deeply affected by what was said about her in the courtroom ('This woman – so low – so degraded (I can still hear the Judge's words)'). Studying the contemporary press reports of the trial alongside Tennyson Jesse's edition of the trial transcript, it is intriguing to note that there are discrepancies between the two. Dr Victoria Stewart, who has made a study of the *Notable British Trials* series, has concluded that it was William Hodge, the publisher, who actually edited the trial transcripts, tidying them up in the interests of making them more accessible to the general reader before passing them on to the likes of Tennyson Jesse to write an introduction. In the case of the Rattenbury trial, Hodge carefully lessened the impact of what the lawyers said about Alma, filleting the text of the more extreme negative language. Hodge might have felt this necessary in the wake of Alma's death as she had been clear in her suicide notes that one of the issues that motivated her to take her own life was what had been said about her in the courtroom. In her suicide letter, Alma mentions two letters she had sent to Stoner in prison, but only one survives. See note 15.

40 Alma's final letters were found in an envelope marked 'Diary' that

contained seven sheets of headed writing paper from the Cleveland Nursing Home. This long first letter was not read out at her inquest and has not previously appeared in print. (DPP 2/263 Part 2)

41   *Daily Express*, 7 June 1935, p. 2
42   DPP 2/263 Part 2
43   Ibid.
44   *Daily Express*, 7 June 1935, p. 2
45   *Daily Mail*, 7 June, 1935, p. 14
46   Ibid.
47   DPP 2/263 Part 2
48   Alma had written two thoughts at different times of her journey on the back of the same envelope, as in this section she has yet to reach her destination (DPP 2/263 Part 2)
49   *Daily Sketch*, 6 June 1935, p. 2
50   DPP 2/263 Part 2
51   When printed in the newspapers or the *Notable British Trials* text, Alma's letters appeared to be continuous, but the letter referred to in note 47 was clearly written before she reached Christchurch, and that referred to in note 50 when Alma had actually reached the water's edge (DPP 2/263 Part 2)
52   DPP 2/263 Part 2
53   *Christchurch Times*, 8 June 1935, p. 1
54   Ibid. Mitchell gave many interviews to the press about the discovery of Alma's body (see *Daily Express*, 6 June 1935, p. 8) but his official story is held in the records of the inquest quoted in Tennyson Jesse, *The Trial of Alma Victoria Rattenbury and George Percy Stoner*, op. cit., Appendix, p. 294–5.
55   Tennyson Jesse, *The Trial of Alma Victoria Rattenbury and George Percy Stoner*, op. cit., p. 294

17.   The Son of Any One of Us

1   Iles, *The Anatomy of Murder*, op. cit., p. 217
2   *Daily Sketch*, 1 June 1935, p. 2
3   *Daily Express*, 1 June 1935, p. 1
4   In 1935, there were about 800 prisoners held at Pentonville at any one time. See Crew, op. cit., p. 169.
5   See letter from Tabuteau to the Home Office regarding the execution of Edith Thompson, 18 June 1951, HO 144 2685 Part 2
6   For the regime at Pentonville, see Crew, op. cit., pp. 169–180
7   Minutes, HMP Pentonville, 3 June 1935, CRIM 1/778
8   *Daily Mail*, 1 June 1935, p. 11
9   *Daily Express*, 1 June 1935, p. 1

10 *Bournemouth Daily Echo*, 3 June 1935, p. 1

11 Casswell, op. cit., p. 115

12 Letter from Travers Humphreys to Casswell, 1 June 1935, printed in Casswell, op. cit., p. 112

13 For the reprieve process and the statistics relating to the recommendation of mercy, see www.capitalpunishment.org/reprieve

14 Ibid.

15 *Daily Mail*, 24 June 1935, p. 8

16 This visit with Marshall Harvey to inform Stoner of his execution date and Alma's suicide is recorded in a statement by the governor of Pentonville, 7 June 1935, CRIM 1/778

17 Minutes, HMP Pentonville, 5 June 1935, CRIM 1/778

18 Minutes, HMP Pentonville, 7 June 1935, CRIM 1/778

19 On Friday 7 June a story appeared in the *Daily Express* – 'Mrs Rattenbury: Stoner Told; tears on hearing of her Fate'– which claimed that it was Marshall who had broken the news to Stoner of Alma's death and that he 'broke down and wept'. That day an incensed Marshall Harvey wrote to Tabuteau, insisting that the leak to the *Express* did not come from him and that he was planning to issue a writ against the newspaper as the story was 'defamatory to me, having regard to my professional position'. By return of post, Tabuteau reassured him that he knew the article to be completely untrue. (Letter from E. W. Marshall Harvey, Argyle Chambers, Bournemouth, to governor, HMP Pentonville, 28 June 1935, CRIM 1/778)

20 *Daily Mail*, 10 June 1935, p. 7

21 Ibid.

22 This would not be the last time that Bickford was involved in an eleventh-hour drama before an execution. In 1955, he would be appointed as the solicitor of Ruth Ellis, who had shot her lover David Blakely on Easter Sunday that year. Like Alma, Ellis was another glamorous woman in the dock of Court Number One at the Old Bailey accused of murder and, thirty years on, her trial was also a tabloid sensation. Though Bickford was aware of Ruth's lover Desmond Cussen's involvement in the murder – providing her with a service revolver and instructing her how to use it – he didn't reveal it at the time of the trial. Ellis was controversially executed and she became the last woman to be hanged in England. The case would haunt Bickford for the rest of his life: 'I can't say it ruined my life, but it had such a profound effect as to change my life.' He would die an alcoholic in 1977. See Carol Ann Lee, *A Fine Day for a Hanging: The Real Ruth Ellis Story* (Edinburgh: Mainstream Publishing, 2013).

18. Leave Her to Heaven

1 W. H. Auden and Christopher Isherwood, *The Ascent of F6* (London: Faber & Faber, 1989), pp. 352–3

2 *Evening Standard*, 5 June 1935, p. 1

3 Agate, *Ego* 2, op. cit., p. 189. As soon as the trial ended, as a theatre critic, Agate note that the verdict 'has given an immense fillip to Emlyn Williams's *Night Must Fall*, a good, highly imaginative play about a murder in an Essex bungalow'. (Agate, *Ego* 2, op. cit., p. 188)

4 *Radio Times*, 25–31 October 1975, p. 7

5 Two conflicting reports illustrate how Alma's elusive character divided the press, even in death. Professor W. G. Clarke, the phrenologist the Rattenburys had consulted in 1932, drew a positive picture of her, which was published in the *Christchurch Times*: 'A most artistic nature, with many marked talents, especially for music. In demeanour and comportment and by natural instinct, I would truthfully describe her as a lady. Vivacious, and apparently quite happy, and there was no note of discord between husband and wife.' However, the *Sunday Dispatch*, again apparently quoting Professor Clarke, seemed to be describing a completely different woman: 'I came to the conclusion that she was a woman of small brains, with weak will, no grit, no backbone. She was one of those people who, when they come under influences, give way to temptation very easily.'

6 J. H. Campbell, 'A Woman's Torment', *Sunday Post*, 9 June 1935, p. 15

7 Ibid.

8 Candidus, *Daily Sketch*, 7 June 1935, p. 7

9 *Daily Express*, 6 June 1935, p. 8

10 *Daily Sketch*, 6 June 1935, p. 22

11 Ibid., 7 June 1935, p. 2

12 Ibid.

13 *News of the World*, 9 June 1935, p. 11

14 *Sunday Dispatch*, 9 June 1935, p. 9

15 *The Times*, 6 June 1935, p. 6

16 Ibid.

17 *Daily Express*, 6 June 1935, p. 8

18 *Sunday Dispatch*, 9 June, p. 8

19 *Bournemouth Echo*, 6 June 1935, p. 1

20 *Sunday Dispatch*, 9 June 1935, p. 8

21 *News of the World*, 9 June 1935, p. 11

22 *Bournemouth Echo*, 7 June 1935, p. 12

23 Ibid.

24 *Sunday Dispatch*, 9 June 1935, p. 13

25 *Western Gazette*, 14 June 1935, p. 11

26 *Daily Sketch*, 10 June 1935, p. 4

27   *Sunday Dispatch*, 9 June 1935, p. 13

28   Cecil R. Cutler was a grave digger at Wimborne Road Cemetery and helped prepare both Rattenbury's and Alma's graves. In eight years as a grave digger, he had never seen crowds as big as the one that gathered in the cemetery to see Alma buried. 'Rattenbury Case: a grave-digger recalls', *Bournemouth Evening Echo*, 27 August 1987, p. 11.

29   *Daily Mail*, 10 June 1935, p. 7

30   *Bournemouth Graphic*, 15 June 1935, p. 10

31   *Western Gazette*, 14 June 1935, p. 11

32   *Sunday Dispatch*, 9 June 1935, p. 13

33   *Daily Mirror*, 8 June 1935, p. 4. After the funeral, the *Daily Mirror* continued to print the public's responses to the case, including criticism of the media's insensitive coverage of the trial and its aftermath, as well as a lack of sympathy in some quarters with Alma, despite the price she'd paid for her part in the death of her husband.

Letter from 'Dispassionate from Coventry', *Daily Mirror*, 8 June 1935, p. 11: 'Presumably the sensational publicity and display of detail in prominent murder cases is intended to serve a useful and moral purpose by deterring would-be criminals. But what of the relations and members of the families of the persons involved? Why cannot these murder cases be heard in camera and all names be suppressed? We are left with the edifying spectacle of a delinquent acquitted by law who ends a life – broken beyond redemption – at the hands of the law – by drowning and the knife.'

Letter from Essex, *Daily Mirror*, 11 June 1935, p. 11: 'If ever a human being has been hounded to death by merciless condemnation, she has. A sensitive woman of genius, "some nobility" of character according to her lawyer, she had been acquitted of the crime of which she had been accused. What remains? That offence of which we are warned that only those without sin might presume to judge.'

Letter from (Mrs) N. Burns, Romola Road, Tulse Hill, *Daily Mirror*, 5 June 1935, p. 11: 'I cannot agree with your correspondents who seem to want to make a martyr of Mrs Rattenbury. She was not hounded to death except by her own rightly distressed conscience. The Judge who said less that he might justly have said, and not a word more than was necessary to present Stoner's case fairly. Mrs Rattenbury's death cannot be deplored. It was best even for her own sake. If she had "a spark of nobility" the thought of Stoner must have tortured her, whether he is hanged or wastes his young manhood in prison. I should hate to be hard on anybody, but I find I need so much sympathy for Stoner's mother, and after that, for Mrs Rattenbury, that my whole supply is exhausted. (Mrs) N. Burns, Romola Road, Tulse Hill.'

34 'Crowd Outside Villa Madeira', *Bournemouth Daily Echo*, 5 June 1935, p. 1

35 'Ghoulish Scenes at Villa Madeira', *Bournemouth Daily Echo*, 17 June 1935, p. 1

36 *Daily Mirror*, 18 June 1935, p. 2

37 *Bournemouth Daily Echo*, 17 June 1935, p. 1

38 Ibid.

39 *Daily Sketch*, 18 June 1935, p. 11

40 *Sunday Dispatch*, 9 June 1935, p. 9

41 Victoria Archives, Rattenbury Probate File, Supreme Court, Victoria Probate/Estate Files, 1859–1941

42 Ibid.

43 Ibid.

44 *Daily Express*, 10 June 1935, pp. 1–2

19. Stay of Execution

1 Robert Anderson, *Tea and Sympathy* (London: William Heinemann, 1957), p. 159

2 *Bournemouth Daily Echo*, 10 June 1935, p. 1

3 Ibid., p. 10

4 Ibid., p. 1

5 Ibid., p. 10

6 Letter from Stoner to Casswell via Mr Bickford, 9 June 1935, DPP 2/263 Part 2

7 Stoner's statements are in the appeal notes, DPP 2/263 Part 2

8 *Daily Sketch*, 12 June 1935, p. 5

9 *Bournemouth Daily Echo*, 14 June 1935, p. 1

10 *Daily Sketch*, 13 June 1935, p. 13

11 Ibid.

12 Ibid.

13 Ibid.

14 *Bournemouth Daily Echo*, 24 June 1935, p. 1

15 Young, op. cit., p. 251

16 *Bournemouth Daily Echo*, 24 June 1935, p. 1

17 The appeal notes are held in DPP 2/263 Part 2

18 Violet Van der Elst, op. cit., p. 89

19 *Bournemouth Daily Echo*, 24 June 1935, p. 10

20 Ibid.

21 Notes of Appeal Judgement Rex *v.* George Percy Stoner before Lord Hewart of Bury, Mr Justice Swift and Mrs Justice Lawrence, Royal Courts of Justice, 24 June 1935, DPP 2/263 Part 2

22 *Bournemouth Daily Echo*, 24 June 1935, p. 1

23 Ibid.

24 *Daily Sketch*, 26 June 1935, p. 3

25 Harold Nicolson quoted in David Dutton, *Simon: A Political Biography of Sir John Simon* (London: Aurum Press, 1992), p. 333

26 Dutton, op. cit., p. 117

27 Lloyd George to Jan C. Smuts, 31 July 1935, Lloyd George MSS G 18/8/6, cited in Dutton, op. cit., p. 221

28 In his diary, Robert Bruce Lockhart wrote, 'Discussed the politicians who were criminally responsible for war and should be hanged on lamp posts in Downing Street. Not many candidates. Nearly everyone agreed that sinner No 1 was Simon.' (Dutton, op. cit., p. 239)

29 Howard Spring, 'Sir John the Coroner', *Evening Standard*, 4 June 1935, p. 7

30 J. A. S. Simon, *Retrospect: The Memoirs of the Rt Hon. Viscount Simon* (London: Hutchinson, 1952), p. 209

31 *Evening Standard*, 25 June 1935, p. 1

32 Letter from the Home Office to the secretary of the Prison Commission, 25 June 1935, CRIM 1/778

33 *Daily Mail*, 26 June 1935, p. 13

34 Ibid., p. 14

35 *Bournemouth Daily Echo*, 26 June 1935, p. 1

36 Ibid.

37 Ibid.

38 Ibid.

39 Ibid.

40 Minutes, HMP Pentonville, transfer to Maidstone recorded, 29 June 1935

41 Minutes, HMP Pentonville, 11 July 1935, CRIM 1/778

42 Letter from Alma Rattenbury, 4 Halkin Place, SW1, to Stoner, HMP Pentonville, 31 May 1935, CRIM 1/778

43 Quoted in Violet Van der Elst, op. cit., pp. 91–2

44 Prison Commission Minutes, 14 July 1942, CRIM 1/778

45 Home Office referred letter, 9 August 1941, confirming that Stoner should be released on 20 May 1942, CRIM 1/778

46 Minutes, HMP Camp Hill, 3 March 1942, CRIM 1/778

47 Notification of Release on Licence or Expiration of Sentence. Date of Licence: 8 May 1942. Date of Release: 27 May 1942. Submitted to the Secretary of State: 10 June 1942. CRIM 1/778.

48 See Stoner's army service record: Army Number: T/14680854

49 The War Diary of 755 Coy RASC, January–June 1944, is held in (NA) WO 171/2545

50 York Membery, interview with Christine Stoner, 'Killer's wife speaks out 67 years later', *National Post*, 30 November 2002

51 See Membery, *National Post*, op. cit.

52   See Patricia Roach's story at www.bbc.co.uk/history/ww2peopleswar/
     stories
53   See George Herbert Tucker's story at www.bbc.co.uk/history/
     ww2peopleswar/stories
54   See Stoner's army service record: Army Number: T/14680854
55   See Membery, *National Post*, op. cit.
56   Ibid.
57   Letter from Yvonne Stoner to Sean O'Connor, 29 April 2013
58   Ibid.
59   Membery, *National Post*, op. cit.
60   *Daily Express*, 6 June 1935, p. 10
61   'Lovers faithful in Shadow of Gallows', in *Books Today*, Compton
     Mackenzie (ed.), *Daily Mail*, 19 December 1935, p. 16
62   Emlyn Williams was interviewed in *The Epic That Never Was*, BBC,
     1965. Korda invited Williams to lunch where they discussed several
     projects for Williams as a writer and actor; 'I was very interested in the
     idea of a film about the Rattenbury murder case for Merle [Oberon]
     and Laurence Olivier.'
63   David Gascoyne, *Lozanne*, in *The Penguin Book of the Prose Poem*
     (London: Penguin Books, 2018), p. 317
64   This lyric originally appeared as a chorus in Auden and Isherwood's
     1936 play, *The Ascent of F6*, op. cit., pp. 352–3
65   Iles, *As for the Woman*, op. cit., p. 246
66   *The Woman in the Sea*, Harper & Brothers, New York, 1948, p. 272
67   *Strand Magazine*, May 1943, p. 76
68   Orwell, *Decline of the English Murder*, in *Collected Essays Volume IV:
     In Front of Your Nose 1945–50*, p. 98, originally printed in *Tribune*, 15
     February 1946
69   'An Actor's Play,' *Daily Telegraph*, 7 March 1940, p. 5
70   '"Belle View" by Francis James', *The Times*, 8 March 1940, p. 6. The
     reviewer also noted that the Alma character, Rita Munden, was 'estab-
     lished early in the play as a woman who makes friends easily with
     servants'.
71   Directed by Auriol Lee and also starring Edmond O'Brien, *Leave Her
     to Heaven* opened at the Longacre Theatre on 27 February 1940, but
     closed on 9 March
72   *Time*, 11 March 1940
73   Gerald Bordman, *American Theatre: A Chronicle of Comedy and
     Drama 1930–1969* (Oxford: Oxford University Press, 1996), p. 189
74   See www.simongray.org.uk
75   *Radio Times*, 25–31 October 1975, p. 7
76   *The Observer*, 25 October 1975, p. 4
77   Ibid., 9 November 1975, p. 25

78   Irving Wardle, *The Times*, 5 July 1977

79   John Barber, *Daily Telegraph*, 5 July 1977, p. 13

80   'Not quite a cause for celebration', *Daily Express*, 9 July 1977, p. 7

81   *Evening Standard*, 5 July 1977, p. 23

82   Benedict Nightingale, *New Statesman*, 3 November 1978

83   Membery, op. cit.

84   *Daily Mail*, 19 August 1987, pp. 18–19

85   Ibid.

86   'Murderer Hits Out Over Film', *Bournemouth Evening Echo*, 21 August 1987, p. 3

87   Ibid.

88   *Daily Mail*, 19 August 1987, pp. 18–19

89   'Murderer Hits Out Over Film', op. cit.

90   Ibid.

91   Ibid.

92   Ibid.

93   Membery, op. cit.

94   Email from Anne Griffiths to Sean O'Connor, 16 April 2015

95   'Naked assault on Boy in Toilet', *Bournemouth Evening Echo*, 29 September 1990, p. 4

96   Ibid.

97   Ibid.

98   Ibid., p. 3

99   *The Guardian*, 29 September 1990, p. 1

100 Membery, op. cit.

101 Kevin Nash, *Bournemouth Daily Echo*, 28 January 1998, pp. 18–19

102 Ibid.

103 Membery, op. cit.

104 Ibid.

105 Ibid.

EPILOGUE: Taliesin, 15 August 1914

1   Ellen Key, *The Torpedo Under the Ark, Ibsen and Women*, trans. by Mamah Borthwick (Chicago: The Ralph Fletcher Seymour Company, 1912), p. 17

2   Quoted in Havers, Shankland and Barrett, op. cit., p. 234

3   York Membery, 'Murder, suicide and the pain of a surviving son', *The Times*, 29 November 2007, Times2, pp. 10–11

4   Ibid.

5   Ibid.

6   The circumstances of John Rattenbury's early life were discussed in an interview with John Rattenbury and Sean O'Connor, 19 June 2013.

7   Ibid.

8   See Membery, op. cit.

9   In researching the books *Francis Rattenbury and British Columbia* and *Tragedy in Three Voices*, Anthony Barrett became well acquainted with John Rattenbury and Christopher Compton Pakenham. He informed the present author about Christopher's life after the Villa Madeira.

10 John Rattenbury, *A House for Life: Bringing the Spirit of Frank Lloyd Wright into Your Home* (Toronto: Warwick Publishing, 2006), p. 19

11 Barrett and Windsor-Liscombe, op. cit., p. 308

12 John Rattenbury, op cit., p. 20

13 John Rattenbury, op cit., p. 19

14 Ibid., p. 22

15 Membery, op. cit.

16 The story of John Rattenbury's extraordinary journey to Taliesin is told in 'Finding Taliesin', the first chapter of his *A House for Life* (op. cit.)

17 John Rattenbury, op. cit., p. 13

18 Ibid.

19 See William R. Drennan, *Death in a Prairie House: Frank Lloyd Wright and the Taliesin Murders* (University of Wisconsin: Terrace Books, 2007)

20 Quoted in Drennan, op. cit., p. 116

21 Wright was buried next to Mamah Borthwick at the Unity Chapel where he rested for the next twenty-seven years. But when Olgivanna Wright died in 1986, there was international controversy when her daughter had Wright's body disinterred from Spring Green, cremated and transported to rest with her mother at Taliesin West, Wright's summer home in the Arizona desert.

22 Membery, op. cit.

23 Ibid.

24 Ibid.

25 Ibid.

26 Ibid.

Afterword

1   Letter from Edith Thompson to Bessie Aitken, 26 December 1922, quoted in Weis, op. cit., p. 269

2   *Daily Mail*, 5 November 1935, p. 18

3   Ibid.

4   Roger Wilkes, *An Infamous Address* (London: Grafton Books, 1989), p. 231

5   Ibid.

6   *Bournemouth Daily Echo*, 28 January 1998, pp. 18–19

7   Wilkes, op. cit., p. 268

8   Ibid.

9   See Barrett and Windsor-Liscombe, op. cit., p. 308

10 See Sean O'Connor, *Handsome Brute: The Story of a Ladykiller* (London: Simon & Schuster), 2013

11 Casswell, op. cit., p. 118

12 Ibid.

13 Email from Yvonne Stoner to Sean O'Connor, 18 September 2018

14 Email from Anthony Barrett to Sean O'Connor, 3 March 2018

15 Napley, op. cit., pp. 217–26

16 *Daily Mail*, 25 August 1987, p. 3

17 *Bournemouth Echo*, 21 August 1987, p. 3

18 Ibid.

19 Letter from Alma Rattenbury, 4 June 1935, DPP 2/263 Part 2

20 'Lasting Memorial for Murder Victim', *Bournemouth Echo*, 18 November 2007

21 Note from Alma Rattenbury, 4 June 1935, DPP 2/263 Part 2

22 Letter from Alma Rattenbury, 4 June 1935, DPP 2/263 Part 2

23 Since my first visit to Alma Rattenbury's grave in 2013, a small stone vase has been placed on the site by Aaron Quirey

Appendix of Songs by Lozanne

1   In order of publication.

2   British Library registration: 16 March 1932, Keith Prowse Music

3   British Library registration: 10 May 1932, Keith Prowse Music

4   British Library registration: 29 May 1932, Keith Prowse Music

5   British Library registration: 3 June 1932, Keith Prowse Music

6   British Library registration: 21 November 1932, Keith Prowse Music

7   British Library registration: 9 September 1932, Keith Prowse Music

8   Published in 1935, text in *Four Love Songs by Alma Clarke 'Lozanne'*, Cambridge, 1992, SJ Music

9   British Library registration: 18 September 1935, Peter Maurice Music Co.

BIBLIOGRAPHY

Books about the Rattenburys:

Anthony Barrett and Rhodri Windsor-Liscombe, *Francis Rattenbury and British Columbia: Architecture and Challenge in the Imperial Age*, University of British Columbia Press, Vancouver, 1983

Sir Michael Havers, Peter Shankland and Anthony Barrett, *Tragedy in Three Voices: The Rattenbury Murder*, William Kimber, London, 1980

Francis Iles, *The Anatomy of Murder: Famous Crimes Considered by Members of the Detection Club*, The Macmillan Company, New York, 1937

F. Tennyson Jesse, *The Trial of Alma Victoria Rattenbury and George Percy Stoner (Notable British Trials)*, Hodge, London, 1935

John L. Motherwell, *Gold Rush Steamboats: Francis Rattenbury's Yukon Adventure*, self-published, Victoria, BC, 2012

Sir David Napley, *Murder at the Villa Madeira: The Rattenbury Case*, Weidenfeld & Nicolson, London, 1988

Terry Reksten, *Rattenbury*, Soni Nis Press, Victoria, BC, 1978

Novels, plays and poems inspired by the case:

W. H. Auden, 'At Last the Secret is Out', from W. H. Auden and Christopher Isherwood, *The Ascent of F6*, Faber & Faber, London, 1989

David Gascoyne, *Lozanne* (1936), *The Penguin Book of the Prose Poem*, Penguin Books, London, 2018

Simon Gray, *Molly*, in *The Definitive Simon Gray II*, Faber & Faber, London, 1992

Francis Iles, *As for the Woman*, Jarrolds, London, 1939

Francis James, *Villa Mimosa*, unpublished typescript, British Library, 1937

Terence Rattigan, *Cause Célèbre* or *A Woman of Principle*, Hamish Hamilton, London, 1978

John Van Druten, *Leave Her to Heaven*, Samuel French, New York, 1941

The Woman in the Sea, Harper & Brothers, New York, 1948

Secondary sources:

Achmed Abdullah and T. Compton Pakenham, *Dreamers of Empire*, George Harrap & Co., London, 1930

Ruth Adam, *A Woman's Place: 1910–1975*, Persephone Books, London, 2011

James Agate, *Ego 2*, Victor Gollanz, London, 1936

Robert Anderson, *Tea and Sympathy*, William Heinemann, London, 1957

W. H. Auden, *Selected Poems*, Faber & Faber, London, 2009

Mary Balf, *Kamloops: A History of the district up to 1914*, Kamloops Museum, Kamloops, 1969

Lady Frances Balfour, *Dr Elsie Inglis*, Hodder & Stoughton, London, 1919

Nicola Beauman, *A Very Great Profession: The Woman's Novel 1914–1939*, Persephone Books, London, 2008

Dorothy Beddoe, *Back to Home and Duty: Women Between the Wars 1918–1939*, Pandora, London, 1989

Paul Begg, *Jack the Ripper: The Definitive History*, Routledge, London, 2004

Pierre Berton, *The Crystal Garden: West Coast Pleasure Palace*, Crystal Garden Preservation Society, Victoria, BC, 1977

Adrian Bingham, *Gender, Modernity and the Popular Press in Inter-War Britain*, Oxford University Press, Oxford, 2003

——, *Family Newspapers? Sex, Private Life and the British Popular Press 1918–1978*, Oxford University Press, Oxford, 2009

William Bixley, *The Guilty and the Innocent: My Fifty Years at the Old Bailey*, The Souvenir Press, London, 1957

Ronald Blythe, *The Age of Illusion: England in the Twenties and Thirties, 1919–1940*, Phoenix Press, London, 2001

Charles Booth, Jess Steele (ed.), *The Streets of London, The Booth Notebooks: South East*, Deptford Forum Publishing, London, 1997

——, *Life and Labour of the People in London, Vol. I: Poverty*, Macmillan & Co., New York and London, 1892

——, *Life and Labour of the People in London, Vol. II: Industry*, Macmillan & Co., New York and London, 1903

——, *Life and Labour of the People in London, Vol. III: Religious Influence*, Macmillan & Co., New York and London, 1902

Gerald Bordman, *American Theatre: A Chronicle of Comedy and Drama 1930–1969*, Oxford University Press, Oxford, 1996

C. Breward, *The Culture of Fashion: A New History of Fashionable Dress*, Manchester University Press, Manchester, 1995

Susan Briggs, *Those Radio Times*, Weidenfeld & Nicolson, London, 1981

Vera Brittain, *Testament of Youth: An Autobiographical Study of the Years 1900–1925*, Virago, London, 2014

Lewis Broad, *The Innocence of Edith Thompson*, Hutchinson & Co, London, 1952

Douglas C. Brown, *Sir Travers Humphreys*, Harrap, London, 1960

J. Burnett, *A Social History of Housing, 1815–1870*, David & Charles, Newton Abbott, 1978

John Camp, *Holloway Prison: The Place and the People*, David & Charles, London, 1974

J. D. Casswell, *A Lance for Liberty*, George G. Harrap & Co. Ltd, London, 1961

Winston S. Churchill, *The World Crisis 1918–1928, Vol. IV: The Aftermath*, Bloomsbury, London, 2015 (originally published 1929)

——, *The World Crisis 1911–1914, Vol. V: The Eastern Front*, Thornton Butterworth, London, 1923

Stuart Cloete, *A Victorian Son: An Autobiography, 1897–1912*, Collins, London, 1972

Claud Cockburn, *The Devil's Decade*, Sidgwick & Jackson, London, 1973

Sean O'Connor, *Handsome Brute: The Story of a Ladykiller*, Simon & Schuster, London, 2013

Eliot Crawshay-Williams, *Stay of Execution*, Jarrolds, London, 1933

Albert Crew, *London Prisons of Yesterday and Today*, Ivor Nicholson & Watson, London, 1933

Eileen Crofton, *Angels of Mercy: A Women's Hospital of the Western Front 1914–1918*, Birlinn Ltd, Edinburgh, 2013

Richard Davenport-Hines, *The Pursuit of Oblivion: A Social History of Drugs*, Orion, London, 2002

E. M. Delafield, *Ladies and Gentlemen in Victorian Fiction*, The Hogarth Press, London, 1937

Charles Dickens, *Bleak House*, Charles Dickens Library, Vol. XI, The Educational Book Co. Ltd, London, 1910

Anne Digby, *The Evolution of General Practice 1850–1948*, Oxford University Press, Oxford, 1999

Frances E. Dolan, *Dangerous Familiars: Representations of Domestic Crime in England, 1550–1700*, Cornell University Press, Ithaca and London, 1994

William R. Drennan, *Death in a Prairie House: Frank Lloyd Wright and the Taliesin Murders*, Terrace Books, University of Wisconsin, 2007

J. C. Dunn, *The War the Infantry Knew: 1914–1919*, Abacus, London, 1987

David Dutton, *Simon: A Political Biography of Sir John Simon*, Aurum Press, London, 1992

R. C. K. Ensor, *England, 1870–1914*, Clarendon Press, Oxford, 1936

J. Macartney-Filgate, *The History of the 33rd Divisional Artillery in the War, 1914–1918*, The Naval and Military Press, Uckfield, 1921

Violet Firth, *The Psychology of the Servant Problem: A Study in Social Relationships*, C. W. Daniel, London, 1925

Kate Fisher, *Birth Control, Sex and Marriage in Britain 1918–1960*, Oxford University Press, Oxford, 2008

C. L. Flick, *Just What Happened: A Diary of the Mobilization of the Canadian Militia*, Chiswick Press, London, 1917

Mark Forsythe and Greg Dickson, *From the West Coast to the Western Front: British Columbians and the Great War*, Harbour Publishing, Vancouver, 2014

Adrian Forty, *Objects of Desire: Design and Society 1750–1980*, Thames & Hudson, London, 1986

Juliet Gardiner, *The Thirties: An Intimate History*, Harper Press, London, 2010

Jonathan Gaythorne-Hardy, *Doctors: The Life and Work of GPs*, Weidenfeld & Nicolson, London, 1984

W. J. Gordon, *The Horse-World of London*, The Religious Tract Society, London, 1893

Robert Graves, *Goodbye to All That*, Octagon Books, London, 1980

—— and Alan Hodge, *The Long Weekend: A Social History of Britain 1918–1939*, Faber & Faber, London, 1940

Harry Gregson, *A History of Victoria 1842–1970*, Victoria Observer Publishing, Victoria, BC, 1970

Llewelyn Wyn Griffith, *Up to Mametz and Beyond*, Pen and Sword Military, Barnsley, 2010

Cicely Hamilton, *Life Errant*, J. M. Dent & Sons Ltd, London, 1935

Thomas Hardy, *The Collected Poems of Thomas Hardy*, Macmillan, London, 1930

Ron Hatch, Elizabeth Duckworth, Sylvia Grupp and Sherry Bennett, *Kamloops: Trading Post to Tournament Capital*, Thompson Rivers History and Heritage Society, Kamloops, BC, 2012

Joan Henry, *Women in Prison*, Doubleday & Co., New York, 1952 (new edition by White Lion, London, 1973)

Matthew Hilton, *Smoking in British Popular Culture 1800–2000*, Manchester University Press, Manchester, 2000

John George Hopkins, *The Establishment of Schools and Colleges in Ontario, 1792–1910, Vol. III*, L. K. Cameron, Toronto, 1910

Chris Horrie, *Tabloid Nation: The Birth of the Daily Mirror to the Death of the Tabloid*, Andre Deutsch Ltd, London, 2003

Catherine Horwood, *Keeping Up Appearances: Fashion and Class Between the Wars*, The History Press, Stroud, 2011

Sir Travers Humphreys, *A Book of Trials*, Heinemann, London, 1953

Henrik Ibsen, *The Collected Works of Henrik Ibsen, Vol. XII, From Ibsen's Workshop; notes, scenarios, and drafts of the modern plays*, William Heinemann, London, 1912

Stephen Inwood, *City of Cities*, Macmillan, London, 2004

——, *A History of London*, Macmillan, London, 1998

Stanley Jackson, *The Life and Cases of Mr Justice Humphreys*, Odhams Press Ltd, London, 1951

Alan Jenkins, *The Thirties*, Willian Heinemann, London, 1976

F. Tennyson Jesse, *A Pin to See the Peepshow*, William Heinemann, London, 1934

Ann Jones, *Women Who Kill*, The Feminist Press, New York, 2009

Enid Huws Jones, *Margery Fry: The Essential Amateur*, Oxford University Press, London, 1966

Michael Joseph, *The Commercial Side of Literature*, Hutchinson, London, 1925

R. Kashar (ed.), *Splintered Classes: Politics and the Lower Middle Classes in Interwar Europe*, Holmes & Meir, New York, 1990

Helena Kennedy, *Eve Was Framed*, Vintage, London, 1992

Marian Wilson Kimber, *The Elocutionists: Women, Music, and the Spoken Word*, University of Illinois Press, Urbana, Chicago and Springfield, 2017

Rudyard Kipling, *Letters of Travel*, Doubleday, Page & Co., New York, 1920

——, *Debits and Credits*, Macmillan, London, 1926

Judith Knelman, *Twisting in the Wind: The Murderess and the English Press*, University of Toronto Press, Toronto, 1998

Ellen Mary Knox, *The Girl of the New Day*, McClelland & Stewart, Toronto, 1919

John Kobler, *The Trial of Ruth Snyder and Judd Gray: Edited with a History of the Case*, Doubleday, Doran and Co., New York, 1938

Marek Kohn, *Dope Girls: The Birth of the British Drug Underground*, Granta, London, 1992

Nicola Lacey, *Women, Crime and Character: From Moll Flanders to Tess of the D'Urbervilles*, Oxford University Press, Oxford, 2008

James Laver, *Between the Wars*, Vista Books, London, 1961

D. H. Lawrence, *Lady Chatterley's Lover*, The Windmill Press, Surrey, 1942

Margot Lawrence, *Shadow of Swords: A Biography of Elsie Inglis*, Michael Joseph, London, 1971

Carol Ann Lee, *A Fine Day for a Hanging: The Real Ruth Ellis Story*, Mainstream Publishing, Edinburgh, 2013

Leah Leneman, *In the Service of Life: The Story of Elsie Inglis and the Scottish Women's Hospitals*, Mercat Press, Edinburgh, 1994

Alison Light, *Forever England: Femininity, Literature and Conservatism Between the Wars*, Routledge, London and New York, 1991

Edgar Lustgarten, *The Woman in the Case*, The Book Service, London, 1976

Norman Macdonald, *Canada: Immigration and Colonisation, 1841–1903*, Aberdeen University Press, Aberdeen, 1966

Cicely McCall, *Looking Back from the Nineties, An Autobiography*, Gliddon Books, Norwich, 1992

J. McDonnell, *Public Service Broadcasting: A Reader*, Routledge, London, 1991

William McElwee, *Britain's Locust Years 1918–1940*, Faber & Faber, London, 1962

Don MacGillivray, *Captain Alex MacLean: Jack London's Sea Wolf*, University of Washington Press, Seattle, 2008

Frances Macnab, *British Columbia for Settlers: Its Trade, Mines and Agriculture*, Chapman & Hall, London, 1898

W. J. Macqueen-Pope, *The Melodies Linger On: The Story of Music Hall 1888–1960*, W. H. Allen, London, 1950

Gordon Martin, *Chefoo School 1881–1951*, Merlin Books Ltd, Devon, 1990

Raymond Massey, *When I Was Young*, Robson Books, London, 1977

Billie Melman, *Women and the Popular Imagination in the Twenties: Flappers and Nymphs*, Palgrave Macmillan, London, 1988

Virginia B. Morris, *Double Jeopardy: Women Who Kill in Victorian Fiction*, Kentucky University Press, Kentucky, 1990

Antonio Navárro, *The Scottish Women's Hospital at the French Abbey of Royaumont*, G. Allen & Unwin Ltd, London, 1917

Beverly Nichols, *The Sweet and Twenties*, Weidenfeld & Nicolson, London, 1958

Virginia Nicolson, *Singled Out: How Two Million Women Survived Without Men After the First World War*, Oxford University Press, Oxford, 2008

Bernard O'Donnell, *Should Women Hang?*, W. H. Allen, London, 1956

——, *The Old Bailey and its Trials*, Theodore Brun Ltd, London, 1950

Sonia Orwell and Ian Angus (eds), *The Collected Essays, Journalism and Letters of George Orwell, Vol. II: My Country Right or Left 1940–1943*, Secker & Warburg, London, 1986

——, *The Collected Essays, Journalism and Letters of George Orwell, Vol: IV: In Front of Your Nose 1945–50*, Secker & Warburg, London, 1968

Richard Overy, *The Twilight Years: The Paradox of Britain Between the Wars*, Viking, London, 2009

T. Compton Pakenham, *Rearguard*, Alfred A. Knopf, London, 1931

Simona Pakenham, *Pigtails and Pernod*, Macmillan, London, 1961

Panikos Panayi, *German Immigrants in Nineteenth-Century Britain 1815–1914*, Bloomsbury, London, 1995

Sylvia Pankhurst, *The Home Front: A Mirror to Life in England During the World War*, Hutchinson, London, 1987

Terry M. Parssinen, *Secret Passions, Secret Remedies: Narcotic Drugs in British Society 1829–1930*, Manchester University Press, Manchester, 1983

Paton's List of Schools and Tutors, J & J Paton, London, 1926

Douglas Perry, *The Girls of Murder City, Fame, Lust and the Beautiful Killers who Inspired 'Chicago'*, Penguin, London, 2008

Margaret Powell, *Climbing the Stairs*, Peter Davies, London, 1970

J. B. Priestley, *English Journey*, William Heinemann, London, 1934

Martin Pugh, *We Danced All Night: A Social History of Britain Between the Wars*, Vintage, London, 2009

John Rattenbury, *A House for Life: Bringing the Spirit of Frank Lloyd Wright into Your Home*, Warwick Publishing, Toronto, 2006

Terence Rattigan, *The Deep Blue Sea*, Hamish Hamilton, London, 1952

Lisa Regan (ed.), *Winifred Holtby: A Woman in Her Time: Critical Essays*, Cambridge Scholars Publishing, Newcastle, 2010

Terry Reksten, *The Illustrated History of British Columbia*, Douglas & McIntyre, Vancouver, 2001

——, *The Empress: The First Hundred Years*, Douglas & McIntyre, Vancouver, 1997

——, *More English than the English: A Very Social History of Victoria*, Orea Book Publishers, Victoria, BC, 1986

Frank Richards, *Old Soldiers Never Die*, Anthony Rowe Ltd, Eastbourne, 2009

J. Ewing Ritchie, *To Canada with Emigrants*, T. F. Unwin, London, 1885

Donald Rumbelow, *The Triple Tree: Newgate, Tyburn and Old Bailey*, Harrap, London, 1982

J. Sadie Clifford, *Expressions of Blame: Narratives of Battered Women Who Kill in the Twentieth Century Daily Express*, VDM Verlag, Riga, 2009

Lizzie Seal, *Capital Punishment in Twentieth-Century Britain: Audience, Justice, Memory*, Routledge, London, 2014

L. B. C. Seaman, *Life in Victorian London*, B. T. Batsford, London, 1973

Francis Sheppard, *London: A History*, Oxford University Press, Oxford, 1998

J. A. S. Simon, *Retrospect: The Memoirs of the Rt Hon. Viscount Simon*, Hutchinson, London, 1952

S. Watson Smith (ed.), *The Book of Bournemouth*, Pardy & Son, Bournemouth, 1934

Stella St John, *A Prisoner's Log: Holloway Prison in 1943*, Howard League for Penal Reform, London, 1943

Olga Samaroff Stokowski, *An American Musician's Story*, W. W. Norton & Co., New York, 1939

Lisa Stead, *Off to the Pictures: Cinema-Going, Women's Writing and Movie Culture in Interwar Britain*, Edinburgh University Press, Edinburgh, 2016

D. H. Stewart, *Kipling's America: Travel Letters, 1889–1895*, ELT Press, University of North Carolina, Greensboro, 2003

Lawrence Stone, *Road to Divorce: England, 1530–1987*, Oxford University Press, Oxford, 1990

Dominic Streatfield, *Cocaine: An Unauthorised Biography*, Picador, London, 2003

Jan Struther, *Mrs Miniver*, Chatto & Windus, London, 1939

Maria Tippett, *Made in British Columbia: Eight Ways of Making Culture*, Harbour Publishing, British Columbia, 2015

Martin Thornton, *Churchill, Borden and Anglo-Canadian Naval Relations, 1911–14*, Palgrave Macmillan, London, 2013

Peter Thorold, *The Motoring Age: The Automobile and Britain 1896–1939*, Profile Books, London, 2003

E. S. Turner, *Call the Doctor: A Social History of Medical Men*, Michael Joseph, London, 1958

Violet Van der Elst, *On the Gallows*, Doge Press, London, 1937

Stephen Wade, *Britain's Most Notorious Hangmen*, Wharncliffe Local History, Barnsley, 2009

Mary and Neville Ward, *Home in the Twenties and Thirties*, Ian Allan Ltd, London, 1978

Robin Ward, *Echoes of Empire: Victoria and its Remarkable Buildings*, Harbour Publishing, Victoria, 1996

Ward Lock, *A Pictorial and Descriptive Guide to Bournemouth, Poole and District*, Ward Lock & Co. Ltd, London, 16th edition, 1934

——, *A Pictorial and Descriptive Guide to Dartmoor*, Ward Lock & Co. Ltd, London, 1934

René J. A. Weis, *Criminal Justice: The True Story of Edith Thompson*, Hamish Hamilton, London, 1988

Roger Wilkes, *An Infamous Address*, Grafton Books, London, 1989

Ella Wheeler Wilcox, *Maurine*, Cramer, Aikens & Cramer, Milwaukee, 1876

Francis Williams, *Dangerous Estate: The Anatomy of Newspapers*, Longmans Green and Co., London, 1957

Kevin Williams, *Get Me a Murder a Day! A History of Mass Communication in Britain*, Arnold, London, 2002

Tennessee Williams, *Summer and Smoke*, John Lehman, London, 1952

——, *A Streetcar Named Desire*, John Lehman, London, 1949

Denis Winter, *Death's Men: Soldiers of the Great War*, Penguin, London, 1979

Jackie Winter, *Lipsticks and Library Books: The Story of Boots Booklovers Library*, Chantries Press, Dorset, 2016

Filson Young, *The Trial of Frederick Bywaters and Edith Thompson* (*Notable British Trials*), William Hodge & Co., London and Edinburgh, 1923 (second edition, 1951)

INDEX